# Faith, Hope and Charity

*Faith, Hope and Charity* explores the interaction between social ideals and everyday experiences in Tudor and early Stuart neighbourhoods, drawing on a remarkably rich variety of hitherto largely unstudied sources. Focusing on local sites, where ordinary people lived their lives, Andy Wood deals with popular religion, gender relations, senses of locality and belonging, festivity, work, play, witchcraft, gossip, and reactions to dearth and disease. He thus brings a new clarity to understandings of the texture of communal relations in the historical past and highlights the particular characteristics of structural processes of inclusion and exclusion in the construction and experience of communities in early modern England. This engaging social history vividly captures what life would have been like in these communities, arguing that, even while early modern people were sure that the values of neighbourhood were dying, they continued to evoke and reassert those values.

Andy Wood is Professor of Social History at the University of Durham. The author of five books, including *The 1549 Rebellions and the Making of Early Modern England* (2007) and *The Memory of the People: Custom and Popular Senses of the Past in Early Modern England* (2013) which won the American Historical Association's Leo Gershoy Award in 2014, his current research focuses on the study of authority and resistance in England from 1500–1640.

# Faith, Hope and Charity

*English Neighbourhoods, 1500–1640*

Andy Wood

*University of Durham*

CAMBRIDGE
UNIVERSITY PRESS

# CAMBRIDGE
## UNIVERSITY PRESS

University Printing House, Cambridge CB2 8BS, United Kingdom

One Liberty Plaza, 20th Floor, New York, NY 10006, USA

477 Williamstown Road, Port Melbourne, VIC 3207, Australia

314–321, 3rd Floor, Plot 3, Splendor Forum, Jasola District Centre, New Delhi – 110025, India

79 Anson Road, #06–04/06, Singapore 079906

Cambridge University Press is part of the University of Cambridge.

It furthers the University's mission by disseminating knowledge in the pursuit of education, learning, and research at the highest international levels of excellence.

www.cambridge.org
Information on this title: www.cambridge.org/9781108840668
DOI: 10.1017/9781108886765

First published 2020

Printed in the United Kingdom by TJ Books Limited, Padstow Cornwall

*A catalogue record for this publication is available from the British Library.*

*Library of Congress Cataloging-in-Publication Data*
Names: Wood, Andy, 1967– author.
Title: Faith, hope and charity : English neighbourhoods, 1500–1640 / Andy Wood, University of Durham.
Description: 1 Edition. | New York : Cambridge University Press, 2020. | Includes bibliographical references and index.
Identifiers: LCCN 2020009396 (print) | LCCN 2020009397 (ebook) | ISBN 9781108840668 (hardback) | ISBN 9781108886765 (ebook)
Subjects: LCSH: Neighborhoods – Great Britain – History – 16th century. | Neighborhoods – Great Britain – History – 17th century. | Social values – Great Britain – History. | Charities – Great Britain – History. | Faith – Great Britain – History.
Classification: LCC HT133 .W66 2020 (print) | LCC HT133 (ebook) | DDC 307.3/362094209031–dc23
LC record available at https://lccn.loc.gov/2020009396
LC ebook record available at https://lccn.loc.gov/2020009397

ISBN 978-1-108-84066-8 Hardback
ISBN 978-1-108-81445-4 Paperback

For my mother and in memory of my father

Though I speak with the tongues of men and of angels, and have not charity, I am become as sounding brass, or a tinkling cymbal. And though I have the gift of prophecy, and understand all mysteries, and all knowledge; and though I have all faith, so that I could remove mountains, and have not charity, I am nothing. And though I bestow all my goods to feed the poor, and though I give my body to be burned, and have not charity, it profiteth me nothing. Charity suffereth long, and is kind; charity envieth not; charity vaunteth not itself, is not puffed up, Doth not behave itself unseemly, seeketh not her own, is not easily provoked, thinketh no evil; rejoiceth not in iniquity, but rejoiceth in the truth; beareth all things, believeth all things, hopeth all things, endureth all things. Charity never faileth: but whether there be prophecies, they shall fail; whether there be tongues, they shall cease; whether there be knowledge, it shall vanish away. For we know in part, and we prophesy in part. But when that which is perfect is come, then that which is in part shall be done away. When I was a child, I spake as a child, I understood as a child, I thought as a child: but when I became a man, I put away childish things. For now we see through a glass, darkly; but then face to face: now I know in part; but then shall I know even as also I am known. And now abideth faith, hope, charity, these three; but the greatest of these is charity.

1 Corinthians 13: 1–13

# Contents

# Preface and Acknowledgements

This book develops the social history of an *idea*: that of neighbourhood. It assesses the ways in which that idea was conceptualized and shows how neighbourhood fed, constantly, into social practice. The book is focused not just on those social groups whom the Levellers called the 'lower and middle sort of people' but also upon the gentry, who are an important part of our tale. Fundamentally, this is a story about the ways in which early modern people – rich, middling and poor – did their best – often in the face of terrible pressures – to make their communities *operate*. The book's title foregrounds the Scriptures as massively powerful yet constantly contested texts with the potential to legitimate or to subvert social order. The title, drawn from 1 Corinthians 13: 1–13, does the following interpretive work:

(a) Faith. Obviously, this alludes to the power of Christian faith within everyday life in Tudor and early Stuart England. Throughout, we return to the significance of readings of the Scriptures for the ways in which ordinary people made sense of their world. Less obviously, it alludes to the capacity of local solidarities – faith amongst one another, amongst neighbours and friends – to weather the storms that threatened otherwise to overwhelm villages and towns.

(b) Hope. In an economy characterized – especially for poorer people – by constant insecurity, what hope was there for the future? Hope is here used as a category against which to situate profound material inequality and political disempowerment and alongside which to locate lower-class agency.

(c) Charity. This critically important concept refers not only to poor relief but also to the *meaning* of charity. Partially, charity was functional: it reinforced practical patterns of paternalism, subordination and deference. Poor folk were expected to beg for support on their knees, with their caps in their hands. Where they did so, their deference legitimated elementary social norms. But charity was also *relational*: poor folk had expectations of their richer neighbours – when demands for charity were frustrated, those expectations could quickly mutate into something far more assertive.

These three concepts – faith, hope and charity – lead us into the unpredictability of early modern people's lives. Most importantly, they lead us to neighbourhood: to the forces that (for all that they were sometimes observed more in the breach than in practice) helped to shape social relations, drawing richer and poorer folk together through a shared investment in community. The book opens with a consideration of one of the dominant beliefs about neighbourhood: the sense that it was in decline or even dead. Charity, contemporaries believed, had 'grown cold'; the rich no longer regarded the poor; litigation and malicious gossip set neighbour against neighbour; the gentry no longer practised good lordship or hospitality but instead oppressed their tenants and ignored the poor. In particular, Tudor and early Stuart people felt that they were trapped within a cash nexus in which the growing commercialization of the economy separated rich from poor. A powerful sign of these divisions was to be seen in the enclosure of the land and the denial of common rights to the poor, generating a set of social practices that were inimical to neighbourly ideals and that were written into the enclosed landscape. In this respect, enclosure was something that was *felt*, *seen* and *read*: it was as much as anything a metaphor, a way of capturing the social conflicts that people felt around them. In the background was a nagging sense of melancholy, nostalgia and loss and a yearning for a golden age of social cohesion. It is important to note that this melancholy was present in 1500 just as it was in 1640; but also that it gained greater voice over the course of our period. There was an important change here. As a discourse, the idea of neighbourhood enjoyed a relative autonomy that lifted it above relations of both production and exploitation. There was a never-to-be-resolved contradiction at work: the more that people complained about the collapse of neighbourhood, the more they reasserted those values. Neighbourliness, it will here be argued, was not so much in decline as it was constantly *contested*. Importantly, economic individualism was constantly *in friction* with corporate ideals that dominated early modern ideas about social structure and social relations, and this contradiction was certainly not resolved by 1640.

We move on from this to consider the characteristics of neighbourhood as an ideal. Collective values, hostility to division and a profound belief in the virtues of social unity coexisted alongside growing economic individualism and increasing polarization. The language of neighbourhood was regularly mobilized in criticism of such forces, which were felt to bring with them atomization. Increased litigation was another force that was felt to be driving society apart; it is therefore important that neighbourly values were regularly linked to informal processes of dispute resolution, which both strengthened communal bonds and reaffirmed social hierarchies. Similarly, while usury was deplored, the practice of providing interest-free loans to the poor was upheld as neighbourly; and, once again, it reinforced the social order. Neighbourhood was a living social virtue, linked to cognate concepts that included love, friendship, charity and equity. Trust and reputation were central to the relationships that neighbourhood generated, and they came with a certain watchfulness: men and women who stood apart from their neighbours, who sought privacy from the public world of the street, village and neighbourhood, were regarded with suspicion. Communal life generated a set of intimate emotional proximities that were to be found within towns and cities just as much as in villages. The notion that urban society was characterized by a placeless anomie is not supported by the evidence: the locus of much of city life was centred on the immediate neighbourhood, street, courtyard or small city parish, and, here, neighbours looked out for one another just like in rural communities.

There were many enemies of neighbourhood: early modern people were sure of that. Litigious lawyers, greedy merchants, oppressive landlords and selfish gentry were joined by those who spread negative gossip about their neighbours. The historical record of litigation concerning tale-bearing and reputation speaks not just to the increased use of the courts but also (contradictorily) to the reassertion of neighbourhood values. Church court litigation, in particular, was as much about sealing social division as it was about getting one over on a local opponent. Importantly, the language of neighbourhood offered a discourse that could be deployed in criticism of the actions of elites, whether gentry, civic governors or middling-sort Puritans. But the most potent enemy of neighbourhood was the witch, who brought dark, malicious, satanic forces into the community. Witches did more than set neighbours against one another; witches personified the reverse of the Christian ideals of charity and moral conduct on which neighbourhood was founded.

Another widely hated figure who stood for anti-neighbourly values was the Puritan, and his or her evangelical predecessors. The early Protestant Reformation was associated for many people with what they called 'new-fangledness'. This was a culture in which innovation might easily be deplored, especially in matters of belief, as the old ways of ancestors were preferred over the divisions that Reformation preachers brought to communities. In the later sixteenth and early seventeenth centuries, Puritans attempted to inflict on working people what one historian has called a 'disciplinary revolution': shutting down alehouses, abolishing communal celebrations, banning festivity, play and good cheer. But

Puritans were largely unsuccessful in imposing their own standards on the 'common sort' of people, who saw in the Calvinist disciplinary revolution an attack on neighbourhood and on the relatively tolerant, easy-going version of Christian religion that ordinary people preferred. In their defence of festive culture, it is significant that religious conservatives and recusant Catholics presented themselves as the friends of neighbourhood. Here, there was an *achievement*. Importantly, when war came in 1642, the embedded hostility towards the godly laid the basis for popular royalism. I will write about this more fully in the future.

According to conventional religious doctrines, all Christians were neighbours. But most early modern people tended to associate neighbourhood with locality – and propinquity. Tudor and early Stuart people did have a sense of national identity, and that could sometimes be mobilized against the Scots, Irish, Walloons, Spanish, French and Dutch. But that sense of patriotism existed alongside an enduring sense of place that was vested in social memory, custom, tradition and the landscape. This was as true in cities and towns as it was in the countryside. One of the things that neighbourhood did was to *localize* social relations. People certainly had a wider sense of a social order, comprising gentry, middling sort, smallholders and the poor: they had a language of social classification that enabled them to think about broader social structures. But those social structures were experienced, understood and articulated on the level of the locality; again, this both helped to reproduce the micro-politics of domination and subordination while – contradictorily – generating horizontal senses of solidarity amongst poorer people that could, in the right circumstances, provide a political resource.

The parish church was one key site within which neighbourhood happened. Another – especially for poorer people – was the alehouse. Then there were what contemporaries called 'merry meetings of the neighbours': parish feasts, gatherings around maypoles or bonfires, events such as Rogationtide and Christmas when neighbourly values were strengthened in ritual drinking. Alcohol was central to such merry meetings: most early modern people liked a drink, and downing ale together could be a way in which friendships were reinforced and hostilities drowned. Customs such as wassailing, wakes and bid-ales drew people together – again, through the ritual consumption of alcohol. For lads, football – what was known as 'camping' – was another way in which parish solidarities could be expressed, as teams from one parish confronted those of a neighbouring settlement. Yet again, alcohol was part of these events, which invariably led to broken heads, blackened eyes and – occasionally – deaths. In this way, a sense of youthful masculinity could be celebrated and linked to a sense of local identity.

Neighbourhood was partly constructed around the bonds that held women together – for instance through working patterns, rituals around childbirth, and gossip networks. Although the harvest saw men and women working alongside one another, for much of the rest of the year – especially in arable and mixed-farming regions – women and adult men seem mostly to have worked apart (the subject requires fuller research). In arable and mixed-farming zones, adult men and older lads worked out in the fields, ploughing and seeding. Women and younger children pastured animals on the commons, did the milking, made cheese, collected honey, cleaned, gleaned, cooked, carried and looked to the very youngest (as a child in the mid-1940s, my father worked on a mixed farm, mostly milking by hand – but by his later-teens in the mid-1950s, his father changed my dad's role and sent him to plough with the great Cheshire shire horses whom they called Captain and Duke and whose presence dominated the farm. This was not so long ago). The result was to generate local solidarities and friendships that were built around gender. Where men assaulted their wives, then, they might confront the collective face of women's disapproval. Violent patriarchs could easily be represented as disturbers of neighbourly values, bringing viciousness and cruelty into a local community. Men had that violent force; but their neighbours knew its deployment to be wrong. Other males despised such men; and, in particular, the evidence speaks of a female solidarity that could be stoked in response to the sight of a woman with bruises and cuts about her face. Yet female solidarity had its limits: there are hard stories to be told in which poor, single women who found themselves pregnant were frozen out by the established women of a community.

Such isolated young women were denied *place*. Having a place allowed poorer folk to access resources through charity, formal relief, employment and clientage. Once again, relations of domination and subordination were reasserted; but the poor got something from that exchange. And so did the rich: they gained the prayers of God's poor. Such prayers eased the gates of heaven. But there were many poor folk who had no such place. The book therefore concludes by considering the other side of the coin: those who were locked out of neighbourhood. These included the transient poor: men, women and children who were to be found frozen to death or perished from starvation, on the road or in fields and barns. But in times of high food prices, even the settled poor might be left to die: times such as the 1550s, the 1580s, the 1590s and the 1620s saw charity grow cold. We finish, then, by considering the ways in which dearth and disease represented challenges to the broad, tolerant, socially inclusive values of neighbourhood that much of this book describes and analyses.

This book is a departure from a large chunk of my earlier work, which has been partly focused on social conflict. One of the criticisms of my earlier work has been that, because I have written about the *agency* of working people in the past, I have somehow *valorized* their efforts to shape the world around them. It has always seemed to me that I have not so much valorized that agency as I have described and analysed it: it is there to be found in the evidence of the archival record. We just need the eyes to see. Historical empiricism – seeking voices in the archive – and historical materialism – an awareness of the social structures within which those voices were heard and recorded – need not be opposed. Historians should be able to write a social history that is rooted in an awareness of the power relations that produced our documents yet also speaks to the stories that those documents tell. As regards this book, although class is always there in the background, it is really about community. I realize, then, that this book represents not so much a *valorization* as a *celebration*. It describes the many ways in which poorer and middling people tried to hold their communities together in the face of often terrible, difficult and profound pressures that, in a post-industrial society, the reader is not always equipped to grasp.

This book will be succeeded by another monograph in which I return to struggles over power, space and resources. My intention is to publish that book in perhaps seven or eight years. I am thinking of calling it something like *Letters of Blood and Fire: Social Relations in England, 1500–1640*. That book, like this one, will deal with the period before the English Revolution. This is not because, like too many social historians of early modern England, I want to avoid the revolutionary decades. Rather, I think that things changed profoundly in the 1640s. The civil wars therefore make a meaningful terminus for both books. In the long run, I want to write a social history of the English civil wars, focusing on their material and human impact; but all of that lies in the future. The year 1640, then, represents a breaking-point.

Every book is a collective endeavour: there is no such thing as the isolated, individual author, labouring away in her or his study. One of the great things in my life has been the endlessly enjoyable experience of being part of a community of historians, along with some stray sociologists, literary critics and anthropologists. Many friendships go back by more than three decades. I am grateful to a great many friends for their encouragement, enthusiasm and criticism. They include John Arnold, Alex Barber, Dom Birch, Andy Burn, Sarah Covington, Barbara Crosbie, Andy Davies, Chris Fitter, Henry French, Adam Fox, Jo Fox, Malcolm Gaskill, Laura Gowing, Adrian Green, Paul Griffiths, Mark Hailwood, Tim Harris, Steve Hindle, Andy Hopper, the late Alun Howkins, Ronald

Hutton, Mark Jenner, Matthew Johnson, Bob Layton, Christian Liddy, Neil Marley, Natalie Mears, John Morrill, Craig Muldrew, Carole Rawcliffe, Hannah Robb, Dave Rollison, Ethan Shagan, Jim Sharpe, Alex Shepard, Simon Sandall, Tim Stretton, Naomi Tadmor, Hillary Taylor, Keith Thomas, Selina Todd, Tim Wales, Garthine Walker, John Walter, Nicola Whyte, Fiona Williamson, Tom Williamson and (most of all!) Keith Wrightson.

Special thanks are due to Richard Cust for making available his High Court of Chivalry material when it was offline (this excellent body of material is now available at www.british-history.ac.uk/no-series/court-of-chivalry/intro-project). John Morrill chaired the advisory board that oversaw the funded elements of the project on which the book was based. John was a source of advice, wisdom, encouragement, enthusiasm and fun. A big part of this project involved work with The National Archives. Collaborating with Amanda Bevan and her marvellous colleagues was a great pleasure. I am enormously grateful to the Arts and Humanities Research Council (AHRC) and to the Leverhulme Trust. The Leverhulme Trust awarded me a Research Project Grant in 2015 and the AHRC gave me a Research Leadership Fellowship in 2017. This funding provided me with the time and resources with which to write this book along with that which will follow it. Going back by more than two decades, the research for this book started to accumulate during a glorious year in 1995–6 when, as a British Academy postdoctoral fellow, I spent almost every day in the Round Room of the old Public Record Office, followed by many evenings in the Institute of Historical Research. In those months, I started to wonder: have historians really captured the double-edged nature of this particular historical epoch? Over twenty years later, as I pulled my thoughts together, I was lucky enough to hold research fellowships at the Folger Shakespeare Library, the Henry E. Huntington Library and Durham University's Institute of Advanced Studies. It was great to work with Amanda Herbert at the Folger. Steve and Louise Hindle made me very welcome at the Huntington. I owe a huge debt to Liz Friend-Smith at Cambridge University Press, who was endlessly patient, running with my ideas, not complaining when one book split into two and allowing me extra time in which to complete the manuscript. I could have no better editor. An anonymous reviewer for Cambridge University Press reminded me of why it all still matters.

Methodologically, this book is an exercise in what might (pretentiously) be called a sort of theorized serendipity. Partly, it involves stumbling on material. That great empiricist Sherlock Holmes would have called it the scientific use of the imagination. More simply, this might mean following one's nose through an archive, albeit with recurrent (yet ever-changing) questions, combined with some sense of those things for which one might be looking. It is also necessary for some such mission to have a rough-and-ready reading of the interdisciplinary, comparative and theoretical literature around one's subject and here, as always, this involved a conversation with social anthropology. The important thing is to allow the archive to surprise you, to let it make you think differently and to listen to the voices in the records that tell you about worlds that are dissimilar from our own.

Historical research does that – or, at least, it should. Here, there is a contest that is methodological, epistemological and political. For historians working in British universities in the early twenty-first century, the bureaucratic demands made for 'rigour', 'targets' and 'outcomes' need always to be muted by the unexpected voices from the past. Times were a'changin' in the years during which I wrote this book, and the deadening strictures of neo-liberalism have become less dominant. The past might provide a few lessons: in the early modern period, neighbourhood was simultaneously an abstract ideal, a local site, a source of mutualities and interdependencies, and a mode of social interaction. The people of Tudor and early Stuart England may have something important to tell us. As social ideals go, neighbourhood is not such a bad place to start.

***

While I have been writing this book, it has been a wonder to watch my children, Max and Rosa Simpson, grow into adults. Lucy Simpson has been my rock. When I was ill with cellulitis, Sally Simpson was a source of considerable support. Pete Herdan carted my books up and down the A1 and did his level best to keep me sane. Along with Barbara Crosbie, Neil Marley, Natalie Mears and Keith Wrightson, Pete and Lucy have been there when I needed them most of all. And Laura Gowing offered kind, thoughtful words at the worst of times. This book was written in two of England's great medieval cities: Durham and Norwich. In 1986, Norfolk set a splinter in my heart. Yet it is good to be back at home in the North, with its rain and egalitarianism. My father, Jim Wood, loved the North. As I was completing the first draft of this book, he passed away. My dad was a marvellous man who meant the world to me. He was clever, funny, erudite and almost wholly self-taught. My dad was intrigued by history and he loved my wonderful mother. We shared both of those things. It is to my father and to my dearest mother that I dedicate this book.

***

All Biblical quotations are taken from the 1611 King James edition. Dates have been modernized.

# Abbreviations

| | |
|---|---|
| BIA | Borthwick Institute for Archives |
| BL | British Library |
| CRO | Cheshire Record Office |
| DUL | Durham University Library |
| *EcHR* | *Economic History Review* |
| EETS | Early English Texts Society |
| FSL | Folger Shakespeare Library |
| HALS | Hampshire Archives and Local Studies |
| HCCO | High Court of Chivalry Online: www.british-history.ac.uk/no-series/court-of-chivalry/intro-project |
| HEHL | Henry E. Huntington Library |
| HMC | Historical Manuscripts Commission |
| *JBS* | *Journal of British Studies* |
| NRO | Norfolk Record Office |
| *P&P* | *Past and Present* |
| *TC&WA&AS* | *Transactions of the Cumberland and Westmorland Antiquarian and Archaeological Society* |
| *TED* | R. H. Tawney and E. Power (eds.), *Tudor Economic Documents: Being Select Documents Illustrating the Economic and Social History of Tudor England* (London, 1924). |
| TNA | The National Archives |
| *TRHS* | *Transactions of the Royal Historical Society* |
| YASRS | Yorkshire Archaeological Society Record Series |

# 1    Charity Never Faileth: Defining Neighbourhood

## The Crisis of Neighbourhood?

Sometimes, social values are only fully transparent when they seem most under threat. For all the significance that the people of Tudor and early Stuart England invested in neighbourhood, throughout the period with which we are dealing, many believed it to be a social virtue that was vanishing from the world. As one ballad of 1571 lamented:

> Wee know wee should forgeve, as wee would be forgeven,
> Yet styll in yre wee live, as though our hartes were reeven,
> Revengements we do keepe, for light occasions geven,
> Our Neighboures greefe we seeke, both every Morne and Even,
> The more wee spie in space, the lesse yet our entraunce,
> Our knowledge without grace, is worse than ignoraunce,
> All falshood and deceite, wee should also abhorre,
> Yet use wee more that sleight, than ever wee did before
> Lingryng still to view, to hurte our Neighbour sore,
> So wee may them pursue, wee care not for no more
> Repression beares the Mace, and Lucre leades the Daunce.[1]

Underlying contemporary discussions of social relations lay a profound melancholy, a yearning for a lost time informed by good neighbourhood and warm communal relations. In 1581, the godly Essex preacher George Gifford reported the opinion amongst his parishioners that whereas their forefathers and mothers had 'lived in friendshippe, and made merrie together, nowe there is no good neighbourhoode: nowe every man for himself, and are readie to pull one another by the throate'. As Gifford glumly concluded, there was 'nowe … no love'.[2] Nine years later, Thomas Nashe wailed: 'Ah, neighbourhood, neighbourhood, dead and buried art thou with Robin Hood.'[3] Similarly, the Essex minister John Gore wrote, in 1636, that 'the world have changed from good

---

[1] Anon., *A New Yeres Gyft* (London, 1571).
[2] G. Gifford, *A Briefe Discourse of Certaine Points* (London, 1582), fol. 5r.
[3] R. B. McKerrow (ed.), *The Works of Thomas Nashe* (Oxford, 1966), I, 293–4.

neighbourhood and good hospitalitie to all manner of basenesse and miserie'.[4] For Robert Greene, writing in 1592, the decline of hospitality was related to the aggressive demands made by landlords upon their tenants. He lamented how 'Hospitality was left off, Neighbourhood was exciled, Conscience was skoft at, and charitie lay frozen in the streets: how upstart Gentlemen for the maintainance of that their fathers never lookt after, raised rents, rackte their tenants, and imposed greate fines'.[5] Phillip Stubbes felt that the emotional economy of social relations had undergone a profound alteration, writing: 'Loove is exiled amongst us, neighbourhood nothing regarded, pitty utterly subverted, and remorse of conscience nothing esteemed, what shall become of us?'[6] In particular, it was felt that hospitality had died. As George Gascogine put it in 1573:

The scriptures say the Lord hath neede, & therfore blame the[m] not.
Then come a litle lower, unto the countrey knight,
The squier and the gentleman, they leave the countrey quite,
Their halles were all to[o] large, their tables were to[o] long,
The clouted shoes came in so fast, they kepte to[o] great a throng,
And at the porters lodge, where lubbers wont to feede
The porter learnes to answere now, hence the Lorde hathe neede.[7]

Past times, many believed, were warmer and simpler. Walter Carey observed: 'Our Fathers in apparel were very plaine ... but living quietly and neighbourly with that they had, they were ever rich, able to give and lend freely.' He noted the widespread conviction that long-gone 'forefathers ... [had] lived bountifully, quietly, pleasantly and (as I may say) like Kings in their little kingdoms: They seldome or never went to London, they did not strive for greatnesse, they did not long for their neighbor[']s land, neither sold of their owne, but (keeping good hospitalitie, and plainely ever attaired), were very rich.'[8]

The gentry's commitment to the provision of hospitality was seen as one of their great contributions to the values of neighbourhood. Even at the start of our period, this was seen as in decline, if not actually dead. A poem written around 1500 complained:

Somtyme nobyll men levyd in [the]er Contre
And kepte grete howsoldis, pore men to socowur
But now in the Cowrte they desire to be;
With ladys to daly, thy sys [th]er pleasure

[4] J. Gore, *Certaine Sermons Preached upon Severall Occasions* (London, 1636), 46.
[5] R. Greene, *A Quip for an Upstart Courtier* (London, 1592), preface.
[6] P. Stubbes, *Two Wunderfull and Rare Examples, of the Undeferred and Present Approaching Judgement of the Lord Our God* (London, 1581), introduction.
[7] G. Gascoinge, *A Hundredth Sundrie Flowres* (London, 1573), 367.
[8] W. Carey, *The Present State of England* (London, 1626), sigs. A3r, B3r.

> So pore men dayly may famyshe for hunger
> Or they com home ... on monyth to remain
> Thy sys the trowth, as I here Certeyne.[9]

A ballad of 1528 expanded on this theme:

> I have hearde saye of myne elders
> That in Englonde many fermers
> Kept gaye housholdes in tymes passed
> Ye, that they did with liberalitie
> Shewayng to poure people charit[i]e
> But nowe all together is dashed.[10]
> Of ryche farme places and halles
> Thoue seist nothynge but bare walles[.]

These anxieties generated a pervasive sense that society had become cold and conflictual. Throughout the period from 1500 to 1640, people worried over that observation from Proverbs 19:4: 'Wealth maketh many friends; but the poor is separated from his neighbor.' One anonymous tract from c.1548 asked of its reader: 'How do we love our neyghbour as our selves when we put them out of their houses and lay our goods in the stretes?'[11] A ballad of 1561 declared:

> What is the cause, neibourhed is gone,
> Which here hath reigned many a daye,
> I heare the poore men make great mo[a]ne,
> And say[e]th his is falne in decaye[.]

The ballad concluded:

> Graunt[,] oh God, for thy mercyes sake
> That neighbourhed, and dealing trewe
> May once agayne, our spirites awake,
> That we our lyves may change a new.[12]

We are dealing, of course, with social stereotypes; but stereotypes matter – they tell us something powerful about the societies that sustain them. The ballad of *The Old and New Courtier* told of an 'old worshipful gentleman' who maintained an 'old house at a bountiful rate', sustained the poor who gathered at his gate, who at Christmas time would feast his poorer neighbours, who hunted regularly 'but in his grand-father's old grounds'. He instructed his son 'to be good to his old Tenants, and to hold old neighbours kinde', but when his son inherited the estate, driven by the

---

[9] F. J. Furnivall (ed.), *Ballads from Manuscripts* (London, 1868–72), 159.    [10] Ibid., 17.
[11] Anon., *The Prayse and Commendacion of Suche as Sought Comenwelthes* (London, 1548?).
[12] Anon., *A Balade Declaring How Neybourhed, Love and Trew Dealing Is Gone* (London, 1561).

expensive demands of his wife, he established a wholly new regime –
a new hall, a new minister, the habit at Christmas of heading for
London – and so 'housekeeping is grown ... cold'.[13] The distance that
many people sensed was coming to separate the gentry from the commons
was something that was greatly regretted. A pamphlet of 1621 exclaimed:

[H]ow may I complaine ... of the decay of Hospitality in our Land, whereby many
poore soules are deprived of that releefe which they have had heretofore. The time
hath bene, that men have hunted after Worshippe and Credite by good Housekeeping, and therein spent great part of their Revenewes: but now commonly, the
greater part of their Livings, is too little to maintaine us and our Children in the
pompe of pride.[14]

Even where lords continued to feast their tenants, it was felt that this
contrasted to their merciless exploitation of their estates, racking rents,
enclosing common land and increasing fines. Writing in 1632, Donald
Lupton provides us with the tenants' view of gentry hospitality: '[M]any
[lords] fill their Tenants['] bodies once, but empty their purses all the
yeare long ...[.] They dare not dislike any meate, nor scarce enter upon
a dish that hath not lost the best face or piece before it come thither, many
of them suppe better at home then they Dine here.'[15] The apparent
decline of hospitality amongst the yeomanry and the gentry was seen as
a litmus test for the wider collapse of neighbourly relations. In 1602,
Nicholas Breton looked back to the days when

Every Farmer kept good hous[e]hold fare
And not a rich man would a beggar rate
But he would give him almes at his gate
... When Ale and Beere was once olde English wine,
And Beefe, and Mutton was good Countrie cheere,
And bread and cheese would make the Miller dine
When that an honest neighbour might come neere
And welcome: Hoh, maide, fill a pot of Beere
And drinke it soundly in a wooden dish,
When wagges were merrie as their harts could wish.[16]

There were material shifts in the economy that were driving harsh
social changes. The most powerful intervention of recent years in the
economic history of early modern England has been Craig Muldrew's

[13] V. de Sola Pinto and A. E. Rodway (eds.), *The Common Muse: Popular British Ballad
Poetry from the 15th to the 20th Century* (London, 1957), 162–5.
[14] M. S., *Greevous Grones for the Poore* (London, 1621), 13–14.
[15] D. Lupton, *London and the Country Carbonadoed and Quartred into Severall Characters*
(London, 1632), 110.
[16] N. Breton, *Olde Mad-cappes New Gally-mawsrey* (London, 1602), sigs. C3v, Dr.

work on credit. Muldrew argues persuasively that, from around the third decade of the sixteenth century, a 'culture of credit' emerged.[17] As consumption expanded, marketing became more complex. But there was only a limited amount of hard cash in circulation and so many financial transactions were conducted on the basis of credit. Because, as Muldrew puts it, '[c]redit relations were interpersonal and emotive'; where people were unable to live up to their obligations, litigation resulted, helping to drive the substantial increase in the use of civil courts observable between the middle years of the sixteenth century and the outbreak of the English civil wars. The experience of increased civil litigation – charted in an influential book by Christopher Brooks – was reflected in the ballad literature of the time.[18] In one such ballad printed around 1630, for example, the old times of neighbourhood and friendship had been replaced with a sharply conflictual and litigious society:

> You that for nothing
> Will goe to Law,
> Vexing your neighbours,
> For a sticke or a straw,
> Because of your lawing,
> Your purse will grow low:
> You'l prove your selves Coxe-combs
> I tell you but so.[19]

In 1615, John Day asked his audience: 'Witnesse those many Quarrels now a foot between Neighbour & Neighbour, especially in the Country. Witnesse that multiplying of Lawyers in our Age more than ever in former times. Witnesse that Thryving of them in our dayes, and those superlative Purchases which they make in Lands, and Lordships.'[20] The character of Bottom in *A Midsummer Night's Dream* – so often portrayed as an ill-educated idiot – had this to say of neighbourliness: '[T]o say the truth, reason and love keep little company now-a-days; the more the pity that some honest neighbours will not make them friends.'[21] This was a sharply perceptive observation for a play that was performed in the hard years of the mid-1590s. The anonymous author of *Pasquil's Palinodia* (1619) harks back to distant days when

[17] C. Muldrew, *The Economy of Obligation: The Culture of Credit and Social Relations in Early Modern England* (Basingstoke, 1998), 3. This periodization is probably wrong; doctoral work by Hannah Robb points to the vitality of the credit market in the fifteenth century.
[18] C. Brooks, *Pettyfoggers and Vipers of the Commonwealth: The 'Lower Branch' of the Legal Profession in Early Modern England* (Cambridge, 1986).
[19] Anon., *A Merry New Ballad I Have Here to Shew* (London, c.1630).
[20] J. Day, *Day's Festivals* (Oxford, 1615), 346.
[21] W. Shakespeare, *A Midsummer Night's Dream*, act III, scene 1, lines 964–8.

> ... raign'd plaine honest meaning, and good will,
> And neighbours tooke up points of difference,
> In Common Lawes the Commons had no skill,
> And publique feasts were Courts of Conscience.[22]

Moreover, as debt increased, downward social mobility occurred, with the consequence that, as Craig Muldrew puts it,

the culture of credit was generated through a process whereby the nature of the community was redefined as a conglomeration of competing but interdependent households which had to trust one another . . .. [T]he idea of the community was interpreted as something problematic, which could only be maintained through trust in the credit of others in the face of increased competition and disputes.[23]

As community became increasingly contested, following the Muldrew thesis, neighbourly relations were strained. Importantly, many reactions to the economic shifts of the period related to movements in the relationship between people and capital, especially what many saw as the growing importance of merchants within local society. This was connected to anxieties about social mobility. An evangelical tract of the mid-1530s, for example, complained: Every pore manes sone borne in labour is suffered to be a merchaunt, bier and seller, which never workith to help his neybores nor never stondith for a comon weale but for his owne singulare weale. Alle suche cane never lyff in charit[i]e, for charit[i]e never seketh his owne thinges.'[24]

One driver for the decay of neighbourliness, it was felt, was the enmeshing of social relations in the cash nexus, especially the practice of usury. As the author of a ballad published around the accession of Charles I put it:

> When such a good world was here in this Land
> Neighbour and neighbour did fall at no strife,
> Then needlesse were bonds and wills of their hands,
> Mens words were not broken but kept as their life.
> But now in these dayes,
> All credit decayes,
> Truth is not used,
> We see any ways.[25]

Usury, it was felt, 'quencheth faith and all neighbourhoode'.[26]

Thinking of usurers, the Ipswich preacher Samuel Bird observed in 1598: 'Men commonly are wont to certifie their neighbours of the estate

---

[22] Anon., *Pasquils Palonidia* (London, 1619), sig. B3r.
[23] Muldrew, *Economy of Obligation*, 4.      [24] *TED*, III, 117.
[25] Anon., *Pitties Lamentation for the Cruelty of This Age* (London, c.1625).
[26] P. Caesar, *A General Discourse against the Damnable Sect of Usurers Grounded uppon the Worde of God* (London, 1578), 10.

of those that purchase and grow in wealth: but this is a meanes to worke envie in them, and to move them to the like worldliness.'[27] Accusations of usury cut into a person's reputation. In 1588, for example, the Yorkshire gentleman John Cracroft sued his neighbour Roger Ringrose, for saying to him, '[T]how art an usurer, a scurvie usurer, & miserable usurer, & a cutter of mens throats.'[28] Similarly, in 1601, two Hull citizens fell out over accusations of usury: John Lister accused Suzannah Dalton, wife of a fellow alderman, of saying that he was 'an usurer and tooke usurie of her husbande above the rate of ten pounds for the hundred for one yere'.[29] The same sense that the love of money drove growing conflict in local communities fed into the language of litigation. Hence, Robert Teasdale was said, in a legal complaint, to be 'a yeoman that liveth by usurie . . . and love of money and by gripinge of poore men by usurious contracts'.[30] Similarly, in 1593, the Star Chamber heard from the Cambridgeshire labourer Christopher Stephenson that, owing to 'the great & outragious prises of corne & other victualles[,] havinge a wiffe & many poore children [, he] was enforced for the supportinge of his charge to selle that catell he had and that not suffisinge was driven to borowe to relive his want & necessitye' and so had become indebted to his 'uncharitable' neighbour Nicolas Shore, who had used the opportunity to dominate Stephenson.[31] Such real-life cases suggest that the laments of the ballad literature had some grounding in economic fact.

Keith Wrightson has emphasized the enduring importance of neighbourliness in underwriting economic transactions.[32] For all that the early modern economy was built upon market relations, aggressive economic individualism could attract criticism as unneighbourly. This mattered. The dealings of Robert Wheeler of Tamworth (Warwickshire) were felt to be so 'vile' and 'base' that his 'neighbours . . . did in course of common humanity reprove . . . Wheeler for his . . . dealing, telling him that he might be ashamed thereof'. In answer, Wheeler said 'that if all that he had done in that behalf were to do again, he would do it'. His neighbours concluded that he was 'past shame and void of all feeling of Christianity'.[33] Neighbourliness could provide the basis of trust that was essential to

---

[27] S. Bird, *Lectures* (London, 1598), sig. B2r.　　[28] BIA, CP.G.2375.
[29] BIA, CP.H.810.
[30] M. Campbell, *The English Yeoman under Elizabeth and the Early Stuarts* (New Haven, CT, 1942), 380.
[31] TNA, STAC5/S53/13.
[32] K. E. Wrightson, 'The "Decline of Neighbourliness" Revisited', in N. L. Jones and D. Woolf (eds.), *Local Identities in Late Medieval and Early Modern England* (Basingstoke, 2007), 24.
[33] J. Chartres, 'The Marketing of Agricultural Produce, 1640–1750', in J. Chartres (ed.), *Agricultural Markets and Trade, 1500–1750* (Cambridge, 1990), 167, 119.

many economic transactions. Bad neighbours, it was felt, were also often bad debtors. Thomas Tusser wrote of one 'envious and naughtie' neighbour:

> His promise to trust to as slipperie as ice,
> His credit much like to the chance of the dice.[34]

Alan Everitt cites the example of a bargain over sheep between two farmers that resulted from neighbourly pressure: one of the neighbours 'did much labour and entreate him' to the bargain 'and commended' the other farmer 'to be a very honest man and a good paymaster'. The matter ended in litigation, but it is indicative of the ways in which marketing and business deals depended upon reputation, credit and social networks.[35] Yet economic individualism, for all its apparently pernicious effects on values such as neighbourliness, found its advocates. Those who took a careful attitude to loans, covenants or other economic dealings with their neighbours found a supporter in the widely read godly author John Dod. In 1607, he maintained a

defence of them which are not flexible to serve every mans turne with bond and covenants, but will first know the person for whome they make their promise, and bee acquainted with his trueth and honestie, and with his state and habilitie; and consider also of their owne sufficiencie, whether they can without any great difficultie, discharge that which they take upon them, if their neighbour should faile. But this is want of good neighbourhood, say they. But this is a point of good wisedome, saith God, who never alloweth that neighbourhood for good, which swarueth from holy discretion. His commandement is: Thou shalt love thy neighbour as thy selfe, and therefore no man is bound to love him more then himselfe, especially when it is with hatred of himselfe, and hurt of many others. And in deede it is no worke of true love, but of fleshly friendship: for love doth never leade a man to doe any thing which God appointeth him to hate, as in this place he doth all rash suretiship.[36]

In this way, growing entanglement in the cash nexus rendered neighbour-hood a contested concept. Who is a good neighbour? What duties do they owe to one another? How circumspect should neighbours be in their dealings with one another?

Merchants, in particular, were held responsible for the commercializa-tion of social relations, their capital-invading communities causing divi-sion and driving downward social mobility to create a new class of

---

[34] T. Tusser, *Five Hundred Points of Good Husbandry* (Oxford, 1984), 140.
[35] Chartres, 'The Marketing of Agricultural Produce', 107.
[36] J. Dod, *A Plaine and Familiar Exposition of the Eleventh and Twelfth Chapters of the Proverbes of Salomon* (London, 1607), 48.

permanent poor. In John Ferne's *The Blazon of Gentrie* (1586), the figure of Columell ('a plowman') complains in vernacular speech about his diminished estate:

[F]ortune ... hath left me a begger, and yet my vather a good yeoman, and lived many a winters season in good repentation, and kept a homely house among his neighbours, and brought up his children cleanly so long as our old lease and Landlord [en]dured, but smoothly, since they ended, and that a Marchant of ... Middlesex had dwelt among us a while, then var[i]e well all our thrift: our sheepe shearing feastes, or beeves in harvest, and the good pirrey in Christmas, been al agone, and turned another way, all is too litt[l]e for him-zelfe ... Gentlefolkes have now small keepe, they beene so straight bent towards us poore men, that by my vathers zoule, they semen most of churles, not of gentle blood ... Vor greater unkinde, how can they be, then to pull downe townes, put in rude beasts, and thrust out men.[37]

Again, the evidence of litigation at central courts suggests that such anxieties informed local understandings of social relations. Just as John Ferne's fictional 'Marchant of Middlesex' had penetrated local society, driving a wedge between neighbours, so the real-life corn merchant William Taylor of Burnham Deepdale (Norfolk) was represented in similar terms in a complaint to Chancery in 1617. The local gentleman Thomas Goword described Taylor as

a man of very covetous mynde & desire and huntinge exceedingly after gayne and Bargaynes in Buyinge and ingrossinge of Corne ... who ys and longe tyme hath bene both hasty and gredy to buye upp and ingrosse into his handes greate somes and quantities of Corne aswell when it was deare as when yt was and ys cheape, and the same beinge so bought and injoyed he hath and doth usually transporte the same beyonde the Seas, one shippe after another, w[i]th as much haste and speede as he canne loade them and send them awaye thirstinge and gredely desiringe to inrich himselfe therby by reason whereof he hath gained w[i]thin thes[e] Fewe yeres the some of Tenne Thousand pounds att the leaste, Albeyt many poore people in the sayd County aswell heretofore as lately doe indewer wante and Fare much the worse.[38]

In this way, mercantile activity – hunting after bargains, sending 'one ship after another' – was presented as socially irresponsible, covetous and oppressive of the poor.

Again, these representations fed into popular literature. The Jacobean ballad *A Dialogue between Master Guesright and Poor Neighbour Needy* has Master Guesright explaining how 'the world is hard' because every occupation and social group seeks only profit. In the end, Neighbour Needy draws the following pessimistic conclusion:

[37] J. Ferne, *The Blazon of Gentrie* (London, 1586), 22.    [38] TNA, C2/JamesI/G13/50.

> Well neighbour Guesright if this same be true,
> Then home we will straight without more adoe
> And what we intend to none we will tell
> But keepe to our selves and so fare-you well[.]

So, Neighbour Needy opts for social atomization.[39] One of the drivers for that atomization, many felt, was the attack by Puritans upon traditional popular festivities and pastimes. Rituals such as wassailing and maypole dancing were felt by many people to provide means by which community could be both celebrated and renewed. One anonymous author of 1619 therefore drew attention to a maypole in his district, which he called

> ... a signe
> Of harmelesse mirth and honest neighborhood,
> Where all the Parish did in one combine,
> To mount the rod of peace, and none withstood:
> Where no capritious Constables disturbe them,
> Nor [J]ustice of the peace did seeke to curbe them,
> Noor peevish Puritan in rayling sort,
> Nor over-wise Church-warden spoyl'd the sport
> Happy the age, and harmelesse were the dayes,
> (For then true love and amity was found)
> When every village did a May-pole raise,
> And Whitson-ales and May-games did abound
> And all the lusty Yonkers in a rout
> With merry Lasses danc'd the rod about,
> Then friendship to their banquets, bid the guests,
> And poore men far'd the better for their feasts.[40]

The end of the wassail-cup was especially painful. In this folk ritual, inhabitants bore cups full of ale around their locality, offering a sip in return for a gift. Often practised during the Christmas season, wassailing was, like rush-bearing, mumming, maypole dancing and a host of other folk customs, something that many contemporaries saw as a source of social unity. It was therefore significant that, once again, Puritans were criticized for their attacks on the wassail-cup:

> And thou my native towne, which was of old,
> (When as thy Bon-fiers burn'd, and May-poles [s]tood
> And when thy Wassall-cups were uncontrol'd,)
> The sommer-Bower of peace and neighborhood,
> Although since these went down, thou ly'st forlorn
> By factious schismes, and humours over-borne.[41]

---

[39] Anon., *A Dialogue between Master Guesright and Poor Neighbour Needy* (London, c.1624).
[40] Anon., *Pasquils Palonidia*, sig. B3r.    [41] Ibid., sig. B4r.

Christmas was the key feast in the calendar. Ronald Hutton notes that, during the twelve days of Christmas, gentry were expected to mount great feasts for their tenants.[42] In 1629 at Hadham Hall (Essex), for example, Sir Edward Capell fed 161 people in the Great Hall, 99 individuals at the entrance hall and 45 poor folk at the gate.[43] Still more impressively, on Christmas Day 1507, the Duke of Buckingham presided over a feast at which 294 people were fed and which included minstrels, trumpeters and actors. Such great feasts could stick in the local memory. For example, in the middle years of the sixteenth century, the earl of Arundel mounted such a huge yuletide feast that many years later it was noted that 'to this day it beareth the name of Greate Christmas'.[44]

Yuletide card games were another way of bringing neighbours together. Christmas was the one time when the Elizabethan juries of Hutton John (Cumberland) and Shap (Westmorland) sanctioned card games.[45] Peak Country miners were also known for their Christmas games: the Derbyshire gentleman Philip Kinder said of them: 'They love to play cards ... ye Miners ... at Christmas tyme will carry tenn or twentie pound about them, gamne freely & returne home againe all the yeere after very good husbands'.[46] Christmas was a key time in the communal calendar. A ballad published around 1625 had it as follows:

> This time of the yeare,
> Is spent in good Cheare,
> kind neighbours together meet:
> To sit by the fire,
> With friendly desire,
> each other in love to greet:
> Old grudges forgot,
> Are put in the Pot, all sorrowes aside they lay:
> The old and the yong,
> Doth Caroll his Song,
> to drive the cold winter away.

[42] R. Hutton, *The Stations of the Sun: A History of the Ritual Year in Britain* (Oxford, 1996), chapters 1 and 6. For the limits on medieval Christmas feasts, see J. Harland (ed.), *Three Lancashire Documents of the Fourteenth and Fifteenth Centuries*, Chetham Society, 74 (Manchester, 1868), 94.

[43] W. Minet, 'A Steward's Accounts at Hadham Hall, 1628–1629', *Transactions of the Essex Archaeological Society*, 15, 2 (1918), 141. For village gossip at a lord's Christmas feast, see P. M. Wilkinson (ed.), *Chichester Archdeaconry Depositions, 1603–1608*, Sussex Record Society, 97 (Lewes, 2017), 206–8.

[44] J. Ross, 'The Noble Household as a Political Centre in the Early Tudor Period', *Harlaxton Medieval Studies*, 28 (Donington, 2018), 87, 92.

[45] N. F. Hudleston, 'Elizabethan Paines Laid at Hutton John', *TC&WAAS*, 2nd ser., 69 (1969), 126; J. Whiteside, 'Paines Made at Shap', *TC&WAAS*, 2nd ser., 3 (1903), 155.

[46] W. G. D. Fletcher, 'Philip Kinder's Ms. "Historie of Darbyshire"', *Reliquary*, 23 (1882–3), 10, 182.

> To Maske and to Mum,
> Kind neighbours will come,
> With Wassels of hot brown Ale;
> To drinke and carouse,
> To all in this house,
> As merry as Bucks in the pale:
> Where Cake, Bread and Cheese,
> Is brought for your fees,
> To make you the longer stay:
> At the fire to warme,
> Will do you no harme,
> To drive the cold winter away.[47]

In 1565, the clerk of the city authorities in Lincoln noted the festive custom of 'Crying Christmas'. This consisted of speeches given by three 'senators'. The second senator spoke as follows:

> Oure intent and purpose is auncyent customes to declare
> That have ben used in this citie manye yeres ago
> And nowe for to breake them we wysshe ye schuld beware
> For ther be grievous ponysshment for them [tha]t wyll do soe[.]

The third senator added the hope:

> Therefore w[i]t[h] a contrite hart let us be merye all
> Having a stedfast faith and a love most amiable
> Disdaynyng no man of power greate or small
> For a crewel oppressour is nothing commendable[.]

The second senator chipped in:

> Therefore Crystmas myrth I wold ye schuld esteme
> And to feare God and scheme [th]e deides of charity both man and wyff
> Orelles the people wyll assemble w[i]t[h] weapons scherpe and keene
> Wherfore it wyll not prevaile to make any stryff[.]

The third senator continued the theme:

> Therefore endevour your selffes to have all thinges well
> That no default be found neyther of riche not pore
> But that tyme help your neighbours as S[aint] James doth [tell]
> Refresshyng the poverty [tha]t cummyth to [th]e dore.

Finally, the first senator concluded by enjoining the people: 'One neighbour to another[,] I wyssh ye schuld be kynde.'[48] Here, the social values of charity and neighbourliness were presented as uniting the city as a whole.

---

[47] Anon., *A Pleasant Countrey New Ditty* (London, 1625?).
[48] HMC, 14th Report, Appendix VIII, Lincoln MSS, Bury St Edmunds MSS, 58–9.

Yet that sense of melancholy that we noted earlier, of paternalist social relations lying only in the past, also found its way into the ballad literature. One ballad ran:

> Christmas beefe and bread is turn'd into stones,
> Into stones, into stones, into stones
> And silken rags
> And Lady Money sleepes and makes moanes
> And makes moanes, and makes moanes, and makes moanes
> In misers' bags
> Houses where pleasures once did abound
> Nought but a dogge and a shepherd is found
> Welladay!
> Places where Christmas revels did keepe
> Are now become habitations for sheepe
> Welladay! Welladay! Welladay![49]

It seemed self-evident to contemporaries that they were living through a period of growing social conflict. Preachers inveighed often and loudly against the oppression of the poor and the decline of communal responsibilities in the face of an avaricious individualism. The godly Essex minister Richard Rogers felt that 'the mighty devise to pill and make bare the meaner sort . . . whereas the predecessors of them both lived together before them in love and good will'.[50] In a 1623 sermon, Robert Sanderson compared rich men to 'Lions, and Wolfs, and Bears . . . the greedy great ones of this world, who are ever ravening after the estates and livelyhoods of their meaner neighbours, snatching, and biting, and devouring and at length eating them up and consuming them'.[51] Seven years later, in a sermon preached at the Devon Assizes, Thomas Foster cited the Book of Ezekiel: 'Thou hast taken Usury, and the increase, and thou hast defrauded thy Neighbours by extortion. Behold therefore I have smitten my hands upon thy Covetousnesse.' He went on to expound

the Morall Law of God: which gives every man his owne, in point of Propriety; and requires this Duty, with all, in point of Community. That the Use of our Goods should be, to help our neighbours in necessity who, in this respect, are called The owners of thy Goods.[52]

---

[49] 'Christmas Lamentation', in J. Payne Collier (ed.), *A Book of Roxburghe Ballads* (London, 1847), 13.
[50] W. Hunt, *The Puritan Moment: The Coming of Revolution to an English County* (Cambridge, MA, 1983), 130.
[51] R. Sanderson, *XXXV Sermons*, 7th ed. (London, 1681), 87.
[52] T. Foster, *The Scourge of Covetousnesse* (London, 1631), 4, 16.

There was a lively sub-genre of complaint literature that focused on the failings of London society. As the capital's population expanded, it seemed that charity grew cold. Henry Brinklow observed, in 1548, that

whereas now London, being one of the flowers of the worlde as touching worldlye riches, hath so manye, yea innumerable of poore people forced to go from dore to dore, and to syt openly in the stretes a beggynge, and many not able to do for other, but lye in their howses in most grievous paynes, and dye for lacke of ayde of the riche, to the great shame of the[e], oh London.[53]

This sense that London was becoming less neighbourly, less hospitable to the poor, fed into social practice. Neighbourly values provided a paradigm within which metropolitan individualism and entrepreneurialism could be criticized. Thus, in 1561, profiteering London poulterers were accused of neglecting 'theire bounden duties towards almightie god and the charitable usinge of their neighbours' and so impairing 'the common welthe of this Cytie'.[54] That Londoners lacked charity and that social relations in the city were cold were common assumptions of the period. In the second section of the Jacobean ballad entitled 'Too Good to Be True', a countryman recently returned from London tells a sceptical local audience that in the city

> The Landlords there are pitiful
> and racke not poore mens rents,
> ... The rich the poore doe love:
> of these there are but few.
> One neighbour sceptically replies
> I never will beleeve this.[55]

The same was true of the ever-expanding centres of proto-industrial activity. In a remarkably perceptive analysis of the economics of the East Anglian textile industry, published in 1603, the godly minister Thomas Carew pointed to the growing immiseration of the weavers as they came under the control of clothiers. Carew wondered, '[W]ill either equity, charity or humanity suffer that they should have their worke without answerable wages?'. In his curiously materialist discussion, Carew identified the increased rates of exploitation within which cloth workers had become ensnared. Their entanglement in that snare led, he felt, to the corrosion of the bonds of village society. The weavers had become so poor that they were unable to afford to dispense charity. Moreover, because they could not 'by

[53] J. M. Cowper (ed.), *Henry Brinklow's Complaint of Roderick Mors ... and the Lamentacyon of a Christen against the Citye of London*, EETS, 22 (London, 1874), 90.
[54] I. W. Archer, *The Pursuit of Stability: Social Relations in Elizabethan London* (Cambridge, 1991), 75.
[55] Anon., *Newes Good and Newe* (London, c.1623).

their labour . . . sustaine themselves, and helpe those that cannot worke', the weavers had become 'so farre from being able to give a penny to those that cannot labor, that . . . they bee most of them beggars and have need to take reliefe'.[56]

The Cornish gentleman Richard Carew also felt that the penetration of mercantile capital was dissolving paternal social relations within the poverty-stricken tin mining communities of his home county. Writing in 1602, he lamented the oppression of Cornish miners by tin merchants who, he suggested, inflicted a truck system upon the tinners:

> To these hungrie flies [i.e., the merchants], the poore labouring Tynner resorteth, desiring some money before the time of his pay at the deliveraunce: the other puts him off at first, answering he hath none to spare: in the end, when the poore man is driven through necessitie to renew his suite, he fal[l]s to questioning, what hee will do with the money. Saith the Tynner, I will buy bread and meate for my selfe and my hous[e]hold, and shooes, hosen, peticoates and such like stuffe for my wife and children. Suddenly herein, this owner becomes a pettie chapman: I will serve thee, saith he: hee delivers him so much ware as shall amount to fortie shillings in which he cuts him halfe in halfe for the price and four nobles in money, for which the poore wretch is bound in Darbyes bonds, to deliver him two hunded waight of Tynne at the next Coynage, which may then bee worth five pound or foure at the verie least.[57]

The ever-fluid land market was also recognized as a driver of social polarization. In a printed dialogue between a surveyor and a woodward, the surveyor says: 'I must nedes say this of most Tenants, that by reason of this greedinesse and spleene one against the other of hyring and buying land, they are more their owne enemies than is either the Surveyor or their Landlord.'[58] But perhaps more than anything it was the practice of usury that seemed to commentators on finance capitalism to combine economic individualism with social immorality, as the traditional gentry class departed the village, leaving its economy to become dominated by 'some rich Grazier, or remorseless Usurer'.[59] No less than ourselves in an age of global exchange, contemporaries found the fluidities of the new capitalist economy hard to capture; there was no straightforward language in which they could express its dynamics. Following a conventional critique of usury, William Perkins perceived his society's discursive limitations, stating: 'No statutes, no laws, can tame usury, for he hath so many turnings & turnagaines, that a man cannot tell wher to finde him. He is in money, in wares, in buying and selling,

---

[56] T. Carew, 'A Caveat for Craftesmen and Clothiers', in T. Carew, *Certaine Godly and Necessary Sermons* (London, 1603), sigs. T8r, X2r.

[57] *TED*, I, 290–1.   [58] R. C., *An Olde Thrift Newly Revived* (London, 1612), 12–13.

[59] Anon., *Muldsacke, or the Apologie of Hic Mulier* (London, 1620), sig. B3r.

for readie money, for time, in borrowing & lending, by himself and by his brokers, the devils huntsmen.'[60]

If the evils of usury represented an easy way of criticizing the growing monetarization of trust, the observable changes in the rural landscape represented the material manifestation of agrarian capitalism. Enclosures, it seemed to many labouring people, were both morally and materially disruptive of the local community. Thus, in 1612, the Norfolk farmer Humfrey Willson was seen as a disruptive presence 'amongest his poore neighbours', threatening them with all sorts of violence. He had enclosed part of a local sheepwalk, saying that, if he were opposed, he would shoot his opponents with arrows.[61] Such people were felt to be the enemies of the neighbourhood.

Neighbourliness therefore confronts the social historian with a question. Was it, as so many contemporaries believed, in decline? Certainly, there were fundamental shifts within the economy that militated against a softening of social relations. Steve Hindle puts this well:

[T]he realities of social and economic differentiation in the century after 1550 ensured that the vision of neighbourliness became fragmented and marginalized, and was perforce restricted to certain degrees and sorts of inhabitants, among whom the habit of political association strengthened the parochial sense of place.[62]

Yet, despite these structural shifts, the discourse of neighbourliness remained strong. Christopher Marsh is right to state that 'there existed in early modern England a deeply rooted and influential consensus about the importance of maintaining a sense of community'.[63] Marsh is less well equipped to deal with the difficult fact that such communal values were shot through with radical inconsistencies and that, for all that they endured, they did so in the face of increased commercialization, social polarization and the growth of capitalist relations of production. This was one of the elementary contradictions of the period.

### Who Is My Neighbour?

In Christian theology, all human beings were neighbours. In a sermon preached in 1613, Francis Rogers spoke condescendingly of how 'the simple sort thinke them onely their neighbours who dwell neare them', explaining

---

[60] W. Perkins, *A Sermon Preached in the Cathedrall Church in Norwich* (London, 1590), sigs. G1v-2r.

[61] NRO, NQS/C/S3/19, articles against Humfrey Willson.

[62] S. Hindle, 'A Sense of Place? Becoming and Belonging in the Rural Parish, 1550–1650', in A. Shepard and P. Withington (eds.), *Communities in Early Modern England: Networks, Place, Rhetoric* (Manchester, 2000), 109.

[63] C. Marsh, '"Common Prayer" in England, 1560–1640: The View from the Pew', *P&P*, 171 (2001), 71.

that '[o]ur Neighbour is not to be esteemed him which is nearest to us in
bloud, or in place, but hee which is our companion in reason: now every man
being a reasonable Creature, every man is therefore our neighbour'.[64] In
answer to the question 'How farre extendeth the name of Neighbour?',
Alexander Nowell's widely read catechism replied: 'The name of neighbour
conteyneth not onely those that be of our kinne and alliance, or frendes, or
such as be knitte to us in any civile bond of love, but also those whom we
know not, yea and our enemies.'[65] In a sermon preached in Oxford on
Easter Day 1615, John Day spoke in similar terms, telling his parishioners:

I purpose to speak to you all, for you are all of you Neighbours: You are not all of
you, or Husbands, or Parents, or Maisters, or Wives or Children, or Se[r]vants, or
Virgins, or Widowes, but Neighbours you are all ... All men are Neighbours to
one another ... Every man is thy Neighbour. He is thy Neighbour, that is born as
thou art, Of Adam and Eve.[66]

Thomas Luspet stated categorically in 1533 that 'everye manne
is neighbour unto other, dwellynge in the smalle compasse of this
e[a]rthe ...[. H]e that loveth not his neighbour, halteth in his charitie
towards God.'[67] And so, as Nicholas Sander put it in 1568, 'everie man is
both our neighbour, and our brother'.[68]

But in practical terms, 'neighbourhood' was understood as a quintessen-
tially local experience. Witnesses in legal cases spoke of their 'neighbourhood'
in small-scale terms – for rural inhabitants, it represented an area (at the most)
five or six miles from their home. For urbanites, neighbourhood was often
thought of as a street or close or alley or maybe the city parish. Commentators
in print sources similarly saw neighbourhood as grounded in the local. For
Thomas Hooker, '[t]he bond of humanity and civilitie' was 'as the bond
of neighbourhood', something that drew together 'people that live in the same
place or towne'.[69] A 1634 translation of Pliny the Elder linked neighbourhood
to 'propinquity', 'Vicinitie' and 'neernesse'.[70] Writing in 1640, Richard Ward
rendered 'the vicinitie, neighbourhood, and brotherhood' deeply
connected.[71] Similarly, Edward Jorden thought of 'neighbourhood and

---

[64] F. Rogers, *A Sermon of Love* (London, 1613), 16–17.
[65] A. Nowell, *A Catechism: or, First Instruction and Learning of a Christian Religion* (London, 1571), sig. F3r.
[66] Day, *Day's Festivals*, 327.
[67] T. Lupset, *A Treatise of Charitie* (London, 1533), fols. 20v–21r.
[68] N. Sander, *A Briefe Treatise of Usurie* (London, 1568), 6.
[69] T. Hooker, *Foure Learned and Godly Treatises* (London, 1638), 65.
[70] Pliny, *The Historie of the World* (London, 1634), introduction and 373.
[71] R. Ward, *Theologicall Questions, Dogmaticall Observations, and Evangelicall Essays* (London, 1640), 18.

vicinitie' as cognate terms.[72] The result was the intense localization of social relations. John Downame argued in 1616 that

wee are bound to relieve before others, our common friends and nearest neighbours, who dwell in the same place & parish, for besides the bond of neighbourhood, we are in this regard also to [prefer] them before others, because through God[']s providence they are first offered to our view, and have the opportunity of discovering unto us their wants and miseries.[73]

Likewise, one didactic tract advised its readers to give alms to 'such as are neerest to us in regard of a domesticall, civill, or christian neighbourhood'.[74] For other commentators, too, neighbourliness was defined by propinquity – what one translator of Calvin called the 'neerenes of neighbourhood'.[75] Henry Burton therefore referred to 'vicinity & neighbourhood of nature & society' as the basis for social organization.[76] Contradicting his proposition that all human beings are neighbours, John Day also identified propinquity as the basis for neighbourhood, stating that 'such may be the Neighbourhood here meant in this place, namely the Neighbourhood, and Nighnes of Such as dwell in the selfe same Streete, or in the selfe-same Parish that we do'.[77]

Neighbourhood represented a powerful affective tie, carrying with it associations of 'love' and 'friendship'. Writing in 1605, the dramatist George Chapman saw 'olde acquaintance and long neighbourhood' as providing strong 'Ties' of 'affection'.[78] Henry Porter's 1599 play *The Pleasant History of the Two Angry Women of Abington* linked 'amity' and 'love' with 'familiar neighbourhood'.[79] The minister of Bermondsey, Edward Elton, argued in 1615 that 'the bond of outward brotherhood, service, societie and neighbourhood' formed 'a perswasion and a powerfull argument urging love'.[80] Writing in the same year, Robert Cleaver set 'neighbourhood' alongside 'love, peace ... and equitie'.[81] Friendship, love and neighbourhood underwrote one another: the English translator of Lambert Daneau's tract on Christian friendship

[72] E. Jorden, *A Briefe Discourse of a Disease Called the Suffocation of the Mother* (London, 1603), 8.
[73] J. Downame, *The Plea of the Poore* (London, 1616), 136.
[74] S. Crooke, *The Guide unto True Blessednesse* (London, 1613), 186.
[75] C. C., *A Commentary upon the Prophecie of Isaiah* (London, 1609), epigraph.
[76] H. Burton, *Israels Fast* (London, 1628), 8.    [77] Day, *Day's Festivals*, 328.
[78] G. Chapman, *Al Fooles a Comedy* (London, 1605), act II, scene 1, line 20.
[79] H. Porter, *The Pleasant History of the Two Angry Women of Abington* (London, 1599), sigs. A2r, B4v.
[80] E. Elton, *An Exposition of the Epistle of St Paule to the Colossians Deliuered in Sundry Sermons* (London, 1615), 82.
[81] R. Cleaver, *A Briefe Explanation of the Whole Booke of the Proverbs of Salomon* (London, 1615), 61.

wrote of the need for 'a continuation of friendlines, & maintaynaunce of neighbourhood'.[82] A 1589 commentator wrote of 'the bond of friendship, neighbourhood, or such like'.[83] In a sermon preached in 1627, Robert Sanderson argued: 'Friendship and Neighbourhood underwrote "kindred", "acquaintance", "covenant, oath, benefits or other natural or civill obligation".'[84] George Gifford's account of the beliefs of the 'common sort' of his parishioners suggested that 'friendship' and 'neighbourhood' were, for them, interchangeable concepts.[85]

In a discussion of intercourse between nations, 'neighborhood' was included alongside 'Religion, aliance, perpetuall unitie' as forming 'natural and civill bonds'.[86] Neighbourhood, then, provided the basis for polities and well as communities: when the English considered the social basis of the French monarchy, for example, they wrote of its roots in 'the rights of neighbourhood, affinitie, honestie and friendship'.[87] A 1576 translation of the Italian humanist Francesco Patrizi's tract *A Moral Method of Civil Policy* understood neighbourhood to form part of the original basis for civil society, writing of how, when early humans 'did playnly see what commoditie was in the societie of man and woman: and howe more easlye and better verye manye lived together, then a fewe: yea more safer from the invasion of wilde beastes: they began to [j]oyne Lordshippe to Lordshippe, and laye Familye to Familye, and also to [j] oyne in neighbourhoode for their owne common utilitie'.[88] This account of early human society presupposed inter-communal cooperation. It was, perhaps, not too far from the truth; in any case, it was presented as a model for early modern villagers and townsfolk.

Neighbourhood was closely associated with kin, suggesting that familial links might have been denser than social historians have tended to suppose. In a sermon preached in Oxford in 1600, it seemed to George Abbot that 'neighborhood' and 'kinred' were cognate concepts.[89] Writing some four years later, George Downame associated neighbourhood with 'kinred, amitie, acquaintance'.[90] A translator of Calvin wrote of the link between 'consanguinitie and

[82] L. Daneau, *True and Christian Friendshippe* (London, 1586), sig. F1r.
[83] T. W., *A Short, yet Sound Commentarie; Written on that Woorthie Worke Called; the Proverbes of Salomon* (London, 1589), 11.
[84] R. Sanderson, *Two Sermons Preached at Paules-Crosse* (London, 1628), sig. A2r, p. 115.
[85] Gifford, *A Briefe Discourse of Certaine Points*, fol. 41r.
[86] T. Palmer, *An Essay of the Meanes How to Make Our Travailes, into Forraine Countries, the More Profitable and Honourable* (London, 1606), 41.
[87] J. de Serres, *A General Inventorie of the History of France* (London, 1607), 187.
[88] F. Patrizi, *A Moral Methode of Civile Policie* (London, 1576), fol. 3r.
[89] G. Abbot, *An Exposition upon the Prophet Ionah* (Oxford, 1600), 518.
[90] G. Downame, *The Christians Sanctuarie* (London, 1604), 79.

neighbourhood'.[91] In 1613, Samuel Crooke advised his readers to pray for those whom God 'hast knit unto us in the bands of consanguinitie, affinitie, neighbourhood, or Christian amitie'.[92] One of the most powerful connections between neighbourhood and another key social ideal was that with charity. 'Neighborhood', 'charity' and 'brotherhood' were conjoined in George Peele's 1595 play *The Old Wives' Tale*.[93] In Thomas Taylor's 1635 discussion of ordinary people's value systems, 'honesty, good neighbourhood, hospitality [and] charity' were presented as connected.[94] It seemed to Henry Chettle in 1595 that 'neighborhood' was as powerful a social norm as 'charitie, pietie, pitie ... friendship [and] equitie'.[95]

A discussion of the sufferings of Germany in the Thirty Years War remarked that 'the bonds of Religion, neighbourhood or commerce' intersected with the desire amongst ordinary people for 'neighborhood, kindred or friendship'.[96] Commerce also mattered to the Northampton physician John Cotta's understanding of neighbourhood: he felt that 'mutuall neighbourhood and Humanity' were connected to 'friendly and [j]ust commerce ... love and loyall reciprocation'.[97] Love was important to Southwark testators: Jeremy Boulton observes that testators nominated the overseers of their wills from amongst their 'long friends', 'good friends' and 'loving neighbours and friends'.[98] For the Essex minister Jeremiah Dyke, writing in 1636, 'peace' and 'neighbourhood' were closely connected.[99] Robert Gomersall believed that 'Neighbourhood' was as powerful a social bond as 'Religion, Language' and 'Bloud'.[100] For John Dod, writing in 1603, 'hospitality' and 'neighbourhood' were interchangeable.[101] Thomas Adams thought that 'God commendeth the inseparable neighbourhood of godlinesse and brotherly kindnesse'.[102] And, in a sermon preached in 1629, Martin Day associated 'company' with the 'neighbourhood of men'.[103]

---

[91] C. C., *A Commentary*, 137.    [92] Crooke, *The Guide unto True Blessednesse*, 59.

[93] G. Peele, *The Old Wives' Tale* (London, 1595), sig. B3r.

[94] T. Taylor, *Christ Revealed: or The Old Testament Explained: A Treatise of the Types and Shadowes of Our Saviour Contained throughout the Whole Scripture* (London, 1635), 169.

[95] H. Chettle, *Piers Plainnes Seaven Yeres Prentiship* (London, 1595), sig. Er.

[96] P. Vincent, *The Lamentations of Germany* (London, 1638), preface, 312.

[97] J. Cotta, *A Short Discoverie of the Unobserved Dangers of Severall Sorts of Ignorant and Unconsiderate Practisers of Physicke* (London, 1612), 47.

[98] J. Boulton, *Neighbourhood and Society: A London Suburb in the Seventeenth Century* (Cambridge, 1987), 238, 242.

[99] J. Dyke, *A Worthy Communicant* (London, 1636), 318.

[100] R. Gomersall, *The Levites Revenge* (London, 1628), 43.

[101] J. Dod, *The Bright Star which Leadeth Wise Men to Our Lord Jesus Christ* (London, 1603), 50.

[102] T. Adams, *The Happines of the Church* (London, 1619), 152.

[103] M. Day, *Doomes-Day: or, A Treatise of the Resurrection of the Body* (London, 1636), 181.

Neighbourhood, then, was a loose and flexible concept. For newcomers to a community, so long as they did not represent a likely burden on the poor rate, they may well often have been welcomed. In the lead mining zone of the Derbyshire Peak Country, for example, male immigrants were taught the free mining customs of the King's Field upon their arrival.[104] Betrothal to an established inhabitant was another way in which a person might become accepted into the neighbourhood. At a betrothal at Folkestone (Kent), the question was put to the soon-to-be bride – 'Which is she that should be our neighbour?' – to which the woman answered, 'I am she.' Patrick Collinson suggests that this may have been 'a customary and almost ritual question'.[105] In many northern communities, it seems to have been common to think of neighbourhood as something that one *did*.[106] In Ousby (Cumberland) in 1602, for instance, 'doing neighbureheade' was understood as a form of social practice. In Penruddock (Cumberland), it was the responsibility of the bailiff to 'charge the Tenantes ... to doe all kinds of neighborheade as neede shall require amongst themselves jointlie together'. In 1607, the tenants of Dilston (Northumberland) were expected periodically to 'come together abowt neghborhead'. Agrarian practice informed neighbourhood. In Malham (Yorkshire) in 1620, the 'order of neighbourhead' meant the arrangement of agrarian practice. In 1621, at Shap (Westmorland), 'good neighborhood' involved maintaining walls between fields. In 1564, the manor court of Dilston ordered that no one was to enter the common field 'but of such tyme that they are on my master service or other thinges nedfull in neighburhed'. The expectation that inhabitants should 'do neighbourhood' was even written into leases. In 1545, the lease of a cottage to Rowland Foster of Dishforth (Yorkshire) required not just that he 'shalbe of good and honeste discrescion emongest his neyghbours' but also that he 'shall doo neighburhed as the case and matter shall require'. Meanwhile, 'evil neighborhode' was prosecuted at the manor court of Extwistle (Lancashire).[107]

---

[104] A. Wood, *The Politics of Social Conflict: The Peak Country, 1520–1770* (Cambridge, 1999), 170.

[105] P. Collinson, *The Birthpangs of Protestant England: Religious and Cultural Change in the Sixteenth and Seventeenth Centuries* (Basingstoke, 1988), 87.

[106] M. Johnston, 'Doing Neighbourhood: Practising Neighbourliness in the Diocese of Durham, 1624–31', in B. Kane and S. Sandall (eds.), *The Experience of Neighbourhood in Late Medieval and Early Modern Europe* (London, forthcoming 2021).

[107] A. J. L. Winchester, *The Harvest of the Hills: Rural Life in Northern England and the Scottish Borders, 1400–1700* (Edinburgh, 2000), 45, 47, 67; J. Healey, 'The Northern Manor and the Politics of Neighbourhood: Dilston, Northumberland, 1558–1640', *Northern History*, 51, 2 (2014), 231; Hudleston, 'Elizabethan Paines Laid at Hutton John', 124; Whiteside, 'Paines Made at Shap', 155; HMC, *Various Collections*, II, 62. For further examples, see Wrightson, 'The "Decline of Neighbourliness" Revisited', 24.

In what might often have felt like a dangerous, unpredictable world, the values of neighbourhood had some power. Rich and poor alike could draw upon those values in times of difficulty. Thomas Tusser reminded housewives:

> No neighbour reprove
> Do so to have love
> The love of thy neighbour shall stand thee in steede
> The poorer, the gladder, to helpe at neede
> Use friendly thy neighbour, else trust him in this
> As he hath thy friendship, so trust unto his[108]

Friendship and trust were two of the core values that underwrote neighbourliness. The assumption was that neighbours *owed* something to one another, even in the most extreme circumstances. Thus, one Wiltshire man who had been accused of assaulting a girl went to a witness against him and asked him to 'use him like a neighbour' and to mitigate his testimony.[109] Then there was the concept of friendship. Friends owed something to one another: friendship was about reciprocity, trust and social bonds. But it was also a hierarchical relationship: one's friends were often one's superiors – a master or mistress, a landlord, older relatives, perhaps a gentleman or gentlewoman or even the lord of the manor. 'Friends' were especially important for young people who hoped to marry. The twenty-five-year old husbandman Ralph Turner of Long Newton (County Durham) told the church court that

being in love wth … helyn by the space of x yeres last past and beinge contract betwyxt them selves and bothe ther frendes agreed thereunto marry for the devision & setting out off the said helyn good [i.e., her dowry] they could not agree and therupon this ex[aminant] and the said helyn sought to Thos Turner of darlington th[i]s depo[nen]t brother to procure them a marriage at darlington wch Thos sent them both to … mr banks to aske them … why and upon what occasion thys ex[aminant] sought nowe to be married at darlington then at long newton he saith that he feired that Rauff colling wold have … forbidden ther marriadge wch was the said helyns uncle.[110]

The ten-year romance between Ralph and Helyn, then, seemed to the young man to be imperilled by his lover's uncle – her 'friend' – who appears to have been in a position to wave through the marriage or to cut it short. Unsurprisingly, young people were sometimes unwilling to accept such

---

[108] Tusser, *Five Hundred Points of Good Husbandry*, 160.

[109] M. J. Ingram, 'Communities and Courts: Law and Disorder in Seventeenth-Century Wiltshire', in J. S. Cockburn (ed.), *Crime in England, 1550–1800* (Princeton, NJ, 1977), 128.

[110] DDR/EJ/CCD/1/2, fol. 253v.

prescriptive marriage advice from their 'friends'. In 1519, for example, the Norfolk woman Agnes Powtwyn told her neighbour Isabel Dyman that she had contracted to marry with John Grygges upon the end of his apprenticeship and 'that if the sayd Grygges wold sett her 20 myle from her frendes she wold be att his commandment, for it is agenst my frendes will that I shuld mary with hym, and if itt plesee hym to cum I will nott moke with him nor disteyne hym'.[111]

## Charity and Neighbourhood

If friendship was something that people felt they should offer but that was manifest within sharp social structures, so, too, was charity. Some wealthier folk were notable for their investment in these powerful moral forces. In 1630, George Hall of Wighill (Northumberland) had this to say of his fellow gentleman Robert Lumsden: 'Dureing all the tyme of his remembrance[,] Lumsden [has been] accounted to be an honest man and charitable to the poore, and ready to doe anie good office of neighbourhood.' Another neighbour, the yeoman Robert Alder, had explained: 'Lumsden lveth 4 or 5 myles from the Scottish ground, and manie poore people, both Scottish and English, repare unto him, and have much reliefe.'[112] Four years later, the Durham gentleman John Richardson was described by Henry Briggs of the North Bailey as 'a verie good and orderly parishioner, and hath moved others to be lyberallie affected towardes the repaireing of St Maries or Bow church in the North Bailey, where he is a parishioner, and hath bene verie bountifull to the poore of that parish'.[113] Obligations to the poor imposed themselves on the mind of the dying. In 1605, the minister Nicholas Diggens of the Sussex parish of Stoughton explained how, as William Lodger was about to pass away, 'twice or thrice he prayed to his mother to be good unto the poor'.[114] Neighbourliness, then, regularly crossed social divisions; there were many occasions on which richer people might do small favours for those poorer than themselves. When old Widow Bennett departed her village of Ashton Keynes (Wiltshire), she was provided with horses and wagons by Mr Robbyns 'in neighbourhood and kindness in that shee was an old sickly woman and his next neighbour'.[115]

[111] E. D. Stone and B. Cozens-Hardy (eds.), *Norwich Consistory Court Depositions, 1499–1512 and 1518–1530*, Norfolk Record Society, 10 (Norwich, 1938), no. 188. By way of contrast, see DUL, DDR/EJ/CCD/1/2, fol. 237r.
[112] W. H. D. Longstaffe (ed.), *The Acts of the High Commission within the Diocese of Durham*, Surtees Society, 34 (Durham, 1858), 24, 26.
[113] Ibid., 91.    [114] Wilkinson (ed.), *Chichester Archdeaconry Depositions*, 139.
[115] B. Howard Cunnington (ed.), *Records of the County of Wiltshire: Being Extracts from the Quarter Sessions Great Rolls from the Seventeenth Century* (Devizes, 1932), 71.

As mentioned, 'neighborhood', 'charity' and 'brotherhood' were presented in George Peele's 1595 play *The Old Wives' Tale* as conjoined.[116] The neighbourly ideal was deeply inscribed within Christian culture. Keith Wrightson has emphasized 'the vitality of the concept of neighbourliness as both a centrally important social relationship and a primary social ideal'. He notes: 'Neighbours were customarily described as "kind", "gentle", "true", "honest", "faithful" or "loving" ...[. T]here were proverbs too: "who hath a good neighbor hath a good morrow"; "a nere neyghbour is better than a farre frende".'[117]

In a 1548 pamphlet, an evangelical shoemaker was depicted articulating a powerful social critique. He explained that the 'true and faythfull christen man ... serveth also his Neighbour, wyth the woorkes of charitie, that is the whole summe of a Christen lyfe'.[118] For all that the godly were seen by many ordinary folk as the enemies of traditional social values, many evangelical and Puritan writers placed great emphasis upon charity as a key virtue, something that bound parishes and communities together. In his *Catechism*, Thomas Becon argued that charity and neighbourhood were linked:

> [W]e should be ready at all times both with our heart, body and goods to help and succor our neighbour ...[. We should] rejoice, when all things go prosperously with our neighbour, and to the uttermost of our power labour that he and whatsoever pertaineth unto him may be safely preserved without all peril and danger. For charity and true neighbourly love seeketh not her own, but the commodity and profit of other.[119]

Charity was, then, a Christian duty, a way in which the rich might redistribute some of their wealth in the certainty that they were following God's commands: 'Such as be rich should deal mercifully and liberally with the poor, helping their necessity and relieving their poverty. For unto this end hath God blessed them with worldly substance, that they should be merciful and bounteous to the poor, and gladly and willingly minister unto them all good things, as faithful and trusty stewards of the Lord's treasures.'[120]

For Dod and Cleaver, in their widely read conduct book, charity was central to the neighbourly ideal: '[E]verie man', they wrote, 'is bound to have a charitable opinion, and good conceit of his neighbour, with a desire

---

[116] Peele, *The Old Wives' Tale*, sig. B3r.

[117] Wrightson, 'The "Decline of Neighbourliness" Revisited', 21–2, 25.

[118] A. Scoloker, *A Godly Dysputacion between a Christen Shoemaker and a Popysh Parson* (London, 1548), no pagination.

[119] J. Ayre (ed.), *The Catechism of Thomas Becon ... with Other Pieces Written by Him*, Parker Society (Cambridge, 1844), 112.

[120] Ibid., 112.

of his good name and credit.'[121] Neighbourliness was deeply rooted in contemporary readings of the Ten Commandments. Naomi Tadmor observes that in catechisms, '[t]he Sixth Commandment was extended to address not only an injunction against murder, but the maintenance of peace, order and good will in local communities'. Tadmor quotes one such text as follows: '[W]e should not only try to preserve the lives of our neighbours, but also seek to love them from the bottom of our hearts, be reconciled should any differences arise, and succor them when in need.'[122]

In 1543, some York citizens were bound over to keep the peace, agreeing not to defame one another but to 'use them selfs with gentyll words, one to an other as honest nebures shuld do'.[123] Likewise, in 1626, the churchwardens of Westhampnett (Sussex) presented their minister 'for that he hath admitted one Robert Taylor to the Holy Communion, being an open contender, and having sued many of his neighbours for matters of small valew, to our great hurt and hindrances, and will not reconcile himself, though it hath bin sought by some of the parish'.[124] Litigious ministers who aggressively pressed their claims to tithes were widely disliked.[125] In 1612, the minister of Clayworth (Nottinghamshire), one John Tunstall, incurred hostility for his unneighbourly dealings. One of his parishioners, Roger Booth, said of him: 'Mr Tunstall is a very troblesome man to his neighbors having vii or viii of them in so many sev[er]all suites att this present.' Thinking better of this, Booth had this remark scored out from the record of the trial. But he went on to explain that he told Tunstall that he was 'a scurvy lyinge fellow'. Tunstall had then threatened to sue him, to which Booth responded '[t]hat he the said Mr Tunstall indeed went about to undoe him and the poore in the parish'.[126]

In 1567, one Kentishman explained that he often 'fortuned to goo into the house of Thomas Haslet nere adjoining to [his] house: as many tymes he did use before that tyme, of neighbour[ho]od to talke and be mery togithers', the happy scene was disrupted when Haslet's wife accused the man of sleeping with a neighbour's wife.[127] Abusing neighbours could

---

[121] J. Dod and R. Cleaver, *A Treatise or Exposition upon the Ten Commandments* (London, 1603), 94v.

[122] N. Tadmor, *The Social Universe of the English Bible: Scripture, Society and Culture in Early Modern England* (Cambridge, 2010), 38.

[123] A. Raine (ed.), *York Civic Records IV*, YASRS, 108 (York, 1943), 94.

[124] H. Johnstone (ed.), *Churchwardens' Presentments (17th Century): The Archdeaconry of Chichester*, Sussex Record Society, 49 (Cambridge, 1947), 116.

[125] For a case-study, see Wood, *The Politics of Social Conflict*, 223–31.

[126] BIA, CP.H.714.

[127] P. Collinson, 'The Cohabitation of the Faithful with the Unfaithful', in O. P. Grell, J. I. Israel and N. Tyacke (eds.), *From Persecution to Toleration* (Oxford, 1991), 67.

carry a heavy sentence: the pains laid down by the manorial court of
Hutton John (Cumberland) in 1576 stated that 'none within this soil
shall revile[,] slander[,] nickname or misreport on another', adding that
Cuthbert Burton would lose his tenancy if he were to be found guilty of
'mysusing anie of his neighbours by himself his false charges or his wife's
evil tongue'.[128] After all, the Book of Psalms offers up praise for '[h]e that
backbiteth not with his tongue, nor doeth evil to his neighbour, nor taketh
up a reproach against his neighbour'.[129]

It was not only within the Christian belief system that values of charity
and neighbourliness were celebrated. There were supernatural rewards
for giving to the poor. An account of the traditions of Cleveland found
that the common folk of the region were 'besotted with ould superstitions', including the belief that

when any dieth, certaine women singe a songe to the dead bodie, recytinge the
jorney that the partie deceased must goe; and they of beliefe (such is their
fondnesse) that once in their lives yt is good to give a payre of newe shoes to
a poore man, forasmuch as after this life they are to passe barefoote through
a greate launde full of thornes and furzen, excepte by the meryte of the almes
aforesaid they have redeemed their forfeyte: for at the edge of the launde an ould
man shall meete them with the same shoes that were given by the partye when he
was living, and after he hath shodde them he dismisseth them to goe through
thicke and thin without scratch or scale.[130]

But within Christian belief there was a powerful link between neighbourhood and charity. Thomas Lupset argued in 1533 that 'If you kepe in you
Charitie, ye be spotless of all gru[d]ges, and therewith ye love in the moste
highest degree of lovynge both god and man, god for hym selfe, and man
for goddes sake . . . Christe saithe, that in charitie is conteyned al the law of
god'. For Lupset, charity transcended social hierarchies. He argued forcefully that 'In charitie is no knowledge of any difference between ryche
and poore, between mayster & servant, between bonde and free, between
faithful and untrue, between male and female, between kynne and no
kynne'.[131]

Charity, love and neighbourhood were cognate concepts. In
a persuasive discussion, John Bossy has shown: 'The state of charity,
meaning social integration, was the principal end of the Christian life,
and any people that claimed to be Christian must embody it somehow, at
some time, in this world.'[132] To William Shakespeare, love and

---

[128] Hudleston, 'Elizabethan Paines Laid at Hutton John', 122, 123.    [129] Psalms, 15:3.
[130] Anon., 'A Description of Cleveland; in a Letter Addressed by H.R. to Sir Thomas
     Chaloner', *Topographer and Genealogist*, II (1853), 429.
[131] Lupset, *Treatise of Charitie*, fols. 2v-3r, 22r.
[132] J. Bossy, *Christianity in the West, 1400–1700* (Oxford, 1985), 57.

neighbourliness slipped easily into each other; so did 'neighbourhood and Christian-like accord'.[133] It was argued that all other Christian virtues were subsumed by charity, 'for yf men be charytable[,] they shall not onely love God[,] feare God and serve God ... but also shal helpe ... sucker and sustayne theyr poore neyghbours with all theyr strength and might'.[134]

Late medieval and early modern people believed profoundly in love – that is, in mutual amity – and understood it to form powerful social cement. In one London guild, 'every brother and sister, in tokening of love and charity and peace, at receiving shall kiss other of them that ben there'.[135] Thomas Lupset suggested in 1550 that while the love of material things separated the covetous from God, true favour to the poor invited divine mercy. Thus, society was held together and humanity redeemed by what W. K. Jordan calls 'the one transcendent virtue of charity'.[136]

Charity was therefore closely linked to Christian faith, such that it could be argued, in 1537, that 'faith must declare itself by deeds of charit[i]e'.[137] Charity might imply a top-down, vertical relationship between giver and recipient; but it was a fluid value that welled up within communities, a synonym for social harmony. One of the meanings of charity – that of being at ease with one's neighbours – is revealed to us in 1623, when the Yorkshireman Robert Layborne was presented to the archdeacon. The churchwardens explained that 'he is in suite w[i]th some of his neighboures & was not in Charitie all Easter last'.[138] The moment of communion could be a time at which disputants might be reconciled to values of good neighbourhood. In Kirkby Overblow (Yorkshire) in 1562, for example, Richard Ampleforth, who was in dispute with one of his neighbours, was called upon by the minister 'to be in charitye and to come up and Receave the hoolye com[mun]ion as other p[ar]ishioners then did'.[139] Ministers sometimes denied communion to those who were not 'in charity' with their neighbours.[140] Richard Purdie of Mettingham

---

[133] Shakespeare, W., *As You Like It*, act II, scene 5, line 1744; *Henry V*, act V, scene 2, line 3329.
[134] W. Conway, *An Exhortacion to Charite* (London, 1550?), sig. A.ii.
[135] Bossy, *Christianity in the West*, 59.
[136] J. A. Gee (ed.), *Life and Works of Thomas Lupset* (New Haven, CT, 1928), 207–31.
[137] Anon., *A Goodly Treatise of Faith, Hope and Charit[i]e* (Southwark, 1537).
[138] BIA, V.1623, fol. 101A.
[139] J. A. Sharpe, '"Such Disagreement betwyx Neighbours": Litigation and Human Relations in Early Modern England', in J. Bossy (ed.), *Disputes and Settlements: Law and Human Relations in the West* (Cambridge, 1983), 177.
[140] For a 1581 example of a Hampshire gentleman who was denied communion 'because he was out of charity', see HALS, 21M65/C3/8.

(Norfolk), for example, was excluded from communion in 1597 because the minister 'said that Purdie was hard to the poore'.[141] The church was meant to be a site of social harmony: the 'mystery of peace', 'bond of love' and 'straight knot of charity' were not available to those who brought unneighbourly attitudes to within its walls.[142]

Charity, then, had multiple meanings – for many, it meant living in quietude and kindness with their neighbours, owing one another reciprocal duties and grounding friendship at the heart of the local community. Christianity itself was felt by some to be reducible to charity and neighbourliness. Philippe de Mornay wrote: 'Religion is nothing els but charitie; that is to say, the performing of a mannes duetie towards his neighbour.'[143] These implications are most often apparent, once again, in their breach. In 1608, for instance, the churchwardens of Tallington (Lincolnshire) presented Thomas Capit 'for carrying of tales betwixt neighbour and neighbour to the breech of charity'.[144] A bill found its way before parliament in 1576, aimed at settling the 'multitude of contentions which for lack of charity rise upon the smallest occasions between neighbours'.[145]

Charity could form a practical response to the massive difficulties faced by the early modern poor. In the face of poverty, dearth and disease, charity saved lives. In 1616, a survey of the population of industrial Hallamshire conducted by 'twenty-four of the most sufficient inhabitants' found that of the 2,207 people who lived in Sheffield, some 725 'are not able to live without the charity of their neighbours. These are all begging poore.'[146] Being good to the poor was an important aspect of being a decent neighbour. In 1597, the neighbours of the Essex woman Elizabeth Westbrowne vouched for her 'very good name', adding that she was 'good to the poor'.[147] These things mattered to the needy,

---

[141] J. F. Williams (ed.), *Bishop Redman's Visitation, 1597*, Norfolk Record Society, 18 (Norwich, 1946), 115. For another example, see Archer, *The Pursuit of Stability*, 79. For a fuller study, see C. Haigh, 'Communion and Community: Exclusion from Communion in Post-Reformation England', *Journal of Ecclesiastical History*, 51 (2000), 721–40. For an example of a man who cared little for his exclusion from communion, see Longstaffe (ed.), *The Acts of the High Commission within the Diocese of Durham*, 143.

[142] A. Walsham, 'Supping with Satan's Disciples: Spiritual and Secular Sociability in Post-Reformation England', in N. Lewycky and A. Morton (eds.), *Getting Along? Religious Identities and Confessional Relations in Early Modern England* (Aldershot, 2012), 35–6.

[143] P. de Mornay, *A Woorke Concerning the Trewnesse of the Christian Religion* (London, 1587), 364.

[144] K. Major, 'The Lincoln Diocesan Records', *TRHS*, 4th ser., 22 (1940), 58–9.

[145] Brooks, *Pettyfoggers and Vipers of the Commonwealth*, 133.

[146] J. Hunter, *Hallamshire: The History and Topography of the Parish of Sheffield in the County of York* (London, 1861), 148.

[147] F. G. Emmison, *Elizabethan Life: Morals and the Church Courts* (Chelmsford, 1973), 79.

allowing them to sustain an independent living. One poor Cheshire women explained to the diocesan court, in 1638, how her scanty earnings were topped up by those around her: she maintained herself and her child through her labour, adding that her 'neighbours are good unto her and doe bestowe some releefe on her'.[148] The Suffolk minister Thomas Carew noted, in 1603, that poor weavers sometimes survived only through 'some furtherance by some friends' who allowed them to 'keepe a cow or two' without which 'they cannot live'.[149]

Ownership of a cow was critical to the household economies of many poor people; the loss of a cow could be devastating, meaning the loss of sources of fat, protein and calcium.[150] For the very poor, those so destitute that they didn't have a cow of their own, there was milk to be taken from those cows that were owned by the parish and whose products were reserved for the poor.[151] Access to pasture land was therefore essential for many poor households, keeping them off such arrangements. It was a live issue in many communities and often the cause of intense conflict. Owning a cow might keep a family off the poor rate: it was noted in Dorset, in 1636, that the consequence of heavy taxation was that 'the greatest part of the are[a]rs falls among the poorer sort who payith like drops of bloud & some doth sell th[ei]r only cowe which should feede the[i]r children & most come to the parish'.[152] But despite this, there were places where landed householders were willing to allow the poor their place on the common. In 1584, for instance, it was recalled how, amongst the tenants of Felmingham (Norfolk), there was 'one poore woman called wedow Andrewes who hadd comon of pasture to her cotage in respecte she did fence parte of the comon ageynste hir cotage'.[153] Piecemeal enclosures by the poor might be tolerated so long as they did not get out of hand. Then there were circumstances in which it made sense to allow a bit of land to the poor. In 1598, the yeoman Raphe Keeling noted that, because of the low quality of some land that he had acquired in Birchover

---

[148] A. Shepard, *Accounting for Oneself: Worth, Status and the Social Order in Early Modern England* (Oxford, 2015), 119.

[149] Carew, *Certaine Godly and Necessary Sermons*, sig. X5r.

[150] For a sharp example of the impact of the loss of a cow to a poor householder, see S. Hindle, *On the Parish? The Micro-politics of Poor Relief in Rural England, c. 1550–1750* (Oxford, 2004), 420–1.

[151] Many parishes had long kept cows, whose milk was available to the poor. For examples, see E. M. Leonard, *The Early History of English Poor Relief* (Cambridge, 1900), 346; N. J. G. Pounds, *The Culture of the English People: Iron Age to the Industrial Revolution* (Cambridge, 1994), 285.

[152] TNA, SP16/333/8.

[153] TNA, E134/26Eliz/East13. For a poor man's exploitation of turbary rights being tolerated by his richer neighbours, see York City Archives, M31/460.

(Derbyshire), he gave it to his 'poore neighbors'.[154] A small matter to Keeling, but for the poor of Birchover, it gave them a bit of ground on which to pasture a few animals. These things mattered.

The greater gentry and nobility were even better placed than were the middle sort to make meaningful changes to the material circumstances of the local poor. The preacher at Lord Montagu's funeral brought the congregation's attention to the virtues of the deceased:

His cottage[r]s payd no fines, & rents so small, th[a]t scarce deserved the name of rents, he kept th[e]m continually in worke, w[hi]ch is a great worke of charity, & the poorest of them had bread, broth, beere, broken meate upon their dole-daies: so th[a]t in fourteen yeares I never knewe a collection for the poore in Weekly. They called indeed the money w[hi]ch his L[or]dship and others gave at Communions & fast dayes, collections, w[hi]ch was distributed amongst the poorest of the parish, but there was never any taxe for the poore in that tyme.[155]

And in some places, there were festive arrangements associated with the agricultural year that were adapted so as to benefit the destitute. By 1624, in Rotheram (Yorkshire), it was customary at the casting open of the fields at Lammastide to feed 'pore beggers at the Gallowtree' with cheese and ale. In that year, this largesse ran to nineteen shillings and four pence.[156]

In many villages, evidence of informal gifts to the poor survive to the historical record only because of some brief aside concerned with other matters. In 1583, for example, in the course of giving evidence to the Court of Exchequer concerning the warren of Brandon Ferry (Suffolk), the eighty-year-old William Edwards mentioned that when he had been warrener there, he had been in the habit of giving 'to pore men ... at the churchinge of their wyves or uppon anye suche occasyon he did nowe and then bestowe a coupell of coneys or more'.[157] A small matter in itself, this was a way of marking the arrival in the community of a new child, whilst ensuring that the families of 'pore men' might enjoy a couple of hot meals. Another small mercy was that practised by the bakers of Hull, who, in 1598, agreed 'that all the ... company will deliver for their breade from time to time xiii.ten to the dozen to the poore women, and other of this towne to retaile the same again'.[158] Then there were men and women like the miller Edmund Allen of Frittenden (Kent), who, along with his wife and four others, was burnt in the reign of Queen Mary for his Protestantism. Allen was remembered not only for his piety but also for his regard for the poor. It was recalled that 'in a dere year when as the

[154] TNA, E134/39&40Eliz/Mich1.     [155] Boughton Hall, Ms 186, article 10, pp. 25–6.
[156] J. Guest, *Historic Notices of Rotheram: Eccelesiastical, Collegiate and Civil* (Worksop, 1879), 360.
[157] TNA, E178/2166.
[158] J. M. Lambert, *Two Thousand Years of Gild Life* (London, 1891), 308.

people wer[e] lyke to starve for foode, then he fed them, and sold his corne better chepe then other did, And did not that onely but also fedd them with the food of lyfe, Readyng the Scriptures and interpreting them'.[159] Piety and charity worked together to reinforce a set of social ethics that this decent man took with him to the stake.

Despite the popular perception of Puritans as grasping individualists, many godly folk had a practical concern for the lives of the poor, an outlook they had inherited from the radical evangelicals of the mid-sixteenth century. In Puritan Shrewsbury in 1595, for instance, the parish authorities held a collection for the relief of an aged poor man, Thomas Shaw, who was not able to work.[160] The 1571 regime established by the mayor and 'bretherne' of godly Northampton ensured that, during communion in the town's churches, '[t]he mynisters often tymes doo call on the people to Remember the poore w[hi]ch is there plentyfully doon, and thus the comunyon being ended, the people doo singe a psalme'.[161]

In contrast to Max Weber's and Karl Max's assumptions concerning the link between Calvinism and capitalism, the godly could be just as hostile to economic individualism as were more conservative writers. In particular, 'self-love' was felt to undermine neighbourly values that Puritans wanted to be seen to uphold. In a sermon preached in 1615, the godly minister of Wethersfield (Essex), Richard Rogers, argued:

Whereto they who will not be subiect, and that readily, knowing that they nourish and uphold neighbourhood and love thereby, they shew that they are willing to breake off this knot. It is hindred by selfe-love, whiles every man regardeth himselfe onely, or for the most part: and especially where men are more frowardly and churlishly disposed, who had neede oft to remember the words of our Saviour, saying, Hereby shall all men know that ye are my disciples, if ye love one another.[162]

Puritan gentry could be as paternalistic as their more conservative peers. Of the godly Cheshire gentleman John Bruen, it was written:

The necessities of the poore in their hunger, and cold, and for want of food and raiment, did ever marvellously affect, and afflict his heart. And as he had a mercifull heart to pitie them, so had hee an open both heart and hand to relieve them. He did usually to his great expence and cost, fill the bellies of great multitudes, which out of his owne and other parishes, did twice a weeke resort unto his house for that end. And in the deare yeares he made provision for them almost every day in the week, and would many times see them served himself.

[159] HEHL, Egerton Ms, Ellesmere 6162, fols. 26r-7r.      [160] HMC Shrewsbury, 59.
[161] J. C. Cox and C. A. Markham (eds.), *The Records of the Borough of Northampton*, 2 vols. (Northampton, 1898), II, 387.
[162] R. Rogers, *A Commentary upon the Whole Booke of Judges* (London, 1615), 13.

As a result of Bruen's charity, especially in the provision of clothing, 'the loynes of the poore did blesse him, being warmed with the fleece of his flocke, or clothed by the cost of his purse'.[163]

The social duty to remember the poor found its way into the material culture. In 1612, the poor box of Holy Trinity, Chester, sat on a table that bore the inscription 'Remember the poor'.[164] In the church of the Norfolk parish of Watton, there survives a carved image of a pauper, dated 1639, inscribed 'Remember the poore', with a slot in his head into which donations can be dropped.[165] Then, as Hannah Robb has shown, there were the early seventeenth-century purses that bore the words 'Remember the poore'.[166] The intimate, personal purse of the middling woman within which she kept her money, then, called upon her to disburse some of her cash to the poor.

The established, resident poor had their place. In many villages and urban districts, they were more than merely tolerated; they were considered part of the neighbourhood. It was therefore upsetting to many propertied people to see the poor mistreated. So when, on 30 August 1604, Mistress Robyns went into the fields to glean, 'as is usuall for all pore to doe', only to be attacked and wounded by the son of the tithe-gatherer, she did not find it hard to find 'goodwives' about her who were willing to sign a petition complaining to the magistracy about the village drama.[167] The needless harassment of poor neighbours was not something that locals found attractive. A Scotswoman called Anne was presented to the Durham diocesan visitation in 1580 because '[s]he is a scoulder of hir neighbours, and namely against Isabell Bullocke, a poore woman'.[168] The violence of the gentleman Henry Leverstone towards the poor folk of Fincham (Norfolk) excited local comment: on 24 August 1615, the inhabitants of that village drew upon a list of complaints against him which explained that he was a common sower of

---

[163] F. R. Raines (ed.), *The Journal of Nicholas Assheton*, Chetham Society, 14 (Manchester, 1848), 83–4.

[164] W. Coster, 'A Microcosm of Community: Burial, Space and Society in Chester, 1598 to 1633', in W. Coster and A. Spicer (eds.), *Sacred Space in Early Modern Europe* (Cambridge, 2005), 130.

[165] T. Barton, 'Notices of the Town and Parish of Watton', *Norfolk Archaeology*, 3 (1852), 394–414. For more on poor boxes, see N. D. Brodie, '"An Ancient Box": The Queen v. Robert Wortley and John Allen (1846); or, A History of the English Parochial Poor Box, c.1547', in A. M. Scott (ed.), *Experiences of Charity, 1250–1650* (Aldershot, 2015), 215–38.

[166] H. Robb, 'Purses and the Charitable Gift', *Journal of Social History*, 49, 2 (2015), 387–405.

[167] W. J. Hardy (ed.), *Hertford County Records: Sessions Rolls 1581 to 1698* (Hertford, 1905), 35–6.

[168] J. Raine (ed.), *The Injunctions and Other Ecclesiastical Proceedings of Richard Barnes, Bishop of Durham, from 1575 to 1587*, Surtees Society, 21 (Durham, 1850), 129.

discord and a violent drunk. Thomas Nicholas signed a statement attesting: 'Mr Leverstone hath beaten divers poor men in the Towne of Fyncham as one Thomas Mattershall, and one John Nicols whome he felled to the grounde & spurned him w[i]th his foote.'[169] A few years later, John Marten, the godly vicar of St John the Baptist, Windsor, complained to the diocesan court against his churchwarden, Thomas Hall. Amongst other things, Marten said that Hall had verbally attacked a poor man during communion, stating:

[T]he said Thomas, at the celebration of the holie sacrament of the Lords supper[,] did with a lowde voyce, expostulate, chyde & wrangle with one Robert Michener[,] a poore labouring man[,] & with Clement[,] his wife: adding moreover these words, except you pay your 2d [a church rate] come no more here, & also adding this threatning I will talke with you in another place: as that not onelie the said Robert & Clement his wife, were much greived, being readie to receive the holie sacrament, but also the minister & diuerse Communicants, were greatlie disturbed.[170]

Even as charity grew cold towards the poor in some places, there remained many propertied folk who saw paupers as fellow Christians and neighbours. In 1625, for example, when the weaver John Throe's house burnt down, he found himself in poverty. Throe was able to draw on local networks to advance his case: the 'better sorte of the same towne' subscribed a petition to the magistracy asking for relief.[171] Three years later, in Melksham (Wiltshire), the Overseers of the Poor and twenty-nine of their neighbours found themselves at odds with the lord of the manor, Sir John Jennings. While Jennings petitioned the bench to ask that Elias More of Melksham, who had built a cottage on the common, should be removed, the neighbours argued that More was 'an honest and poore man ... [. P]ittying his Distressed estate in regard of himself, his wife and Five small children who are likely to perish through want of harbour', they asked that he be left in his humble home.[172] In 1612, William Dench of Longdon (Worcestershire) explained: '[B]eing a very poor man and having a wife and seven children all born at Longdon[, I] was, at Michaelmas ... desititute of any habitation, whereupon one William Parsons of Longdon, yeoman, in charity, without any consideration,

---

[169] NRO, NQS/C/S3/20, articles against Henry Leverstone.
[170] A. F. Johnston, 'English Puritanism and Festive Culture', *Renaissance and Reformation*, 15, 4 (1991), 289.
[171] W. Le Hardy (ed.), *Calendar to the Sessions Books and Sessions Minute Books and Other Sessions Records of the County of Hertford, Vol. V: 1619–1657* (Hertford, 1928), 69.
[172] J. Bettey (ed.), *Wiltshire Farming in the Seventeenth Century*, Wiltshire Records Society, 57 (Trowbridge, 2005), 324–5.

gave to the petitioner a little sheepcote of his.'[173] With the consent of the rest of the village, the 'little sheepcote' was converted into a home. William Dench and his family had found their place. It came with its own expectations of social submission, but it was better than life on the road. The aid of the richer villagers of a community could make the difference between having a place within a community and being ejected.

James C. Scott's words perhaps made best sense of the social place occupied by the Dench household in Jacobean Longdon:

Village redistribution worked unevenly and, even at its best, produced no egalitarian utopia. We may suppose that there was always some tension in the village between the better-off who hoped to minimize their obligations and the poor who had most to gain from communal social guarantees. The poor, for their part, got a 'place', not an equal income, and must have suffered a loss of status as a result of their permanent dependence. Nevertheless, this pattern did represent the minimum moral requirements of village mutuality. It worked through the support or acquiescence of most villagers and, above all, in normal times it assured the 'survival of the weakest'. What moral solidarity the village possessed *as a village* was in fact based ultimately on its capacity to protect and feed its inhabitants. So long as village membership was valuable in a pinch, the 'little tradition' of village norms and customs would command a broad acceptance.[174]

Perhaps most powerfully of all, the deathbed could be a site at which neighbourliness was made real. Here, an old man or woman might pass on their knowledge of the customs of the parish and manor.[175] As their kin, servants, friends and neighbours gathered about them, the dying parishioner would set their affairs to right, sorting out creditors from debtors, perhaps promising a payment to the poor, indicating who would be beneficiaries to land, capital and goods. The glover George Laborne remembered, on 26 July 1569, how 'the satt[e]rday byfore the said wedoo died she cauld or neighbors to come in wher she was in the said mathewes house to here hir will that then was written by the wordes of hir owne mouth by one [Christ] ofer wright'.[176] The deathbed, then, was a location within which neighbourliness was celebrated – it was a communal site, as the soul of one of the parish passed from one world to the next. The dying parishioner was reminded of their bonds to the parish community: one

---

[173] HMC, *Various Collections*, I, 296.

[174] J. C. Scott, *The Moral Economy of the Peasant: Rebellion and Subsistence in Southeast Asia* (New Haven, CT, 1976), 43–4.

[175] A. Wood, *The Memory of the People: Custom and Popular Senses of the Past in Early Modern England* (Cambridge, 2013), 8–10.

[176] DUL, DDR/EJ/CCD/1/2, fol. 144r.

London woman explained how she had 'saluted and comforted the said testatrix as neighbours comonlie doo'.[177]

The process by which the goods of the departed were distributed was itself a ritual in which friendship and neighbourliness were recognized and celebrated. The Durham yeoman Jasper Horsley explained, in 1569, how 'Robson & Rich[ard] M[ar]shall haith been longe fellowes & frends to gyther and that this ex[aminant] & his wyffe haith often tymes h[e]ard the said Robson say that the said m[ar]shall shuld have the order of his the said Robson goods yf any thinge came to him but good at any tyme'.[178] Difficult property relations – and, of course, *emotional* relations – were established at the deathbed. Ellen Gyles of St Gregory's parish in Norwich recalled, in 1582, how, a year earlier, she had visited her neighbour Agnes Betts, who died that Palm Sunday. She told the Court of the Duchy of Lancaster that

she h[e]arde the sayd agnes speake upon her dead bed and div[er]s tymes before that she had done her sone George Betts great wronge so that she thought she could not dep[ar]t out of this world wth quiet mynde but wherfor she this deponent remembreth not ...[. A]gnes tould her that her husband betts did gyve her the house att aylsh[a]m for term of her lyfe and that after her decease her sone George Betts was to have yt.[179]

Now, Agnes sought to put things right, seeing that this son of her first marriage was to inherit her Aylsham house. The neighbours who gathered about her attested to her will. The process of the transmission of home and land was charged without emotional electricity: these were more than material relationships. For the deathbed was also a key site at which other social bonds were recognized. As he lay dying of the plague in 1593, James Ballidon called his sub-tenants to him and passed to them his lands.[180] Perhaps Ballidon felt little social distance between himself and his sub-tenants – all lived in the lead mining village of Bonsall (Derbyshire), the poverty of which was almost equally shared. Within this little world, it might have been that neighbourliness was an especially potent and integrative force.

### Christian Neighbours

One of the most powerful sites within the early modern community was the parish church – and, more broadly, the *idea* of the parish. For many women and men in pre-Reformation England, the parish was about social unity. The bede roll, in which the benefactors of the church were recalled,

[177] Archer, *The Pursuit of Stability*, 76.     [178] DUL, DDR/EJ/CCD/1/2, fol. 175r.
[179] TNA, DL4/24/5.     [180] TNA, DL4/49/39.

told the members of the parish about their ancestors' investment in the place. The rite of perambulation inscribed in landscape and memory the bounds of the parish, giving a larger meaning to trees, hedges, crosses, standing stones, street corners, houses and farms. Church ales were a way both of funding the affairs of the parish and of celebrating, in however hazy a fashion, the values of social concord. In such moments, society was made whole.[181] The interior of the church itself was a reminder of the continued financial and emotional investment of ordinary folk in the church – funding chantries, paintings, sculpture, elaborate rood screens and even the priest's vestments.[182]

Importantly, popular religion was grounded upon an organic sense of community, one that linked Christian belief to neighbourly practice. Thomas Tusser articulated this connection very clearly, including the following principles amongst his 'Principall points of religion':

> To use thy neighbour honestly,
> To looke for death still presently,
> To helpe the poore in miserie,
> To hope for heaven[']s felicitie,
> To have faith[,] hope and charitie.[183]

Faith, hope and charity: these were some of the keywords of English folk belief. At the start of our period, it seemed self-evident to the author of a collection of proverbs that a sense of Christian charity underwrote social relations:

> At owur begynny[n]ge, god be owur spede
> In grace & virtue to prosede!
> Be petuus & eke merciabyll
> To nedy folke be Cherytabyll
> A man with-owte mercy, or mercy shall mys
> & he shall have mercy [th]at mercifull ys.
> By mereye & mekenes all thynge chevythe.[184]

Trust was just as important to the concept of neighbourhood as were friendship and love. One translator of Jean Calvin argued that 'he that doth defraud and deceave his neighbours after that he hath used the name of God for it, doth iniury, not to men onely, but to God'.[185] Richard

---

[181] J. Bossy, 'Some Elementary Forms of Durkheim', *P&P*, 95, 1 (1982), 3–18.

[182] The best study of this sense of place is E. Duffy, *The Voices of Morebath: Reformation and Rebellion in an English Village* (New Haven, CT, 2001).

[183] Tusser, *Five Hundred Points of Good Husbandry*, 190.

[184] W. M. Rosetti and E. Oswald (eds.), *Queene Elizabeth's Academy*, EETS, 8 (London, 1869), 68.

[185] E. P., *A Harmonie upon the Three Evangelists, Matthew, Mark and Luke* (London, 1584), 177.

Mulcaster argued that neighbourhood was grounded on mutual trust, asking his reader:

[W]hat is it else but to thinke of thy neighbour, as thou wouldest be thought on thy selfe, when thou beleevest him in thine, as thou wouldest be beleeved in his? A true president of naturall humanitie, a religious patterne of honest neighbour-hoode, which in no other thing can declare more good will, in no other thing can do one more good, then in respect to his children, whether ye consider the children[']s persons, or the thing which is wished them.[186]

Given the epistemic importance of neighbourliness, parishioners were angry when their ministers became an unneighbourly presence. The petition of 'the more part of the parishioners' of Jacobean Westhatch (Somerset) complained that their minister, Mr Jeffery Smithe, 'threatenth your said suppliants with process and suites and molesteth us with suites and is a disturber of his neighbours and will not be contented with his tithes due and accustomed to be paid and with threatening words puteth his said neighbours in fear so that by no means we can be quiet by him'.[187] In 1589, the curate of Great Braxted (Essex) was said to be 'in the alehouse at inconvenient times and will be overtaken with drink and useth hard speeches of his neighbours'.[188] In Caroline County Durham, the minister John Vaux brought his calling into disgrace not only by using magic to find lost goods but also by manipulating the legal system against his flock: as the High Commission heard, he was 'troublesome amongst his neighbours, and cited verie manie of them to appear at Durham, and then would have compounded with them'.[189] The High Commission also heard, in 1635, about the breach of neighbourly relations by the minister of Thorpe Bulmer (Northumberland). He was, his flock explained, often so drunk that he 'could not reade the service at the afternoon praiers, nor scar[c]e utter any word soe as the people might understand . . .[.] Many neighbours did see soe much, and were greatlie offended.'[190] Yet many ministers were seen as good neighbours, fitting easily into village society. When Thomas Pestell, the vicar of Packington (Leicestershire), came under attack, his flock explained to the church court, in 1632, that he was 'a painfull preacher and catachizer in his p[ar]ishe . . .[. H]e liveth peaceablie w[i]th his neighbors.'[191]

---

[186] R. Mulcaster, *Positions wherein Those Primitive Circumstances Be Examined, which Are Necessarie for the Training Up of Children* (London, 1581), 286–7.

[187] E. H. Bates (ed.), *Quarter Sessions Records for the County of Somerset: Vol. I, James I, 1607–1625*, Somerset Record Society, 23 (London, 1907), 26.

[188] Emmison (ed.), *Elizabethan Life*, 227.

[189] Longstaffe (ed.), *The Acts of the High Commission within the Diocese of Durham*, 40.

[190] Ibid., 128.    [191] HEHL, HAL5/9.

In the annual ritual of Rogationtide, the yearly custom in which inhabitants followed their ministers around the key points in their parish boundaries, Christian neighbourliness was written into the land.[192] Rogationtide did more than merely map the bounds: it also celebrated the parish as a key unit within which values of trust, friendship, obligation and neighbourliness were made real. And it need not be restricted to any single parish. In some places, as one parish procession met that of its neighbour at some customary spot, there could be drinking and rejoicing. Thus, in 1556, the seventy-two-year-old cordwainer William Robynson of Hinderscliffe (Yorkshire) explained the custom whereby 'the Curate of Bulmer upon Weddynsday in Crose weke when Hardie Flate is sawne goeth in procession about Hardie Flate and saith a Gospell at the Sowth nowke of the same and hath a pott with aill the which the inhabitants of Welburne giveth'.[193] Richer neighbours would be expected to provide processioners with drink and food as they passed by. Sometimes, this was something that was more lodged in communal memory than practised in the current times.[194] Failure to live up to such expectations – deemed a part of parochial custom – could upset neighbours. Thus, in 1621, George Staple of West Itchenor (Sussex) was presented to the Archdeacon's court 'for that he made no provision of dyet for the poore that went about the bounds of the parish in the perambulation, according to the ancient custom'. In the same year in Yapton (Sussex), ten parishioners were presented to the Archdeacon for failing to provide cakes in the perambulation, including '[t]he farmer of the great farme, where now Mr William Edmonds dwells, [who] was wont to give a dynner upon every Thursday in the Rogacion weke to the greatest number of the people in the parrishe, and now there is nothing given for that farme'.[195]

For ordinary people, Christianity was not just some set of abstract theological precepts. Rather, folk Christianity fed into everyday patterns of social interaction. In 1587, three neighbours of Barker Gate in Nottingham, along with 'the whole streete', complained about John Grinefield, saying not only that he was noisy and threatening but also that 'he [is] not doinge as a Christian ought to doe or as

---

[192] For more on this, see S. Hindle, 'Beating the Bounds of the Parish: Order, Memory and Identity in the English Local Community, c.1500–1700', in M. Halvorson and K. Spierling (eds.), *Defining Community in Early Modern Europe* (Aldershot, 2008), 205–27; Wood, *The Memory of the People*, 188–246.

[193] J. S. Purvis (ed.), *Select XVI Century Causes in Tithe*, YASRS, 64 (York, 1947), 92.

[194] Collinson, *The Birthpangs of Protestant England*, 53.

[195] Johnstone (ed.), *Churchwardens' Presentments*, 3, 16; see also 11, 36, 96, 100, 119.

a member of Christe his Churche, for that he hathe not be[e]n a partaker of the Sacrament theis twoe yeares ne[i]ther come to the Churche'.[196] The key rites of passage were observed by neighbours in the parish church: the Prayer Book ordered 'that persons to be married should come into the body of the church "with their friends and neighbours"'; some magistrates enforced the expectation that people should attend funerals of their neighbours. Religious duties, then, constructed everyday obligations.[197]

---

[196] W. H. Stevenson et al. (eds.), *Records of the Borough of Nottingham*, 7 vols. (London, 1885–1947), IV, 219.

[197] K. Thomas, *The Ends of Life: Roads to Fulfillment in Early Modern England* (Oxford, 2009), 191.

## 2    Charity Suffereth Long:
Neighbourhood and Community

---

### 'A Nere Neyghbour Is Better than a Farre Frende': The Social Logic of Neighbourhood

The working people of early modern England knew that it was essential that they had some *place* in their local communities. For this remained in some respects a corporate society in which households, kin, neighbourhood, country, parish, fraternity, sisterhood and (in urban communities) guilds and companies were all ways in which the social order was both structured and made real. For some people, the early modern neighbourhood could be an oppressive place, in which communal, collective values were set above those of the individual. In a highly significant discussion of the topic, Keith Thomas observes: 'Those who failed to adhere to conventional expectations, whether in their religion or their tastes or their personal behavior, were accused of the great vice of "singularity", of following their "private fancy and vanity".' He quotes one Jacobean minister: 'Desire not to be singular, nor to differ from others for it is a sign of a naughty spirit, which hath caused much evil in the world from the beginning.'[1]

So, for the migrant poor or for newcomers in a village or district, their place could be tenuous: Who were they? What did they bring with them? Would they become a charge upon the parish? This was one reason that urban migrants settled in places where they had friends or kin or at least might be amongst others from their country or shire. Neighbourhood was a powerful, vital relationship. To be a neighbour might be almost the same as being a brother or a sister: when the Yorkshirewoman Elizabeth Hardwiche explained to the Archdiocesan authorities that she had been rescued from her violent husband by her 'neighboures', she also referred to them as her 'brethren'.[2] Ordinary people held tenaciously to that sense of place: that sense of enjoying a site within the moral order of the village or urban district. Thus, when the husbandman Richard Miller of

---

[1] Thomas, *The Ends of Life*, 27.    [2] BIA, CP.H.5094.

Compton (Wiltshire) and his family were the victims of a cruel mocking rhyme in 1620, he emphasized to the magistracy that he and his wife 'have lived honestly and peaceably amongst their neighbours, and albeit their estate in wealth be none of the richest, yet he thanketh God that there hath beene allwayes a good opinion held of them for their honestyes and good behavior'.[3]

What was true of individuals and their households could also be true of parishes. Division was to be avoided at all costs. When, in 1633, the minister of the neighbouring settlement of Broxborne fell out with Thomas Hassall, the minister of Amwell, Hassall recorded sorrowfully: 'Hence grew much unquietnes in the towne, parts-takinge and unkindness amongst frends and neighbours. What the issue wilbe is yet uncertayne, but presageth much evill.'[4] There were always those who would sow division. The parochial and legal records are full of examples of those who were 'knowen to be lewd persons[,] deryders and scoffers of there neighbors' who 'care not what they sey or what they doe in depraving & dyscredytyng ther neybors'.[5] Thomas Tusser wrote powerfully of the ways in which 'envious and naughtie' neighbours stored up grudges over the years, observing:

> An envious neighbour is easie to finde,
> His cumbersome fetches are seldome behinde ...[.]
> His head is a storehouse, with quarrels full fraught,
> His braine is unquiet, till all come to naught.
> His memorie pregnant, old evils to recite,
> His mind ever fixed each evill to requite.[6]

The proper neighbour, in contrast, regarded communal values as highly as she or he might regard the values of an orderly household. In 1550, Thomas Heywood made the following observations of 'a quiet neighbour':

> Few more commodious reason sees,
> Than is this one commoditee,
> Quietly neighboured to bee.
> Whiche neighbourhood in thee aperes ...
> I neuer heard thy seruauntes brall
> More than thou hadst had none at all ...
> Thou art to them, and thei to thee
> More mylde than muet. mum ye bee.

[3] Howard Cunnington (ed.), *Records of the County of Wiltshire*, 69.
[4] S. G. Doree (ed.), *The Parish Register and Tithing Book of Thomas Hassall of Amwell*, Hertfordshire Record Society, 5 (Cambridge, 1989), 221.
[5] J. A. B. Somerset, *Records of Early English Drama: Shropshire* (Toronto, 1994), I, 224.
[6] T. Tusser, *Five Hundred Points of Good Husbandry* (Oxford, 1984), 140.

I heare no noise mine ease to breake:
Thy buterie doore I heare not creake.
I never heard thy fyre once sparke,
I never heard thy dog once barke,
Of all thy guestes set at thy boorde
I never heard one speake one woorde . . .
For this neighbourlie quietnesse
Thou art the neighbour neighbourlesse.[7]

Above all else, division was to be avoided. In his account of the opinions of his Essex parishioners, the godly minister George Gifford put the following words into the mouth of the conservative character who personified traditional values:

Is it not our dutie to maintaine love, and charitie with our neighbours? Indeede they bee great swearers, and sometime they use to speake against Gods worde, if they bee awry, I thinke they shall answere for themselves, if wee should gainsay, or seeme to reproove them, they would not take it well, therefore I thinke good not to disquiet them.[8]

Charity, truth, neighbourhood and love were cognate concepts and they slipped easily into one another. Writing in 1560, Thomas Palfreyman argued:

Concorde must be kepte: we may not breake unitie: we muste be all of one mynde: there may bee no discension amongst us . . . If true love and charitie, by the good lawe of God, to his praise, and to the profyte of our neighbour, onely belongeth unto us; then nothynge at all verily, of our vayne talking, detraction, rashe and blynde foolyshe judgement, or otherwise, wherbye we may hurte our neighboures, belongeth unto us. For the peace of god and unitie is our possession: and the virtue of charitie, true friendship, and godly love should be always our very hungre and luste, for our honest preferment to the estimation of God; ye it is the fulfyllyng of his lawe. But to use folishe babbling, detraction, or undirect judgement, to the hurt of our neighbour belongeth not to us.[9]

Thomas Cartwright felt that neighbourhood was socially vested in Christian values and built upon the parish. In 1575, he argued that

the church as much as may be conveniently should have her partes not onely in a spiri | tuall bond off charitie but in neighbourhood of dwellinges well trussed one with an other: yt is apparant that although the scripture doth not mention parishes nor precisely define off the compasse yet yt giveth the rule wherby they are squared owt. For when a parish well bounded is nothing els but a nomber of those families which dwelling neere together may have a commodious resort: and the assemblies

[7] J. Heywood, *An Hundred Epigrammes* (London, 1550), sigs. B2r-v.
[8] G. Gifford, *Foure Sermons upon the Seven Chiefe Vertues or Principall Effectes of Faith* (London, 1582), fol. D2r.
[9] T. Palfreyman, *A Myrrour or Cleare Glasse* (London, 1560), sigs. C.v–C.1r.

off the churches owght so to be ranged as they may be neerest the place off their spirituall refelection: yt followeth that the scripture hathe after a sort gyven the churches tarriers and that a parish well bounded for the spiritu | all intercommuning hath testimonie owt off the word off God.[10]

For all that contemporaries felt neighbourhood to be under threat, throughout the period with which we are dealing, it was *also* felt to be alive and well. This represents the fundamental contradiction in the history of the concept. A didactic ballad of 1601 stated that people should

> Deale with thy neighbour mercifully,
> deceive no man by guile:
> Take heed of all extortion,
> it will thy soule defile ...[.]
> Give almes unto thy children deare,
> and turne not from the poore:
> Lend to the needy man thy goods,
> his pledge to him restore.
> Hurt not thy neighbour wittingly,
> in body goods or name:
> Remit offences willingly,
> lest God revenge the same ...[.]
> Keepe not thy hyrelings wages backe,
> God will his cry regard:
> In poore mens matters be not slacke,
> the Lord will thee reward ...[.]
> Oppresse no man by usury,
> refuse unlawfull gaine:
> Give plenteously unto the poore,
> Christ will thee pay againe.[11]

The Essex Puritan Richard Rogers saw love and neighbourhood as synonymous.[12] An anonymous writer of 1598 felt that 'the greatest love in us, next to God, ought to be love towards our neighbours'. Christian duty was interlaced with a love of neighbours: 'Whatsoever duties we perform in kindlinesse towards our neighbours, wee performe unto God.' Love underwrote both familial and social ties: 'Love is the first foundation of marriage, & [the] conjunction of neighbourhood.' Critically, neighbourhood was based upon common humanity: 'Neighbours are our likes or similitudes, and our duties to them is charitie, and love equal with ourse[l]ves.' Most importantly, humans were *social*

---

[10] T. Cartwright, *The Second Replie of Thomas Cartwright: Agaynst Maister Doctor Whitgiftes Second Answer, Touching the Churche Discipline* (London, 1575), 360.

[11] Anon. *A Right Godly and Christian ABC, Shewing the Duty of Every Degree* (London, 1601?).

[12] Rogers, *A Commentary upon the Whole Booke of Judges*, 13, 14.

beings: 'Men are not borne for themselves, but for their country, parents and neighbours.'[13]

Neighbourhood found its way into material culture through kitchen implements, pots and pans that bore the inscription 'Love thy neighbour'.[14] And neighbourly ideals were also expressed in proverbial culture. In 1545, an 'englysshe proverbe' observed the importance of social propinquities, observing: 'A nere neyghbour is better than a farre frende.'[15] A long-lived 'common Proverbe', noted in 1598, had it '[t]hat who so hath a good neighbor, hath a good morrow'.[16] It was axiomatic that people should 'live friendly and lovingly together as neighbours'.[17] To live in charity with one's neighbours was, then, to be on easy terms with them.[18] This is not unlike the social values uncovered by the anthropologist Robert Layton in his 1969 fieldwork amongst small-scale farmers in Franche-Comté. Layton observed the hostility amongst villagers 'to even the smallest of gestures that might be construed as setting oneself apart from the body of the community'. The value of being *gentil* informed village life in Franche-Comté. As it was explained by one of Layton's informants, being *gentil* 'meant to respect people, and even animals; to like everyone, to be amiable towards your neighbours, to say good-day to those whom you meet'. Another informant explained 'that to be *gentil* meant to be calm, to be gracious towards your wife and children, to be content and not to pick quarrels with your neighbors'.[19]

Something like the idea of being *gentil* was at work in Tudor and early Stuart England. It was important for neighbours to be aware that they lived 'in upright godlie and Christian manner to the generall good likeing and approcacion of all their neighbours, friends and familiars'.[20] Love for one another was understood as a Christian ethic that underwrote neighbourliness: one Tudor Londoner advised people: 'Love thy nayghber and turne all that he saith or dothe to good, for that pleasith me [i.e., God]

---

[13] N. L., *Politeuphuia: Wits Common Wealth* (London, 1598), 164–6.

[14] For an example, see S. Pennell, '"Pots and Pans History": The Material Culture of the Kitchen in Early Modern England', *Journal of Design History*, 11, 3 (1998), 213.

[15] R. Taverner, *Erasmus' Proverbes* (London, 1545), sig.

[16] G. de la Perrière's *The Mirrour of Policie*, sig. Oiij. For the same proverb in the fifteenth century, see H. B. Wheatley (ed.), *Merlin, or The Early History of King Arthur*, EETS, 10, 21, 36, 112 (London, 1856–99), No. 21, 434.

[17] HCCO, 45: *Billiard* v. *Robinson*.

[18] J. S. Purvis (ed.), *Tudor Parish Documents of the Diocese of York* (Cambridge, 1948), 224. For the later period, see W. M. Jacob, '"In Love and Charity with Your Neighbours": Ecclesiastical Courts and Justices of the Peace in the Eighteenth Century', *Studies in Church History*, 40 (2004), 205–17.

[19] R. Layton, *Anthropology and History in Franche-Comté: A Critique of Social Theory* (Oxford, 2000), 184, 185, 186. For the decline of this ideal in the face of growing social polarization, see ibid., 204–6.

[20] TNA, STAC8/92/10.

more than if thowe every day enspired to heven.'[21] That sense of ease that
Layton's informants of Franche-Comté alluded to seems to have been
present in the mind of Robert Skeet of Hickling (Norfolk) in 1632, when
he explained to the Exchequer Court how he allowed his neighbours to
walk across his lands 'not of dutie but ... by curtesie or good
neighbourhood'.[22] Such 'curtesies' made life liveable in early modern
communities. Early modern people were highly sensitive to boundaries
– between fields and lanes, between houses, between manors and parishes
– and so it meant something important that Robert Skeet took so relaxed
an attitude to access to his fields; it was a way in which 'good neighbourhood' was built into the local landscape.[23]

The normative significance of neighbourliness was transparent to local
people. In the course of a 1605 dispute in which allegations of cuckoldry
were thrown about, the tailor Thomas Floate explained that he was 'a
friend and wellwisher' to both sides in the dispute, 'in matters of equity
and right, as one neighbour should be to another'.[24] Offenders against
neighbourhood values were, at first, gently encouraged to resort to better
behaviour. Faced with his drunken statement that 'he ne[i]ther cared for
God, nor for the devell, nor for any thinge th[a]t any Justice of the Peace
could do unto him', the neighbours of the Norfolk man Edmund Dawson
came to him and 'exhorted [him] to cease this evell course of life and to
carye himself in a more sober course of lyfe'. It was only when he scorned
them 'verye dispitefullye' that they brought him before the magistrates.[25]
The law, here as in so many contexts, was not so much a forum within
which conflict could be perpetuated as a means of binding local society
together, settling feuds and reasserting basic social norms.

Yet in some places, the values of neighbourhood required institutional
support. In the hard year of 1596, the court leet of Manchester declared
that 'touching encroachments and other difficulties betwixt neighbour
and neighbour', they would meet again and hear all complaints concerning this sensitive matter.[26] In 1602, things seem to have fallen apart

---

[21] S. Brigden, 'Religion and Social Obligation in Early Sixteenth Century London', *P&P*,
103 (1984), 67.

[22] TNA, E134/7ChasI/Mich18.

[23] For the sensitivity to boundaries, see N. Blomley, 'Making Private Property: Enclosure,
Common Right and the Work of Hedges', *Rural History*, 18, 1 (2001), 1–21. While the
material facts of enclosures have been extensively explored and heavily debated, their
*meaning* to ordinary people remains less clear. The generation and maintenance of
boundaries – both urban and rural – deserves closer attention.

[24] Wilkinson (ed.), *Chichester Archdeaconry Depositions*, 135.

[25] NRO, NQS/C/S3/17/2, articles against Edmund Dawson. For more in this case, see
NRO, NQS/C/S3/17/2, Information of John Buck.

[26] J. Harland (ed.), *Court Leet Records of the Manor of Manchester, A.D. 1586–1602*, Chetham
Society, 55 (Manchester, 1865), 44.

altogether in Weardale. Here, the Forest Court established new rules for the 'reformac[i]on' of the locality. The orders were recited by the court

for the better saiftie of theire goodds & chattels and p[ro]fiting one of another. And that through the wilfull obstinance of sundry the Inhabitants there & slacknes of the said officers, the said orders have not been p[er]formed accordingly[.] By meanes whereof div[er]s of the said Inhabitants have lately susteyned great damages through the stealing of their goodds & chattels, as also other losses by reason of unneighbourly dealings amongest themselves in over eating one another pastures & meadowes by reason of all hedges & ditches.[27]

The provision of credit to the poor on easy terms, or even better on no interest at all, was felt to be one of the social duties of wealthier parishioners. After all, the Book of Ezekiel was clear that lending on interest was a sin: 'That hath taken off his hand from the poor, that hath not received usury nor increase, hath executed my judgments, hath walked in my statutes.'[28] Similarly, Proverbs conceptualized kindness to the poor as a loan to the Almighty: 'He that hath pity upon the poor lendeth unto the Lord; and that which he hath given will he pay him again.'[29] Thomas Tusser advised yeoman farmers to build their local reputations by offering easy credit to the poor, telling them: 'Lending to neighbour, in time of his neede, / winnes love of thy neighbour, and credit doth breede.'[30] Breeding credit – social standing – was therefore just as valuable as lending credit – lendish cash. For this reason, wealthier people were regularly enjoined to make loans at no interest to the poor. Nicholas Sander argued in 1568 that 'everie lending ought to be made unto the poore. For lending is a kind of charitie, or of alms deedes, which was instituted chiefly and only for the poore.'[31] Sometimes, an awareness of the cash nexus into which people were being drawn under-wrote some sense of the local economy. Edwin Sandys, Archbishop of York, conceptualized neighbourly relations as a form of generous loan, preaching: 'Everie man is to his neighbour a debtor not onely of that which himself borroweth, but of whatsoever his neighbor needeth, a debtor not onely to pay that he oweth, but also to lende that he hath and may conveniently spare: to lend I say according to the rule of Christ, lend, looking for nothing thereby.'[32] Hence, in 1597, Henry Arthurton wrote: 'If anie of thy brethren be falne pore . . . ye shall lende and give him (as necessitie requireth, without any grudging . . .) that the Lorde thy God may prosper thy proceedings.'[33] Writing in 1611, Roger Fenton stated that just as inviting 'poore

---

[27] DUL, WEC/45. 1602. Orders of the Forest Court in Weardale.    [28] Ezekiel, 18:17.
[29] Proverbs, 19:17.    [30] Tusser, *Five Hundred Points of Good Husbandry*, 19.
[31] Sander, *A Briefe Treatise of Usurie*, 5. For a fuller discussion of loans to the poor, see Hindle, *On the Parish?*, 77–81.
[32] Sandys, *Sermons*, sig. L8v.
[33] H. Arthurton, *Provision for the Poore* (London, 1597), sig. B3v.

neighbours to dinner' was 'a worke of charity' and 'an act of kindnesse, of neighbourhood, of friendship', so '[l]ending is a worke of mercy to the poore, of kindnesse to thy neighbor'.[34] Parish elders sometimes took control of the matter, establishing parochial credit unions upon which the poor could draw.[35] In Pittington (County Durham), for example, the local poor benefited from a bequest that established a fund from which loans were made. The poor were expected to have neighbours who would stand surety for the loans: a powerful example of the ways in which social relations were *localized* in the period.[36] Alan Macfarlane has suggested that those making such loans gained what he called 'social' interest – that it created dependencies and loyalties. In this way, the extension of credit reasserted the reciprocities on which *local* social structures rested.[37] Thus, some of the least attractive effects of the market economy might be mitigated. Moreover, the extension of credit might strengthen hierarchical bonds, drawing poor people into clientage links at the centre of which were their richer creditors.[38]

## Paternalism and the Reinforcement of Hierarchy

Neighbourliness crossed social boundaries, transcending the growing divisions of the period. Neighbours may be poor, many thought, but they remained just that: neighbours. John Markay, a minister in Newcastle upon Tyne, said of William Dickson that 'he is th[is] depont[s] neighbour a very honest poore ma[n]'.[39] A yeoman of Elizabethan Whickham (County Durham) identified a fellow parishioner as 'a very poore man and his neybor'. Another villager was 'a Skotish man[,] a poore man and went from dore to dore ... and a simple ma[n]'. Despite the common northern hostility to Scots, the man was accepted in the community.[40] Richer people were expected to adhere closely to the values of neighbourhood, distributing charity and loans where they were needed.

Those of the middling sort had a special position in this regard, for it was they – not the gentry – who came into daily contact with the poor. It was assumed that a proper yeoman would be

---

[34] R. Fenton, *A Treatise of Usurie Divided into Three Books* (London, 1611), 99.

[35] For a discussion of parish loans to the poor, see Hindle, *On the Parish?*, 181–2.

[36] J. Barmby (ed.), *Churchwardens' Accounts of Pittington and Other Parishes in the Diocese of Durham from 1580 to 1700*, Surtees Society, 84 (Durham, 1888), 78, 80, 82, 91–2.

[37] A. Macfarlane, *The Family Life of Ralph Josselin: An Essay in Historical Anthropology* (Cambridge, 1970), 55–6.

[38] Boulton, *Neighbourhood and Society*, 139. For a case-study of the lending habits of one urban gentleman, see ibid., 87–92.

[39] DUL, DDR/EJ/CCD/1/2, fols. 129v-30r.     [40] DUL, DDR/EJ/CCD/1/2, fol. 3v.

bountyfull both to strangers and poor people ...[.] In a time of famine he is the Joseph of the country and keeps the poor from starving ... and to his poor neighbour abateth somewhat of the high price of the market. The neighbouring gentry court him for his acquaintance, which either he modestly waveth, or thankfully accepteth, but in no way greedily desireth.[41]

According to traditional social values, the yeomanry were expected to provide for poor travellers. In the play *A Knacke to Knowe a Knave* (1592), the disguised King announces that his father had told him

> that piers plowman was one of the best members in a commo[n]wealth
> For his table was never emptie of bread, beefe and beere,
> As a help to all distressed traveilers.[42]

Such values may have been observed more in the breach than in practice, but they remained powerful standards against which many felt they had to judge their actions. Thus, in a 1574 complaint to the Star Chamber, Roger Beckwith of Thorpe (Yorkshire) presented himself as an ideal yeoman, telling the court that all his life he had been 'accompted and reputed ... of honest fame good credit ... [and] hath bene a housekeeper in his cuntre[y] not only to the Releife of the pore and Impotente people thereaboute dwelling and inhabitainge to thuttermoste of his power But also to the settinge on worke [of] div[er]s daye laborers'.[43]

For all that they remained at a remove from the village community, the gentry were also meant to practise good neighbourhood – especially bountiful hospitality. Writing in 1592, Robert Greene stated forthrightly that a gentleman should be a

> mortall enemy to pride ...[. H]e regardeth hospitality, and aimeth at honor with releeeving the poore: you may see, although his lands and revenewes be great, and he able to maintain himself in great bravery, yet he is content with his home-spun cloth, and scorneth the pride that is now adaies used among young upstarts: he holdeth not the worth of his gentry to be and consist in velvet breeches, but valeweth true liberality, housekeeping and almes-deeds. Vox Populi vox Dei: his tenants and farmers would, if it might bee possible, make him immortal with their praiers and praises. He raiseth no rent, racketh no lands, taketh no income, imposeth no mercilesse fines, envies not an other, buyeth no house over his neighbours head, but respecteth his country, and the commodity thereof, as deere as his life. He regardeth more to have the needy fed, to have his boord garnished with full platters, then to famous himself with excessive furniture in apparel.[44]

---

[41] T. Fuller, *The Holy and Profane States* (Cambridge, 1831), 89.
[42] Anon., *A Knacke to Knowe a Knave*, lines 1247–9.    [43] TNA, STAC5/B69/8.
[44] Greene, *A Quip for an Upstart Courtier*.

At any moment in the sixteenth and seventeenth centuries, it seemed to contemporaries that the values that Greene described had passed away. Yet reports of the death of neighbourhood were clearly exaggerated. Such values remained powerful social norms against which gentlemen and women gauged their own actions, and according to which they were judged. Many 'village' gentry – those who didn't hold the Commission of the Peace but were nonetheless recognized as a cut above a yeoman – nonetheless saw themselves as a part of the local community.[45] On one occasion, for instance, the lesser gentleman Fabian Haywood gathered with his neighbors at Studeley Hall (Yorkshire) 'at a drinking to helpe & give some monies towards the relief of a poore man'.[46] The squire William Harman, of Crayford (Kent), was anxious to assure the Henrician Star Chamber that

all the day[s] of his lyff [he] hathe lyvyd honestly and quyetly amongst his neyghbours and hathe byn takyn and acceptyd aswell by all persones of worshupp and to be noo busy persone … butt always hathe indeveryd hym self truly and feythfully to the utt most of his power to save the kinges majestie his most gracious sovereign lord in all such his affayres wherin your sayd orator hathe had other aut[h]orytie or comandement to travayle as your seid orator will stonde to be tryed by all honeste persones.[47]

Despite their reputation for aggressive economic individualism, the elites of textile districts also felt a sense of duty to the poor. In the hard year of 1598, for example, the wealthy Gloucestershire clothier Robert Taylor invested £2,000 in buying Danish rye which he intended to sell to those 'of the worshipful and better sort of men who he thought to be most careful for the relieving of the poorer sort of people … as also to divers men of great account of other countries thereunto adjoining … [whom he] thought were likewise well affected to their poorer neighbours' and promised to sell the rye to them at decent prices, with the intention that they should give it to the poor.[48]

For the greater gentry, a financial and emotional investment in charitable giving was also important as it did more than validate their social position; it underwrote their claim to embody Christian ethics. The social responsibilities of the Christian gentleman were self-evident to the Cheshire baronet Sir Richard Grosvenor. In 1636, he advised his son to '[b]ee charitable to the truly poore. Receive strangers, cloath the

---

[45] 'Village' gentry were very significant figures, yet they lack a proper study.
[46] TNA, STAC8/227/1.102.     [47] TNA, STAC2/33/52.
[48] A. Everitt, 'The Marketing of Agricultural Produce, 1500–1640', in J. Chartres (ed.), *Agricultural Markets and Trade, 1500–1750* (Cambridge, 1990), 126.

naked.'[49] The Elizabethan gentleman Sir William Petre of Ingatestone (Essex) provides a clear example of consistent informal giving combined with investment in charitable institutions that would outlast him. Looking over Petre's accounts, his biographer observes: 'Many small sums went "in alms", "to a poor man", and so forth.' Petre also gave cash handouts to poor folk, along with several shillings or even a sovereign to tenants or local craftsmen who had fallen sick and similar generosity to servants who were leaving to get married. He invested in institutional charity: in 1556, Petre founded an almshouse for the poor and endowed it with lands valued at £50 per year, followed, in 1564, by a fund that paid out £16 a year, to be distributed to ten poor folk. Petre was sure to provide hospitality at Christmas: his Great Hall was crowded with tenants, neighbours and unexpected poor visitors who were treated to food and drink. Weddings, too, were occasions when villagers might expect to be invited to receive food in the Great Hall. And the charity continued in more everyday contexts, with workmen, travellers, tenants and paupers all fed at the Great Hall. Poor-quality bread was regularly baked for the poor in the kitchen of Ingatestone Hall.[50] Generosity and inequality were thereby literally swallowed down.

Sir William Petre personifies one social virtue that has received attention from historians: that of hospitality.[51] The values of good lordship continued to emphasize the provision of hospitality. A 1596 ballad mourning the passing of the third earl of Huntington emphasized that the earl was noted for his provision for the poor:

> The naked he clothed with garments from cold,
> And ... bestowed his silver and gold
> His purse was still open in giving the poore
> That alwaies came flocking to Huntington's doore
> His tenaunts that daily repaired to his house
> Was fed with his bacon, his beefe and his souse
> Their rents were not raised, their fines were but small,
> And manie poore Tenaunts paide nothing at all.[52]

---

[49] R. Cust (ed.), *The Papers of Sir Richard Grosvenor, 1st Baronet (1585–1645)*, Lancashire and Cheshire Record Society, 84 (1996), 32. He followed his own advice. See references to casual gifts 'to divers poore'; 'to a poore woman'; 'to 2 poore women'; 'to a poor man'. Ibid., 66–7.

[50] F. G. Emmison, *Tudor Secretary: Sir William Petre at Court and Home* (London, 1961), 123, 127, 132, 134, 277–8.

[51] For a detailed discussion, see F. Heal, *Hospitality in Early Modern England* (Oxford, 1990).

[52] Anon., *The Crie of the Poore for the Death of the Right Honorable Earle of Huntington* (London, 1596). For a full study, see C. Cross, *The Puritan Earl: The Life of Henry Hastings, Third Earl of Huntington, 1536–1595* (London, 1966).

Hospitality defined the gentry ideal: just as lords shouldn't raise rents, enclose commons, oppress the poor or leave their 'Country', so they were expected – like Sir William Petre – to keep an open house to visitors, whether they be the wandering poor, their tenants or their gentry neighbours. The funeral sermon of Edward, Lord Montagu, celebrated the same values. The preacher spoke of how Montagu's

housekeeping was liberal & bountiful for entertain[men]t of resorters to him, who were very many, & of the poorest sort of people ...[.] It is better to give one his dinner, th[a]t knows not elsewhere to have it, th[a]n twenty able to answere feast w[i]th feast, according to our Saviour's divine direction ...[.] When y[o]u makest a dinner or supper, call not thy friends nor thy kinnesmen, nor thy rich neighbors least they also bid thee againe & a recompense be made thee. But when y[o]u makest a feast, call the poore[,] the maimed[,] the lame & the blinde &c wh[o] at christide was such, th[a]t it[']s scarce credible, save to those who were eyewitnesses a long time all the poore men women & children were placed at tables furnished w[i]th victuals, from whence arising, they were sent away & others placed, until all had beene set downe.[53]

The Suffolk gentleman Sir Edward Lewkenor went so far as to have a special structure built in which food was provided to the poor.[54] In the dearth year of 1623, another Suffolk gentleman, John Winthrop, wrote to his wife to tell her: 'I praye thee let provision be made; and all our poore feasted, though I be from home, so I shall be the less missed: and such as are of the middle sort let alone till I come home.'[55] The central state did its best to encourage such instincts amongst the gentry. So, also, Biblical precedent encouraged wealthier people to provide hospitality to the poor: in an earlier dearth year, 1597, the 'godly Cittisens of Corinth of Philippi' were upheld as an example to the Tudor gentry. They 'were not onely willing to releeve their neighbours, but in the time of scarcitie in other countreyes, did freely bestow their alms in money (above their abilitie) and sent the same to supply theyr wants that were converted and become Christians'.[56] For some poor folk, it was possible to survive by moving from one gentry house to another, seeking support. In 1590, for example, Edward Jeffrey told the magistrates of Leicester that, since Lady Day, 'he hathe had no service butt wandered to and froe to gentlemens houses where he was best knowne, to get a meales meate to kepe himself from follye'.[57]

[53] Boughton Hall, Ms 186, article 10, p. 23.
[54] T. Oldmayne, *Gods Rebuke in Taking from Us ... Sir E[dward] Lewkenor* (London, 1619), 27.
[55] A. P. Forbes (ed.), *Winthrop Papers*, 5 vols. (Boston, MA, 1929–47), I, 293.
[56] Arthurton, *Provision for the Poore*, sig. D4v.
[57] M. Bateson (ed.), *Records of the Borough of Leicester ... 1509–1603* (Cambridge, 1905), 268.

In the fiercely competitive world of the English gentry, those who failed to deliver proper hospitality could be held up to scorn. In 1608, for example, the Yorkshireman Sir John Bentley criticized one of his peers who 'neyther hath good chear, good company nor gives ought to the poore'.[58] Fundamental to gentry identity was the provision of largesse. As Humfrey Braham explained in his 1568 handbook on gentry virtues: 'To gentlemen of the c[o]untry which have lands or lyving therto, it hath been a greate prayse in tymes past, and is truly a thing praise worthy, to be good hous[e]kepers, to relieve their neighbours with meate and drynke, to fede many and be themselves fed of fewe.'[59]

So, too, the burden of past social practices lay heavy upon the middle sort. They, too, were meant to maintain hospitality for their workers and the poor, to extend credit, to dispense charity, to look out for the interests of the community. And here, too, these expectations found expression in dramatic form. In *A Knacke to Knowe a Knave*, a yeoman called Dunston, who maintains a flock of 1,200 sheep along with 100 oxen, has this to say:

> That everie Winter feed within my stalles
> And twentie poore men living neere my house,
> I daylie feed, and all upon my farme:
> Go but among my neighbours where I dwell,
> And here what good report they give of me,
> The poore man never went from my dore,
> But to my power I did relieve his want:
> I was no farmer that inricht my selfe:
> By raysing markets and oppressing poore,
> But I have sold my corne full manie tymes
> At better rate, then I could wel afford.[60]

Dunston wasn't some social imaginary. Despite all the pressures upon them, richer people sometimes provided succour to their poorer neighbours, feeding them from their doors, even taking the poor into their houses. In 1622, dearth conditions were worsened in the Gloucestershire clothing districts by industrial depression; here, it was noted by the magistracy that 'one William Benett[,] a very ancient & good Clothier[,] doth offer to live by browne bread & water rather then his great number of poore people should want work, yf he had meanes to keep them in worke'.[61] The poor came more often came into contact with their immediate richer neighbours – the better sort of people – than they did

---

[58] Sheffield Archives, BFM2/2/216.

[59] H. Braham, *The Institution of a Gentleman* (London, 1568), sig. D8v.

[60] Anon., *A Knacke to Knowe a Knave* (London, 1594), lines 859–70.

[61] F. H. Clutterbuck, 'State Papers Relating to the Cloth Trade, 1622', *Transactions of the Bristol and Gloucestershire Archaeological Society*, 5 (1880–1), 157.

with the gentry. The relationship between poor and middling people was complex, intimate and sometimes conflictual.[62] Heavy expectations were often made of richer farmers, especially at times of high food prices, regarding their responsibilities to the local poor. Charles Fitz-Geffrie wrote in 1631, for example:

[T]the way to heaven is not so narrow, nor the gate so strai[gh]t, but that a courteous Farmer, with his Cart load of Corne may enter into it, who is ready to releeve the Countrey by charitable selling. Behold how God esteemes that mercy to others, which brings a commodity to our selves; and faith, in effect, to you that are of ability, in these extremities; Thy neighbour hath need, yea, I my selfe in him, doe suffer want, now enrich thy selfe. At other times (and so now too especially) Hee that giveth to the poore, lendeth to the poore; at this time, Hee that selleth unto the poore, giveth unto the Lord, and the Lord will repay him with a blessing on the bargaine.[63]

Alongside this text, Fitz-Geffrie cited Proverbs 19:17: 'He that hath pity upon the poor lendeth unto the Lord; and that which he hath given will he pay him again.'

But, in all too many cases, the entrepreneurial, prosperous middling sort did not live up to their social duties. In 1621, the jurors of Forehoe Hundred (Norfolk) presented a number of their wealthier neighbours for failing to maintain the standards that were expected of them. There was William Rowse, a Wymondham brewer, who held land worth £300 but 'keepeth no howse[, has] but one childe & he richely maryed'. Then there was the yeoman Thomas Hobs, who was 'riche in money, gathereth wealth very much, never a childe and liveth at a meane Rate'. In Crownthorpe, Richard Ken was described as 'a great usurer, Riche in stock besides & useth a great estate by farme'. In Hingham, there was the brewer John Long, who was 'a very great usurer'; his son was an attorney '& very rich also'. Neither contributed much to the poor. In Wicklewood, the gentleman Jonas Pytts was known to be 'very Rich, very miserable, gotten much wealth'. In the same village, the yeoman John Bale possessed 'a good estate in lands, a great & griping usurer'; Edmund Bale lacked any spirit of hospitality. It was recorded that he 'kepeth no howse: [worth] 60. li in lands, riche in money & an usurer & may as well as any'. The yeoman George Fynderne held £100 per year in land yet was 'an usurer & lyveth at a meane rate & gathereth much wealth'. In contrast to such people, there were always folk like the yeomen Phillipp Cullyer and Henry Gay, both of whom, it was said, were 'good to the poore'.[64]

---

[62] It is a relationship that warrants much closer scrutiny.

[63] C. Fitz-Geffrie, *The Curse of Corne-Horders* (London, 1631), 42.

[64] W. Hudson, 'Assessment of the Hundred of Forehoe in 1621: A Sidelight on the Difficulties of National Taxation', *Norfolk Archaeology*, 21, 3 (1922), 285–309.

Although early modern England was far from the 'precapitalist' economy imagined by James C. Scott, his comments on the vulnerability of subsistence workers to shifts in food prices remain apposite: 'The precapitalist community was, in a sense, organized around this problem of the minimum income – organized to minimize the risk to which its members were exposed by virtue of its limited techniques and the caprice of nature. Traditional forms of patron-client relationships, reciprocity, and redistributive mechanisms may be seen from this perspective.'[65] Such mechanisms might, in years such as 1587, 1596–7 or 1622–4, prevent starvation amongst the established poor. In his brilliant discussion of the subject, John Walter has therefore cautioned against '[a]n anachronistic reading of early modern society as a market society marked by the triumph of economic individualism'. Rather than reading social relations off from price indices, Walter suggests that early modern society is better understood 'by considerations of oeconomy, rather than economy'. In this world, at the moments of its greatest tests – dearth – 'protection against harvest failure was ... to be found in a much wider set of relationships: amongst others the relationship between landlord and tenant, farmer and labourer, master and servant, rich and poor'.[66] And a critical role was played by the magistracy in enforcing such social expectations – backed, as they were, by the force of the law. In years of high food prices, the county bench was meant to see that food was sold at reasonable prices. Not all farmers would always go along with this. When, in 1594, William Lambarde and other Kentish justices went into the country to question farmers about how much food they could spare for the poor, they were met with one obstinate farmer who stated bluntly that he knew much richer men than he who had refused to spare any and that he thought the Queen's orders were unreasonable.[67]

Working under even greater pressure than in rural areas, urban authorities often did their best to treat the settled poor with compassion and fairness. In the small coastal towns of Kent, urban rulers were prepared to see that, in years of high food prices, their own poor were properly provided for.[68] The problem lay, they felt, with the mobile poor, for whom they felt no responsibility. In conditions of food scarcity, and in those places where the poor had little credit, the exact nature of measures

---

[65] Scott, *The Moral Economy of the Peasant*, 9.

[66] J. Walter, 'The Social Economy of Dearth in Early Modern England', in J. Walter and R. Schofield (eds.), *Famine, Disease and the Social Order in Early Modern Society* (Cambridge, 1989), 121–2.

[67] R. M. Warnicke, *William Lambarde: English Antiquary, 1536–1601* (Chichester, 1973), 108.

[68] S. Hipkin, 'The Structure, Development, and Politics of the Kent Grain Trade, 1552–1647', *EcHR*, 2nd ser., 61 (2008), 106–19.

in food in the marketplace might matter a lot. In 1520, the Leicester authorities laid down a requirement that, '[f]or the comonwelth off the towne', there should be some set standards as of the quality of bread sold to the poor.[69] In King's Lynn, from the 1550s onwards, a stock of grain was maintained, to be sold to the poor at a 'reasonable price'; this stock was supervised by six 'honest men'.[70] Urban rulers went out of their way to see that food and fuel were sold to the poor at prices they could afford. In May 1631, for example, the trader Thomas Turner found himself in trouble with the Reading authorities for having 'denyed to deliver fourth his wheate to the poore at suche rates and prices' as they had set as reasonable; in the end, the constables took Turner's corn from him and sold it to the 'poorer sort' for seven shillings per bushel.[71] In 1552, after John Carr of Wymondham (Norfolk) was prosecuted for selling his pigs at an inflated price, the Norwich authorities instructed that all market traders were 'to utter and sell their wares at Reasonable pryces'.[72] In York, the lord mayor personally supervised the markets of that great city. In 1555, he 'went through the market to see reasonable pricez of vitalls'; on observing a butcher 'sellyng his fleissh excessyvely', the mayor ordered the man to sell at prices 'reasonable to the poor'.[73]

Perhaps just as important to the poorer sort as cheap food was the deeply contested question of access to fuel.[74] In Bristol, the authorities carefully supervised fuel supplies.[75] Traders and shopkeepers who sold goods at excessive prices, along with rich urbanites who stockpiled food, were held up for public censure. In 1574, those London victuallers who sold at excessive prices were accused of 'forgetting both their bounden duties and obedience to our sayd sovereign lady the queen and her laws and the godly and charitable dealings they owe and shew unto their neighbors'. Those traders who failed to sell food at reasonable prices were felt to have 'regard onlie to there owne pryvat lucre and gayne', driven as they were by 'gredy, unsatiable, covetous minds and appetites'.[76] It was essential that urban elites weren't seen to buy up or stockpile food. This was an allegation set against the 'substantial people'

[69] Bateson (ed.), *Records of the Borough of Leicester*, 15–17.
[70] S. M. Battley, 'Elite and Community: The Mayors of Sixteenth-Century King's Lynn', PhD, State University of New York (1981), 249.
[71] J. M. Guilding (ed.), *Reading Records*, 4 vols. (London, 1895), III, 66.
[72] NRO, NCR16A/6, p. 143.    [73] D. M. Palliser, *Tudor York* (Oxford, 1979), 63.
[74] I hope to write more fully about fuel, entitlement and social relations in the future.
[75] L. Toulin Smith (ed.), *The Maire of Bristowe Is Calendar*, Camden Society, 2nd ser., 5 (London, 1872), 83–4.
[76] R. M. Benbow, 'The Court of Aldermen and the Assizes: The Policy of Price Control in Elizabethan London', *Guildhall Studies in London History*, 4, 3 (1980), 93.

of Colchester in the dearth of 1527, and Cardinal Wolsey intervened to make sure that grain was sold to the inhabitants.[77]

There were times when the charity of wealthy householders mattered enormously to the urban poor.[78] During the dearth of 1597, 'the most prosperous of the Worcester citizens took into their homes "above two hundred poor and aged persons" and supported them'.[79] City authorities wanted to show not just that their wealthier burghers had stood up for Christian values of charity and kindness but also that they had been *seen* to do so. The rich hoped that, by virtue of such kindnesses, they would win everlasting fame. Just as lasting as such institutional investments were those bequests that sustained the supply of food to the poor. Here, too, the assumption was that such bequests would win eternal fame on the behalf of the generous civic figure that had made such an offering. When Henry Manship wrote his history of Great Yarmouth in 1619, he made sure to mention Catherine Rogers, the daughter of a Yarmouth merchant, who left, in 1556, the annual sum of £100 to be spent on grain for the town's poor. As Manship put it, her object was 'to beat down the covetous minds of those greedy cormorants, who never cease to grind the faces of the poor, by inhancing the prices, making a dearth when God sendeth plenty'.[80] Civic institutions also played their part in the maintenance of this culture of giving: in an order of 12 July 1596, for example, the Exeter Guild of Merchant Adventurers noted that they had already agreed that money normally spent on a dinner on election day for officers of the guild should instead be spent on buying corn to be given to 'poore householders of this Cittie'. They now ordered that the guild will raise further funds for the poor, amounting to £8 8s 6d.[81]

For the gentry, such gifts were supposed to form a bond with those further down the social hierarchy.[82] At the 1640 funeral of the gentleman Sir Thomas Lucy, the preacher told those gathered before him:

---

[77] J. S. Brewer et al. (eds.), *Letters and Papers, Foreign and Domestic, of Henry VIII*, 21 vols. (London, 1862–1910), IV (2), 1629, 1781.

[78] I. W. Archer, 'The Charity of Early Modern Londoners', *TRHS*, 6th ser., 12 (2002), 223–44.

[79] A. D. Dyer, *The City of Worcester in the Sixteenth Century* (Leicester, 1973), 166.

[80] C. J. Palmer (ed.), *The History of Great Yarmouth by Henry Manship Esq., Temp. Queen Elizabeth* (London, 1854), 129. For more on Manship, see A. Wood, 'Tales from the "Yarmouth Hutch": Civic Identities and Hidden Histories in an Urban Archive', in L. Corens, K. Peters and A. Walsham (eds.), *The Social History of the Archive: Record Keeping in Early Modern Europe*, *P&P*, 230, Supplement 11 (2016), 213–30.

[81] W. Cotton (ed.), *An Elizabethan Guild of the City of Exeter* (Exeter, 1873), 122–3.

[82] For a perceptive account of this social ideal, see M. E. James, *Family, Lineage and Civil Society: A Study of Society, Politics and Mentality in the Durham Region, 1500–1640* (Oxford, 1974), 32–5.

A Noble Lady hath lost, not an Husband (as shee saith) but a Father.
Many children have lost, not a Father, but a Counsellor.
An house-full of servants have lost, not a Master, but a Phisitian, who
   made ... their sicknesse his, and his physic and cost teirs.
Townes-full of Tenants have lost a Land-Lord, that could both protect
   and direct them in their owne way.
The whole Neighbourhood have lost a Light.
The Countie a Leader.
The Countrey a Patriot; To whom he was not wanting, till he was
   wanting to imselfe, in his former vigor and health.[83]

The lesser gentleman Robert Furse advised his children:

Be good and gentyll to your Tenantes and love them and have always ther good
wylles and reporte. Performe ther leses and that wythe owte vexsasyon or sute
...[.] Burden them not wythe more fynes, rents, or serves more then theye be well
abell to paye you. Dysplase not an honeste fryndely tenant for a tryfell or smalle
some of money. Rejoyse and be gladde to se[e] your tenantes to proser for then
your londes shall prosper and yf they growe in welthe then no dowte when you
com to ther howses they will fryndelye intertayne you, and yf you need anye
thynge that theye have they will surelye helpe you and be alwayes at your com-
mondemente and redy to do you and yours good. Therefore esteem an honeste
fryndelye tenant more then moneye.[84]

The 'love' of tenants and the poor could be a useful cultural resource for a
gentleman. When the status of the London merchant Daniel Dobbins was
challenged following his acquisition of the manor of Kidderminster
(Worcestershire), his tenants came to his aid, proferring to the High Court
of Chivalry enthusiastic statements of his standing in the local community.
The clothier Elias Arche, for example, told the court: 'Daniel is a man of
good life and conversation, a charitable minded man to releeve the poore and
ever since he purchased parte of the manor, he hath freely and liberally given
towards the maintenance of the poore of Kidderminster, twelve pounds per
annum; and Daniel Dobbins is a gentleman well beloved of all his neighbours.' The public notary Arnold Collwall agreed, adding that he had known
Dobbins' family for sixty years during which time 'they were allwaies
accompted, reputed and taken and stiled gentlemen and never heard them
stiled otherwise'. Just like Daniel Dobbins, his father had been reputed a
'man of honest life and good conversation', well 'esteemed amongst the
better sorte of the gentlemen ... very charitable to the poore and a peacemaker amongst his neighbours'.[85]

[83] R. Harris, *Abners Funerall, or A Sermon Preached at the Funerall of ... Sir Thomas Lucie*
   (London, 1641), 25–6.
[84] A. Travers (ed.), *Robert Furse: A Devon Family Memoir of 1593*, Devon and Cornwall
   Record Society, new ser., 53 (Exeter, 2012), 19–20.
[85] HCCO, 624: *Stepkin v. Dobbins*.

Letters of advice by older gentlemen to their sons are replete with instructions to look after tenants and be kind to the poor. In 1604, for instance, Sir William Woodhouse advised his son: 'Avoide usury and selling anie thing to pore men to a long daie for a great pryce ...[.] Never take a cruell advantage upon a mortgage, bonds &c of pore men.'[86] The Cheshire gentleman Sir Richard Grosvenor was conscious that seigneurial oppressions would bring down divine displeasure upon the family, warning his son in 1636: 'Let your fines bee modderate & accept of such scirvises as may bee performed without just cawse of repineing, lest otherwise the poor tenant cry (with the oppressed Israelites) unto God for ease & hee take thire cawse in hand.'[87] Sir Walter Raleigh was also aware that gentry oppressions would incur divine wrath, telling his son that he should not 'take any thing from the poor: for the cry and complaint thereof will pierce the heavens ...[. U]se thy poor neighbours and tenants well.'[88] Edward, Lord Montagu, advised against depopulating villages, telling his son that the Almighty 'hath made you a Landlord of many tenants: Counte that a greate[r] blessing then if he had made you a master of ten thousand of sheepe.' Citing Mark 12:15 ('A man[']s life standeth not in his Riches'), Montagu went on:

Know you are but a Steward and must make an accounte of the usage of your tenants and estate. Place therefore Firmly Resident Conscionable ministers over them to Instruct the[i]r soules. Be moderate in taking of fines: and sharing in raysing of Rentes That they may have cause both to pray and prayse God For you ...[.] Shun altogether oppression ...[.] Travayle not too much to be Rich.[89]

The poor, thought Robert Furse, should be nurtured by the gentry, rather than stand as figures of scorn, instructing his descendants: 'Mocke not nor dyspyse the power sympell and innosente person but geve god thankes that he hathe induede the[e] better.'[90] Conventional paternalist thought was clear that the poor would always be favoured by God and that they deserved protection: hence, William Vaughan advised his readers: 'The poore, being an inferior familie in Gods Church, are recommended by him to our charge, namely, that wee should relieve them in their distresse, and consider that whatsoever wee do unto them, wee do unto Christ himself.'[91] The aged – especially old servants – were also supposed to be recipients of gentry paternalism. Sir Richard Grosvenor encouraged his son to look after his former servants:

[86] J. P. Cooper (ed.), *Wentworth Papers, 1597–1628*, Camden Society, 4th ser., 12 (1973), 21.
[87] Cust (ed.), *The Papers of Sir Richard Grosvenor*, 34.
[88] Anon., *Practical Wisdom; or The Manual of Life* (London, 1824), 25.
[89] Boughton Hall, 186, article 13.    [90] Travers (ed.), *Robert Furse*, 17.
[91] W. Vaughan, *The Golden Grove* (London, 1608), book 2, chapter 23.

[S]ome I have who have benn carefull of my business and scirvisable to mee in my troubles. Amonge the rest Bearde hath spent many years, even the prime of his time, in my scrvis; and out of love to mee hath benn contented to imprison himself never leaving not forsaking mee. I have donn little for him proportionable to his scrvis. Hee hath ever been painefull, faithfull & trusty to you. I leave him to be cherished and better provided for, that he want not in his age.[92]

The paternalist ideal was perhaps best summarized by the Isle of Wight gentleman Sir John Strode, who (drawing on Matthew 25:35–45) advised his son in 1597:

In thy Conversation, be then Curteous, and Respectfull to all, not prowde, nor disdainfull to any ...[.] Be thou Pittifull to the poore, mercifull to the Aflicted, And Redy to Relieve, According to thy power ... visit thou those that ar Sick, Comfort them that ar in prison, Relieve the oppresst, harbor the stranger, cloth the naked, feede the hungry, Be a father to the fatherles, and a husband to the widowes, So shalt thou be beloved of God, more then of they father and mother.[93]

The practice of generosity and hospitality helped to oil the machinery of social relations. In 1568, Humfrey Braham opined that 'liberalitie is ... a thing whiche sheweth for the th[e] [h]onour of a Gentle heart ...[. L] iberalitie is to helpe and succour with worldy goodes the man which is poore and standeth nedefull therof, or to geve money to the marriage of poore maydens.'[94] The gentry liked to think of themselves as paternalists: in 1588, for example, William Lambarde described himself as the 'professed proctor of the poore'.[95] These expectations fed into the role of the gentry as brokers in local social relations. The Norwich gentleman Edward Younges was encouraged by his peers to support the inhabitants of nearby Thorpe against the lessee of the parochial tithes 'for that [the case] ... did concerne a sort of poore men'.[96] Similarly, an epitaph of 1590 said of Sir Francis Walsingham:

Farewell Sir Francis Walsingham, that usurie sore didst hate
That still didst good to rich and poore that came to thy gate
Farewell the comfort of the poore, that do almes did give
... Farewell the su[i]tor for the poore, that seldome let thee rest
... Farewell the care for counties good, when corne was prisde so hie.[97]

---

[92] Cust (ed.), *The Papers of Sir Richard Grosvenor*, 33.
[93] Isle of Wight Record Office, OG/SS/1.
[94] Braham, *The Institution of a Gentleman*, sig. D5r.
[95] Warnicke, *William Lambarde*, 51.    [96] TNA, E178/4940.
[97] T. Nelson, *A Memorable Epitaph ... for the Death of Sir Francis Walsingham* (London, 1590).

Elite benevolence could lodge itself in local memory. In John Stow's nostalgic *Survey of London*, he recalled how, in 1532, the Bishop of Ely 'dayly gave at his Gates besides bread and drinke, warm meate to two hundred poore people'. Likewise, Stow noted that, in 1500, the Bishop of Ely gave 'reliefe to the poore, wheresoever he was lodged. In his travailing, when at his coming, or going to or from any towne, the belles being rung, all the poore would come together, to whom he gave every one 6.d. at the least.' In his own time, Stow had seen, 'in that declining time of charity . . . at the Lord Cromwels gate in London, more then two hundred persons served twise every day with bread, meate and drinke sufficient, for hee observed that aunicent and charitable custome as all prelates, noble men, or men of honour and worship his precedessors had done before him'.[98] These practices generated powerful expectations.[99] The notion that the gentry should be merciful and benevolent to the poor was invoked where such expectations were frustrated. Critical comment was passed in 1530, for example, upon an Oxfordshire landlord who, it was reported, had undone the poor of Woodstock by summoning them to London courts before which they could not afford to sue.[100]

For all that the godly were often criticized for their lack of support for traditional social virtues, they, too, were capable of exercising mercy to the poor – at least so long as the poor showed sufficient adherence to Puritan ethics and demonstrated proper deference. The orders agreed by the Puritan governors of Dedham (Essex) in 1585 laid down the injunction that 'so many as be of habilitie' should 'invite to their howses one couple of such of their poore neighbors as have submitted themselves to the good orders of the Churche, and walke Christianly and honestlie if their callings, and others of less hability any one such person providing no more for them then ordinary and so longe as they shall thankfully accepte of the same'.[101]

The capacity of local inhabitants to sustain hospitality was taken as an indication of the social stability of their communities. In Terrington, located within the frequently flooded Marshland district of Norfolk, the older inhabitants explained, in 1600, that the costs of maintaining their defences against the sea had impoverished the community. Whilst the

---

[98] C. L. Kingsford (ed.), *A Survey of London by John Stow*, 2 vols. (Oxford, 1908), I, 88–9.
[99] Although Steve Hindle sounds a note of caution, observing: 'Despite the rich fund of prescription and nostalgia expressed in funeral sermons and family memoirs, evidence for the actual practice of gentry hospitality is rather limited, and even where it can accurately be measured it constituted only a tiny fraction of the income of the landed elite.' Hindle, *On the Parish?*, 105.
[100] TNA, SP1/59, fol. 116r.
[101] R. G. Usher (ed.), *The Presbyterian Movement in the Reign of Queen Elizabeth*, Camden Society, 3rd ser., 8 (London, 1905), 100.

numbers of poor in the village had rocketed, there remained only three householders who were capable of maintaining hospitality, where once there had been twelve.[102] Likewise, in 1592, the old men of Petworth (Sussex) looked back on earlier years when their lords had been less rapacious than the current earl of Northumberland. One explained to the Court of Chancery that whereas the 'predecessors' of the current tenants 'were wealthy men & able to doe for theire frends of neede', now the copyholders were of 'veary bare and naked estate'.[103]

Clergy were also expected to be solid providers of charity and hospitality. Sir Simonds D'Ewes inherited the story about his clerical grandfather 'giving good examples to his neighbours by his constant hospitality, [that] earnest he was and sincere in the right cause of his client, pitiful in the relief of the distressed, and merciful to the poor'.[104] The godly Elizabethan minister Bernard Gilpin was remembered for his generous provision for the poor. On every Sunday between Michaelmas and Easter, in his parish of Houghton-le-Spring (County Durham), Gilpin kept a table for all parishioners. Gilpin made sure that people sat according to their social place. His biographer noted that 'he had the gentlemen, the husbandmen and the poorer sort sat every degree by themselves, and as it were ordered in ranks'.[105] Hospitality, in Houghton-le-Spring, provided for the poor while renewing social bonds and articulating social hierarchies.

Sometimes, clerical hospitality was expected to take a festive form. In 1622, the churchwardens of Rustington (Sussex) presented their parson William Waters 'for not making our drincking at harvest last past for the parishioners of Rustington; which is a custome in our parrishe'.[106] Until they were painted over during the civil wars, inscriptions in Gawsworth parish church (Cheshire) recorded, underneath depictions of two pre-Reformation priests, the following words:

> To Rectors all these two may be,
> Rare patterns of greate Piety;
> The Chancell fitton raised from ground,
> The Rectory did Baguley found;
> Such Rectors should be but such are
> Wonders these days they be so rare;
> For charitie with us growes cold,
> Worse in this age than 'twas of old;

---

[102] NRO, MC1872/17 (866x2).

[103] A. Wood, '"Some Banglyng about the Customes": Popular Memory and the Experience of Defeat in a Sussex Village, 1549–1640', *Rural History*, 25, 1 (2014), 10.

[104] A. T. Hart, *The Man in the Pew, 1558–1640* (London, 1966), 45.

[105] G. Carleton, 'Life of Bernard Gilpin', in C. Wordsworth (ed.), *Ecclesiastical Biography*, 6 vols. (London, 1818), IV, 158.

[106] Johnstone (ed.), *Churchwardens' Presentments*, 49; see also 57.

Yet good cause why, the clergies store
Is threefold less than 'twas before.[107]

The belief that the charity of clergy 'grows cold' was something that came
with the Reformation and that coloured relationships between the laity
and their ministers. Complaints concerning the failure of ministers to
provide hospitality to their neighbours or charity to the poor are not hard
to find.[108] Chris Fitter has observed that, in late Elizabethan and early
Stuart drama, 'the saying that "Charity grows cold" became proverbial:
variant between 1590 and 1607 as "So cold is charitie in these times",
"Charitie waxeth cold", and "Charitie is frozen and neum'd with
colde"'.[109] These were no mere abstractions: when the poor man James
Mason and his family were thrown out of their home and forced to live in
the streets of Little Paxton (Huntingdonshire) in 1638, he remarked upon
'the frozen charitie of our towne governors'.[110] This reflected a growing
sense that integrative social values were coming under increasing threat: it
was part of the depressive mood-music of the early modern period. And
yet, so much of the evidence points to the continued investment by elites
and institutions such as parishes and boroughs in paternalist social practices throughout the period with which we are dealing.

The attachment of early modern people to the values of hospitality – in
however attenuated and contested a form – illustrates something of the
ways in which individualistic notions of the accumulation of land and
capital were constantly bisected by traditional values that emphasized
communal belonging and mutual interdependence. In this, the idea of
neighbourhood was central: in its ideal form, everyone in a community –
the landless poor as well as the lord of the manor, the richer farmers and
the minister – had an investment in the maintenance of a social relationship in which all sides owed something to the others. This is what Pierre
Bourdieu has called a 'good faith' economy, where there is a permanent
need to reaffirm and reassert personal ties.[111] We might push the concept
further. In her study of Zapotec villagers, the anthropologist Laura Nader
invoked the concept of the levelling mechanism. As she explains it:

Because hierarchy refers to rank relationships where each role is defined as
subordinate to the one above, the levelling dimension, the value placed on

---

[107] R. Richards, *The Manor of Gawsworth, Cheshire* (Congleton, 1957), 66.

[108] For examples, see HMC, 14th Report, VIII, Lincoln MSS, 62; DUL, DDR/EJ/CCD/1/
2, fol.bis. 207r.

[109] C. Fitter, '"As Full of Grief as Age": Protesting against the Poor Law in King Lear', in
C. Fitter (ed.), *Shakespeare and the Politics of Commoners: Digesting the New Social History*
(Oxford, 2017), 218. See also Matthew, 24:12.

[110] Hindle, *On the Parish?*.

[111] P. Bourdieu, *Outline of a Theory of Practice* (Cambridge, 1977), 171–97.

symmetry, may be seen as either contradictory or complementary. The concept of levelling, of balanced proportions, operates in many of the same contexts in which hierarchy is found, as well as in additional situations. Levelling mechanisms serve to mediate the harsher aspects of hierarchy, but at the same time they do not function to sabotage superordinate/subordinate relationships.

One example of a levelling mechanism provided by Nader is that of richer people providing the funds for fiestas. What she identifies as 'symmetry' is seen amongst the Zapotec as the preferred mode within which social relations are conducted: 'It is unappealing to be too rich or too poor ...[.] Asymmetry is often the underlying cause of envy, witchcraft accusations, or disputes in courts.' What Nader calls 'harmony ideology' operated amongst the Zapotec villagers; this comprised 'an emphasis on conciliation, recognition that resolution of conflict is inherently good and that its reverse – continued conflict or controversy – is bad or dysfunctional'.[112] To any student of early modern society, there is much that is familiar here. Something very similar seems to have been at work in early modern communities – a sense that the growing inequalities between rich and poor could be mitigated – or perhaps even transcended – by a belief in Christian values that emphasized mutual interdependence.

Underpinning the values of neighbourhood, reciprocity and hospitality was a profound belief in charity as a Christian virtue, a sort of social glue that held an otherwise fractious society together. In particular, charity was seen as a necessary corollary of a belief in an organic, hierarchical society in which all knew their place. In a sermon of 1619, John Donne observed:

Rich, and poor are contrary to one another, but yet both necessary to one another; but the poor man is the more necessary, because one man might be rich, though no man were poor, yet he could have no exercise of his charity, he could send none of his riches to heaven, to help him there, except there were some poor here.[113]

Addressing hoarders of corn in 1631, Charles Fitz-Geffrie demanded of them:

Why art thou rich, and hee poore? Certainely, for no other cause, but that thy fulnesse might supply his want, and that both might, doing their duties, obtaine of him a reward; thou of faithfull distributing, and hee of his patient enduring. If all were rich, what praise were there of patience? If all were poore, who should be able to shew charity? If there were, in this kinde, an equality, two precious vertues would be vile or not at all, Charity and Patience.[114]

---

[112] L. Nader, *Harmony Ideology: Justice and Control in a Zaoptec Mountain Village* (Stanford, CA, 1990), 2, 36.
[113] E. M. Simpson and G. R. Potter (eds.), *The Sermons of John Donne*, 10 vols. (Berkeley, CA, 1953), II, 214.
[114] Fitz-Geffrie, *The Curse of Corne-horders*, 40–2.

Writing in 1615, Thomas Lupton invited his readers to imagine a rich man conversing with Satan in Hell. The rich man was sure that, if he had his time back on Earth again, he would have cared more for the poor:

If I were on the earth againe ... I would goe from house to house, to releeve the poore, I would ... releeve them that are in miserie, according to my power: I would not banquet the Rich, nor feed the flatterers, but most the poore and miserable wretches: yea, the lame, the blind and the sore, that lie in the streetes I would send for, and they should be my guests, and they should feede on my foode: and if my rich neighbours disdained me for it, yet Christ that is richer then they, would not mistake me for it. My purse should never be shut from the poore, and I would always be readie to lend the needie.[115]

Gentlemen and women therefore invested in charity not only as a virtue in itself but also to save their souls and to win lasting honour as a parent to their country. The preacher at the funeral of Edward, Lord Montagu, explained:

Charity is comunicated goodnes, w[i]thout wh[ic]h a man is no other th[a]n a beast preying for himself alone ...[.] It is the glory of Christianity when works goe w[i]th wordes, practise with profession, and faith is shewed by its fruits ...[.] This charity is th[a]t w[hi]ch makes riches worth the owning ...[.] Such was his L[or]dships goodness & charity, that he did not onely good to the good, to make th[e]m better, but also to the bad least they should grow worse[,] he wel[l] knowinge th[a]t only use gives praise to worldly possessions. ... [H]e by bountie & beneficence cheered[,] co[m]forted & refreshed many, by w[hi]ch he hath honoured God and himself for liberality & expense breedeth & maintaineth honour.[116]

In giving to the poor and helping his neighbors, then, Lord Montagu's reputation and 'honour' were thought to live beyond the grave. And his way into heaven, it was hoped, was eased by the grateful prayers of the poor.

Lord Montagu was not the only wealthy individual who hoped that his good name would endure beyond the grave. The neighbourly ideal was strong enough to make its way into the otherwise mute record of the parish register. In Aston (Warwickshire), Jess Eagles was buried on 25 December 1607, 'a good churchwoman and good to the poor'. On 5 April 1624, in Burstall (Suffolk), the widow Jane Salter was buried, the clerk observing that 'she had lived in the favour of God and all good people lxxi yeares'. A few years later, in St Peter's Cornhill (London), the weaver David Powell was buried. It was noted:

This Powell was a plaine man and led an honest life
Hee loved peace and amitie, and shun[ne]d debate and strife[.]

[115] T. Lupton, *A Dreame of the Devil and Dives* (London, 1615), sig. C4v.
[116] Boughton Hall, Ms 186, article 10, p. 20.

## Alcohol, Alehouses and Good Neighbourhood

The parish church often seems to historians to represent the central site for the articulation of communal values. Yet, for many labouring people, as Mark Hailwood has recently demonstrated, the alehouse was at least as important.[117] In his earlier study, Peter Clark quotes a contemporary who felt that poor customers in alehouses 'strive so after community . . . They think it some ease and comfort in misery to have companions . . . [that] sorrows divided among many are borne more easily'.[118] In neighbourhoods where the poor were supposed to know their place, some alehouses were felt by richer folk to represent a challenge to the dominant order. In 1612, for instance, the Norfolk bench heard that at South Pickenham there was an alehouse run by Thomas Whitby 'who harbours a fellowe which is a disobedient person & a drunkard unknowen to the townsmen'. This was part of a pattern: Whitby 'drawes divers poore to spend their time & money otherwise then lawe requires'.[119]

Some alehousekeepers were held up as examples of unneighbourly people. From Griston (Norfolk), it was reported that, since John Falks had been licensed to keep an alsehouse, he had 'growen into such an humor of drunkenness & lewde behavior that he is neither meete for that purpose, nor yet to lyve in a common wealth'.[120] Likewise, in 1590, Ellen and Hugh Smythe of Norton (Staffordshire) were accused of running an unruly alehouse. Ellen was said to be a 'strumpet . . .[. H]er greate shewes of overmuch famyllierytie towards many men w[i]thin the parishe hathe bred suche disquyetnes between them and theire wiefes that theire hathe byn . . . redie to parte companye, wherapon she hathe gretlie rejoysed.'[121] In this respect, Ellen Smythe represented an existential threat to the patriarchal order of the village. A similar taint of sexual and moral disorder hung over John Stanfield's drinking establishment in Layston (Hertfordshire) in 1597, it being 'a howse of great disorders as well in intertayninge of the worst sort of people as also by suffering swearing, gamynge, drunkenness, quarrellinge, and great suspicion of whoredom'.[122]

In the early seventeenth century, the minister of Offord Cluney (Huntingdonshire) complained about the increased number of alehouses

---

[117] M. Hailwood, *Alehouses and Good Fellowship in Early Modern England* (Woodbridge, 2014).

[118] P. Clark, *The English Alehouse: A Social History* (London, 1983), 156.

[119] NRO, NQS/C/S3/18, presentment of Hundred of Launditch.

[120] NRO, NQS/C/S3/18, certificate of William Story.

[121] S. A. H. Burne (ed.), *The Staffordshire Quarter Sessions Rolls, II: 1590–1593*, Collections for a History of Staffordshire (Kendal, 1932), 51–3.

[122] Hardy (ed.), *Hertford County Records*, 27.

in his parish. He explained that 'whereas the inhabitants of ... Offord Cluney' some twenty years ago had maintained sixteen ploughs, had 'lived in peace and love, and kept good hospitalitie for the poore', now they were reduced to seven ploughs due to the alehouses, which 'live most of them idlye upon the sinnes and distempers of the people'; they constituted 'temptacons and snares to devoure mens time, meanes and soules'.[123] Some alehouses were depicted as sites of unneighbourly punch-ups and fracas. In 1614, the jurors of Freebridge Hundred (Norfolk) presented Thomas Heckleton of Grimston because he 'doth suffer unlawfull games in his howse being an Alehowse And that he doth suffer some of his neighbors there to drinke until they fall together by the eares'.[124] In 1611, the leading inhabitants of Barton Bendish (Norfolk) petitioned against the alehousekeeper Christopher Wade, explaining that he kept

very evill order in his house, having mens servants and other poore Laborers playing at cardes, tables, dyce, on the Saboth daye, and in the tyme of devyne s[er]vice, And some of them there drinking untyll they be drunck & not able to goe home[.] And further there are some poore laborers there drinking and playing at cardes And some mens servants lykewyse playeinge & drinking there at tenne of the clock in the night.[125]

The problem in Barton Bendish, it seemed, was that of labour discipline: Wade's alehouse had become an alternative centre for conviviality and hearty cheer amongst the poor of the village.

Yet, for many people, collective drinking was no more than an unproblematic form of 'good fellowship'. In 1597, Thomas Preston and his friends from Bridlington (Yorkshire) were presented to the diocesan visitation for being 'common dronkardes ... [who] rejoice in their dronkennes etc., counting them selfes good felowes so to do'.[126] In Elizabethan Westmorland, after receiving the sacrament, parishioners would 'goe for good fellowship to the tavern or alehouse'. And at Danby Wisk (Yorkshire), following communion, local people would go to an inn to 'drink together as a testimony of charity & friendship'.[127] In 1598, the churchwardens of Corringham (Essex) presented an especially revealing instance of the association between alcohol and friendship:

[123] BL, Add Ms 34401, fol. 224r.

[124] NRO, NQS/C/S3/19, presentment of Hundred of Freebridge.

[125] NRO, NQS/C/S3/17/1, 'Articles of Evill Behaviour of Christopher Wade'. The story continues at NRO, NQS/C/S3/17/1, 'Certayne Articles of the Misdemeanors of Grace Wade'.

[126] W. J. Sheils (ed.), *Archbishop Grindal's Visitation, 1575: Comperta at Detecta Book*, Borthwick Texts and Calendars, 4 (York, 1977), 87.

[127] Walsham, 'Supping with Satan's Disciples', 44.

One John Smith of this parish, Robert Cottes of Orsett and George Landish of Barking, after great abuse in drinking, did at their parting take with them into the field at the town's end, where they meant to part, four or six pots of beer, and there setting them down did kneel upon their bare knees, humbly kneeling down and kissing the pots and drinking one to another, prayed for the health of all true and faithful drunkards, especially for Mr Andrew Browghton, as they said, the maintainer and upholder of all true and faithful drunkards; and having done kissed each other, and for a memory of their worthy act did every man make his mark upon an ashen tree that stood there.[128]

This represents an example of what Hailwood has identified as the positive communal function of drinking, as one man put it in 1600, 'for neighbourhood's sake'.[129] The collective consumption of alcohol bonded these men – just as, before the Reformation, during the Rogationtide perambulation of the parochial bounds, villagers might drink beer together at key points of the procession, sometimes out of the handbells that they carried with them.[130] In many post-Reformation parishes, a link was retained between festive drinking and the custom of Rogationtide. Some richer folk failed to live up to the expectation that parishioners on perambulation be met at their houses, farms and mills with firkins of beer. They were held up for censure: thus, in James I's reign, the churchwardens of Cropredy (Oxfordshire) presented Mr Arthur Coldwell, Mr Robert Mancell and Mr Joseph Plamer 'for that they do not allow in rogation weeke such charges by drinkinges so called at the severall mylnes in rogation weeke as hath bene before accustomed'.[131] Alcohol fulfilled a social function: its collective consumption built social bonds and, however hazily, made community happen.

Neighbourly values were often imagined within the landscape. The yearly parish perambulation at Rogationtide, or the less frequent circuit of the manorial bounds, marked out key jurisdictions within the twists and turns of well-known and recognizable features in the land: crosses, buildings, streets, farms, hedges, walls, piles of stone walls. Rogationtide did more than merely map some administrative district: it was tied into senses of neighbourly belonging. It was also about the deep linkage between the church, the parish and the people, combining religious observance with the social practice of marking the bounds of the community. As George Withers put it in 1635,

---

[128] Emmison (ed.), *Elizabethan Life*, 70.
[129] Hailwood, *Alehouses and Good Fellowship*, 190.
[130] For a detailed example, see NRO, PD254/171.
[131] S. A. Peyton (ed.), *The Churchwardens' Presentments in the Oxfordshire Peculiars of Dorchester, Thame and Banbury*, Oxfordshire Record Society, 10 (Oxford, 1928), 245.

... wish I could, Men better did regard
Those Bounders, which Antiquity hath rear'd;
And, that, they would not, with so much delight,
There, make incroachments, where they have no right
That, ev'ry man might keep his owne Possessions,
Our Fathers, us'd in reverent Processions
(With zealous prayers, and with praisefull cheere)
To walke their Parish-limits, once a yeare:
And, well knowne Markes (which sacrilegious Hands
Now cut or breake) so bord'red out their Lands,
That, ev'ry one distinctly knew his owne;
And, many brawles, now rise[n], were then unknowne.
But, since neglected, sacred Bounders were,
Most men Incroachers, and Intruders are:
They grieve each other, and their Dues they steale,
From Prince, from Parent, and from Common-weale.[132]

This was code for anti-Puritanism, for it was overwhelmingly from the godly that hostility to Rogationtide traditions arose.

Rogationtide celebrated vertical social ties based upon propinquity and Christian fellowship. Perambulations could, in times of food scarcity, be a means by which richer parishioners could fund the needs of the poor – with food dispensed at key points in the bounds. Thus, in 1595, the churchwardens of St Margaret's Westminster paid eight pounds and ten shillings 'for bread, drink, cheese, fish, cream, and other victuals, when the worshipfull of the parish, and many others of the poorest sort, went the perambulation to Kensington, in this hard and dere time of all things'. Two years later, the costs of feeding the poor during Rogationtide, 'being a yere of great scarcity and dereness', stood at seven pounds, eight shillings and eight pence.[133] Likewise, in Bocking (Essex) in 1564, it was noted that 'the poorer women' of the parish '(as God knew) that lacked work ... were glad of the relief that was accustomably provided for them' during the Rogationtide procession.[134] It therefore mattered a lot when some neighbours transgressed local boundaries. In 1590, articles exhibited to the Staffordshire bench against William Alcocke of Little Onn stated that he

very unorderlie ... suffreth his fence to lye open against his neighboures grounde and ... against the comon feildes wherebye he procureth and ys the original of manye sutes ... against his neighbours. And no curtesye or neighbourlie perswacions will reforme the same ... [. H]e provideth not any fuell at any tyme of the yere But what he or his Famyl[i]e have ys by tearing his neighboures hedges and leying open theire inclosures ... and he will not spare to coppe other mens trees ...

[132] G. Wither, *A Collection of Emblemes, Ancient and Moderne* (London, 1635), 161.
[133] J. E. Smith (ed.), *A Catalogue of Westminster Records* (London, 1900), 51.
[134] J. Strype (ed.), *The Life and Acts of Matthew Parker*, 3 vols. (Oxford, 1821), I, 303–5.

because he thinketh hym selfe a man Lawlesse and therefore lyvethe without the compasse of good order.[135]

In disrupting boundaries within the landscape, Alcocke also disrupted the social order. Early modern people liked to feel that they lived in an orderly world and this was as true of the landscape about them as it was of patriarchal norms.

In order to interrogate a culture, we need to seek sources that reveal quotidian, everyday assumptions. We need access, in other words, to texts that articulate and reproduce ordinary worlds. As Mark Hailwood has shown in some brilliant essays, ballad literature gives us privileged access to those worlds, eavesdropping on them as they gave voice to song after a couple of pints.[136] The repetitive nature of such ballads made them especially suitable to the alehouse environment, whose values they celebrated:

> Good morow neighbour Gamble,
> Come let you and I goe ramble,
> Last night I was shot
> Through the braines with a Pot,
>     and now my stomacke doth wamble:
> ... My bones I doe not favour,
> But honestly doe labour:
> But when I am out,
> I must make a mad bout
>     come heres halfe a pot to thee neighbour
> ... Now lest our Wives should find us,
> Tis fit we should look behinde us,
> Lets see what is done,
> Then pay and be gone.
>     as honesty hath assignd us.
> Tis strong Ale I conceive it,
> Tis good in time to leave it,
> Or else it will make,
> Our foreheads to ake.[137]

Then there was the widespread celebration of the role played by the Three Wise Men in the Christmas drama, noted by Thomas Tusser:

---

[135] Burne (ed.), *The Staffordshire Quarter Sessions Rolls, II*, 25–6.
[136] M. Hailwood, 'Alehouses, Popular Politics and Plebeian Agency in Early Modern England', in F. Williamson (ed.), *Locating Agency: Space, Power and Popular Politics* (Newcastle, 2010), 51–76; M. Hailwood, 'The Honest Tradesman's Honour: Occupational and Social Identity in Early Modern England', *TRHS*, 6th ser., 24 (2014), 79–103.
[137] Anon., *Mondayes Worke: or The Two Honest Neigbours Both Birds of a Feather* (London, 1632).

> At Christmas we banket, the rich with the poore,
> who then (but the miser) but openeth [h]is doore?
> At Christmas of Christ many Carols we sing,
> and give many gifts in the joy of that King[.]
> At Christmas in Christ we rejoice and be glad,
> as onely of whom our comfort is had;
> At Christmas we joy altogether with mirth;
> For his sake that joyed us all with his birth.[138]

Church ales and parish festivals drew people together. They represented one way in which community was made real. There is a palpable sense of excitement in the churchwardens' minutes for Crondall (Kent) in 1587, as they recorded expenditure on their church ale. This included disbursements on malt, and a brewer, minstrels, chickens, meat, wine, a calf, eleven lambs, four bushels of wheat, a hogshead of beer, bread and 'spice and sawce'.[139] John Day commended 'those Neighbourly Meetings, when at certaine times of the Yeere, whole Parishes meet together, & friendly feast with one another'.[140] Yet, here, too, social values were becoming contested: one account of 1635 suggested that

a Faith hath entered into many peoples minds, contrary to that which is prescribed throughout the three books of the Divine service. Also that a great cause of the decay of much charity and good neighbourhood, hath bin the forbidding of the ancient feasts of the Church, & of ordinary meetings, & of the like nourishings of unity & godly love.[141]

Alcohol and neighbourhood could be funny subjects and were much commented upon in the ballad literature. Understanding jokes, as Robert Darnton has suggested, takes us close to a culture, to its conventional assumptions.[142] The relationship between alcohol and neighbourhood, then, points to the ways in which, as labouring men necked a few after work, their womenfolk looked down upon them for their failure to invest in the needs of the plebeian household, spending too much time and money in the alehouse. This was stuff that people found funny, for it was a common, everyday experience for both genders: in one ballad, a man observes:

> At home I confesse, with my wife honest Besse,
> I practise, good husbandry well.
> I followed my calling, to keepe me from falling,

---

[138] Tusser, *Five Hundred Points of Good Husbandry*, 62.
[139] R. P. Butterfield, *Monastery and Manor: The History of Crondall* (Farnham, 1948), 53.
[140] Day, *Day's Festivals*, 338.
[141] E. Reeve, *The Communion Booke Catechisme Expounded* (London, 1635), 108.
[142] R. Darnton, *The Great Cat Massacre and Other Episodes in French Cultural History* (New York, 1984).

>     my neighbours about me that dwell,
>     Wil praise me at large, for maintaining my charge
>     but when I to drinking incline,
>     I scorne for to shrinke, go fetch us more drinke.[143]

Beer, cider, meat, cheese, bread, nuts, fruit and pies: these could provide the basis for a neighbourly commensality that drew people together. In 1577, for example, the Company of Mercers, Ironmongers and Goldsmiths of Shrewsbury considered it 'a necessary thing for the incre [a]se of amytie & Love amongst them that a Dyner be kept once a yere'.[144] Ronald Hutton suggests that the custom of wassailing (wassail was hot mulled cider) originated in the early Tudor period, as neighbours would progress around their communities with dishes of the drink, crying out:

>     Wassail, wassail, out of the milk pail
>     Wassail, wassail, as white as my nail
>     Wassail, wassail, in snow, frost and hail
>     Wassail, wassail, that much doth avail
>     Wassail, wassail, that never will fail.[145]

Wassailing represented one especially enjoyable way of reasserting local solidarities. Albeit within a wholly different context, wakes could be a time at which communal bonds were reinforced, celebrating the passage of the soul of a member of the parish community to the aftermath. It was quite usual, when writing wills, for early modern people to provide for food and beer at wakes, such that both 'poor and rich neighbours' would attend.[146] Then there were those communal drinkings that brought neighbours together to support poor folk who were in need. Bishop Piers noted, in 1633, that in Somerset '[t]here is another kind of publique meetinge called a Bid-ale when an honest man decayed in his estate is sett up agayne by the liberall benevolence and contribution of friends at a feast'.[147] Similar customs were to be found elsewhere in England. In 1605, for example, Henry Harris of Yatton Keynell (Wiltshire) explained that 'having lost a cow[,] being all the goods he had[he] was advised by a friend of his to provide a stand of ale and he would bring him company to help him towards his losses'.[148]

---

[143] Anon., *A Health to All Good-Fellowes* (London, c.1615).

[144] Somerset, *Records of Early English Drama*, 222.

[145] R. Hutton, *The Rise and Fall of Merry England: The Ritual Year, 1400–1700* (Oxford, 1994), 13–14; Hutton, *The Stations of the Sun*, 13–14, 22, 62–4.

[146] D. Cressy, *Birth, Marriage and Death: Ritual, Religion and the Life-Cycle in Tudor and Stuart England* (Oxford, 1997), 445.

[147] TNA, SP16/250/56.

[148] M. Ingram, *Church Courts, Sex and Marriage in England, 1570–1640* (Cambridge, 1987), 100.

Clergymen would be expected to join in this culture of alcoholic good fellowship. The godly held ministers who did so in contempt and, by the later sixteenth century, many diocesan authorities were concerned to root out alehouse-haunting clergymen. The story of Richard Mylner, the curate of Lanchester (County Durham), might stand for many, for he was part of an earlier generation of ministers who saw no harm in immersing themselves in the life of their village. When Mylner was hauled before the consistory court in 1575, his friends presented him as a well-liked member of the community. In contrast, Mylner's opponents said that he was often drunk in the village alehouses and that he could be violent. William Gelson, one of Mylner's supporters, conceded that the minister 'wilbe some time mery and light with drink, and short tonged, but not drunken nor given to feightinge'. The alehousekeeper George Harrison told the court that Mylner 'doith often use to aile howses in the said township of Lanchester, ass moche for compenye as for drinke'. The gentleman William Hall said of Mylner that he is 'a right honest and discreat man'; he had often been with him 'at many feastes, weddings, ma[t]ches, shotyngs, dynners and drinkin[g]s'; and that he was 'an honest man and a good companion'.[149] It was of such men that Shakespeare wrote. In *Love's Labour's Lost*, the parson, Sir Nathaniel, is referred to as 'a foolish, mild man, an honest man, look you, and soon dashed. He is a marvelous good neighbour, faith, and a very good bowler.'[150] The godly held such clergy in contempt.

In contrast to negative assessments of the alehouse culture, many local inhabitants presented alehouses as centres of conviviality, rest and succour.[151] When Ellis Pawley of Martock petitioned the Somerset bench in 1627 for a licence to run his alehouse, his neighbours signed a certificate in his support, saying that

rather he hath a convenient cleanly house for the parishioners sometimes to refresh themselves in, being so far from the parish church that often times on the Sabbath day and other hollydaies they cannot go home and come again to church the same day; and for that the women of the parish when they bring theire young children to be christened do often stay there to warm their babes, coming sometimes a mile, sometimes two, from home in the cold.[152]

---

[149] J. Raine (ed.), *Depositions and Other Ecclesiastical Proceedings from the Courts of Durham Extending from 1311 to the Reign of Elizabeth*, Surtees Society, 21 (London, 1847), 286–92. For another clergyman who was fond of a drink with his neighbours, see DUL, DDR/EJ/CCD/1/2, fol. 229r.

[150] *Love's Labours Lost*, act V, scene 2, lines 575–8.

[151] See, for instance, HMC, Various Collections, I, 77. On alehouses as a positive communal presence, see Hailwood, *Alehouses and Good Fellowship*, 21, 51.

[152] E. H. Bates (ed.), *Quarter Sessions Records for the County of Somerset: Vol. II, Charles I, 1625–1639*, Somerset Record Society, 24 (London, 1908), 34.

Clearly, Pawley's neighbours believed that his hitherto unlicensed alehouse was fulfilling a valuable role. Similarly, in 1590, some sixty-three inhabitants of Norton (Staffordshire) signed a certificate in support of Hugh Smyth and his wife Elyn, 'our neighbours'. They had been accused at the Quarter Sessions of selling corrupted beer; to which charge, the signatories, in order to

preserve the credytte of our sayd Poore neyghboures[,] doe by these presents notyfye that wee have of longe tyme knowen the said Hughe and his wife to have kepte an Inne within Norton ... where her majesties subjectes and our neyghbowres traveling thorowgh the sayd towne or having occasion to use lodging and victualinge have bene ever very honestly and reasonably used and enterteyned to there generall good contentment.[153]

The role of alehouses as informal sources of succour to the local poor received particular attention. In 1616, the Assize Judges received a petition from 'a great number of poor people' of Bury St Edmunds (Suffolk). Its authors explained:

[W]e have many years been relieved by those innkeepers which had the liberty to brew their beer in their own houses, not only with money and food, but also at several times of their brewing (being moved with pity and compassion, knowing our great extremities and necessities) with such quantities of their small beer as has been a continual help and comfort to us with our poor wives and children.

By 1616, however, these compassionate alehousekeepers had been replaced by a bunch of rich brewers who refused to help the poor.[154] Elsewhere, it was also assumed that a good alehousekeeper would look to the poor: in a petition of 1611, the inhabitants of Beeston (Norfolk) told the county bench that their neighbor 'Rob[er]t Feazer of Beeston hathe of longue tyme used to kepe an Alehouse in Beeston, and is thought by the Inhabitants theare very mete and fytt to contynewe the same, in respect of his honest & good useage of the poore people there, wch doe many tymes want those necessaryes w[hi]ch he would helpe them w[i]th'.[155] In the same year, the inhabitants of Warham (Norfolk) wrote in support of George Towting's wish to set up an alehouse, observing that the result would be to 'better relieve the pore'.[156] Elsewhere, the business of running an alehouse was felt to keep poor folk off the parish dole: in 1595, the Staffordshire bench heard that Richard Mason, 'beinge a poore man and laboringe hard for his living by the daye', was responsible for the support of his blind mother and so kept her off the poor rate. His neighbours

[153] Burne (ed.), *The Staffordshire Quarter Sessions Rolls, II*, 69–70.
[154] HMC, 14th Report, Appendix VIII, Bury St Edmunds MSS, 142.
[155] NRO, NQS/C/S3/17/1, certificate of inhabitants of Beeston.
[156] NRO, NQS/C/S3/17/1, letter to Sir Henry Sydney from the inhabitants of Warham.

therefore appealed to the bench, asking that Towting be granted a licence to run an alehouse 'and for his honestie and good behaviour his neighbours ... have sett there handes'.[157]

### Festivity, Play and the Celebration of Neighbourhood

Alehouses were regarded as one site at which informal conceptions of community could be celebrated and renewed. Another site at which community might be given meaning was the camping field. In East Anglia, many villages and towns had a dedicated strip of land, often alongside the parish church, at which young men would, after a few drinks, go camping – that is, play the rough-and-tumble, occasionally lethal, game of football.[158] This game would often set the lads of one parish against those of their neighbouring parish. In Norwich, for example, there was a camping field alongside St Augustine's church, on a strip of land called the Gildencroft. Likewise, camping is also recorded in the adjoining parish of St Martin at Oak 'on a holydaye at the camping ball'.[159] As some undergraduates of Cambridge University discovered when they encountered a band of youths from Chesterton (Cambridgeshire), camping matches could be violent affairs. The yeoman James Bats explained:

[T]he townes me[n] and yought[h] of chesterton ... [were at] playe at the footeball & lookynge for schollers procured staves & other weapons to be putt in the church porche of chesterton. and after ward when they were hotte in playe sodenlye one called staves. [A]nd ... some cam[e] forth wth the staves and so fell upon the schollers and did beate divers of them and some runying awaye the[y] did folowe & cawsed to swym ov[e]r the watter.[160]

In 1549, the rebellions of that year were remembered in East Anglia as the 'camping time': the term had a double meaning. It referred to the formation of rebel camps on sites like Mousehold Heath, from which insurrectionaries drew up lists of complaints for the attention of Protector Somerset. But it also alluded to football: a game played by slightly drunk,

---

[157] S. A. H. Burne (ed.), *The Staffordshire Quarter Sessions Rolls, III: 1594–97*, Collections for a History of Staffordshire (Kendal, 1933), 109. See also Bates, *Quarter Sessions Records for ... Somerset: Vol. I, James I, 1607–1625*, 27.

[158] D. Dymond, 'A Lost Social Institution: The Camping Close', *Rural History*, 1 (1990), 165–91. The locations of camping fields remain in place-name evidence; a regional survey would be valuable. For deaths while playing at camping, see J. S. Cockburn (ed.), *Calendar of Assize Records: Essex Indictments, Elizabeth I* (London, 1978), nos. 308, 1323, 1361.

[159] NRO, NCR, 12A/1 (c), fol. 73r.

[160] Cambridge University Library, V.C.Ct.I.70(2.c).3.

fairly violent young men – those who made the rank-and-file of the rebel hosts.[161]

Deep play, then, could be about rebellion. The practice is also apparent in the large-scale riots of the late 1630s inspired by the Crown-sponsored drainage of the Cambridgeshire fens. In 1638, the magistrates of that county received news of the gathering of hundreds of men under cover of a football match; they were to meet at Whelpmore Fen in Littleport 'at a foot ball play or camp, which camp should be called Anderson's camp, who should bring an hundred strong with him'. At that time, Whelpmore was common to Littleport, Downham and Ely. The following day there were enclosure riots involving 200 men. One man, Edward Anderson, said that he would not leave his commons until he saw the warrant and signet of the monarch, for that he would obey God and the King but no other man. He asked if one might be inspired to do the poor good and help them to their commons again.[162]

Festive play, then, could be about drawing social divisions – between the young men of neighbouring villages; between the lads of Chesterton and the Cambridge undergraduates. It was, thereby, also about communal unity, drawing local inhabitants together in rough-and-tumble games. In this respect, games and festivities fulfilled a social *function*, generating local solidarities that crossed class boundaries and defining neighbourhood as a shared social value. As the Somerset gentleman Sir Edward Parham of Poyntington explained to the Star Chamber in 1606, the Mayday revels that took place 'in Country p[a]rishes ... hath byn heretofore commonly used for norishing of love and famyliarity amongst neighbours'.[163] Elsewhere, festive cheer provided a means of defining a particular trade identity. The Court of the Star Chamber, in Henry VIII's reign, heard:

It hath ben used tyme out of mans remembraunce within [Whitby] ... being a havyn towne inhabyted with maryners, and within all other havyn townes thereboute so inhabyted, that yerely on Midsomer even, Sent Peter even and Seynt Thomas even, at the time of the bonefiers accustomed to be made in the honour of God of tyme oute of mans remembraunce within this realme, that all maryners and masters of schippes, accompnayed with other yong peple, have used to have carried before them on a staf halfe a terbarell brennyng, and the maryners to folowe too and too ... and to syng throught the srttes, and to resorte to every bonefier, and there to drynke and make mery with songes and other honest pastymes.[164]

---

[161] D. MacCulloch, 'Kett's Rebellion in Context', *P&P*, 84 (1979), 41.
[162] TNA, SP16/392/45.   [163] TNA, STAC8/291/12.
[164] W. Brown (ed.), *Yorkshire Star Chamber Proceedings, III*, YASRS, 51 (Leeds, 1914), 198.

Festive meetings sometimes commemorated key events in local history. Writing around 1624, Sir John Oglander observed:

There is a lane near Newport [Isle of Wight] called 'Dead Man's Lane'. The French, improvidently coming down that lane towards Carisbrooke Castle, were most slain by an ambush of our archers, wherefrom the lane took its denomination. They were buried in a bury now called 'Noddies' Hill: because so indiscreetly they came to their ends. The youth of Newport, in remembrance thereof, meet there at cudgels every Shrove-Sunday.[165]

Longstanding local games and festivities were locked into popular memory. In 1635, the aged men of Dundry (Somerset) explained to the court how a field called Church Hay lying alongside the parish church had been the location for 'recreations[,] sportes & playes of sev[er]all sortes . . . as setting upp of mayploes . . . daunceing, sporting, kissing, bulbayting, coyting, bowling[,] shootinge att Butts[,] cudgle playing[,] tennis playing and dvers other sportes and playes'. The sixty-six-year-old carpenter Henry Lukins added that he had 'manie tymes' been 'an actor & player himselfe, and heeretofore div[er]se & sundrie tymes seene heades broken att cudgells & fighting'.[166] A few cracked skulls seemed, to the old men of Dundry, a cheap price to pay for the festive articulation of communal spirit. Then there were customs such as that practised before the civil wars in Pagets Bromley (Staffordshire). This involved dancing a hobby-horse through the streets along with a pot, which was kept in turn by four or five of the chief inhabitants of the town, who provided cakes and ale to put in the pot; these would be distributed to the poor; the payment for the cakes and ale was given to the church.[167]
Certain occupational groups were especially known for their enthusiasm for strenuous games, a way of asserting plebeian masculinity and strength: in 1630, Thomas Westcote noted that labourers and tin-miners recreated themselves with games that are 'toilsome and violent, as wrestling, hurling, foot-ball, leaping, running, dancing with music, especially in their festivals'.[168] Sometimes, local festivities had a larger underlying meaning. In the case of the grain loaders who carried their goods to the millers of Warwick, their customary celebrations were intended to imprint an awareness of the rights of the town. On Midsummer Day, the loaders rode on their horses up and down the streets of the town, some with bells, some with tabors and pipes, some with bagpipes and some with

[165] F. Bamford (ed.), *A Royalist's Notebook: The Commonplace Book of Sir John Oglander Kt. of Nunwell* (London, 1936), 9–10.
[166] Somerset Record Office, D/D/Cd/81.
[167] R. Plot, *The Natural History of Stafford-Shire* (Oxford, 1686), 434.
[168] T. Westcote, *A View of Devonshire in MDCXXX* (Exeter, 1845), 54.

fiddles, until they reached Castle mills, the loader of which they called out – if any of the loaders failed to appear, then they had no right to load within the town for the next year. Thomas Heywood, a fifty-eight-year-old loader, explained in 1633 that 'the reason of such ridinge of the said loaders is to continue a remembrance that noe loader belonging to any other mill ought to be priveledged to loade or fetche and carrye any griste from the said towne of Warwicke'.[169]

In many places, music was provided with pipes and drums. The Derbyshire gentleman Philip Kinder observed: 'For generall inclination & disposition the Peakard & moorlander are of the same ayre, they are given much to dance after ye bagg-pipes, almost every towne hath a bagg-piper in it.'[170] Elsewhere, there were dramatic enactments to be enjoyed: from before the Reformation, the young men of the parish of Calstcok (Cornwall) were responsible for organizing the Whitsun ales and worked with the village maidens in staging dramatic productions of Robin Hood and St George.[171] And, for young men and boys, the practice of archery was much enjoyed. The location for archery practice in Methwold (Norfolk) was a set of what seem to be prehistoric or Iron Age cist tombs, known in the 1580s as Robin Hood's butts.[172] Meanwhile, in 1634, the attempt on the part of the city authorities to trespass on Exeter's common fields was resented by poorer folk of the city, who explained that the land was used for archery practice, fairs and taking the air.[173]

Many ordinary people, then, would have agreed with the sentiments expressed by the character of the Plowman in Rastell's 1520s play, 'Of Gentylnes and Nobylyte':

> There is no joy nor pleasure in this world here
> But hyll bely, fill bely, and make good chere![174]

Festivity and games were considered by many to be a way of celebrating togetherness. In 1618, Nicholas Breton set the following words into the mouth of his idealized countryman:

[169] M. W. Farr, 'Midsummer Riding: A Seventeenth-Century Custom of the Millers of Warwick', *Warwickshire History*, 7, 3 (1988), 80–2.

[170] Fletcher, 'Philip Kinder's Ms. "Historie of Darbyshire"', 10, 181.

[171] S. Pittman, 'The Social Structure and Parish Community of St Andrew's Church, Calstock, as Reconstituted from Its Seating Plan, c.1587/8', *Southern History*, 20 (1998), 62. For further details on church ales and Robin Hood, see E. E. Trotman, 'The Church Ale and the Robin Hood Legend', *Somerset and Dorset Notes and Queries*, 28 (1961–7), 37–8.

[172] TNA, MPC1/75.        [173] TNA, E134/9ChasI/East25.

[174] R. Axton (ed.), *Three Rastell Plays* (Woodbridge, 1979), 'Of Gentylnes and Nobylyte', lines 427–8.

[A]t our meetings on the holydayes betweene our Lads and the Wenches, such true mirth at honest meetings, such dauncing on the greene, in the market house, or about the May-poole, where the young folks smiling kisse at every turning, and the old folks checking with laughing at their Children, when dauncing for the Garland, playing at stooleball for a Tansie and a banquet of Cords and Creame, with a cup of old nappy Ale, metter of small charge, with a little reward of the Piper, after casting of sheepes eyes and faith and troth for a bargaine, clapping of hands are seales to the truth of hearts, when a payre of Gloves & a handkerchiffe are as good as the best obligation, with a cappe and courtesy, hie the home maides to milking and so merrily goes the day away.[175]

But festive culture had its opponents. Much ire was directed at women's sociability. In 1575, the aldermanic council of Kendal (Westmorland) decreed that drinking at weddings, after women's churchings and on All Hallows Eve was to be banned.[176] Seven years earlier, the Leicester authorities had ordered that 'there shal be no feastes made at churchings ... saving only one competent messe of meate provided for gossips and mydwyves'. This was to prevent poor people from coming into the city to eat at churching feasts.[177] Back in 1541, the Chester authorities had suppressed churching feasts on the grounds that too much food and drink was consumed during these revels; they ordered instead that, henceforth, only the midwife and relatives of the new mother should be allowed into the woman's house.[178] It was not only women's sociability that some urban authorities were coming to restrict. Ronald Hutton provides the instance of Marlborough (Wiltshire) where, in 1590, the aldermen decided that they would invite the householders in each of their wards to 'drink together as neighbours and friends'. Following this alcoholic celebration of local fellowship, the mayor would host a party for the whole town. But, at some point, the record of these gatherings was scored through in the minute book and so discontinued.[179] In 1623, the churchwardens of Yapton (Sussex) presented the fiddler William Witcher of Boxgrove, who every Sunday came to Yapton with a crowd of up to thirty or forty others from the nearby area and led them in dances. Many, the churchwardens sniffed, were youths and should have been at their catechism in church.[180] The author of *Pasquil's Palinodia* was very aware of the hostility of the godly to festive culture; the writer recalled how, in the past,

---

[175] N. Breton, *The Court and the Country* (London, 1618), sig. B2v.
[176] R. S. Ferguson (ed.), *A Boke off Recorde or Register of the Burgh of Kikby Kendal* (Carlisle, 1892), 89–91.
[177] Bateson (ed.), *Records of the Borough of Leicester*, 122. See also Cressy, *Birth, Marriage and Death*, 201–3.
[178] CRO, ZAB/1, fol. 70v.    [179] Hutton, *The Rise and Fall of Merry England*, 122.
[180] Johnstone (ed.), *Churchwardens' Presentments*, 66.

[t]hen Lords of Castles, Mannors, Townes & Towers
Rejoyc'd when they beheld the Farmers flourish
And would come downe unto the Sommer-Bowers
To see the Country gallants dance the Morris
... But since the Sommer-poles were overthrown,
And all good sports and merryments decayd,
How times and men are chang'd, so well is knowne,
It were but labour lost if more were said.[181]

But the godly didn't have things all their way; people could be tenaciously aggressive in defence of their customary pleasures. There was a sense that, in targeting local festivities, Calvinist disciplinarianism represented an attack on neighbourhood. One godly writer noted:

[A] Faith hath entered into many people[']s minds, contrary to that which is prescribed throughout the three books of the Divine service. Also that a great cause of the decay of much charity and good neighbourhood, hath bin the forbidding of the ancient feasts of the Church, & of ordinary meetings, & of the like nourishings of unity & godly love.[182]

Defenders of customary feasts noted that, in the New Testament, Christ himself had attended village festivals. Feasting, it was argued, was understood by the Israelites to represent 'assemblies of good neighbourhood' that fostered 'brotherly love and concord'.[183] Ordinary people were more than willing to stand up in defence of their traditional festivities. In 1617, the minister William Jeffries petitioned the Worcestershire bench to complain that the youth of Longdon on the Sunday nearest May Day held May games, morrises and dancing such that 'rude ruffians and drunken companions' converged on the village from the nearby area. In 1615, some of the youth of Longdon procured an excommunicated woman to enter the church during divine service and tell the minister 'that this excommunicate person was in the church hoping thereby to put an end of God's service that so they might again return to their sports'. The following year, Jeffries was assaulted while trying to suppress festive games.[184] Bear-baiting was another popular pastime that was becoming increasingly contested. In 1581, for example, angry at the number of Cambridge University scholars who had gone to Chesterton to see a bear-baiting, the vice-chancellor went to the village to see the custom suppressed. The locals told him, in no uncertain terms, that he had no

---

[181] Anon., *Pasquils Palonidia*, sig. B3v.
[182] Reeve, *The Communion Booke Catechisme Expounded*, 108.
[183] P. Heylyn, *The History of the Sabbath in Two Bookes* (London, 1636), 107.
[184] J. W. Bund (ed.), *Calendar of the Quarter Sessions Papers, Vol. I: 1591–1643*, Worcestershire Historical Society, 22 (Worcester, 1900), 254–5.

jurisdiction there.[185] Likewise, when, in 1629, 'Baxter the bearward' was put in the stocks by the constables of Wilmslow (Cheshire), the result was only greater displays of festive disorder. As the magistracy were later told:

Forthwith there came one Henry Orrell Butcher ... unto the said Baxter, and hee affirmed hee would fetch an axe, and therewith Knocke the same stockes in peeces ...[. A]fterwards the said Henry Orrell, together alsoe with one William Kellsall and one John Robinson[,] went upp & downe the Towne in an outdaring manner, and caused the drummer to drumme, whilst the said Baxter sate in the same stockes; saying, hee should drumme, in dispite of any Justice of the peace whatsoever.[186]

---

[185] Cambridge University Library, V.C.Ct.I.70(2.c), 1–2.

[186] E. M. S. Baldwin, 'Entertainments in East Cheshire before 1642', *Transactions of the Lancashire and Cheshire Antiquarian Society*, 89 (1993), 122.

# 3   Now Abideth Faith, Hope and Charity: Place, Neighbourhood and People

## Words as 'Sharpe Weapons': Public Worlds

In early modern England, there was an intense watchfulness to local life that fed into the ways in which people related to one another. Alexandra Shepard cites a case at the York consistory court in 1574 that 'provoked discussion of whether witnesses for the plaintiff were both "taken to be rich men" and "counted Richer man" than the witnesses produced on behalf of the defendant . . . [T]his included endorsement of the plaintiff's witnesses in general terms as "welthy yomen and good housekeepers and of verrey good and honeste reputacon" and as "honest substantiall men"' and also included assessment of the witnesses' landed and movable estate as it was 'reputed by his neighbours'.[1] In contrast, the testimony of Emma Carpenter of Chalgrave was little regarded by her richer neighbours. Elizabeth Burnam said of her that 'she is a poor woman & will sometymes be drunke & then . . . will safely be persuaded to swear any thing'.[2]

Within the local social environment within which so much of the working population of early modern England lived their lives, reputation was key to their place in the community.[3] Within these small worlds, what was said mattered. As Jane Kamensky observes about New England, speech was 'part of the dynamics of face-to-face communities in which the small scale of daily life makes words loom large'.[4] Thus, in 1548, the Cheshire man John Wright sustained his evidence in a matrimonial case on the basis of what he 'knoweth and harde say as beyng neybor in the towne'.[5] A few months later, John Cropper of Oldham (Lancashire) told the Chester consistory court that he knew the time of the birth of the child of Elisabeth Travers 'as he remembreth and th[a]t he doth knowe because he is a

---

[1] Shepard, *Accounting for Oneself*, 49.
[2] W. O. Hassall (ed.), *Wheatley Records, 956–1956*, Oxfordshire Records Society, 37 (Banbury, 1956), 45.
[3] DUL, Special Collections, DDR/EJ/CCD/1/1, fol. 4v.
[4] J. Kamensky, *Governing the Tongue: The Politics of Speech in Early New England* (Oxford, 1997), 5.
[5] CRO, EDC2/4, p. 3.

neybor ... and harde honest wom[en] th[a]t were pr[esen]t att the birth depose the same to this deponent to be true'.[6] Neighbourhood sustained stories about one's place in the moral and social order of the locality. Words had a special power in early modern society, and they could rip communities apart. George Webbe warned in 1619: 'It is the tongue which breaketh the peace betweene neighbours, giveth shrewd wives sharpe weapons to fight against their husbands, breedes quarrels among servants, and setteth men together by the eares.'[7]

Quietitude was, for many early modern people, synonymous with order, neighbourhood and easy living. Those who disrupted communal norms were frequently represented as having also created noise, commotion and dissension. In 1600, the Yorkshire gentleman John Savile was said to have

upon a Saboth day and in tyme of devine service w[i]thin the parish church of wakefield ... not onely by words quarrel Chide and brawle w[i]th ... Gervase Hatefeild Esquier[.] And in great anger and w[i]th lowd and vehement speeches ... molest troble and dysturbe ... Gervase being att his prayers in his own Pew But also did smite and lay violent hands of the said Gervase Hatefield Esquire.

Elizabeth Sawener explained that she was kneeling in her stall when she heard 'a shofflinge' and saw Savile attack Hatefield 'and plucke him by the cloke in despitefull and angrye manner in the sight of a great number of the p[ar]ishioners beyinge in the ... church'. Margaret Hewerdyne added that Savile had attacked Hatefield with kicks and punches 'in angry & despiytefull manner and in such sorte that the most of the p[ar[ishioners then and there assembled loked at him & his evill dealing ...[. H]is saide dealing was offensive to the [parishioners] & then one Edward Alderson speaking to ... Savell & willing him to be a q[u]yet he left his unquietnes then & there.' These were ordinary folk responding to a dispute amongst their social superiors – gentlemen whom they represented as disruptors of quietude and proper order.[8]

Women's speech and action might easily be represented in terms of noise and disruption. In 1555, Thomas Woodward of Glaisdale (Yorkshire) told the consistory court that he had witnessed James Wyn

come in a furie ... to ... Jayne [Burton] sitting in her stall ... and would have plucked here forth ... [but] the said Jane mad[e] such shifte that he did not plucke here forthe of the stall but he did remove here and sett hys wif[e] where she did sitt in the said stall and said that he woiuld make here to knowe here better.

---

[6] CRO, EDC2/4, p. 39.
[7] G. Webbe, *Arraignment of an Unruly Tongue* (London, 1619), 28.     [8] BIA, CP.H.778.

Wyn continued to berate Burton with a 'lowde vo[i]ce and in gre[a]t furie' in front of most of the people of the chapelry. This verbal attack in the public space of the parish church had undermined Burton's place in the village such that 'the said jayne is worse used with here husbande since the relacon of the saide words then she was before'. Neighbours had tried to settle the matter: Woodward had been part of a meeting in the church to take order as to the use of the women's pews. They called James Wyn and Myles Burton (husband of Jayne Burton) to appear before them, in the course of which meeting James Wyn told Myles Burton 'that he the said myles co[u]ld not order his wif[e] and said that his wif[e] had need to be ridden with a colte halter and said that she was garded and ruffed like a ... jenny of jellygate and that she wold have mad[e], or wold make man's morther'.[9] So the attempt to seal the social drama failed, and the articulacy of Jane Burton was held up to public scorn.

For poor people, a good name was essential: with it might come employment, charity, favour and friendship. It mattered a lot to William Bell of Elizabethan Black Heddon (Northumberland), for example, that he was 'countyd for an honest poore fellow'.[10] Likewise, when the husbandman George Atkinson told the Durham consistory court that his neighbour Edward Garnet of Ryton, whom he had known for twenty years, was 'an honest trewe poore man', it bolstered Garnet's place in the local community.[11] In contrast, in 1635, the yeoman Robert Fletcher of Chester-le-Street (County Durham) reported that 'Elizabeth Bulmer is ill reported on amongst her neighbours, and is addicted to drinkeing in idle companie. She is not worth 20s debtlesse.'[12] Even amongst the poor, lineage mattered. Elizabeth Leigh, for example, was reputed to be 'an honest poore woma[n] of a poore ma[n] dowghter as any is in Lansley p[ar]ish'.[13] Neighbourhood often overrode class. A yeoman of Elizabethan Whickham (County Durham) said of one man that he 'is a very poore man and his neybor'.[14]

Those poor folk who worked hard and thereby maintained independent households were often seen as valued members of the community. In May 1567, for example, the gentleman Thomas Spenser of Hurstbourne Priors (Hampshire) said that he had

herd all men for the most parte to have reported ... Isarne and Prowtinge to be honest pore men & of honest conv[er]sac[i]on at all times for eny thinge that this depo[nen]t ever knewe or harde ... the said Prowting and Izarne be w[i]th ther

---

[9] BIA, CP.G.3538.　　[10] DUL, DDR/EJ/CCD/1/2, fol. 137v.
[11] DUL, DDR/EJ/CCD/1/1, fol. 15r.
[12] Longstaffe (ed.), *The Acts of the High Commission within the Diocese of Durham*, 153.
[13] DUL, DDR/EJ/CCD/1/2, fol.bis. 215v.　　[14] DUL, DDR/EJ/CCD/1/2, fol. 3v.

labor able to get their owne meate and drink & so they doth and also of this depo[nen]ts knowledge they fereth God to much to p[ro]cure them selves for any mans sake.[15]

The standing of poor people might be buttressed by their good name amongst wealthier folk. In the 1560s, for instance, the yeoman Robert Smith reported of Thomas Legg of Durham that he 'is of good honestie and credence although a poore ma[n] . . . and hath for his honestie & truthe bene put in truste and credence w[i]th me[n] of worship'.[16] The Newcastle minister John Markbray said of William Dickson that 'he is th[is] depont neighbour a very honest poore ma[n]'.[17] Likewise, Sir Ralph Ewyire of Darlington (County Durham) told the consistory court that, in a defamation case in which Elizabeth Heweth had been called a whore by a man called Branston, whereas Heweth possessed a good name, 'the talk & report of the said Branston is of litle credit or acomptyd upon so yt amongst ancient & discret of the p[ar]ish'.[18]

In contrast, the fact that a man or woman might live in poverty could be enough to blacken their name.[19] In 1636, the Norfolk consistory court learnt:

There is noe faith nor credit to be given to the deposicions and sayengs of the foresaid Katherine Goodwyn . . . for that [she] . . . was and is a poore needy woman and takes almes or releife of the towne of Foulsham a very bad woman of evill life and con[ver]sation one that for gaine reward and lucre wilbe easily drawne to sware and depose unto any thinge that is false and untrue, a com[m]on breaker of other mens hedges and a purloiner of their firing one also that doe not frequent her p[ar]ishe church of Foulsham upon Sondaies and holiedaies . . . but is a com[m]on prophaner.[20]

That a man or woman worked for wages, or depended upon charity, was, for some of their richer neighbours, enough to damn them. In 1634, the gentleman Edmund Finch of Warkworth (Northumberland) said of two of his neighbours: 'Turner and Heppell are of noe great creditt or estimacion where they live. The one is houshold servant to Mr Heslehead, and liveth on his wages. The other not worth 20 s[hillings] debtless.'[21] Six years later, the High Court of Chivalry was advised:

No faith or credit is to be given to the testimony of William Rutt; and John Pricklove is a poore needy fellow and oftentimes when he wanteth work receiveth relief from his neighbours. Pricklove is soe poore and needy that he, his wife and

---

[15] HALS, 21M65/C3/4, p. 136.    [16] DUL, DDR/EJ/CCD/1/2, fol. 202r-v.
[17] DUL, DDR/EJ/CCD/1/2, fols. 129v-30r.    [18] DUL, DDR/EJ/CCD/1/2, fol.bis. 209r.
[19] DUL, DDR/EJ/CCD/1/2, fol. 153v.    [20] NRO, DN/CON/15/, part 3, fol. 140r.
[21] Longstaffe (ed.), *The Acts of the High Commission within the Diocese of Durham*, 102.

children are upon the almes of the parish and are such as are beleeved may easily be drawne to depose an untruth for reward or gaine.[22]

Poor women and men who failed to show proper deference in their proceedings within their communities might be damned by their assertiveness. The miller Thomas Marche told the Durham consistory court, for example, that 'John als Jenkyn Burden is and hath been the tyme he dwelt among th[i]s ex[aminant's] neighbors very troblesom & toilsom, and of smale credit and for his substaunce or habilitie he cannott depose, but he thinks th[a]t was not very moche'.[23] Similarly, in 1573 Richard Gyll said of his neighbour John Long of Alresford (Hampshire) that he 'is a pore froward old man'.[24] Poor folk were not meant to be 'froward' – that is, to speak out of place. Suspicion might attach to outsiders: the national origins of one beggar in Whickham (County Durham) were much remarked upon: one of his neighbours reported that he was 'a Skotish man a poore man and went from dore to dore ... and a simple ma[n]'. A labourer said of the same man that he was a 'poore beggar and a Skotish ma[n]'.[25]

Boundaries between public and private worlds were loose, and if one's moral reputation was impugned, it hurt. John Day argued in 1615 that 'the chiefest Harme of all that may be intended against our Neighbour is in respect of the Evill, or Hurt, that may be done to our Neighbours Good Name ...[. I]f once we wrong our Neighbours Name, and slander his Reputation, we doe him a lasting injury.'[26] After James Jackson called George Jackson a knave in 1579, adding that he was 'as ill beloved' of his 'neybors as a dogg', George Jackson felt obliged to sue for defamation at the consistory court.[27] Common fame could damn a man or woman – the mere fact of its spread was considered sufficient evidence to bring a legal case. Thus, in 1621, the churchwardens of Limister (Sussex) presented William Berry 'for incontinency with Joane Bastow, as the common fame goeth'.[28] Fourteen years later, after Alice Greaves had called Joan Bane of Stockport (Cheshire) a whore, it was felt that her 'good name ... is much impaired and much called into question amongst her neighbours by reason of the words [spoken by Alice Greaves] saving the said Joan Bane hath beene accomted to live in good fame and name amongst her neighbours'.[29] In 1622, the churchwardens of Chiltington (Sussex) presented 'Widdow Parram, for a common fame of incontinency with William Coates'.[30] And so Widow Parram's reputation was destroyed.

---

[22] HCCO: 692, *Watts* v. *Elliott*.     [23] DUL, DDR/EJ/CCD/1/2, fol. 157v.
[24] HALS, 21M65/C3/5, p. 309.     [25] DUL, DDR/EJ/CCD/1/2, fol. 3v.
[26] Day, *Day's Festivals*, 333–4.     [27] BIA, CP.G.1955.
[28] Johnstone (ed.), *Churchwardens' Presentments*, 15.     [29] CRO, EDC5/1635/21.
[30] Johnstone (ed.), *Churchwardens' Presentments*, 37.

The 'common voice' could be dangerous: it was insidious, an ever-present threat to the fortunes of those whom it found lacking. It was therefore very important that, in those cases where a person's reputation had been successfully defended, she or he should have the satisfaction of seeing their accuser publicly confess their error. Thus, in 1616, William Phelipps of Pitmister (Somerset) was bound over for spreading malicious stories about Mary Gill, for which the magistrates ordered that 'on his open acknowledgement ... he was ... to make public confession and to ask forgiveness of the same in the parish church on Sunday next after morning prayer'.[31]

As Malcolm Gaskill has suggested, in Tudor and early Stuart communities, 'lives were, for the most part, lived in plain sight of all, and for most part people's privacy was not just unobtainable but undesirable'.[32] The gossip in the Sussex village of Middleton in 1606 went that when Agnes Nashe had lived in London she had 'committed or lived in adultery or fornication ... and was burned there [i.e., acquired venereal disease] and came home from London by committing the most foul act of adultery or fornication'. William Holden held forth to this effect 'at Felpham mill before 20 people'. In consequence, 'the good name and fame of Agnes Nashe is much impaired and hindered by reason of the words of defamation amongst all the neighbours and friends of her ...[S]ince William Holden did utter the words there hath been a great speech within the parish and never before.'[33]

Even when behind locked doors, early modern people could not be certain that they had escaped prying eyes. Physical boundaries between households were rarely respected. In 1577, for example, three Southampton women testified as to the sexual immorality of neighbours after watching their illicit conduct through a hole in the wall.[34] But accusations that were thrown about in the open street were accorded a special force: in Elizabethan Newcastle, John Hopert reported that 'upo[n] the mondaye at afternoyn next after corp[us] x.pe. daye he herd willi[a]m armstronge call thomas hettells wyfe Isabell hettell [w]hor[e] and th[i]ef ... in westgate in newcastle openly in the quenes high strete where many he[a]rd & might here'.[35] Much of plebeian life was lived in the street, and local dramas were enacted openly. In May 1617, the

---

[31] Bates (ed.), *Quarter Sessions Records for ... Somerset: Vol. I, James I, 1607–1625*, 180.

[32] M. Gaskill, 'Little Commonwealths II: Communities', in K. E. Wrightson (ed.), *A Social History of England, 1500–1750* (Cambridge, 2017), 89.

[33] Wilkinson (ed.), *Chichester Archdeaconry Depositions*, 189–91.

[34] G. H. Hamilton (ed.), *Books of Examinations and Depositions, 1570–1594*, Southampton Record Society, 16 (Southampton, 1914), 30–1.

[35] DUL, DDR/EJ/CCD/1/2, fol. 12v.

people of the Birley district of Leeds witnessed one such drama. As George Eastburne later recalled,

Thomas Brooke being in the towne gate or street of Burley ... did goe unto the dore of the house of John Beamond ... and willed him ... to come forth of the house into the said streete & threatened to fight w[i]th him whereupon ... John Beaumond spooke unto the said Thomas Brooke through a windowe of his ... house & tould him that he had three sonnes, the worst of w[ji]ch would answere him, And thereupon ... Thomas Brooke tould ... John Beamond that both he & his wife were witches ... & ... that the said Isabell Beamond had bewitched his goodes & had bene a wi[t]ch for fortene yeres last of his knowledge then & there being p[re]sent and hereinge the same words he this ex[aminan]te henrie.

These were dangerous words: the accusation might, were it to be sustained before the common law, lead the Beaumonds to the gallows. That the whole affair had been performed in public, before a number of witnesses, added further force to Brooke's words. It was essential, therefore, that things be set right, and so the Beamonds sued Brooke for slander at the York church court.

Men and women certainly did not inhabit separate spheres. But it does seem that, for all their daily interactions, some sites and social interactions were more gendered than others. This seems to be confirmed by another slander case involving accusations of witchcraft that appeared before the York church court, this time in May 1622. Anna Mellor recalled how

aboute the feast of St Peter the Apostle now last past (a more certaine tyme she remembreth not) she ... coming to drawe water att a common well in the towne gate of Almondbury ... found ... Anne Coke and Jane Kay chiding together and att angry speaches each against other, where and when she ... did hear ... Anne Coke say unto ... Jane Kay away witche for thee betwitched Parkin's childe that it never thrive after.

Hester Stolefield was standing in the threshold of Jane Kay's house when she too heard the two women arguing, throwing allegations of witchcraft. Sara Williamson was another local woman who overheard the accusation of witchcraft: as she remembered things,

she ... being sitting & working att her husbandes howse dore situate in Almondbury ... did hear & see ... Jane Key and Anne Coke chiding & att angry speaches together where and when ... Anne Coke did call ... Jane Kay witch saying unto her go thy way witch as thou arte, and sayd further that she the sayd Jane had betwitched Parkins childe that it never thrive after, upon speaking of w[hi]ch words ... Jane Kay took witness & called this exa[m]i[n]a[n]te unto her & desired her & other witnesses then & there p[rese]nte to remember her words.[36]

36 BIA, CP.H.1504.

If allegations of witchcraft needed to be stamped upon at once, to be
called a thief could be almost as damaging. In small-scale communities
where people depended closely upon one another, and where houses
might easily be entered, trust was central to social relations.[37] Thus, the
neighbours of George Chikin reported that he 'is not a ma[n] off good
name & fame amongest his neighbors for he was put frome his m[aste]r
Mr Wetley for steilinge & withdrawinge of his said m[aste]r corne'.[38]
Thomas Watson explained that he had known Robert Layton of
Sedgefield (County Durham) for more than twenty years and he had
always taken him for an honest man, but that since Thomas Gibson 'in
a great rage cauld the said Rob[er]t Layton theff and that he had been
longe a false fellow & a theffe', the result was that Layton had been 'moch
impared by the said report & sklander'.[39] Likewise, for the Yorkshireman
Henry Jackson, it hurt that in 1584 his neighbours felt no hesitation in
explaining to the church court that he 'hath bene & hereb[e]fore commonly reputed and taken for a man of very evell Liffe and con[ver]sation
amongst his neighboures and hath bene heretofore sclaundered and
vehemently suspected for stealing of sheepe and upon the said vehement
suspytion apprended and comytted to prison'.[40]

What was 'comonly reported' concerning a person's behaviour might
destroy their moral standing.[41] When Thomas Waples of Stanford-le-
Hope (Essex) was accused in 1584 of having committed adultery with
Mistress Day, the result was 'only for the defaming of her good name and
fame amongst the neighbours, being esteemed since of worse credit than
before'.[42] Similarly, in Elizabethan Darlington (County Durham), 'there
was a great vo[i]ce or slander' that either Mistress Nickolson or Mistress
Hall of the town had been 'plainge the hore upon a donghill'. Alicia Clark,
'beinge an honest mans wyff & ashamed to here th[a]t ungodly report',
did her best to stop the rumour.[43] The minister of Stampton
(Northumberland) was 'judged and p[ar]tly vo[i]ced to have lyvyd
ungodly wth dyv[e]rs women viz one watson, Eliz hunter & Eppy
Lawrence'. When a married woman of the parish chose to give birth at
her sister's house at Barnard Castle, the rumour grew that she, too, had
been impregnated by the vicar.[44] So, also, in 1586 the churchwardens of
Gainford (County Durham) reported that 'there is a verie great talke and

[37] See, for instance, the following allegations of theft, which ended up as defamation suits at
the church court: DUL, DDR/EJ/CCD/1/2, fols. 13v, 22v.
[38] DUL, DDR/EJ/CCD/1/2, fol. 136r. For a similar example, see Hamilton (ed.), *Books of
Examinations and Depositions, 1570–1594*, 104.
[39] DUL, DDR/EJ/CCD/1/2, fol. 213r.    [40] BIA, CP. G/2192.
[41] DUL, DDR/EJ/CCD/1/7, fol. 93v.    [42] Emmison (ed.), *Elizabethan Life*, 57.
[43] DUL, DDR/EJ/CCD/1/2, fols. 21v-22r.
[44] DUL, DDR/EJ/CCD/1/2, fols. 229r-230r.

common fame in the parish ... that ... [their minister] Sir Ralph lyveth very ungodlie and naughtilie with ... Carr's wyfe'.[45] All of this undermined the moral standing of the minister and, by extension, of the Church itself.

If the authority of the clergy could be undercut by a low sexual reputation, so too the gentry were profoundly concerned to ensure that their status was protected in the eyes of their social inferiors. William Vaughan wrote all too easily in 1608 '[t]hat Gentlemen must not greatly respect what the common people speake of them'. For, recognizing the importance of gentry reputation amongst the commons, he went on to explain that the gentleman should strive 'to keepe a good name, especially among their neighbours'.[46] Certainly, in everyday life, gentlewomen and men were concerned to maintain their moral standing within their 'Country': as the Kentish gentleman Thomas Parramoure explained to the Star Chamber in 1608, he was 'knowne [and] hath evermore bene taken and reputed worthie [of] the companie, acquaintance familiaritie and frendshippe of the best sorte that lived about him'. So when scurrilous libels concerning his sexual honour were circulated in Canterbury, he understood that the purpose was 'to 'deprive him of his good name and reputation w[hi]ch he doth hold and esteeme as precious as his life and by w[hi]ch he hath injoyed and received much comfort and sweete contentment'.[47]

Gentry honour was not just about their sexual behavior: it also had to do with their place in the local hierarchy. So, when Robert Furse remembered his kinswoman Johan Rolande, he wrote that she was

a wyse woman and decente in her apparel, an excellente good hussewyfe and carefull, a parfytee woman to doo anye thynge wythe her nele to knytt to make bonelase. She was a fine coke and well esteemed of all peopell, she was myche bente to faste praye and geve almese to the pore, she was a plesante woman in company and was ever of honeste lyfe and conversasyon, nevere charged or suspected wythe anye evyll, she was a fryndely woman and lyberall to all her brothers ... [at her funeral] she gave to Cxx pore persones iiii.d a pese and penye dole.[48]

Clearly, whereas Isabell Bele was regarded as having failed to live up to the social expectations of a gentlewoman, Johan Rolande's standing remained lodged in collective memory.

---

[45] Raine, J. (ed.), *The Injunctions*, 131.
[46] Vaughan, *The Golden Grove*, book 3, chapter 17.    [47] TNA, STAC8/232/2.
[48] Travers (ed.), *Robert Furse*, 137.

## Nation, Country and Neighbourhood

Early modern social historians have had relatively little to say about
national identities. Yet it is clear that many English people saw themselves
as very much apart from other nations. In the northern border counties,
there was considerable antipathy towards the Scottish. In 1600, the town
authorities of Berwick-upon-Tweed ordered that 'no Scotishe borne
persons oughte to inhabite within this towne'. They also passed the
injunction that 'it is not lawfull for the Scotts repayeringe to this towne
to walk about the streats after the watch bell is ronge at night'. All Scots
had to surrender their weapons upon entering the town.[49] Rules for the
company of goldsmiths, glaziers, plumbers, pewterers and painters in
Newcastle upon Tyne in 1536 stipulated that no Scotsmen were to be
taken as apprentices.[50] If any brother of Newcastle's Goldsmiths'
Company called another 'a Scott, a murderer [or] a thefe', he was to be
expelled from the company.[51] In 1561, controls were established over
Scots selling goods in Carlisle and other market towns, and over Scottish
tailors.[52] In 1561, the Carlisle authorities laid down that '[n]o unchar-
tered Scott shall dwell within this citie ...[.] Noe Scottsman nor woman
shall walk within this citie after the watch bell be rounge at thare perill
onless thei have a freman his son or servant with them.'[53] Suspicion was
widespread. In 1501, the York authorities ordered that no Scot was to
enter without first knocking upon the city gates.[54] Perhaps in an indication that a north-east accent might be misheard, a letter to the York
aldermen from a Durham gentleman affirmed that the bearer, Richard
Hammylton, is 'a trewe Englishman born' and 'that he shall not suspect
for a Skott'.[55]

Scots were widely regarded as dishonest, and to be identified as
Scottish was, for many English people, highly insulting. In 1575, the
allegation of being Scottish was sufficient to cause a fist-fight in
Wolsingham (County Durham).[56] Six years earlier, the suggestion that
a neighbour was 'a skot' resulted in a defamation suit.[57] Likewise, in
Elizabethan Newcastle, being called a 'Skotts magerell' or a 'Skotts
browll' provided grounds for a defamation case.[58] For the neighbours of

[49] HMC, Various Collections, *I*, 24.
[50] R. Welford (ed.), *History of Newcastle and Gateshead*, 3 vols. (London, 1884–7), II, 151.
[51] W. Tomlinson, *Life in Northumberland during the Sixteenth Century* (London, 1897), 144–5.
[52] R. S. Ferguson and W. Nanson (eds.), *Some Municipal Records of the City of Carlisle, TC&WA&AS*, 4 (Carlisle, 1887), 94–5, 148.
[53] Ibid., 68.    [54] A. Raine (ed.), *York Civic Records*, II, YASRS, 103 (York, 1943), 165.
[55] Ibid., 168.    [56] Raine (ed.), *Depositions ... from the Courts of Durham*, 305–7.
[57] Ibid., 89.    [58] DUL, DDR/EJ/CCD/1/1, fols. 13v-14r.

the Scotsman James Naysmith, it was a fine question whether or not he was to be trusted. Some put their faith in his status as a neighbour, explaining to the Durham church court that 'James Naysmith is a skottsma[n] and an honest trew ma[n] ... and is reportyd amongest there an honest ma[n] wher he dwelleth to be of good credit & estimac [ion]'. But John Hopper said of Naysmith that 'he is thought to be a man of evil conscience being a skottish man'; similarly, William Hopper stated that 'James Naysmith ... is a skottishman born [and] is not to be creddit ... as any indifferent witness'.[59]

The union of the Scottish and English Crowns in 1603 probably did little to lessen this Scottophobia. The Carlisle Merchants' Guild stated in 1624 that no Scotsman was to 'retayle eyther in market or houses'.[60] The name of '[t]heife, carle and Gallowaie knave' was considered an unpleasant insult in Northumberland in 1637.[61] Being Scottish was, in some Northumberland villages, not merely an insult but actually an *accusation*. Nor was it only on the northern borders that the Scots were disliked. Around 1524, William Wilson of Gorleston (Norfolk), outraged at some unstated infraction of his rights within the village, exclaimed: 'I cannot see but ... an horeson Scotte hath more privilege and liberties in the town than an Englishman.'[62] In 1611, Phillip Pattrick of Castle Acre (Norfolk) called Randall Coock 'rogue rascall branded rogue & Scottish rogue: then Randall Coock demaunded Phillip what a Scott was: as Randall hath reported the sayd Phillip should make his answer that a scott was a Rogue & a rascall for all scotts are rogues & rascalls'. A year earlier, Phillip Patrick and Randall Cooke had 'rayled one against the other in very unseemly manner, the sayd Patricke calling Cooke Rogue & Scottish Rogue and sayd that he did come to the Towne lyke a Roague: wherupon Cooke demanded of Patryke what a Scott was, whoe answered ... that the sayd Cooke was a Roague well known'.[63]

Other people of the Atlantic archipelago were also seen as distinct from the English. Chester parish registers show that Welsh and Irish folk were to be found in the city in the seventeenth century. They may not entirely have fitted in: when the Welshman Evan ap Rees died in the city in 1610, the parish clerk recorded his burial, noting that he was a 'yeoman and stranger'. Two years earlier, an Irishman who was buried was recorded as

[59] DUL, DDR/EJ/CCD/1/3, fols. 2r, 11r, 14r.
[60] Ferguson and Nanson (eds.), *Municipal Records*, 95.
[61] Longstaffe (ed.), *The Acts of the High Commission within the Diocese of Durham*, 182–3.
[62] Stone and Cozens-Hardy (eds.), *Norwich Consistory Court Depositions*, no. 317.
[63] NRO, NQS/C/S3/17/1, 'words delivered from the mouths of Randall Coock and William Pintcher'; NRO, NQS/C/S3/17/1, information of William Pynchard. For more on the case, see NRO, NQS/C/S3/17/2, petition of Randall Cooke.

'a stranger called John [who] came out of Ireland'.[64] The famines in early seventeenth-century Ireland cast many Irish folk onto English roads, desperate travellers who were easily identified as outsiders. In 1582, Alice Wynn – known as Welsh Alice – was expelled from Liverpool; she had been living with a married woman in the town whose other lodgers included Manx, Irish and 'northern men' described by the town clerk as 'loiterers and quaines'.[65] In the early sixteenth century, Cornwall appears to have been conceived of as a separate entity, rather like Wales. Mark Stoyle has suggested that it formed part of 'an essentially tripartite structure' in which Cornwall was 'the smallest of the three distinct "provinces" which made up the kingdom of England'. As late as 1616, one contemporary observed: 'England is … divided into 3 great Provinces or Countries … every [one] of them speaking a several and different Language, as English, Welsh and Cornish.' English observers regarded the Cornish commons as rough and 'boorish'.[66]

English attitudes to the people of France and the Low Countries were more ambiguous. Back in 1381, Kentish rebels had heaped in the streets of London the bodies of the Flemish weavers they had murdered.[67] Something similar might have been in the minds of Londoners in 1517 when, following rising tensions between the native population and the Flemish and French population, a seditious bill was circulated in the streets. This found its way into the hands of a hothead minister, who, in the course of an inflammatory sermon, read it aloud:

To all you the worshipful lordes and masters of this citie, that will take compassions over the poore people your neighbours, and also of the great importable hurtes, losses, and hynderaunces, whereof procedeth the extreme povertie too all the kynges subjectes that inhabite within this citie and subsurbes of the same, for so it is that the alyens and straingers eate the bread from the poore fatherles chyidren, and take the livynge from all the artificiers, and the entercourse from all merchauntes, whererby povertie is so muche increased that every man bewaileth the misery of the other, for craftesmen be brought to beggery and merchantes to nedynes; wherefore the premisses considred, the redresse must be of the commons, knyt and unite to one parte, and as the hurt and dammage greveth all men, so must all men set to their willyng power for remedy, and not to suffer the sayd alyens so highly in their wealth, and the naturall borne men of this region too come to confusion.[68]

[64] Coster, 'A Microcosm of Community', 137.
[65] J. A. Twemlow (ed.), *Liverpool Town Books*, 2 vols. (London, 1935), II, 308, 397, 423.
[66] M. Stoyle, *West Britons: Cornish Identities and the Early Modern British State* (Exeter, 2002), 31–2, 34–5.
[67] R. B. Dobson, *The Peasants' Revolt of 1381* (Basingstoke, 1970), 162.
[68] E. Hall, *Hall's Chronicle: Containing the History of England during the Reign of Henry the Fourth and Succeeding Monarchs, to the End of the Reign of Henry the Eighth* (London, [1548]1809), 586–91.

Social unity and xenophobia combined in 1517: for the commons to 'knyt and unite to one parte', they had to turn on their foreign neighbours.

The 1517 rising – for all it that remains under-explored by historians – was a significant moment in the history of London, leading to the suspension of civic authority and to executions in the streets. This was not the only sign of complaint about the French and Low Country folk. In Henry VIII's reign, for instance, The London Cordwainers' Company complained to the Star Chamber about the liberties that foreign shoemakers were taking in the city. The cordwainers explained that the alien shoemakers were meant to be limited to forty-four householders, but that they seemed to be constantly increasing in number. As the cordwainers put it:

[A]lways the said strangers doo mocke and skorne your said orators and saith that they have made a worshipfull acte. And soe as soon as any of the seid estrangers dothe aryse and growe in substance the doo a voyde theymselffe and suche goodes as they have goten there in that realme in Continent they convey and Carry theym home into theyer owne Contreys to the great hortte and losse of this realme, And so immedyatly after other that be of theyer owne contryne and but bare persones and sett in theyer howsis to occupye in theyer howsis and so within short space all weyes they become Rich and greatly advanced in substance.[69]

There was a continuous sense in Tudor and early Stuart London that the alien population threatened the interests of poor and middling householders. Repeating the contents of the rebel bill that had initiated Evil May Day in 1517, the depiction of the events of that day in the multi-authored drama *Sir Thomas More* brought the rebel leader Captain Lincoln onto the stage. In imposing order amongst rebel ranks, he cries out: 'Peace, hear me: he that will not see a red herring at a Harry groat, butter at elevenpence a pound, meal at nine shillings a bushel, and beef at four nobles a stone, list to me.' He suggested that famine was caused by the greed of the aliens: 'Our country is a great eating country, *argo* they eat more in our country than they do in their own.'[70] Such works resonated with many working people's feelings in London in the 1590s: some of the drama of that decade took the concerns of the London groundlings and wove them into stage productions.[71] In the dramatic depiction of the events of 1381 in the 1593 play *The Life and Death of Jack Straw*, the horrifying violence against the Flemish weavers was shown in festive, comedic terms: the rebel Nobs entered the stage with a captured Fleming, crying out:

---

[69] TNA, STAC2/9/44.     [70] *Sir Thomas More*, act II, scene 3, lines 1–4, 7–8.
[71] A. Wood, 'Brave Minds and Hard Hands: Work, Drama and Social Relations in the Hungry 1590s', in C. Fitter (ed.), *Shakespeare and the Politics of Commoners: Digesting the New Social History* (Oxford, 2017), 84–103.

Sirra here it is set downe by our Captaines that as many
Of you cannot say read and cheese, in good and perfect
English, ye die for it, & that was the cause so many strangers did
die in Smithfield.[72]

It was not only in London that this kind of hostility was exhibited to the Flemish, Walloons and French. In East Anglia, with its notably multi-national composition and close trading links to the Low Countries, there were periodic outbursts of hostility towards aliens. In early sixteenth-century Suffolk, to be called a Fleming represented an insult. In 1502, Robert Sancrofte of Fressingfield (Suffolk) said of his neighbour Thomas Gurlyng that he 'was a fals flemmyng, he and all his brethren'. Eight years later, John Humme of Southwold (Suffolk) told Hugh Wylliamson: 'Thou art a false flemmyng and a false styknyng cokald.'[73] In Elizabethan Colchester, the poor of that divided town petitioned against enclosures that had been made on their commons and against the arrival of rich strangers who, they felt, had stolen away their livelihoods.[74] In an under-investigated 'insurrection' in Suffolk in 1569, it was reported that 'very meane personag[e]s' were in arms 'againste the multitude of straun-gers and forreyne Artificers, by whose number & faculties the natural was oppressed they said. But their intent was playnlie (as the custome is) to have spoiled all the gentlemen & welthie p[er]sonages.'[75]

The picture is more complex than a straightforwardly xenophobic hostility to immigrants, however: we can also detect a large degree of acceptance of strangers amongst many native East Anglians. The evidence suggests that the strangers were welcomed in Norwich for their contribution to the local skills-base and providing employment for the poor.[76] Certainly, this was the implication of a report prepared by the Norwich authorities for the Privy Council, which stated clearly that the strangers had

brought grete comoditie thether, viz., the making of bayes, moccados, grograynes, all sorts of tuftes, etc, which were not made there before, wherby they do not onely set on worke their owne people but do also set on worke our owne people within the cittie as also a grete number of people nere xx myles about the cittie to the grete relief of the porer sorte there . . .[. T]hey for the moste parte feare God, and do diligently and laboriously attende upon their severall occupations, they obey all magistrates and all good lawes and ordynaunces, they live peaceablie amonge themselves and towarde all men, and we think our cittie happie to enjoye them.[77]

---

[72] Anon., *The Life and Death of Jack Straw* (London, 1594), lines 616–19.
[73] Stone and Cozens-Hardy (eds.), *Norwich Consistory Court Depositions*, nos. 23, 122.
[74] TNA, SP12/240/115. See also TNA, SP12/193/83.
[75] BL, Cotton Ms Titus B.II, fol. 492r-v.    [76] *TED*, I, 315–16.    [77] TNA, SP12/20/49.

The evidence of Flemish and Walloon Protestant immigrants, fleeing the Spanish Terror, suggests strongly that they found a welcome in godly Norwich.[78] In 1567, the hatmaker Clais van Wervekin wrote to his wife back in Ypres: 'You would never believe how friendly the people are together, and the English are the same and quite loving to our nation. If you came here with half our property, you would never think of going to live in Flanders. Send my money and the three children.' In the same year, Clement Baet wrote to his wife: 'I let you know that we are merry and happy with each other. May God give you the same loving peace and riches as we have here in Norwich. It is very dear to hear the word of God peacefully.' Also in 1567, Giles Navegeer told his grandmother that his father and his siblings were all well and that 'we have been at Norwich a little less than two years, where we are living in great quietness and peace, and the word of God is much preached among us'.[79] It was not only in Puritan Norwich that immigrants from France and the Low Countries found that they were able to integrate. At Mildenhall, in the Suffolk Brecklands, John Bocking, 'cooper and Ducheman', wrote his will in 1557, leaving his money for the repair of the parish church, along with twelve shillings to be given on the day of his burial to the poor. He was owed money by other Dutch men in Friesland; so he told his wife to travel to London to pursue these debts. John Bocking, it seems, had become part of Mildenhall society, yet retained links to a wider world.[80]

So, how did ordinary people understand their national identity? This is difficult to answer. Much of the source material available to the social historian concerns local identities – depositions in cases concerning customary law, parish accounts, testamentary evidence and so on. It is harder to answer the question of how the English perceived themselves as a people. But the evidence concerning popular politics provides some clues. As has been suggested, there was a powerful xenophobic urge amongst the English, perhaps especially in urban communities. Englishmen and women were pretty sure that the common people of France were kept in a state of subordination that contrasted to their own liberties and freedoms. In 1549, it was charged that the French commons 'be caytives and wretches, lyvyng in lyke thraldom as they did to the Romaynes, and gevyng tribute for theyr

---

[78] For the positive reception of protestant strangers, see R. Esser, '"They Obey All Magistrates and All Good Laws ... and We Thinke Our Cittie Happie to Enjoye Them": Migrants and Urban Stability in Early Modern English Towns', *Urban History*, 34 (2007), 64–75.

[79] *TED*, I, 299–300.

[80] *TED*, I, 296. For an example of a Huguenot glazier asking an English neighbour to act as the executor of his will, see A. Gregory, 'Witchcraft, Politics and "Good Neighbourhood" in Early Seventeenth-Century Rye', *P&P*, 133 (1991), 44.

meate, drinke, bre[a]des and salte'.[81] Robert Crowley suggested a year later that Kett's rebels had believed that 'we must nedes fight it out, or else be brought to the lyke slavery that the Frenchmen are in!'[82] The English tended to think that whereas their own commons lived in a state of freedom, the ordinary people of France were mere 'peasants', labouring under the yoke of an oppressive nobility. Similarly, English writers wrote easily of the 'peasantly' tenants of Scottish lords, who were felt to lack any independence.[83]

Sir Thomas Wyatt's rising against Queen Mary was underpinned by an anti-Spanish impulse that came from her impending marriage to Philip II, along with deeply rooted Kentish anxieties about vulnerability to foreign invasion. For instance, on 22 January 1554, William Isley had ridden into Ightham and declared 'that the Spanyards was commynge into the realme w[i]t[h] harnes and handgonnes, and would make us Inglish men wondrous vile'. The villagers had responded 'these be wondrous words and we shall be hanged if we stir'. But Isley responded that the people were 'alredy upp in Devonshire'.[84] One of Wyatt's former rebels told a Norwich man that 'the Rysing was for the quenes Marryage, and if that shuld goo furth, we shuld lye in swynestyes and caves and the Spanyerdes shuld haue o[u]r houses & we shuld lyve lyke slaves & be gladd to drynke a potte w[i]t[h] water'.[85]

Reported conversations about military and foreign policy also suggest the existence of a strong national identification. In February 1559, a rumour spread across Norfolk that 'certeyne sedicyus p[er]sons' backed by the French, Scots and Spanish would set market towns and villages on fire. These forces intended to 'com[e] clothed having beggars clokes for ther uttermost garment and under that having sylke dubletts'. In particular, these 'strangers' intended the destruction of Norwich.[86] A few years earlier, in 1552, the Norwich man Henry Ussher made the mistake of asking his fellow weaver Andrew Kegell the provocative question 'What newes?' Kegell provided a shocking response, telling Ussher '[t]hat the gates of yermouth were Rampered in and that there were many strangers in the towne . . .[. T]here ar[e] nere xviii.ay strangers come to London and . . . they were dryven out of the lande because of the newe lernyng.'[87]

Ordinary English people could become quite inflamed by seemingly distant questions such as the claim of the Tudors to the French throne.

[81] *TED*, III, 6.

[82] J. M. Cowper (ed.), *The Select Works of Robert Crowley*, EETS, 15 (London, 1872), 133.

[83] C. Hill, *Society and Puritanism in Pre-revolutionary England* (London, 1964), 233.

[84] D. M. Loades, *Two Tudor Conspiracies* (Cambridge, 1965), 52.

[85] NRO, NCR12A/1(a), fol. 135r.

[86] NRO, NCR12A/1(b), unpaginated, 3 February 1559.    [87] NRO, NCR16A/6, p. 104.

On 6 May 1553, Thomas Aldersen of the Norfolk village of Cringleford found himself drawn into a verbal confrontation with a Frenchman. As he explained things to the Norwich magistrates, he had been in Frauncis Metcalf's house in Thorpe when 'a frencheman cam[e] into the same hous[e] and among other comynycaon [he] ... seid that he hadde sene the kynge of fraunce in pareis xx.tie tymes', to which Aldersen answered 'felowe talke not of suche thyngs ... for the kyng oure maister is kyng of fraunce'. The Frenchman responded:

[N]oo for herry the ... kyng of fraunce was borne in fraunce and kyng herry the viii was his godfather. Wherfor this kyng Edwarde was never Crowned in fraunce & therfor he hathe nothing to do there. And if your kyng sholde be kyng of fraunce our kynge shulde be aswel kynge here. And then this deponent said felow thou talkest like a fole for our kynge writithe his stile kynge of englond & fraunce & yrelonde. And then he said if he writithe so then he writithe otherwise then it is for it is not soo. Wherunto on[e] of the company said whoo ... thow Spekitt like a fole recant for thei sayeing is naught[.] Wherunto he answered rather then I wulle recant I wulle be hewen as small as this orange pille whiche he then hadde in his hande.[88]

Aldersen's outrage at the suggestion that Edward VI may not have enjoyed a legitimate claim to the French throne reminds us that English national identities could be held by ordinary people with great power and conviction. Yet at the same time, there were those who brought a critical acumen to their assessment of the state's military and foreign policies. In 1545, William Rye told the Norwich mayor's court that he and Antony Sprowston 'ded ryde togyther from North Walsh[a]m to Holte' and that 'beyng in comunycacyon the said Will[ia]m said that it is an hard worlde for poor folks and prayed to God that yf yt war his pleasure to send a peace', to which Sprowston said 'that yt wer not pease shortely yt should make a bare Ynglond'. Rye replied:

[I]f yt wer bar[e] w[i]t[h] Inglond other Realms which wer in warre as wele as Inglond, which the Kyng's most noble Grace has moste vyctoryously and nobely in all his affaires ov[er]come as France and Skotland thei shuld then be very bare. Unto the whiche the said Antony made answer and said I praye you what ded the Inglyshe men in Skoteland but cam[e] in on a Sundaye in the mornyng when some wer[e] in bedde and some at chyrche, and by a false traytor of Edinborow cam[e] in to Edinborow and ther did but robbe and ste [a]le, but if thei had taryed but the space of iii or iiii [h]owers lenger thei[r] de [e]d thes[e] shuld have knowen the peyce.[89]

[88] NRO, NCR 12A/1(a), fols. 87r–88r.
[89] W. Rye (ed.), *Depositions Taken before the Mayor and Aldermen of Norwich, 1549–1567; Extracts from the Court Books of the City of Norwich, 1666–1688* (Norwich, 1905), 93–4.

There are the merest hints in the records of that enduring English obsession: the divide between the North and the South. In 1536, seditious speech accusations emanating from the South sometimes provide evidence of people speaking about the intentions of the 'northern men'. These 'northern men' composed a rebel ballad that spelt out a clear sense of a correspondence between regionalism and religious affiliation:

> The northorne pepull in tyme longe paste
> Haith lytyll beyn Regardyde of the awstrall [i.e., southern] nacione
> But now I doo trust, evyn at the Last
> Renowne we shall wyne, to oure holle congregacyon
> Off these Southourne herytykes, devode of all vertu
> And them over-thorwe: ther faithe is untrewe.[90]

What is clearer is that rich and poor alike had a strong sense of what they called their 'country'. For the greater gentry, this sometimes corresponded to the county; although that sense of country identity could cross county boundaries, especially where kinship and other affinities were involved.[91] Sometimes, parliamentary elections could be occasions for the celebration of a united 'country' identity amongst the gentry, who would proffer preselected candidates to a freeholder electorate for their apparently passive assent.[92] Serving the country in this way could be seen by gentlemen not just as a duty but as an honour.[93] However, in contrast to the view that a sense of country was inevitably harmonious, gentry of families often found themselves at odds with one another, especially where issues of religious loyalty were involved.[94] Country loyalties did not, then, preclude religious or political conflicts. Moreover, national identities mattered: Clive Holmes has shown the ways in which early Stuart gentry identified within a shared, national political culture, one founded on constitutionalist ideas about the common law that would prove a roadblock to the Jacobean and Caroline absolutism.[95] These national loyalties were held alongside – sometimes in tension with – an

---

[90] Furnivall (ed.), *Ballads from Manuscripts*, 305.

[91] For early modern country identities, see V. Morgan, 'The Cartographic Image of "The Country" in Early Modern England', *TRHS*, 5th ser., 29 (1979), 129–54. For country identities in the earlier period, especially amongst the gentry, see M. L. Holford, 'Pro Patriotis: "Country", "Countrymen" and Local Solidarities in Late Medieval England', *Parergon*, 23, 1 (2006), 47–70.

[92] M. A. Kishlansky, *Parliamentary Selection: Social and Political Choice in Early Modern England* (Cambridge, 1986).

[93] See, for instance, HMC Montagu, 109.

[94] See, for instance, the account of a contested county election in Worcestershire that pitted Catholic against Protestant candidates: TNA, STAC8/201/17.

[95] C. Holmes, 'The County Community in Stuart Historiography', *JBS*, 19, 2 (1980), 45–73.

identification with the country. The country ideal underwrote gentry identity. We should not be surprised to see it sometimes honoured only in the breach; yet it continued to influence the ways in which the gentry perceived themselves, their class and the wider world. This was their 'neighbourhood'. William Lambarde articulated with great clarity the link between local officeholding, duty to the Crown and duty to the country in an address to the grand jury of Kent in 1583. He told them: '[C]onsider that you represent the body of your natural country, which lieth now afflicted with many griefs and putteth you in trust to seek help for her weigh the danger and harm that may ensue if weeds be suffered to overgrow the corn, and think ourselves weeders into the cornfield of the commonwealth.' In another address in 1587, he told the grand jurors: 'You are a body gathered of diverse parts, dispersed through the shire (as if it were so many eyes put into one head) that nothing might escape your sight and knowledge.' Loyalty to country, Lambarde said, should stand above more finely tuned local connections: '[H]owsoever our kins-folk, neighbours, and friends be dear unto us, yet the love of God and our country ought to be nearer and dearer than they all.' Two years later, he remarked upon the importance of the legal process being vested in 'those of the same shire and neighbourhood', telling the grand jurors that they were there to maintain 'the common good of your native country'. And in 1592, he addressed the grand jurors as 'good neighbours and friends' who were there 'to serve their country'.[96] It was not only in Kent that 'Country' identities maintained a powerful hold over the county gentry. As Hassell Smith observes, following Sir Nathaniel Bacon's protracted absence in Norwich, the rector of his home village of Stiffkey (Norfolk) wrote to explain that, with Bacon away, '[t]he country hereabowt is lefte as shepe without a guyde: God send your worshippe an happy returne to this your house.'[97]

The correspondence of one west Midland gentry family, the Bagots, in the late sixteenth and early seventeenth centuries illustrates the nexus amongst country, obligation and clientage. Their connections straddled Staffordshire and Shropshire – an area that they called their 'country'. The Bagots were not especially distinguished: they were the sort of gentry who held local society together, holding office as magistrates, sheriffs and commissioners for recusants. A part of this involved the regular maintenance of links based upon clientage. Kinship – an ever-elastic quality amongst the gentry – meant

[96] C. Read (ed.), *William Lambarde and Local Government* (Ithaca, NY, 1962), 75, 88, 89, 99, 109, 111.
[97] A. H. Smith, 'Puritanism and "Neighbourhood": A Case Study in Late 16th and Early 17th-Century Norfolk', in E. Royle (ed.), *Regional Studies in the History of Religion in Britain since the Later Middle Ages* (York, 1984), 85.

that the Bagots could expect to receive periodic correspondence from other gentry who felt themselves obligated in that behalf. In 1610, for example, Sir Walter Chetwynd wrote to Walter Bagot on behalf of a 'kynsman' in a struggle with a 'troublesom[e] parson'.[98] Kinship was not necessarily genetic; to be the 'cousin' of a gentleman might mean a social connection, rather than any familial bond. In either case, gentry were unembarrassed about calling on favours from one another. One gentlemen who had fallen on hard times – 'I am by birth a gent', he insisted – wrote to Richard Bagot in 1590 to ask for help, explaining that when young he made the mistake of leaving 'my contry and al[l]iance' and venturing abroad and had lost all his money.[99] The assumption was that, as a cousin, Bagot was meant to relieve the man; in this way, the values of country and of gentry 'alliance' would be sustained. In the same year, Roland Lacon wrote to Walter Bagot to explain that his tenants in Knightly (Shropshire), 'being in deed the poorest lordship w[i]thin yo[u]r Country', had been very heavily taxed and therefore 'I would entreat you (good cosen) as you may, [to] extend yo[u]r favorable respect towards those my tenaunts'. Were Bagot to find it within himself to help Lacon's tenants, 'they shall be much bounden and I beholding unto you'.[100]

Friendship – an ambiguous concept, just as elastic as kinship and country – was much called upon. Hence, Sir Charles Egerton wrote '[t]o the Right worshipfull [and] verie muche esteemed and worthie good frend Mr Walter Bagot' on 13 June 1618:

As one of my chefest frends amongst others I intrete you wilbe pleased to dyne w[i]th me upon mydsomer day nex[t] att my tenant widdo[w] hir Eleis house in thorny layne whooes daughter is th[a]t day to bee maried unto my sarvant evanes Flloyd & you shall com[m]end me much more in any thinge wherein my poore abylletie shall extend[.] Thus w[i]th Remembraunce of [my] trewe affection unto your selfe [torn] … or worthy good bedfello[w] I take le[a]ve and [re]st, Youre assured loving fr[i]end Charles Egerton.[101]

Country, just like kin and friendship, imposed duties. In particular, the gentry had little difficulty in recognizing their collective interests as a class. And so, when Philip Draycote wrote to Walter Bagot in 1600 concerning the impending parliamentary elections in Shropshire, he encouraged Bagot not to press too hard for his own candidate; this would be, Draycote said, 'for the benyfytt of owre cuntrey'.[102]

Neighbourhood – spanning a far wider geography for the gentry than it did for poor and middling folk – was also something that placed obligations upon the Bagots.[103] In 1607, for instance, Walter Bagot wrote to William Lord Paget to remind him that the last time he had been in

---

[98] FSL, L.a. 377.     [99] FSL, L.a. 865.     [100] FSL, L.a. 610.     [101] FSL, L.a. 439.
[102] FSL, L.a. 429.     [103] FSL, L.a. 617.

Paget's company, at the request of 'my honest neighbour' Mr John Swaynton, he had craved Paget's favour to three of Swanton's servants who had trespassed in a warren. Bagot explained that they had confessed the offence and bound themselves to be of good behaviour, but that he now learnt that the servants were to be prosecuted at the Assizes. Doing his best to pull strings on the men's behalf, Bagot asked that Paget see that the case be dropped. So a web of obligations was generated – that between Bagot and Paget, between Swaynton and Bagot, and finally between Swaynton and his servants.[104] Twelve years later, the gentleman William Church wrote to Walter Bagot, seeking to activate a similar set of obligations. Once again calling upon his status as the Bagots' neighbour, Church explained:

I ame boulde to Intreat youre frendshipe to wardes this bearer whome tells mee that he is much wronged by a neighboure of his as hee will showe you more at learge[.] I knowe the p[ar]tie to be a very [h]onest mane & hathe marryed a neghbours doughter of mine one Mr Savage daughter. [H]ee lived twenty yeares & more my next neighbor in nantwiche & nowe dwells w[i]thin a mille of mee in Staffordshire. [M]y request is that you wold doe him whatt good you maye in his good & honest cause & I will ever rest thankfull to you.[105]

There was a social electricity generated here, surging up and down the hierarchy. Friendship, country and clientage had been called upon, and now a series of dependencies and obligations had been created, dependencies that helped to reinforce the social order. The same energy was at work when Sir Thomas Heanage wrote to Richard Bagot in February 1593. Heanage explained that the esquire Raphe Adderley had entered suit against John Ashton, 'a very poore man', concerning a cottage in Needwood Forest; he asked that Bagot examine the matter and see that Ashton was restored to the cottage. The poor man was 'as muche unwilling as he is unable to contend against Mr Adderley'.[106] This time, the claim made depended upon ideas about proper gentry behaviour: it was unseemly to drive a poor cottager and his family from their home. Gentry paternalism was here invoked, at the same time as a new web of dependencies was spun.

The Bagots were, in many ways, a very ordinary gentry family. They held no great office, and imposed themselves only very slightly on the history of the realm. But they retained respect within their country. They occupied their place as respected members of the gentry community, one that straddled county boundaries but was, at best, regional in its character. They did deals for those below them and represented the interests

104 FSL, L.a. 124.     105 FSL, L.a. 389.     106 FSL, L.a. 537.

of the humble to those further up the food chain. They would have felt out of place at the royal court, but, when riding through a village in their own country, would have expected their subordinates to doff their caps or curtsey. They might count for the many thousands of gentry families across England upon whose loyalty and activity the state depended. Sometimes, as in the carriage of the Queen's and King's peace, this took the official form of magistracy; but a lot of the time, it was communicated in informal ways, in forms that recognized the Bagots' status as mothers and fathers of their country, as people who could get things done. Like the East Anglian families whom Roger Thompson has studied, the Bagots and their clients 'were bound together by the intersecting vines of kinship, clientage and neighbourliness'.[107]

If, for the gentry, there was a kind of creative tension between loyalty to the country and to the nation, for poorer and middling people there was another seeming contradiction. On the one hand, this was a society that experienced constant movement – up and down the social scale and geographically, across the realm. Vagrants might wander for hundreds of miles in search of shelter and employment. This corresponded to the needs of the capitalist economy, one of the most fundamental aspects of which is always the need for a flexible labour force that is willing to get up and move to wherever is required. Yet, at the same time, it was also a world in which many people lived out their lives within a very localized area. This locality – also referred to as their 'country' or 'neighbourhood' – was of perhaps five or six miles' radius, the specifics of which were determined by ecology, economics, transport links and geography. This country was the world within which many people migrated. Certainly, village society was fluid, with many people getting up and moving sometimes quite frequently in the course of their lives. But, unlike the long-distance movement of the vagrants and the agrarian proletariat, for established people – many of whom could be quite poor – it was within this smaller-scale 'country' that they moved. These migration patterns provided the grounds for a cultural association with the landscapes of a local area. Movement, then, had a cultural meaning as well as an economic one. Charles Phythian Adams has put this well, arguing:

Where physical mobility is highly localized the memberships of particular communities may be constantly changing, but over the same area as a whole there may

---

[107] R. Thompson, *Mobility and Migration: East Anglian Founders of New England, 1629–1640* (Amherst, MA, 1994), 186.

well emerge comparatively dense networks of blood relationships, the perpetuation of which in one form or another over generations will be likely to engender traditionalized modes of local self-identification and hence, in cultural terms, some sense of local exclusiveness.[108]

Studying migration patterns and kinship links within a particular district of Nottinghamshire, Anna Mitson has discerned the existence of 'a social space encompassing a wider area than that of the parish: an entity comprising a group of parishes which together formed what might be termed a loose but identifiable "neighbourhood area"'.[109] For Mitson, the central component of the neighbourhood area was 'the dynastic family, a stable group of core families resident over several generations in the same parish or, more significantly, dispersed over a group of contiguous parishes'.[110] These were the sort of people who might, in their later years, be expected to give evidence in disputes over customary law, in which they would explain the boundaries and customs of villages in which they had been born, and from which sometimes they had moved – but, in many cases, only a few miles away, and sometimes then to return.

Within these localized districts, established people came to know one another well. Relationships were conducted, mediated and understood within small, intimate, face-to-face contexts, in which neighbours knew one another all too well. The fifty-year-old George Lane of Biging (Derbyshire) provided a glimpse of these close bonds. In 1561, he told the Duchy Court that he could remember the age of his neighbour Edward Sortred because 'he being a weyfer by his occupacion dyd weyffe the swedlyng bonds of the sayd Edwards upon the Saterdaye next after Corpus chrysti daye w[hi]ch was xxviii ye[a]res ago last past'.[111] Such intimate memories caught neighbours together in webs of association and local meaning. Neighbourlinesss was strengthened by long residence. When George Grinham of Norton-under-Hamdon (Somerset) sought to secure a cottage in that village in 1609, he reminded the county bench that he was 'a towne borne childe [th]er[e] myselfe'.[112] In some

---

[108] C. Phythian-Adams, *Re-thinking English Local History* (University of Leicester, Dept of English Local History, Occasional Papers, 4th ser., No. 1, 1987), 27.

[109] A. Mitson, 'The Significance of Kinship Networks in the Seventeenth Century: South-West Nottinghamshire', in C. Phythian-Adams (ed.), *Societies, Cultures and Kinship, 1580–1850: Cultural Provinces in English Local History* (Leicester, 1993), 24. For a later period, Keith Snell also senses such areas in rural England, referring to 'groupings of parishes which shared certain historical concerns, dense kinship networks, dialect, working habits, costume, certain key employers, estate structures or other such features'. K. D. M. Snell, 'The Culture of Local Xenophobia', *Social History*, 28, 1 (2003), 4.

[110] Mitson, 'The Significance of Kinship Networks', 25.     [111] TNA, DL4/3/7.

[112] Bates (ed.), *Quarter Sessions Records for ... Somerset: Vol. I, James I, 1607–1625*, 41.

ways, the experience of neighbourhood – everyone knowing one another's business, remembering gossip about one another that might go back decades – might have seemed oppressive.

The ways in which middling and poorer people spoke about common opinion was often highly localized. In 1598, Hugh Wright couldn't remember who it was that him told him stories of past troubles amongst the local gentry over the enclosure of Greenfairfield (Derbyshire), simply 'but as it was thought amongst the Neighbors'.[113] Back in 1548, the Cheshire man John Wright sustained evidence he gave to the church court about a matrimonial dispute with reference to what he 'knoweth and harde say as beyng neybor in the towne'.[114] In 1600, John Dawson spoke of a 'voice & a common fame w[i]thin the p[ar]ishe of hart & other places thereabouts that ... Rob[er]t Watson hath com[mi]tted incontinencye w[i]th ... Anne Tyndale'.[115] In similar cases, witnesses spoke of what was 'comonly reported', of 'a verie great talke and common fame in the parish' of 'the comon report of the people'; of what 'ys comenyd amonge the p[ar]yshioners'; of 'the comon report off neighbors & p[a]rishioners'; of 'the como[n] report & fame in the p[ar]ishe'; of the 'public voice, fame, and report within the parish'.[116] Sometimes, merely being a neighbour was enough to justify a particular point of view: in 1548, John Cropper of Oldham (Lancashire) felt able to give evidence concerning the birth of an illegitimate child in his community 'th[a]t he doth knowe because he is a neybor'.[117]

Collective speech formed the basis for local moral judgments, forming a buzz of rumour that comprised what was 'judged and p[ar]tly vo[i]ced' amongst the neighbours.[118] 'Country', in these contexts, became a living entity that could 'speak'. So, there were those witnesses who spoke of the talk of the country: of how, in 1606, Edward Graye called Rose Harris 'whore and arrant whore and so the country should yield her', or of how, in 1578, '[t]he report in the Country' was that Widow Fourde of Titchfield (Hampshire) 'is a naughty woman by reason of the clamourment' in the village concerning her sexual behaviour.[119] In the 1570s, it

---

[113] TNA, DL4/40/29.    [114] CRO, EDC2/4, p. 3.

[115] DUL, DDR/EJ/CCD/1/7, fols. 87r-v.

[116] DUL, DDR/EJ/CCD/1/7, fol. 93v; DUL, DDR/EJ/CCD/1/2, fols. 121r, 229r; Raine (ed.), *The Injunctions ... of Richard Barnes, Bishop of Durham*, 131; CRO, EDC2/10, fol. 20v; Longstaffe (ed.), *The Acts of the High Commission within the Diocese of Durham*, 136–7; HALS, 21M65/C3/8, p. 135.

[117] CRO, EDC2/4, p. 39.

[118] DUL, DDR/EJ/CCD/1/2, fol. 230r. For the earlier context, see T. Fenster and D. Lord Smail (eds.), *Fama: The Politics of Talk and Reputation in Medieval Europe* (Ithaca, NY, 2003).

[119] Wilkinson (ed.), *Chichester Archdeaconry Depositions*, 208; HALS, 21M65/C3/8, p. 134.

was reported by the bailiff of Black Heddon (Northumberland) 'that George Chikin is not a man of good name and fame emongst his neighbours'; indeed, the 'voice of the contree' was that he was a thief.[120] At the same time, the Durham church court learnt that 'their gooith a great voice in the contree' concerning the corrupt handling of the will of Mr Jarrerd, a rich man who owned a great store of gold.[121]

The sense that the 'Country' could speak, that it had a memory, an identity and that it possessed agency, is especially significant given that sometimes the 'Country' was deployed as a synonym for the common people of a locality. In April 1640, for example, an agent of the sponsors of fenland drainage in Lindsey Level reported that 'the country begins to Rise up in arms' against them.[122] Four years earlier, during large-scale rioting in the fens, Christopher Clarke of Boston (Lincolnshire) exclaimed 'that the Country would not rest thus, but make all as plain, as ever it was, before they had done'.[123] Likewise, in 1612, the lord lieutenant of Gloucestershire reported disorder in the Forest of Dean in which 'some fifteen desperate knaves' had set fire to piles of cordwood, after which they danced around the fire crying 'God save the King'. He explained that 'they still walk the wood with weapons and oft I hear weak shot; they call their neighbours cowards for not assisting them; they give out that they look for more help; the Justice has given order for their apprehension but the country favour them'.[124] In the 1620s, during trouble over enclosures in Braydon Forest (Wiltshire), the Crown's agent reported that '[t]he country is in a miserable combustion, and have w[it]h a general consent combined themselves together'.[125] In 1617, Sir Fulke Greville, writing to the Privy Council, said of the proposed purchase of the Lammas Commons by the Crown:

The last weeke I had notice that the Steward of Waltham Forest being in hande with the necessarie worke for setting out the true boundaries of it, the contry growing jealouse of some further intention of inclosing their Comons began to mutyn[i]e ...[.] Wherin ye may see how easily this tight Sea of busie people is raysed up with every wynde; so as a tender proceeding with them can be no prejudice.[126]

Perhaps the most resonant, and yet also the most ambiguous, use of the term 'country' was that employed by Dorothie Berry. In the aftermath of

[120] Raine (ed.), *Depositions ... from the Courts of Durham*, 113.
[121] DUL, DDR/EJ/CCD/1/2, fol. 122r.
[122] K. Lindley, *Fenland Riots and the English Revolution* (London, 1982), 109.
[123] Ibid., 88.   [124] TNA, SP14/70/49.
[125] E. Robson, 'Improvement and Epistemologies of Landscape in Seventeenth-Century English Forest Enclosure', *Historical Journal*, 60, 3 (2017), 604.
[126] TNA, SP14/91/50. See also TNA, E178/3765.

the grain riots in which she had been involved in Maldon (Essex) in 1629, when she was asked by the magistracy 'whoe p[ro]cured her' to riot, Berry answered 'the Crie of the Country and hir owne want'.[127] By 'Country' did she mean the locality? Or did she mean the common people? Either way, the Country 'cried'. What is striking about all of the above references is that they all use the term 'country' to refer to an *active* commons. The 'Country' – whether composed of fenmen and women breaking drainage works, or West Country forest inhabitants protesting against enclosure, or Essex women refusing to accept high food prices – is depicted as a living, collective agent.

Certainly, local identities could provide the basis for political agency on the part of the middle and poorer sort of people. For many people, there was a strong identification with the land. When the tenants of Thornbury (Gloucestershire) wrote, in 1519, to Sir John Daunce asking him to intercede on their behalf with the Duke of Buckingham, who intended to enclose their fields into his deerpark, they emphasized that this was land 'that they were borne unto'.[128] Neighbourhood often underwrote plebeian assertiveness. The people of Wetwang (Yorkshire) remembered, in 1554, how, twelve years earlier, enclosures had stood upon the common field but they had complained to the Council of the North 'by cause the neighboures was not contented with the inclosing thereof' and the enclosures were pulled down within a year.[129] The Warwickshire miller William Wright mobilized the language of neighbourliness when he wrote to the gentleman Sir John Newdigate in 1607 to tell him that he should behave 'like a neighbour amongst us and offer our pore neighbors no wrong'. He advised the knight to keep his pigs and sheep out of the common woodlands, stating unequivocally that 'you have no right there at all – it belongeth to the poore'.[130]

In 1525, when the Duke of Suffolk appealed to his tenants to serve under him against the rebels at Lavenham, who were in arms against Cardinal Wolsey's Amicable Grant, 'they came to hym [and] saied, that they would defende hym from all perilles, if he hurte not their neighbors, but against their neighbors they would not fight'.[131] The values of

---

[127] Essex Record Office, D/B3/3/208, no. 14. For the full story, see J. Walter, 'Grain Riots and Popular Attitudes to the Law: Maldon and the Crisis of 1629', in J. Brewer and J. Styles (eds.), *An Ungovernable People: The English and Their Law in the Seventeenth and Eighteenth Centuries* (London, 1980), 47–84.
[128] TNA, SP1/22, fol. 97r.    [129] Purvis (ed.), *Select XVI Century Causes*, 52–5.
[130] S. Hindle, 'Self-Image and Public Image in the Career of a Jacobean Magistrate: Sir John Newdigate in the Court of Star Chamber', in M. J. Braddick and P. Withington (eds.), *Popular Culture and Political Agency in Early Modern England: Essays in Honour of John Walter* (Woodbridge, 2017), 133.
[131] Hall, *Hall's Chronicle*, 699–700.

neighbourliness informed the old Staffordshire man John Harley's view of the enclosure riots that the women of his village had carried out in 1611. He told Anne Swamme that 'that w[hi]ch the women had done about the casting open of the inclosures liked him well, And that if he were A yo[u]ng man as he was then olde he wo[u]ld him self have been amongest them, And that so longe as he was worth A groate he wold stycke to his neighbors and not forsake them'.[132] The values of neighbourliness also underwrote the ways in which rioters thought of themselves as a collectivity. Whereas the enclosing lord of Haddenham (Cambridgeshire) described the women and men who had destroyed his fences as 'pore and simple people' who had come together in an 'uprore and Tumulte of a multitude of people', the rioters preferred to think of themselves as 'the company' and 'the townesmen'.[133] Neighbourhood, then, as a plebeian value, had a purchase amongst ordinary people, giving them a sense of collectivity and agency.

Such commitment to communal norms and values generated local solidarities amongst poorer people. In 1562, 300 'lewd fellows' destroyed enclosures on the commons of Lichfield (Staffordshire). When some of their number were arrested and questioned as to those who had led them, they replied that they had done it with 'common consent and that every of them is at faults as much as any other'.[134] In contrast, those who failed to stand together with their neighbours might be denounced as 'false brothers and untrustie and treacherous men'.[135] Sometimes, brute intimidation underwrote the assertion of local norms. The weaver Raphe Edge and his wife, Alice, experienced the rough end of the stick in Wetton (Staffordshire) in June 1600, when their house was invaded by their neighbours, who believed them to be unmarried and so to represent a threat to the moral order of the village. Led by the headboroughs and churchwardens, twenty-eight men and two women stormed the Edges' cottage, beating them and driving them outdoors. Raphe Edge told the Star Chamber that he knelt before the crowd and begged them not to attack his wife as she was with child, but they ignored this and drew them along, 'sayinge they should be carted', throwing them into a wagon, tying them, and finally sinking them into a pond. As a result, Alice Edge was shortly after 'deliv[er]ed of a Child longe before her tyme in most unnaturall manner'. The defendants explained that the 'comon reporte of the said Town of Wetton' was that the Edges were living out of wedlock, and that they therefore decided to cart the Edges for incontinency.[136] Similarly, in 1619, the constable of Burton-on-Trent (Staffordshire) led a shaming ritual against a man and a woman suspected of living together

---

[132] TNA, STAC8/12/7.    [133] TNA, STAC8/5/21.    [134] BL, Add MS 35380, fol. 141r.
[135] TNA, STAC8/284/24.    [136] TNA, STAC5/E13/17.

outside of matrimony. The pair were dragged through the streets, while their neighbours banged pots and pans and chanted 'a whore, a whore and a thefe'. The couple having been set in the stocks, their neighbours then urinated upon them. All of this was done, said the constable, according to the 'auncient usage and custome of longe and very auncient tyme within the towne'.[137] Returning to Wetton, back in 1552, the tenants of that village had collected a common purse in order to take central legal action against their lord, who was attempting to enclose their commons. They bound themselves 'to stick to each other against him' and assaulted those neighbours who would not join with them. A year later, as the case against their lord unfolded, a number of the villagers turned against a neighbour called Wynche who had refused to contribute to the common purse; as Wynche explained things to a local gentleman, because he 'would not stick to them', his neighbours disliked him.[138] In the intense, communal world of the early modern village, to be frozen out like this could be a damaging experience.

An important aspect of neighbourly values lay in the celebration of social collectivity, of a world where boundaries between public and private were only hazily sketched and where people lived in one another's pockets. Unity was celebrated and could be an enabling force in popular politics. The late Elizabethan and early Jacobean period saw intense conflict between the tenants of Petworth (Sussex) and their lord, the earl of Northumberland.[139] When the Star Chamber demanded of the Petworth weaver James Barton which of his neighbours had complained that the earl had dealt 'extremely' with his tenants, he suffered a sudden failure of memory, telling the commissioners that 'hee doth not nowe p[e]rfectley remember' who that might have been.[140]

Oppressive, enclosing landlords and farmers were often represented as avaricious individualists who, in driving poorer people off the commons or out of their villages, wished to live alone. One oppressive farmer in Gimingham (Norfolk) was described by his tenants as 'gredye, covetous ... very malicious, troublesome and contentious ...[. He] respecteth his oune privacie, will and pleasure [more] than he regardeth the common good, comoditie of his pore neighbours.'[141] Likewise, on 26 March 1589, a group of women in Hassop (Derbyshire) stood up against their lord, the

---

[137] J. R. Kent, '"Folk Justice" and Royal Justice in Early Seventeenth-Century England: A "Charivari" in the Midlands', *Midland History*, 8, 1 (1983), 73, 78.

[138] W. K. Boyd, 'Star Chamber Proceedings: Henry VIII and Edward VI', *Collections for a History of Staffordshire*, 37 (1912), 181–7, 197–201.

[139] For which see Wood, 'Some Banglyng about the Customes'.

[140] TNA, STAC5/N1/16.

[141] C. M. Hoare, *Records of a Norfolk Village, Being Notes on the History of the Parish of Sidestrand* (Bedford, 1914), 93.

widely disliked recusant gentleman Rowland Eyre, who was trying to snatch their common land. The women came as a crowd to intimidate Eyre's servants, who were attempting to drive off the villagers' sheep from the common. When Eyre sued the women at the Star Chamber, they responded with a searing critique of his failings as a lord. Eyre was, the women said, 'a man verye covetous & extreamelye impatient of their neighbourhood, thinking to engrosse their whole lyvinge unto his owne hands, usethe most indirect & unchristian practices' in an attempt to grind down popular opposition.[142] 'Covetous', 'impatient' of 'neighbourhood', 'unchristian': within the discourses of the sixteenth and seventeenth centuries, it was harder to think of a sharper or more powerful critique. So, also in July 1549, at the height of the commotions of that year, the commons of Landbeach (Cambridgeshire) complained that the lessee of the manor was 'so small a frend to the Comon Weale . . . he intentyth the dystruccon the rest of the towne for he wysshyth th[a]t ther were no more houses in the towne but his owne and no more'.[143] Likewise, the Warwickshire rebels of 1607 wrote to their fellow Diggers to denounce those 'incroaching Tirants w[hi]ch would grinde our flesh upon the whetstone of poverty, and make our loyall hearts to faint w[i]th breathing, so th[a]t they may dwell by themselves in the midst of theyr heards of fatt weathers'.[144] Something similar was going on around the same time in a libel distributed around Warwickshire concerning Sir John Newdigate of Chilvers Coton (Warwickshre). The authors criticized his 'malice & ill will . . . to the Commonwealth of [the] country & neighbors', arguing that, in pursuing the enclosure of their commons, he was driven by 'covetousness' and a desire to 'inlarge demeynes of [his] . . . owne'. Whereas hitherto the fields had been 'used in Comon where reliefe & hospitality for the poore hath bin', Newdigate's enclosures were 'only for the private benefit of one gentleman'.[145]

Neighbourliness, then, had a politics.[146] In providing poorer and middling people with a way of speaking about community, entitlement and

[142] R. Meredith, 'The Eyres of Hassop, 1470–1640: I', *Derbyshire Archaeological Journal*, new ser., 84 (1964), 25–6.

[143] Corpus Christi College, Cambridge, Parker Library, XXV/194, 'Articles against Richard Kyrby'.

[144] J. O. Halliwell (ed.), *The Marriage of Wit and Wisdom, and Ancient Interlude, to which Are Added Illustrations of Shakespeare and the Early English Drama* (London, 1846), 140–1.

[145] J. Walter, 'Public Transcripts, Popular Agency and the Politics of Subsistence in Early Modern England', in M. J. Braddick and J. Walter (eds.), *Negotiating Power in Early Modern Society: Order, Hierarchy and Subordination in Britain and Ireland* (Cambridge, 2001), 136.

[146] K. E. Wrightson, 'The Politics of the Parish in Early Modern England', in P. Griffiths, A. Fox and S. Hindle (eds.), *The Experience of Authority in Early Modern England* (London, 1996), 10–46.

place, it gave them a terminology that they could mobilize to criticize the world around them. Neighbourhood, in evoking fuzzy but powerful ideas about social obligations, constructed powerful norms – albeit ones that were constantly contested. While seemingly a normative language that was about consensus, the concept of neighbourliness provided a way of assessing social *conflicts*.

## 'A Packe of People'? Urban Neighbourhoods

This section offers a corrective to the view of urban society as characterized by placelessness and anomie. We shall see that the 'vibrant community culture' that Peter Earle notes as being part of pre-Reformation England, which he claims had mostly vanished with the Reformation, in fact survived in an attenuated but nonetheless highly meaningful form.[147] Earle is not alone as seeing early modern urban society – perhaps, especially, London society – as characterized by a certain rootlessness. Keith Thomas has argued: 'In London and other large cities, the growing anonymity of daily life set people free from the constant invigilation and moral surveillance which was a feature of smaller communities. In the metropolis, neighbours took less interest in each other's affairs than they did in country villages, and people passed each other in the street as strangers.'[148] Thomas's point draws on contemporary senses of the nature of urban society: it was axiomatic to many Tudor and early Stuart writers that towns and cities were characterized by a cold, empty anomie. In a dialogue of 1579, for example, the Countryman was made to observe:

That opinion I conceave, because I finde there, much love & charity, which as I take it, are two speciall markes of godlines, and seldom found in Citties, where every man almost, lyveth to him selfe: For wheras Neighbours doo meete often without ceremony, chearing, and conversing one with an other, without disdayne, or envie, (as wee do in the Countrey,) there I [j]udge is love, and good neighbourhood: Likewise where hospitalitie is liberally kept, and many Children and Servauntes daily fed, with all other commers: there (as I also thinke) is much charitie: in the Towne it seemeth the contrary, there is no meeting of neighbours,

---

[147] P. Earle, *The Making of the English Middle Class: Business, Society and Family Life in London, 1660–1730* (London, 1989), 243.

[148] Thomas, *The Ends of Life*, 182. This is in contrast to the tendency to read Italian and French urban spaces as sharply distinguished. See D. V. Kent and F. W. Kent, *Neighbours and Neighbourhood in Renaissance Florence: The District of the Red Lion in the Fifteenth Century*, Villa I Tatti Series: 6 (Locust Valley, NY, 1982); N. A. Eckstein, *The District of the Green Dragon: Neighbourhood Life and Social Change in Renaissance Florence* (Florence, 1995); D. O. Hughes, 'Kinmen and Neighbours in Medieval Genoa', in H. A. Miskimin, D. Herlihy and A. L. Udovitch (eds.), *The Medieval City* (New Haven, CT, 1977), 95–111; D. Garrioch, *Neighbourhood and Community in Paris, 1740–1790* (Cambridge, 1986).

without special convitation, no salutation, without much respect, & ceremony, no
number of Servaunts, but those that for necessary uses are imployable. So as in
breefe, there seemeth to bee litle love amonge equals, and lesse liberality to
inferiours: Wherupon I inferre, that in Citties and Townes, is lesse plenty of
both these properties: (I meane love and charity,) then is with us in the
Country.[149]

In later Tudor London, it was widely believed that neighbourhood was
under threat. While digging through the medieval records detailing its
local history, the parish clerk of St Andrew's Holborn, Thomas Bentley,
found 'Sume Monuments of Antiquities' which spoke to a vanished world
of warm neighbourhood in which parish life had been funded by 'good
people then used to be gathered by the men & wome[n] of the p[ar]ishe in
boxes, as ales, shootings & common meetings for the onely purpose
thorow the parish, weekly during the tyme of those works as by theyr
accompts yet remaining may & doth appere'.[150] There was a sense of
desperation in the overstated sermon preached by the Bermondsey minister Edward Elton in 1615. He argued that

it is hard to finde neighbours to agree together, even because they are neighbours,
and daily converse one with another, what [j]arres and differences do dailie rise
betweene neighbour and neighbour, and betweene such as dwell the next doore
one to another, we finde it too common a thing; well, let us remember, that our
neighbourhood ought to binde us more neerely together in spirituall love one to
another, and when thou art stird up by the Devill, and thine owne corruption, to
[j]arre, and to fall out with thy neighbours, thinke thus with thy selfe. Shall I fall
out with him? no; besides the common bond of Christianitie I am bound to him,
with a more speciall bond of neighbourhood, he is of the same parish, and of the
same particular congregation with mee, and therefore I ought the more to love and
regard him.[151]

In the mid-Tudor period, there was a sense that London was a place
devoid of any neighbourly solidarities. Robert Crowley had a dark view of
social relations in the city:

> For the charitie of rich men
> Is nowe thorowe colde
> And this is a Citye
> In name, but, in dede,
> It is a packe of people
> That seke after meede
> For Officers and al
> Do seke their owne gaine,

---

[149] Anon., *Cyvile and Uncyvile Life: A Discourse Very Profitable* (London, 1579), fol. 14r.
[150] London Metropolitan Archives, P82/AND/B/008/MS04249, fol. 221r.
[151] Elton, *Epistle of St Paule to the Colossians*, 1338.

But for the wealth of the commons
Not one taketh paine.
An hell with out order,
I maye it well call,
Where everye man is for himself,
And no manne for all.[152]

Yet, for all this, the recent social history of urban communities suggests a different picture from Crowley's depressing vision of cities as but 'a packe of people'.[153] In his study of the calamitous Newcastle plague of 1636, Keith Wrightson senses that, even under the pressure of the plague, there existed 'tendrils of connective tissue generated by kinship, neighbourhood, the practice of trades, and the conduct of business'. All of this, Wrightson suggests, provided sources of 'cohesion' in which his 'tendrils' grew within close senses of place, embedded within the urban landscape. Wrightson observes of the testators who died during the plague that, in their bequests, they employed 'a language of place' that was 'evident from the many references to places that occur throughout the testamentary and deposition evidence', which suggested that 'people had both a broad sense of the topography of what was still a relatively small city and an intimate knowledge of the neighbourhoods in which they lived'.[154]

Senses of urban parochial space were, if anything, even more intense than in rural areas. When the old men of All Saints' parish of Southampton described the bounds of their parish in 1577, they mentioned 'a crosse w[hi]ch stode on right the lane commonly called the kings orchard lane wher now standyth a stone', street turnings, fields, another site where a cross had once stood, and a particular walnut tree in the garden of a neighbour. Some of the witnesses had long acquaintance with the parish – the sixty-four-year-old labourer Nicholas Gobbes, for example, recalled a dispute over tithes demanded by a chantry priest some fifty years earlier.[155] In contrast to such finely drawn discussions of parish bounds, when plebeian witnesses were asked to give an account of the circuits of a city as a whole, they were rather more vague, happier to talk about the streets and lanes around them than the whole of the urban

---

[152] Cowper (ed.), *The Select Works of Robert Crowley*, 11.
[153] For a useful survey, see D. Garrioch and M. Peel, 'The Social History of Urban Neighbourhoods', *Journal of Urban History*, 32, 5 (2006), 663–76. For a detailed case-study, see P. Baker and M. Merry, '"The Pore Lost a Good Frend and the Parish a Good Neighbour": The Lives of the Poor and Their Supporters in London's Eastern Suburb, c.1583–c.1679', in M. Davies and J. A. Galloway (eds.), *London and Beyond: Essays in Honour of Derek Keene* (London, 2012), 155–80.
[154] K. E. Wrightson, *Ralph Tailor's Summer: A Scrivener, His City and the Plague* (New Haven, CT, 2011), 94, 146–7.
[155] Hamilton (ed.), *Books of Examinations and Depositions, 1570–1594*, 45–6.

polity, which appears to have been something of an abstraction to them. What William Camden called 'the neighbourhood of a great citie' seems, then, to have been too vast a spatial construct for many ordinary people to hold on to.[156] Neighbourhoods – for all that they were fluid – 'continually disappearing, but at the same time being recreated' – remained the key unit of many ordinary city-dwellers' worlds.[157]

Neighbourliness, then, was not just a rural ideal. The Tudor parish clerk of St Botolph Billingsgate (London) composed the following:

> Even as stickes may easselly be broken
> So when neighbours agre not then ther is a confucion
> But a great many of stickes bound in one boundell will hardly be broken
> So neighbours being joynjed in love together can never be severed.[158]

For all the rapid turnover of population and the dynamics of economic interaction, there were forces for social stability within urban communities, and neighbourliness remained an important paradigm. In towns and cities, '[a]n exemplary neighbour was one who "carried himself to gain love and good opinion of the neighbours", or who was "well-esteemed and thought of" by "the best and chiefest inhabitants"'.[159] Neighbourly relations were built on tangible foundations. Jeremy Boulton's study of seventeenth-century Southwark points to the continuing importance of local interactions, such as acting as overseers of wills or of choices of marriage partner, creating surprisingly close kinship links between some households.[160] Boulton notes 'the inherent tendency towards localism within metropolitan society'.[161] Similarly, Paul Seaver explains how, in 1618, as a twenty-year-old apprentice, the Londoner Nehemiah Wallington

was not a lonely apprentice far from his family and isolated in a strange city. Rather, he lived in the midst of a large family: his father and second stepmother were very much in evidence, as were a brother and four sisters, a half sister, two brothers-in-law, and three nephews and nieces ...[H]e was surrounded ... by more than a dozen close kin all living a stone's throw away from one another in a tiny parish.[162]

---

[156] W. Camden, *Britain, or A Chorographicall Description of the Most Flourishing Kingdomes, England, Scotland, and Ireland* (London, 1637), 324. I hope to write more fully about urban senses of space in the future.

[157] Garrioch and Peel, 'The Social History of Urban Neighbourhoods', 671.

[158] Archer, *The Pursuit of Stability*, 84.

[159] P. Griffiths, J. Landers, M. Pelling and R. Tyson, 'Population and Disease, Estrangement and Belonging, 1540–1700', in P. Clark (ed.), *The Cambridge Urban History of Britain: Vol. 2, 1540–1840* (Cambridge, 2000), 229.

[160] Boulton, *Neighbourhood and Society.*     [161] Ibid., 231.

[162] P. S. Seaver, *Wallington's World: A Puritan Artisan in Seventeenth-Century London* (London, 1985), 72.

For many people, then, urban society was not a world of *anomie*. Most people in the capital had been brought up outside it. It was a city of migrants, in which particular areas were defined by a very rapid population turnover. Of David Cressy's sample of East London church court witnesses in the 1580–1640 period, only 12 per cent had been born in Stepney, Whitechapel or London. The rest came from across the realm.[163] Yet, once they moved to London, those possessed of sufficient capital to set up as householders appear to have integrated quickly. They seem rapidly to have developed a sense of parish identity, along with a fuzzier sense of their 'neighbourhood'.

The city appears to have been abstractions to many poorer people. It was with this local world that ordinary people engaged.[164] For artisans and traders, urban neighbourhoods created opportunities for marketing and for employment. Amongst the stable core of residents, those who constituted the social structures through which others moved, the street, courtyard and urban parish were the most important units of identification. When the plebeian inhabitants of Gloucester were asked in 1589 to give an account of the city, they spoke about their immediate locale – its streets and closed spaces – rather than about the larger world of the city.[165] Likewise, when regulations for Elvet district of Durham were drawn up in 1610, they focused on social life in individual streets.[166] In Jacobean Leeds, the most immediate attachment that ordinary urbanites felt was to their 'streets' and 'fields', and then to their districts, such as Burley, and only lastly to Leeds as a whole.[167] The social topography of early modern towns and cities was structured by social zones that separated richer from poorer areas; yet, these nonetheless existed alongside one another in close proximity.

The ordering of the streetscape was fundamental to this experience of the city. In his study of Worcester, Alan Dyer noted: 'The broad trend of social zoning was for the rich to live along the main commercial streets as close to the centre of the city as possible.'[168] Such social zones did not correspond neatly to parochial boundaries. Once an individual moved away from the main street, as Jeremy Boulton has demonstrated for Southwark, she or he encountered poorer households – yet these households lay within the boundaries of parishes that still included the rich

---

[163] D. Cressy, 'Occupations, Migration and Literacy in East London, 1580–1640', *Local Population Studies*, 5 (1970), 58.
[164] L. Gowing, *Domestic Dangers: Women, Words and Sex in Early Modern London* (Oxford, 1996), 21.
[165] TNA, E134/31Eliz/East15. For parish identities in Worcester, see Dyer, *The City of Worcester*, 347–8.
[166] Durham Cathedral Library, Allan 8 (8).    [167] BIA, CP.H. 1296.
[168] Dyer, *The City of Worcester*, 177–8.

households located on the main road. Boulton observes of early seventeenth-century Southwark: 'The High Street was dominated by the wealthier inhabitants. Of the 192 households located on the High Street, 108 (56.3%) were subsidy payers and 57 (29.7%) were poor-rate payers. Only 14% of the householders on the High Street were not rated for either tax.'[169] Other than as regards suburbs subject to rapid expansion (such as the Sandgate district of Newcastle upon Tyne, which was a fundamentally proletarian area, or the eastern and northern suburbs of London which were noted for their poverty), longer-established parish communities included both rich and poor.[170]

Just like in rural parishes, people who dwelt in the same street in Elizabethan Norwich addressed one as 'neighbour'.[171] Within the streetscape of that great city, generations seem to have been brought up in the same claustrophobic worlds of the courtyards that remained a defining part of the city's landscape until the mid-twentieth century.[172] Norwich parishes were felt to have their own distinct identities and religious traditions. In 1561, for example, inhabitants of the nearby parishes of St Peter Parmentergate and St Andrews were caught up in an argument about their differing responses to the reintroduction of Protestantism: while riding to Walsingham market, Lawrence Hodgen and a man called Blome fell to argument. Hodgen asked his fellow traveller, 'Ys your perke [i.e., rood screen] downe in St Andrewes?', to which Blome answered, '[Y]ea and so shall yor in St Peters shortly; as for that ... I have nothing to do neyther in the pluckinge it downe nor setting it up. Well sayd Hodgen you have a sight of Rebellyus harts in that p[ar]isshe ... yet notwth standing ... yt shall downe in yor p[ar]isshe as well in or p[ar]isshe.'[173] Just like in London,

[169] Boulton, *Neighbourhood and Society*, 175.
[170] This pattern has long been recognized; yet the contemporary *sense* of social zoning has received less attention than it deserves.
[171] NRO, NCR, 12A/1 (c), fols. 18r-19v. For other references to this mode of address, see HALS, 21M65/C3/5, pp. 48, 301; Wilkinson (ed.), *Chichester Archdeaconry Depositions*, 24; Anon., *A Knacke to Knowe a Knave*, lines 1039-41; W. Shakespeare, *Much Ado about Nothing*, act III, scene 3, lines 7, 1329, 1334 and act III, scene 5, line 1610; *Henry IV, Pt 1*, act II, scene 1, line 683 and act II, scene 2, line 819; *Henry IV, Pt. 2*, act II, scene 1, line 1333; *Henry VI, Part 2*, act II, scene 3, line 1110; *Richard III*, act II, scene 3, lines 1431, 1438; *The Taming of the Shrew*, act II, scene 1, lines 880-1, 917, 1183, 1252; BL, Harl Ms 207, fols. 3v, 7r, 9v, 10v, 11r; F. O. Mann (ed.), *The Works of Thomas Deloney* (Oxford, 1912), 260-1.
[172] The Norwich courts deserve closer analysis; little survives of them today, other than as place-names. Many were destroyed in wartime bombing and the rest in mid-twentieth-century slum clearance programmes. On life in London alleyways and courtyards, see Laura Gowing's ground-breaking piece: L. Gowing, '"The Freedom of the Streets": Women and Social Space, 1560-1640', in P. Griffiths and M. S. R. Jenner (eds.), *Londinopolis: Essays in the Cultural and Social History of Early Modern London* (Manchester, 2000), 130-51.
[173] NRO, NCR, 12A/1 (c), fol. 1v.

Norwich parishes were very small. Walking briskly through a major thoroughfare such as St Benedicts Street, a person could, within two or three minutes, pass through two or three parishes. Yet the boundaries between these small worlds were intensely felt and carefully guarded. The corner of a building, an outhouse or a small patch of garden might mark out a parish boundary.[174] There were also shared spaces: the wide city field of Gildencroft, in which families pastured their cattle and where young men played football, lay at the intersection of the three poor northern parishes of St Augustine's, St Martin's and St Clements at the Bridge and it had its own distinct tithing customs.[175] Then there were the city's fields and commons. On the west side of Norwich lay grounds where poor people pastured animals and gleaned after the harvest. To the north and east lay the great expanse of Mousehold Heath. Here, too, the city's poor pastured their cows, dug for lime and collected fuel.[176]

Urban people identified closely with their parish.[177] Just like in rural communities, the city parish was imagined as possessing a 'common voice'.[178] Longevity of residence was one guarantee of status as a neighbour: the Newcastle man John Hopert told the Durham consistory court in the 1560s that he had known contending parties in a suit 'a Longe tyme beinge neighbors'.[179] In the Elvet district of Durham, officeholding and the payment of dues allowed one to 'belong to good Neighbourhood' and entitled them to pasture rights on the adjacent common. Neighbourliness in that district extended to the poor: the 1610 orders included an injunction that

if any frend or well disposed p[er]son will lend a poor man or woman a horse to lead there winter coals they having none of theire owne nor theire full stinte on the common that the said horse shall be suffered to goe one month on our common and likewise for a cow to such as have none of there owne so long as she giveth the p[ar]tie milck and noe longer the same being done upon a necessitie and without fraud or guile.[180]

---

[174] Stone and Cozens-Hardy (eds.), *Norwich Consistory Court Depositions*, no. 412.

[175] Ibid., nos. 115, 410.

[176] The long history of Mousehold Heath deserves a book-length study. For the early modern period, see Nicola Whyte's brilliant essay: N. Whyte, 'Remembering Mousehold Heath', in C. J. Griffin and B. McDonagh (eds.), *Remembering Protest in Britain since 1500: Memory, Materiality and the Landscape* (Basingstoke, 2018), 25–52. For the later period, see N. MacMaster, 'The Battle for Mousehold Heath, 1857–1884: "Popular Politics" and the Victorian Public Park', *P&P*, 127 (1990), 117–54.

[177] See F. Williamson, *Social Relations and Urban Space: Norwich, 1600–1700* (Woodbridge, 2014), 57–62.

[178] D. M. Palliser, 'Civic Mentality and the Environment in Tudor York', *Northern History*, 18, 1 (1982), 107.

[179] DUL, DDR/EJ/CCD/1/2, fol. 12v.    [180] Durham Cathedral Library, Allan 8 (8).

Economics, then, underpinned urban neighbourliness. Just like in Jacobean Elvet, so also in Jacobean Southwark, trading relations were enmeshed in a closely felt sense of urban belonging. One Southwark tailor complained in 1624 that, following a dispute with his employer, he had been

enforced to ... depart from his said house and liberty albeit to his utter undoing in driving your said subject from amongst all his acquaintance and custom of trade into a strange unknown place where he was and yet is lost of all acquaintance and friends, and hath thereby lost all his custom of work to his utter overthrow and decay of his trade and maintenance.[181]

So, this man's 'custom of work' – that is, his trading links – depended upon having close 'acquaintance and friends' nearby.

There were many ways of celebrating urban neighbourliness. Parishioners of pre-Reformation St Margaret Pattens (London) had a cup engraved on the outside with the message 'Of Gods hand blessed be he that taketh this cup and drinketh to me' and on the inside with 'God that sitteth in Trinity, send us peace and unity'.[182] Another way of celebrating social unity took the form of downing a few pots of ale with one's neighbours while gathered around the elemental flames of a bonfire: in Tudor Warwick, money was bequeathed to allow the 'neyhboures of the other thre[e] bonfyres' within one of the wards of the city 'to make merry withall'.[183] Eating and drinking together could reinstate broken bonds. Members of London craft guilds who had fallen out were some-times required by the company masters to 'supe together lyke neyghbours and fryndes'.[184] Something similar was at work in the memories of John Stow. When he looked back on the summer feasts of his London youth in the 1530s, he remembered how

there were usually made Bonefeirs in the streetes, every man bestowing wood or labour towards them: the wealthier sort also before their doors ... would set out Tables ... furnished with sweete breade, and good drinke, and on the Festivall dayes with meates and drinks plentifully, whereunto they would invite their neighbours and passangers also to sit, and bee merrie with them in great famil-iaritie, praysing God for his benefites bestowed on them. These were called Bonefiers as well as food amitie amongst neighbours that, being before at

[181] J. Boulton, 'Neighbourhood Migration in Early Modern London', in P. Clark and D. Souden (eds.), *Migration and Society in Early Modern England* (London, 1987), 135.

[182] Brigden, 'Religion and Social Obligation', 72.

[183] C. Phythian Adams, 'Ceremony and the Citizen: The Communal Year at Coventry, 1450–1750', in P. Clark and P. Slack (eds.), *Crisis and Order in English Towns, 1500–1700: Essays in Urban History* (London, 1972), 65–6.

[184] J. Bishop, 'Speech and Sociability: The Regulation of Language in the Livery Companies of Early Modern London', in J. Colson and A. van Steensel (eds.), *Cities and Solidarities: Urban Communities in Pre-modern Europe* (London, 2017), 219.

controversie, were there by the labour of others, reconciled, and made of bitter
enemies, loving friendes.[185]

In 1558, the York authorities observed that the parish feasts had a utility,
explaining that 'metyng of neighburghes at the sayd fests and dynars and
there makyng mery togiders was a good occasion of contyneweyng and
renewing of amytie and neighburghly love one with another'.[186]
Occupational identity also provided a way in which people might ground
their sense of collective belonging. The Merchant's Company of
Newcastle decreed that it would be considered 'most godly and most
loving neyghberhed' to attend all marriages and burials of other members
of the company, as well as their children and servants.[187]

    In a small city like Durham, settled inhabitants often knew one another
well. Hugo Ford explained that 'he hathe knowen george wilkynson and
his wife synce they were yong children for they were both born in saynt
oswald p[ar]ishe'. This long association with the parish hadn't prevented
Mistress Wilkinson from denouncing one of her neighbours as a whore; in
answer she had been called a whore and a thief.[188] In such a small, densely
settled city, just like in villages, people worried about the 'comon fame'
that attached to their name.[189] Parish loyalties mattered in Durham. In
1575, it was reported that there had long been a feud between the parishes
of St Oswald's and St Margaret's. The sixty-year-old yeoman Thomas
Wayman explained the roots of this animosity. He told the consistory
court that he had been born in St Margaret's parish and had lived there all
his life save for six months when he moved to St Oswald's. Wayman
described the feud as follows: back in the 1520s, his father had been
one of the keepers of the keys of a chest in St Oswald's church that
contained the jewels of that church and for which St Margaret's also
retained a key. Upon the occasion of a marriage, the parishioners of St
Oswald's had their key ready to open the chest, but they didn't have the
key held by his father on behalf of St Margaret's and so they broke open
the lock, 'whereupon grew a groudge, and haith contynewed ever sence
bytwixt the said parishes'.[190] A seemingly trivial matter in itself, the story
of the conflict between the two parishes was embedded in the local
memory of the city and by 1575 had become part of its cultural fabric.

    We might expect a small city like Durham to retain a strong sense of
parochial identification. But in big conurbations like Newcastle upon

[185] Brigden, 'Religion and Social Obligation', 73.
[186] A. Raine (ed.), York Civic Records, V, YASRS, 110 (York, 1944), 17.
[187] Tomlinson, Life in Northumberland, 64.    [188] DUL, DDR/EJ/CCD/1/2, fol. 18v.
[189] DUL, DDR/EJ/CCD/1/2, 209v.
[190] Raine, J. (ed.), Depositions . . . from the Courts of Durham, 279–80.

Tyne, for all its constantly energetic dynamics, there was also room for neighbourliness. That a Scotswoman who settled in the city 'had nether frend nor kyn' was a matter of comment amongst her neighbours.[191] There was a strong sense of the value of residential proximities in shaping communal relations: in 1562, Margaret Resh singled out Agnes Gawen as an important figure in her life. As she told the consistory court, 'she saith she is her doore neighbor'.[192] The assumption was that a 'doore neighbour' would know one's doings, would be in the street gossiping and in and out of one's own home. 'Doore neighbours' would know one another's intimate affairs. A year later, the weaver John Pattenson expressed his surprise at hearing defamatory speech concerning young William Richardson: he 'mervaled moch att that sodden talk, for although he was the next neighbor he hard of no such bifore that tyme'. Mistress Anderson was clear about her regard for William Richardson, calling him 'cosyn and moved him to cast his love to . . . Margaret Joycy, and required [John Pattenson] to drink a pott of ale and bere of ther communing, and so he did . . . They dranke to gather and aither said th[ey] loved [the] other well.'[193]

Just like in London, so in Newcastle, there were families that had lived in the same neighbourhood for one generation after another. In the 1570s, the sixty-year-old William Michaelson described himself as a 'neighbor borne & yett dwellinge' next to a neighbour caught up in a legal case, who had been born in that house, 'w[hi]ch this ex[aminan]t knowe verye well & all his brethren and sisters being the children of Richard Robson w[hi]ch dwelte in the said towne nigh a place caulde the cowpoint'. The blacksmith Joseph Browne also knew the parties in the action, 'longe being all children togyther & borne in Saint Andrew p[ar]ish in newcastell'; he knew this 'for this ex[aminant] beinge a neighbor childe borne wthin fyve houses' of the litigants had grown up with them. All of this was well known 'throughout the towne of newcastell'.[194]

Part of the experience of urban living was the constant movement of population. As one London parson observed, 'the most part of the parish changeth as I by experience know, some goinge and some comminge'.[195] A study of Elizabethan Cambridge points to very high levels of population turnover, with migrants attracted from across the whole country.[196] Yet many migrants to urban centres had some kin or friends upon whom they could rely to help them set themselves up. Peter Clark has shown that of a sample of female migrants to London in the period 1565–1644, some

---

[191] Ibid., 66.  [192] Ibid., 70.  [193] Ibid., 78.  [194] DUL, DDR/EJ/CCD/1/2, fol. 174r.
[195] L. Stone, 'Social Mobility in England, 1500–1700', P&P, 33 (1964), 31.
[196] M. Siraut, 'Physical Mobility in Elizabethan Cambridge', Local Population Studies, 27 (1981), 65–70.

37 per cent had kin in the capital and more than a fifth were living with relatives. The result was that kinship links could, for many young Londoners, be a key way in which they developed a place in the capital.[197] Migrants to other great cities might be able to make the expectation of receiving some welcome. Ilana Krausman Ben-Amos cites one migrant to Southampton who, on presenting recommendations from his neighbours back home, was provided with food and clothing.[198]

In any case, anthropological studies suggest that rapid population turn-over does not always equate to social anomie. One contemporary study of village society in the North of Ireland, for example, has found that stable, wealthier families interact with one another less frequently than do transient labouring households. These poorer neighbours need one another more than do their richer, landed employers. One poorer infor-mant said that good neighbourhood was an economic necessity: 'You could not afford to fall out with your neighbours … because you could never be certain that tomorrow you would not need their assistance.'[199] Importantly, urban authorities assumed that, within their immediate local-ities, aldermen and constables would be able to distinguish insiders from outsiders. And so, in 1540, the Chester authorities stated that due to the

greate number and multitude of valiant idell p[er]sons and vacabonds wch be stronge and able to serve and Labor for ther livinges and yet daylye go on beggynge wtin the same Citie so that the pore impotent & indegent people inhabitinge wthin the same citie & having no other meanes to get their lyvinges but onelye be the charytable Allmys of good Cristen people dayly want & be destitute of the Same to the greate displeasure of allmightye god and contrarye to good conscience[,]

they had decided to compile a register of all the needy beggars in each ward. Such needy folk were licensed to beg in their own ward but in no other, 'ther names to be written in a byll & set upp in every mans house w[i]t[h]in ev[er]y warde for knowledge to whome they shall gevether allmys and to no other'.[200] If the evidence from Henrician Chester suggests that the urban poor were not an amorphous, anonymous mass, so that from Jacobean Brighton paints a similar picture. Here, in 1618, the governing council

---

[197] P. Clark, 'Migrants in the City: The Process of Social Adaptation in English Towns, 1500–1800', in P. Clark and D. Souden (eds.), *Migration and Society in Early Modern England* (London, 1987), 272.
[198] I. Krausman Ben-Amos, '"Good Works" and Social Ties: Helping the Migrant Poor in Early Modern England', in M. C. McClendon, J. P. Ward and M. Macdonald (eds.), *Protestant Identities: Religion, Society and Self-Fashioning in Post-Reformation England* (Stanford, CA, 1999), 131.
[199] A. Buckley, 'Neighbourliness: Myth and History', *Oral History*, 11, 1 (1983), 44–51.
[200] CRO, ZAB/1, fol. 60r-v.

known as the Twelve, assigned to themselves 'some streete or circuit, neare to his dwelling house, over which he ... [has] the keepinge of good order'.[201]

Differences between insider and outsider were closely observed in many urban communities. There was often a sharp delineation between city folk and rural outsiders. Deponents to the Norwich Court of Mayoralty often drew a distinction between urbanites and the 'men of the contrith'. Likewise, in 1520, the Leicester authorities ordered that 'all bakers off the cuntre[y] that bryng bred to sell make goode bred and holsom for mans body, and weygh after the [as]syse, and that no baker off [th]e contre[y]bring in no maner off bred into [th]e towne bot on the market days'.[202]

## 'A Kynde of Murdering My Neighbor': Disputes and Their Settlement

Like all social norms, neighbourly values were often most clearly revealed in their breach. This was true of the ways in which disputes were settled, which had a ritualistic cast, whereby the values of neighbourliness were restated, reasserted and celebrated. After John Ashby, minister of Aschurch (Gloucestershire), got snarled up in disputes with his neighbours in 1596, he was instructed by the High Commission to

preache a s[er]mon of Charitye and love to be houlden amongst neighbours and the [said] ashbye in full performance of reconciliasion betweene hi[m] and his p[ar]ishioners taking with hi[m] two honest men of the said parish w[i]t[h]in these five dayes shall goe to three or fower of his greatest adv[er]saryes ... and shall desire theyre good willes and theyre frendshepes and shall p[ro]mise by gods grace he will geve the[m] noe justie cause of offence hereafter.

If Ashby found any of his neighbors unwilling to reconcile with him, he was instructed to refer them to the diocesan court. Just to make sure that the social wounds were properly bound, after seeing to the High Commission's instructions, Ashby was to see that four of the 'sufficient and honest' men of the parish were to certify that he had done as he had been ordered.[203] In this way, a breach was sealed.

Writing in the early 1560s, Sir Thomas Smith felt that increased litigiousness was one of the forces that was pulling English society apart.

[201] E. Turner, 'The Early History of Brighton, as Illustrated by the "Customs of the Ancient Fishermen of the Town"', *Sussex Archaeological Collections*, 2 (1849), 48.

[202] Bateson (ed.), *Records of the Borough of Leicester*, 15.

[203] J. Hitchcock, 'A Decree of the High Commission, 1596', *Transactions of the Bristol and Gloucestershire Archaeological Society*, 88 (1969), 216–17.

The preferred alternative, he felt, was for disputes to be settled within the community. Smith suggested that unlike those who were 'but idle, whot heads, busie bodies, and troublesome men in the common wealth' who preferred to take cases to court, '[g]ood labourers and quiet men could bee content to ende their matters at home by judgement of their neighbours and kinsfolke without spending so their money upon procurers and advocates whom we call attornies'.[204]

Where field boundaries lay, where one parish abutted onto another or in the densely packed cities where one household's back fence extended into someone else's courtyard could all be interpreted as breaches of neighbourliness. In such struggles, local knowledge held by older people was often called upon. And so, in 1566, in Edale (Derbyshire), the yeoman Raphe Barber explained that, some thirteen years earlier, there had been disagreement amongst neighbours over access to their land 'whereupon they submitted them selves to the arbiterment of this deponent and other there neighbours who by there consent ordered that ev[er]y of them sh[o]uld use his severall waies over the sev[er]all grounds of the other according to suche order as they then appointed w[hi]ch was other wise then before had be[e]n used'.[205] Neighbours looked to one another to find pragmatic resolutions to disruptive local struggles. No one, it seemed, wanted their village to divide over questions of whose backyard lay over whose garden or where a field strayed onto the common. Hence, in 1558, in the course of a dispute over the will of a villager in Bidston (Cheshire), neighbours tried to settle the matter through local arbitration. A sixty-year-old explained how he had been 'desired as a neybor' to help achieve a settlement. In the end, an agreement was reached by 'iiij.or indifferent men', meeting in the parish church, who were 'sworne by the hollie evangelist' to find a neighbourly settlement.[206] Propinquity underwrote many practices of dispute settlement. But nearness could create problems all of its own. According to John Saltmash in 1639: 'When you observe there will be any discord or jarring in your neighbourhood, the best remedy is to remove: if your nearnesse bee as it were incompatible with the other, yet first looke well with what conveniency it may bee done, and doe not take your leave at one place till you be secured by another.'[207]

[204] T. Smith, *De Republica Anglorum: The Maner of Governement or Policie of the Realme of England* (London, 1583), 53–4.

[205] TNA, DL4/8/4.

[206] E. K. M. Jarman (ed.), *Justice and Conciliation in a Tudor Church Court: Depositions from EDC 2/6, Deposition Book of the Consistory Court of Chester, September 1558–March 1559*, Record Society of Lancashire and Cheshire, 146 (Bristol, 2012), 38–9.

[207] J. Saltmarsh, *The Practice of Policie in a Christian Life* (London, 1639), 15.

Jim Sharpe's groundbreaking study of dispute resolution cites a sequence of cases from the York consistory court that show gentlemen and ministers adjudicating in disputes. One Pontefract gentleman, addressing the parish minister, told him that 'heare is a matter between your neighbour Browne and Christ[ofer] Hurst... I wold yow and I might make them frendes ...[Y]ow and I will take this matter upon us & make them frendes.'[208] Where neighbours could not find a way of burying an argument, they might appeal to the local gentry. In his widely read textbook for magistrates, *Eirenarcha*, William Lambarde wrote that the Justice of the Peace should 'occupie himself ... in pacifying the suits and controversies, that do arise amongst his neighbors'. He should act as a 'Compounder, as a Commissioner of the Peace: and I thinke him so much the meter to step in betwixt those that bee at variance, as (by reason of his learning, wisedome, authoritie & wealth) he is like to prevaile more by his mediation and intreatie, then is another man'.[209] Humfrey Braham wrote in 1568 that, rather than spending his time hunting and feasting, the true gentleman but should develop a solid knowledge of the law. Moreover, 'for the better furtherance of their naighboures['] just causes', Braham recommended that the ideal gentlemen should 'geve them good counsel fre[e]ly [and] ... make an ende of debates and strives'.[210] In 1509, Edmund Dudley had been of a similar opinion: he wrote that the nobility and gentry should

be gentle and courteous in Wordes and deedes, both sobre and honest in demeanour and countenaunce; Be trew and stedfast in all wordes to the riche and pore, and be the makers of endes and lovedaies, charitable, bytwene neighbors and neighebors, frindes and frindes; Be the helpers and the relevers of poore tenantes, and also be the maynteynors and supporters of all poore folks in godes causes and matters.[211]

So, in 1571, we find the Lancashire gentleman John Towneley writing to his fellow esquire William Farington to request that he settle a quarrel between two local men who were at odds and who said that 'they are contented to stande to any soche order as two or fower men shall make amongst them'. However, the conflict had become so embedded in the local fabric that it 'cannot be decyded by ordre of neiybures'.[212]

In some contexts, there might be an institutional impulse that pushed magistrates to settle neighbourly disputes. Thus, the magistrates of

---

[208] Sharpe, 'Such Disagreement betwyx Neighbours', 175.
[209] W. Lambard, *Eirenarcha: or Of the Office of the Justices of the Peace* (London, 1599), 10.
[210] Braham, *The Institution of a Gentleman*, sig. C.3r.
[211] D. M. Brodie (ed.), *The Tree of Commonwealth: A Treatise Written by Edmund Dudley* (Cambridge, 1948), 45.
[212] S. M. Farington (ed.), *The Farington Papers*, Chetham Society, 39 (Manchester, 1856), 127.

Elizabethan Norfolk ordered that, following their general sessions, they would take dinner together, during which village constables were to present difficult cases in their communities, '[a]nd if besides all this, ther be anye private controversies between pore neighbours, wherof the hundred had wonte to be full, they bestowe the rest of the day in intreatinge them to peace one with another by accorde betweene themselves or by arbytrament of ther nearest neighbours'.[213]

The lesser gentleman Robert Furse instructed his children to 'geve blameless cownsell to your nyghebures, have a grete desire wylle and pleasure to make pease, concodres and agrementes between your nyghebures when anye of them be yn varyence, for so shalte thow be called the chylde of god'.[214] The absence of a gentry family that could settle disputes was felt deeply: in early sixteenth-century Morebath (Devon), when conflicts between neighbours occurred, it was to the Sydenhams across the border in Somerset that the parishioners turned to settle their differences.[215] In their capacity as magistrates, greater gentry might also be drawn into the settlement of disputes. In 1599, for example, concerning the 'variance & controv[er]sie between Alexand[e]r Firth and John Turner of Hudd[e]rsfield whereof ther is great unkyndnes fallen & misdemeanors committed to th[e] end her ma[jes]t[ie]s peace may be the better p[re]served and tranquilitie between them made', the West Riding magistracy ordered that the dispute be settled and arbitrators appointed who 'shall make a final ende of all controv[er]sies'.[216]

In a subtle, gentle manner, dispute settlement therefore reinforced the authority of local elites.[217] All too often, though, the gentry seemed far away from the world of the village. Disputes might then appear before the manor court, which was more vigorous in providing local justice than has often been assumed. Edward Coke, for example, observed that leets were established 'for the ease of the people ... [so that they] should have ... justice done unto them at their own doors without any charge or loss of time'.[218] Courts leet sometimes persuaded leading neighbours to reconcile disputes: Walter King observes that '[o]ftentimes, neighbors were the

---

[213] A. H. Smith, 'Justices at Work in Elizabethan Norfolk', *Norfolk Archaeology*, 34, 2 (1967), 84.

[214] Travers (ed.), *Robert Furse*, 17.    [215] Duffy, *The Voices of Morebath*, 8.

[216] J. Lister (ed.), *West Riding Sessions Rolls, 1597/8–1602*, YASRS, 3 (Worksop, 1888), 139.

[217] For an example, see Ingram, 'Communities and Courts', 126.

[218] W. J. King, 'Early Stuart Courts Leet: Still Needful and Useful', *Histoire Sociale/Social History*, 23, 46 (1990), 290. For the continuing vigour of courts leet, see B. Waddell, 'Governing England through the Manor Courts, c.1550–1850', *Historical Journal*, 55, 2 (2012), 279–31; C. Harrison, 'Manor Courts and the Governance of Tudor England', in C. W. Brooks and M. Lobban (eds.), *Communities and Courts in Britain, 1150–1900* (London, 1997), 43–60.

first to attempt to resolve disputes, sometimes at the request of leet officials'. He provides the examples of how the friends of Edward Stockley and Peter Kenwrick mediated a 'difference of hedgement' and how the friends of John Webster and William Lyon settled a dispute over a watercourse.[219] Small towns such as Burford (Oxfordshire) issued ordinances that were designed to settle neighbourly differences before they came to the law courts. In 1605, the Burford authorities ordered that were any disagreements to arise within the town, the 'Aldermen and Stewarde with other of their bretheren shall or maye make a brotherly concorde and agreement betweene them by the treasonable conformytyes of the said partyes'.[220] Likewise, in 1577, it was recorded by the authorities of Beverley (Yorkshire) that Robert Bell and four others, arbitrators in the dispute between William Allanson and Robert Pynder, had settled the dispute between them, noting that they should set aside all 'evell will and mallyce' and henceforth should be 'lovers and frends', and if either of them renewed their quarrel, they should be fined five pounds.[221] In this way, painful struggles within the intimate world of the small market town might be brought to an end.

Where courts leet or town councils were not engaged in neighbourly differences, and where the gentry seemed too distant from village life, it often fell to the wealthier landholders – the yeomanry – to resolve disputes. The preacher of an assize sermon at Norwich in 1619 observed that many of the disputes that found their way before the courts were sufficient to be settled through local arbitration, by 'a Common Yeoman' deciding the matter sitting 'in his chaire at home'.[222] Sometimes, disputes might be settled in the charged site of the parish church. An argument between two Yorkshire folk, Margaret Jackson and Edward Norrison, concerning Jackson's sexual reputation, was, at least initially, settled in 1584 by 'the ordering and arbitremente of foure of there honeste neighboures who all met in egton church or chapple upon all soules day last paste for the endinge of the said matter'.[223]

Such occasions might be deemed worthy of register within the local record of village affairs. The Staffordshire yeoman Simon Rider recorded in his commonplace book that, in 1592, he settled a controversy between two argumentative neighbours whom he persuaded to settle 'all matters whatsoever betweene them depending or being from the beginning of the world till that date'. Another settlement provided that 'all suits,

[219] King, 'Early Stuart Courts Leet', 293–4.    [220] HMC, *Various Collections*, *I*, 36.

[221] J. Dennett (ed.), *Beverley Borough Records, 1575–1821*, YASRS, 84 (Wakefield, 1933), 6.

[222] S. Garey, *A Manuall for Magistrates: or A Lantern for Lawyers: A Sermon Preached before Judges and Justices at Norwich Assizes, 1619* (London, 1623), 1.

[223] BIA, CP. G/2192.

controversies, debts and demands between them ... should cease and be void & so to be lovers and friends without any money giving either to the other'. In some cases, settlements were concluded with the drinking of beer and shaking of hands. In such ways, neighbourhood was made real.[224]

The convivial site of the alehouse was one place at which neighbours might bury their differences. Following the 'earneste intreatie of neighbours and freendes', a defamation suit between two Tudor Londoners was settled in an alehouse.[225] Friends, family and neighbours gathered at meals or drinkings to see disputants settle their conflicts: in 1621, one such drinking was opened with a former disputant calling out, 'I drincke to you and all the malice or hatred I beare to you I putt into this glasse.'[226] Alcohol helped to ease enmities, renewing social bonds.[227] In this way, neighbourhood was made real. To give one example: in 1639, the Cambridgeshire gentleman Thomas Castell was insulted at a cudgels match by William Crispe, 'an ordinary country fellow'. Witnesses explained to the High Court of Chivalry that 'there being a feast or wake kept ... and a great concourse of people from severall parishes meeting together, there was playing of cudgells (as is usuall at such feasts) and those which were of the severall parishes of Cambridge held up the bucklers or hilts against all comers out of the Isle of Ely where Mr Castle dwells'. Crispe objected to Castell's judgment over the match, 'calling Mr Castle, Base, cowardly fellowe, and that he was a better man or better gentleman than Mr Castle'. On the following day, Castell wrote to the minister of Crispe's parish asking him to settle the feud,

whereupon Crispe, ... did come and submitte himselfe in manner and forme following ... saying, Mr Castle for the wordes and language I gave you yesterday I am heartily sorry, and confess that it was unmanerly spoken, and I pray remitt it. And Mr Castle therupon replied and said it was sufficient, or he was satisfied with Crispe his acknowledgement and submission, and then and there tooke a glasse of beere and dranck to Crispe in a very courteous and friendly manner.[228]

London companies and guilds took it upon themselves to resolve disputes amongst their members. Similar practices were followed by guilds in smaller urban centres. The ordinances of the Merchants and Mercers of Beverley that were drawn up in 1596 instituted a system of arbitration for disputes amongst its members.[229] Just as in villages, dispute settlement

[224] Campbell, *The English Yeoman*, 385.    [225] Archer, *The Pursuit of Stability*, 80.
[226] Gowing, *Domestic Dangers*, 136.
[227] See, for instance, DUL, DDR/EJ/CCD/1/6, fol. 26r.
[228] HCCO: 99, *Castell* v. *Crispe*.
[229] Dennett (ed.), *Beverley Borough Records*, 53. The Drapers Company made a similar order in 1596. See ibid., 60.

often involved the public consumption of ale. Stephen Rappaport notes that '[s]haking hands in court, drinking together, these and other public demonstrations of good will were ordered frequently by [company] assistants when interpersonal disputes were resolved' and that they were 'intended to publicise and thus to cement the settlement or perhaps to warn disputants against further trouble'.[230]

Collective drinking eased the settlement of the struggle between Bartram Mytforde of the Durham district of Elvet and his opponent Charles Shawe, who had been required to make a public confession concerning defamatory words regarding Mytforde. Their neighbour Richard Hutcheson drew the men together and, '[a]fter certain unquiet words caste betwixt the parties at their meatinge', they were 'pacified . . . and perswayded . . . to be frendes, and drincke togyther, as they dyd [at] length, shaking merilye hands togyther'. Charles Shawe said that 'nowe that we be frends and lovers, yf Bartram have any matter against me, let hym trye the lawe . . . [H]e [Richard Hutcheson] was a mover thereof, as a neighbour.'[231] The implication was clear: having settled the conflict over a pint, were the conflict to flare up once again, it would be before the law. And, indeed, this is what happened: the struggle between Mytforde and Shawe eventually found its way before the Durham consistory court. Similarly, after Margaret Jackson of Whitby (Yorkshire) was accused of being a whore, she and her accuser sat down and 'did drynke th[e] one to th[e] other vereie frendlye and familiarlye and did us beare and behave theme selves at the said dynner as loving neighboures and frends',[232] but the settlement broke down and the parties found themselves before the York consistory court.

Christian social ideals informed much of the rhetoric of neighbourliness and charity. After there were harsh words between Robert Bishoppe and Agnes Daniell of Selsey (Sussex) in 1603, the minister and the churchwarden interceded, explaining that they 'wished Robert Bishoppe and Agnes Daniell to be at unity with one another and live together like neighbours, in so much that both were content to remit and forgive all offences and speech'; the disputants then made up, saying 'that they did forgive one another and that hereafter they would become good friends and neighbours'. The minister and the churchwarden, in settling the dispute, 'had only respect unto the Christian reconciliation of Robert Bishoppe and Agnes Daniel and to bring both into Christian charity'.[233] In 1578, a sense of neighbourly reciprocities muted a fierce feud between

---

[230] S. Rappaport, *Worlds within Worlds: Structures of Life in Sixteenth-Century London* (Cambridge, 1989), 204, 209.

[231] Raine, J. (ed.), *Depositions . . . from the Courts of Durham*, 206.    [232] BIA, CP. G/2192.

[233] Wilkinson (ed.), *Chichester Archdeaconry Depositions*, 7–9.

an older woman and her daughter-in-law. Emma Holdway of Ashermersworth (Hampshire) had been at words with her daughter-in-law, Elizabeth, saying that Elizabeth caused the death of Emma's son. The minister of the parish intervened and 'thereupo[n] the sayde Em[ma] desiered the sayde Elizabeth if she had offended her to forgive her saying God forgive us all. And the said Elizabeth asked her forgiveness like wise[.] And soe they were then made frends.'[234]

Easter communion – when the whole parish would be expected to attend service – represented *the* key moment in the celebration of social unity. Arnold Hunt observes:

If a dispute could not be settled, then people would often stay away from communion. Visitation records are full of cases like that of Christopher Boreman of South Newton (Oxfordshire), presented in 1584 for not receiving communion at Easter, who explained that 'ther was some controversie in lawe betwene this respondent and two other of his neighboures, and by that meanes he was not in perfyct love and charitie'.[235]

Then there were those moments of dispute settlement that would be regarded as of sufficient importance to find their way into the parish register. In April 1568, the parish clerk recorded how 'in the presence of the hole paryshe of Twycknam was agreement made betwixt Mr Packer and his wyffe, and Hewe Rytte and Sicylye Daye upon the aforesaid Mr Packer'. A week later, the same clerk noted that Thomas Whytt and James Herne 'have consented that whosoever geveth occasion of the breaking of Christian love and charity betwixt them, to forfeit to the poor of the paryshe three shillings and four-pence, being dewlye proved'.[236]

These things seared themselves into the soul. The early Tudor Londoner Richard Allington 'never wente to [the] church . . . bycaus' as he put it 'I dyd condeme my consyence for sufferynge me to commite suche abominable usery and other most detestable synnes'.[237] Within the public world of the village or the street, people felt it their duty to settle disputes between husband and wife. In Elizabethan Newcastle, it was 'comonly reported amongste hir neighbors' that Isabel Walker had left her husband and set off for Darlington. The collapse of the Walker household was no private matter. When Isabel eventually came home, William Walker 'by intreaty of neighbours was content to take hir [a]gain' as his wife. Marital violence was part of the story – one neighbour exlained that

---

[234] HALS, 21M65/C3/8, p. 25.
[235] A. Hunt, 'The Lord's Supper in Early Modern England', *P&P*, 161 (1998), 48.
[236] T. F. Thistleton-Dyer, *Old English Social Life as Told by the Parish Registers* (London, 1898), 179–80.
[237] Brigden, 'Religion and Social Obligation', 79.

'he thinketh th[a]t w[i]l[liam] walker ys morr lyke to beat Isabel his wyff then she the said will[ia]m'. But Isabel also had some violent thoughts about her husband; when two neighbours (one a gentleman) tried to reconcile them, Isabel declared 'that rather then shee wolde aske hym the said w[i]l[liam] foregiveness she had rather see this throte cutt'.[238]

One of the expectations placed on ministers was that they would settle parish disputes.[239] This was a commonly shared assumption across western Christendom.[240] The parishioners of Cropredy and Borton (Oxfordshire) may well have felt themselves to be fortunate in their minister: in 1619, the churchwardens reported that '[o]ur minister ys knowen to be a modest man in all things and maker of peace not cawsinge dissension'.[241] Settling quarrels reinforced Christian values of amity and neighbourhood. In 1636, for instance, John Hill and John Taylor of Stratford Tony (Wiltshire) signed an agreement to end all controversies between them, this having been negotiated by the minister; the men explained that 'they heartily forgive each other all wrongful passages'.[242] So was Christian amity restored in one village.

Sometimes, the minister was assisted by his wife in settling parish disputes – especially where they involved disputes within the household. In 1589, for example, the Norfolk woman Anne Felmingham had been subject to consistent, extreme violence by her husband, to such an extent that she sought a separation. The matter came before the parish minister and his wife, who tried to arrive at a settlement, the minister telling Thomas Felmingham that he should 'live quietly with his said wife, or else to put her away'.[243] Success in such matters reflected well upon the clergy. The Sussex clergyman James Pellett was said by one of his flock in 1605 to be 'a peacemaker and persuader of his neighbours over whom he hath charge to love and quietness'.[244] In 1564, the vestry of St Mary Magdalen Milk Street in London established the practice of holding

---

[238] DUL, DDR/EJ/CCD/1/2, fols. 230v, 236r.

[239] For examples, see Emmison, *Elizabethan Life*, 60; A. R. DeWindt, 'Witchcraft and Conflicting Visions of the Ideal Village Community', *JBS*, 34, 4 (1995), 48; Sharpe, 'Such Disagreement betwyx Neighbours', 175, 184; DUL, DDR/EJ/CCD/1/6, fols. 21v, 26r. Some clergy acquired a wide reputation for their role in settling local disputes. See S. Hindle, 'Exclusion Crises: Poverty, Migration and Parochial Responsibility in English Rural Communities, c.1560–1660', *Rural History*, 7, 2 (1996), 132.

[240] Bossy, *Christianity in the West*, 64.

[241] Peyton (ed.), *The Churchwardens' Presentments*, 249.

[242] HMC, Various Collections, I, 102.

[243] S. D. Amussen, '"Being Stirred to Much Unquietnesss": Violence and Domestic Violence in Early Modern England', *Journal of Women's History*, 6, 2 (1994), 70–89. For other examples of informal dispute resolution, see S. D. Amussen, *An Ordered Society: Gender and Class in Early Modern England* (London, 1988), 173–5, 177–8.

[244] Wilkinson (ed.), *Chichester Archdeaconry Depositions*, 46.

monthly meetings with the minister 'to hear matters of variance'.[245] Fourteen years later, the minister of Epsom (Surrey) wrote to Sir William More, nervously emphasizing that he lived in peace with his neighbours, adding that 'I ... have bin glad alwaiese to make peace and agreement between any of my neighbours which have bin at any discorde'.[246] Sometimes, ministers felt compelled to keep matters out of court. In 1629, when two little-regarded labourers tried to take out a warrant against a well-respected woman of their Norfolk village, the minister, 'a learned and good man', did his best not to pursue the matter.[247]

Ministers were also expected to settle boundary disputes. In 1618, the vicar of Walford (Herefordshire) did his best to establish the whereabouts of a footpath. He explained that he had consulted with the 'auncient neighboures' and settled in favour of one of the disputants on the basis of what they had said; yet still the matter ended at Chancery.[248] Likewise, in 1628, the minister of Layston (Hertfordshire) noted that he had 'mediated betweene my Fower upland parishioners about the number of their acres and making their rates'. The minister had persuaded them to enter into a written settlement.[249] The expectation that the Church existed in part to bring peace to communities was also implicit in much litigation at church courts. As Sharpe observes: 'It was ... a principle of the canon law that litigants should be given every opportunity to reach a reconciliation, and there is some evidence that the ecclesiastical authorities encouraged such practices.'[250] Even the highly charged accusation of witchcraft – something that could easily split a community down the middle – could potentially be resolved through ritual purgation ordered by the church courts. Thus, after Robert Singleton of Yedingham (Yorkshire) attacked Janet Milner and 'called her witch because she useth to heal cattle by charmings', he was required by the diocesan authorities to ask her forgiveness, which he did by kneeling before her in the consistory court and acknowledging that she was an honest woman.[251]

Given the expectation that ministers should bear some responsibility for dispute resolution and the neighbourly functioning of community, it was therefore maddening for parishioners to have to deal with ministers

---

[245] Archer, *The Pursuit of Stability*, 80.
[246] A. J. Kempe (ed.), *The Loseley Manuscripts* (London, 1836), 256.
[247] NRO, NQS/C/S3/27, complaint of Hamon Lestrange.   [248] TNA, C115/52/3651–3.
[249] H. Falvey and S. Hindle (eds.), *'This Little Commonwealth': Layston Parish Memorandum Book, 1607–c.1650 and 1704–1747*, Hertfordshire Record Society, 19 (Hertford, 2003), 52.
[250] Sharpe, 'Such Disagreement betwyx Neighbours', 174.
[251] P. Tyler, 'The Church Courts at York and Witchcraft Prosecutions, 1567–1640', *Northern History*, 4, 1 (1969), 100.

like George Methwen, the curate of Bamburgh (Northumberland). In 1634, John Shipperd explained to the Durham High Commission: 'Methwen doth often stir upp strife amongst his neighbours, and is addicted to quarrelling and feightinge, and doth boost thereof after he hath done it.' Methwen's violent reputation had spread way beyond his parish: Shipperd added that 'about Lammas last' he had 'heard it reported in Newcastle that Mr Methwenn had there reported how he used John Conyers and that his face did beare his badge for a moneth'. This was not behaviour to be expected of a clergyman and it did nothing to sustain neighbourly values.[252]

Despite the popular sense that the godly were a divisive presence, Puritans were also strongly motivated to find ways of settling local disputes.[253] In the 'orders and dealings in the Churches of Northampton' laid down in 1571, it was agreed that every fortnight before communion, the minister and the churchwardens would make a circuit

from howse to howse to take the names of the Comunycantes and to examyne the state of their lyves, amongst whom yf any discorde be founde the parties are brought before the Maior and his bretherne being Assisted with the preacher and other gentillmen before whome there ys reconcilement made, or ells Correction and puttinge the partie from the Comunyon which will not dwell in Charitie.[254]

Likewise, the articles agreed by the Puritan minister and 'Auncients' of Dedham (Essex) in 1585 stated that

so many as shalbe admitted to the Communion promise and professe to live charitablie with all their neighbors, and if any occasion of displeasure arise, that they refraiginge from all discord or revenging by words, actions or suites will firste make the minister and two other godlie and indifferent neighbors acquainted w[i]th the state of their cawses before they proceed further by lawe or complaint out of the towne.[255]

Godly ministers were just as concerned as many of their conservative colleagues to play their role in settling local disputes. In 1588, the minister of Wenham (Suffolk) sought advice from the Dedham Classis as to how to deal with neighbours who were not in charity. He asked the Classis

---

[252] Longstaffe (ed.), *The Acts of the High Commission within the Diocese of Durham*, 106.

[253] Significantly, in towns in Puritan New England, local regulations laid down instructions that disputes between neighbours should be subject to informal resolution before proceeding to the courts. T. H. Breen and S. Foster, 'The Puritans' Greatest Achievement: A Study of Social Cohesion in Seventeenth-Century Massachusetts', *Journal of American History*, 60, 1 (1973), 15.

[254] Cox and Markham (eds.), *The Records of . . . Northampton*, II, 386–7.

[255] Usher (ed.), *The Presbyterian Movement in the Reign of Queen Elizabeth*, 99.

how he might deale w[i]th a couple of persons that were in hatred one against thither for words defamatory, viz., saying that he had killed a sheepe; whether he might admit them to the Communion, it was answered if they wold professe love one to another he might, because he cannot worke love but onlie admonish them of the danger of it, but if they be in open hatred the booke warrantes him not to reveive them.[256]

Significantly, one of the orders decided upon between the 'Auncients' and the minister of Dedham (Essex) in 1587 was that

so many as shalbe admitted to the Communion promise and professe to live charitablie with all their neighbors, and if any occasion of displeasure arise, that they refraiginge from all discord or revenging by words, actions or suites will firste make the minister and two other godlie and indifferent neighbours acquaynted w[i]th the state of their causes before they proceed further by lawe or complaint out of the towne.[257]

For all that their plebeian opponents saw the godly as a disruptive force, then, Puritans saw part of their role within their parishes as that of bringing harmony and charity amongst their neighbours.

Sometimes, the tightly controlled parish vestries of counties like Puritan Essex could provide sites for dispute resolution. In Finchingfield, in December 1626, a 'controversie between George Perrye and Robert Julyon' was settled at a meeting of the parish governors held at the minister's house.[258] Just like others, in their everyday dealings, the godly knew best to respect neighbourly relations. In December 1640, Nehemiah Wallington wrote a harsh letter to his neighbour Constantine Waddington in which he criticized Waddington for breaking the sabbath. In his conclusion, Wallington tried to soften the blow, writing 'and now neighbor, take this my admonition in love';[259] for Puritans such as Wallington often had their own methods of dispute resolution. The Dedham Classis allowed into their company only those who were at peace with their neighbours. Those in conflict had to refrain from litigation until the matter had been considered by the minister and two godly neighbours.[260]

Love, neighbourhood, friendship: these were all Christian virtues to which the godly believed themselves to adhere. In this respect, the godly built upon the earlier traditions bequeathed to them by mid-Tudor evangelicals. Thomas Becon stated unequivocally that

---

[256] Ibid., 71.    [257] Ibid., 99.
[258] F. G. Emmison, *Early Essex Town Meetings* (Chichester, 1970), 109.
[259] Seaver, *Wallington's World*, 103.
[260] Usher (ed.), *The Presbyterian Movement in the Reign of Queen Elizabeth*, 99.

seeing we are all men, and cannot at all times so circumspectly live, but sometime one of us offend another; if any such thing chance between his neighbour and him, let the labouring man and artificier straightways seek a reconciliation, and procure the renewing of love and amity so soon as is possible, as the holy apostle saith: 'Be angry, and sin not. Let not the sun go down upon your wrath; neither give place to the backbiter.'[261]

In some places, there were semi-official means for settling local struggles. The duties of the Sixteen Men who governed Holm Cultram (Cumberland) included the settlement of disputes.[262] However, despite many people's best efforts, these arrangements sometimes collapsed. In 1604, a body of rules for the settlement of disputes was drawn up in Houghton le Spring (Durham). They had been formulated by the minister along with

the gentlemen, and the fower and twentie of this parish, that all controversies present, and which shall hereafter arise and growe, betwixte anie of the parishioners of this parish shalbe referred to the arbitrement and judgement and endinge of foure of the gentlemen, or of foure of the foure and twentie.

The parson will be the 'umpier in everie arbitrement'. If the controversy was weighty, then it was decided that two counsels should be consulted, at the costs of both parties. But by 1633 this local system had broken down: village governors observed that the 'pious order' of 1604 had

lyen fruitlesse for divers yeares last by past, by reason whereof the parishioner . . . is growne to such a height of malice and contention as it hath caused the knights, the parson of Houghton . . . the gentlemen and 24 of the said parish, to take into there considerations what might be the causes why the aforesaid order, being made to so good and religious an end, should worke no better effect.[263]

It is important not to overdraw the boundary between legal culture and local culture. Just as the failure of neighbourly sanctions led to litigation, the law sometimes fell back on neighbourly sanctions.[264] Sharpe observes that 'the initiation of a suit [at church courts] for defamation might be interpreted as the first step towards bringing neighbourly tensions to a close'.[265] Litigation before church courts formed a way of sealing breaches. Thus, Martin Ingram notes that those ordered by church courts to perform penances

---

[261] Ayre (ed.), *The Catechism of Thomas Becon*, 402.
[262] F. Grainger and W. G. Collingwood (eds.), *Register and Records of Holm Cultram* (Kendal, 1929), 225.
[263] Barmby (ed.), *Churchwardens' Accounts*, 282, 300.
[264] For a fuller discussion of litigation and the settlement of disputes, see C. Muldrew, 'The Culture of Reconciliation: Community and the Settlement of Economic Disputes in Early Modern England', *Historical Journal*, 39, 4 (1996), 915–42.
[265] Sharpe, 'Such Disagreement betwyx Neighbours', 178.

often had to stand before the congregation during the whole service, which not uncommonly included a sermon or homily ...[T]o conclude the proceedings, culprits asked God, and sometimes also their neighbours, for forgiveness, and joined with the congregation in saying the Lord's Prayer in what was intended to be a ritual of reconciliation ...[S]uch penances bore hard, and it is scarcely surprising that some people broke down and wept as they performed them.[266]

Thus, in 1635, the Durham High Commission, having heard a case of adultery against Anne Marshall of Haltwhistle (Northumberland), decreed that she should purge herself by the hands of twelve persons of good note and quality, being Marshall's neighbours 'whoe knew her life and conversacion', and that the intention was that 'soe far as by lawe they could', Marshall should be 'restored ... to her former credit'.[267]

Indeed, the function of the church courts in dispute resolution seems often to have been sufficient to provide a forum in which anger, resentment and hostility could be articulated, without necessarily reaching settlement: they were places within which story-telling could occur, and opinions registered.[268] Nonetheless, some of the sentences that the church courts could hand out, were their authority to be recognized, could be humiliating, as Charles Shawe discovered in 1570 when he was sentenced to stand 'in lynen apparell' in his parish church during divine service and say:

Beloved neighbours I am now comen hither to shewe my self sory for slannderinge one Bartram Midforde, namely in that I called him openly 'beggarly harlot and cutthrote' sainge that he was 'a covetous snowge and such as he by Godd's worde aught to be weded out of the Coomenwealthe'. I acknowledge that thus to slander my Christian brother is an heynouse offence, first towards God, who haithe straightly forbidden it in his holy laws accomptinge it to be a kynde of murdering my neighbor and threatening to punyshe it with hell fire and the losse of the kyngdome of heaven. ... Agayne, my unruly tonge, it were not punished, it wolde not onely set mo[re] of yow on fire, but also it wolde bolden others to doe the like.[269]

Charles Shawe's recantation is indicative of the intense power attached to neighbourhood: his slander of his 'Christian brother' represented, remember, 'a kynde of murdering my neighbor'.

Given such stakes, settling disputes could be a great pleasure. In 1574, James Wawton ran into the curate of Lanchester (County Durham), Richard Mylner, who seemed in a good mood. Wawton asked the minister, 'What mak[e]s you so hye, Sir Richard?'. Mylner answered that he

[266] M. Ingram, 'Puritans and the Church Courts, 1560–1640', in C. Durston and J. Eales (eds.), *The Culture of English Puritanism, 1500–1700* (Basingstoke, 1996), 65. On dispute resolution, see L. Nader (ed.), *Law in Culture and Society* (Chicago, 1969).
[267] Longstaffe (ed.), *The Acts of the High Commission within the Diocese of Durham*, 138.
[268] Gowing, *Domestic Dangers*, 42–3.
[269] Raine (ed.), *Depositions ... from the Courts of Durham*, 107–8; see also 111–12, 117–18.

had settled a quarrel between John Haswell and William Grinwell. James demanded of him, 'What have ye adoo with that?', to which Mylner answered, 'Yes, I have to do ther[e]with, bycause they ar[e] my parishioners', adding that 'yf the partie greved sought to me, I wold have to doo therein by the auctorit[i]e I have under my lord of Durham, to bringe them to good order and quietness'.[270] Order and quietness: these were two of the things that neighbours expected of one another. Dispute resolution – by the clergy, the gentry, the yeomanry or just by near neighbours – reasserted those critical social norms.

## The Gender of Neighbourhood

The concept and practice of neighbourhood were heavily inflected by ideas and social practices rooted in gender. As Elizabeth Hallam has put it, '[t]he involvement of women and men in distinct (but sometimes overlapping) networks of social relations and everyday practises informed ... gendered orientations'.[271] In her 1970s research on the Aragonese village of Oroel, Susan Harding argued that patterns of gossip were highly gendered and that this was rooted in a sharp sexual division of labour. Men talked about the fields; women talked about the village.[272] Something similar might have happened in arable villages in early modern England.[273] It was suggested in a ballad of the early 1630s that, when in mixed company, men and women broke into separate conversational groups. Men spoke about land, prices, stock and the institutional arrangements of their community:

> Well I noted as they sorted
> all their speech in order,
> Men by themselves, women likewise,
> men they talkt of Tillage,
> The prises of wheat, of sheep and Neat,
> and orders of their Village.[274]

---

[270] Raine (ed.), *Depositions ... from the Courts of Durham*, 286–92.
[271] E. A. Hallam, 'Turning the Hourglass: Gender Relations at the Deathbed in Early Modern Canterbury', *Mortality*, 1, 1 (1996), 68.
[272] S. Harding, 'Women and Words in a Spanish Village', in R. R. Reiter (ed.), *Toward an Anthropology of Women* (New York, 1975), 284. See also J. Riegelhaupt, 'Saloio Women: An Analysis of Informal and Formal Political and Economic Roles of Portuguese Peasant Women', *Anthropological Quarterly*, 40 (1967), 109–26.
[273] Although possibly less so in pastoral-industrial regions. Differing patterns of work, social structure, community and gender in contrasting regional economies deserve closer attention. Essex would make a good contrast, as would Gloucestershire. Both have excellent church court records.
[274] Anon., *The Country Mens Chat* (London, c.1632).

Yet men's gossip could be just as personal – and as damaging – as that of women. In a 1636 case that speaks to men's sociability as rooted in their labour beyond the village, the York consistory court heard from husbandman Robert Chambers of Houghton (Yorkshire). He explained that 'John Anderson & this Ex[aminan]te beinge (w[i]th divers others) comeing from the Comon day worcke' passed their neighbours Robert and William Graveley. He 'did heare the said Willi[a]m Graveley in very angry and fierce mann[er] say that he mother of the said Rob[er]t Graveley (meaneinge ... Mary Graveley), was a queane, and an old witch, & said further that the said Rob[er]t Graveley was a witches Cub'.[275] The case resulted in a defamation suit brought by Mary Graveley – one that called upon male witnesses to depose as to the gossip amongst their ranks concerning her moral standing in the village and her supernatural powers. All of this stemmed from an angry confrontation amongst the men of the village, out in the fields.

In their daily patterns of interaction, urban people may have lived more closely together than in many rural districts: and yet, at least for male artisans, they may have felt a need to define labour still more tightly. English urban artisans did not possess the same hard rules as their counterparts in the Low Countries and Germany.[276] Nonetheless, there was still a strong sense amongst those in authority in towns and cities that the patriarchal household formed the basic building block of urban society. Guilds and companies played up to this. The Northampton shoemakers – the most numerous craftsmen in that town – might be taken as typical. In ordinances of 1552, they established that if any outside shoemaker set up shop without having served an apprenticeship, he had to pay thirty shillings; in contrast, the fee for a Northampton man to set up shop was one shilling. No master shoemaker was to employ another master's apprentice, unless their parting from their former master was harmonious. Shoemakers were not to sell their wares at the market. There were significant restrictions on enfranchised master shoemakers employing outside journeymen; in particular, in an attempt to control the labour market, any outside journeyman who had wrought within the town and then moved on, should he wish to return to

---

[275] BIA, CP.H.2102.
[276] M. E. Wiesner, 'Guilds, Male Bonding and Women's Work in Early Modern Germany', *Gender and History*, 1, 2 (1989), 125–37. As Sheilagh Ogilvie explains, male institutional controls were weaker in England than in Germany; see S. Ogilvie, 'How Does Social Capital Affect Women? Guilds and Communities in Early Modern Germany', *American Historical Review*, 109, 2 (2004), 349. For the sharply articulated labour identities in the cities of the urbanized Low Countries, see J. Dumolyn, '"I Thought of It at Work, in Ostend": Urban Artisan Labour and Guild Ideology in the Later Medieval Low Countries', *International Review of Social History*, 62, 3 (2017), 389–419. An international study of urban labour organization (especially regarding gender) that is focused on the North Sea and Baltic economies of differing towns and cities would be very revealing.

work in Northampton, was required to work with his former master. The masters were in charge of quality control: every year, they were to choose two 'discret men' to check on the quality of leather used by the shoemakers; a further two 'discret men' maintained order amongst the shoemakers. Depositions taken in 1581 revealed that, following the dissolution of the White Friars' priory in Northampton, the shoemakers had taken over the building and renamed it St George's Hall, using it for their feasts, drinkings and official proceedings.[277] These were all ways in which the plebeian master was able to assert control over labour markets, skill, identity and relations of production. They informed a vision of the urban economy that was underwritten by patriarchal assumptions.

The underlying logic of the Northampton shoemakers' arrangements was that the skilled, enfranchised master remained paramount; collective male drinking rituals at St George's Hall reinforced a sense of mutuality and belonging. According to their regulations, the labour market was placed under guild control, as was the sale of leather and shoes. The consequence was to underwrite the patriarchal authority of the master over his apprentices, his class authority over his journeymen and his predominance in the governance of the trade. Something similar was going on in Hallamshire (Yorkshire) after 1624, where the Sheffield Cutlers' Company laid down orders concerning the government of the labour market such that masters retained control over the industry. After serving their seven-year apprenticeships, it was common for journeymen to enter into indentures to work with a master for a further six years, dwelling in his household.[278] Possession of a recognized skill and membership of a guild or company might set an artisan apart from his fellow workers, who were thought of as 'only comen labourers'.[279] This helped to sustain an occupational xenophobia in which workers inside a polity (most obviously, that of the town or city) might strive to squeeze out those from outside. In 1629, for example, the joiners of Hull complained against incomers to the town who were taking their work and 'are strangers and unskilfull'.[280]

Artisanal identities underwrote a strongly masculine sense of community that remains to be explored properly by historians. In cities and towns where trades were concentrated in particular parishes or streets, this may have strengthened an overtly male sense of urban neighbourhood. Mark Hailwood has recently shown that there existed a broad artisanal identity in the period, encompassing different trades in a homosocial model of

---

[277] Cox and Markham (eds.), *The Records of ... Northampton*, 183–5, 293–4.
[278] R. E. Leader, *History of the Cutlers in Hallamshire, in the County of York*, 2 vols. (Sheffield, 1905), I, 44–5.
[279] Phythian Adams, 'Ceremony and the Citizen', 58.
[280] Lambert, *Two Thousand Years of Gild Life*, 251.

male bonding that was articulated in ballads. Phrases such as 'The gentle Craft [i.e., shoemakers] doth beare good will, to all kind hearted trades-men' articulate what Hailwood calls an 'occupational-cum-social identity'.[281] Work was, for many artisans, a source of pride and identity. In one of Hailwood's ballads, a hard-working porter says of lazy workers who cannot stand the price of a drink:

> Such men as these I hold in scorne,
> I'le rather rise at four i'th morn
> And labour hard til nine at night
> Ere I in shirking take delight . . .
> . . . No man shall say he paid my shot.[282]

Likewise, another balladeer said:

> When we have spent all, to labour we fall,
> For a living wee'le dig or wee'le delve;
> Determined to be bounteous and free.[283]

A ballad concerning the foundation of a company for London porters provides confirmation of Hailwood's interpretation. It ran:

> Thrise blessed is that Land
> where King and Rulers bee,
> and men of great Command,
> that carefull are to see,
> that carefull are to see,
> the Commons good maintained
> by friendlie unitie
> the proppe of any land[.]

Importantly, though, this excludes a certain segment of the population: in its terms, the Corporation

> excludes, and shuts out many
> that were of base esteeme.[284]

How this worked out in textile villages – rural communities where men and women worked more closely together than in arable communities – remains to be investigated. Meanwhile, in free mining communities in which men claimed the right to dig for tin, coal or lead ore wherever it was to be found, those who were 'of base esteeme' often included their

---

[281] Hailwood, 'The Honest Tradesman's Honour', 86.
[282] M. Hailwood, 'Sociability, Work and Labouring Identity in Seventeenth-Century England', *Cultural and Social History*, 8, 1 (2011), 14.
[283] Ibid., 15.
[284] Anon., *A Newe Ballad, Composed in Commendation of the Societie, or Companie of the Porters* (London, 1605).

womenfolk, who (by the late sixteenth century, as works became deeper and more complex, and as men seized control of highly paid and valued underground labour) were relegated to poorly paid surface work.[285] Where women were allowed access to high-status underground work, it was often – as in the northern coalfield – in conditions of labour scarcity, and it was remarked upon by men as rather unusual. In contrast, the underground labours of free miners in regions such as the Peak Country, the Somerset Mendips, the northern Pennines, the Forest of Dean and the tin mines of Devon and Cornwall generated powerful social solidarities, creating bonds that were every bit as strong as those amongst urban artisans. Such workers found ways of crafting identities and relationships that made the experience of labour about much more than the dull compulsion of economic relations. In 1517, the cobblers of Helston (Cornwall) drew up a set of rules for the government of their guild in which collective welfare was central. They ordained that 'if any brother fall in poverty that then every brother and sister help him after their degree'.[286] Symbolically, socially and politically, such workers' guilds could be a powerful presence in a community, carving an institutional and organizational space within the local polity for the self-organization of working people. Critically, this form of labour organization crossed gender divisions, drawing on a sense of local solidarity that drew 'brother' together with 'sister'.

   Male and female spheres were partly structured by the sexual division of labour. Bernard Capp has suggested that women were 'interdependent, and their work (whether domestic ... [or] waged) [w]as closely integrated with their social lives'.[287] Capp ignores the significant regional variations, defined by the rural economy, that were at work here. In agrarian regions such as South Essex, Amanda Flather has shown that men worked out in the fields, while women stayed within the open streets of the village, working alongside one another (due to the need for light) while spinning. Alternatively, women were often to be found engaged in dairying, milking cows, churning butter and making cheese. In an instructive study, Laurel Thatcher Ulrich has argued that, in New England, 'the economic lives of women and men were clearly differentiated', such that women 'lived and worked in less visible communities of their own',

---

[285] Wood, *The Politics of Social Conflict*, 174. See also S. C. Karant-Nunn, 'The Women of the Saxon Silver Mines', in S. Marshall (ed.), *Women and Reformation in Counter-Reformation Europe* (Bloomington, IN, 1989), 29–46.

[286] A. L. Rowse and M. I. Henderson (eds.), *Essays in Cornish History by Charles Henderson* (Truro, 1963), 78.

[287] B. Capp, *When Gossips Meet: Women, Family and Neighbourhood in Early Modern England* (Oxford, 2003), 52.

constituting 'a community of women'. Thus, while men worked in the fields, woodland or at sea, women's working day was spent in the village, engaged in 'cooking, washing, plain sewing, milking, tending a garden . . . feeding swine . . . cheese making, spinning, knitting, poultry raising, [and] cultivation of flax'. This generated intense links amongst women. As Thatcher Ulrich puts it: 'Because families in early America were neither socially nor economically self-contained, a good housewife was of necessity a "friendly Neighbor".'[288] Something similar surely went on in the England that these people had left.

Women's lives were lived in the street – spinning, sewing, looking to children, carrying water, bargaining and bartering. Amanda Flather mentions women sitting 'in the doorway of the house, to take advantage of the light, and from this vantage point women were able to chat with passers-by and observe the goings on in the neighbourhood while they worked'. And, within the household, they spent time in the dairy. Then there were also the commons, where women worked in pasturing animals and collecting food and fuel. Importantly, 'work was . . . shared and it remained a sociable activity'.[289] Flather observes that there were important annual rhythms:

For much of the winter different work in separate places kept contact between husbands and wives to a minimum, whereas in the spring women were employed in the fields planting and weeding, sometimes working alongside their husbands. Most important, during haymaking in June and when harvesting of corn began in July, whole households worked together out in the fields reaping, gathering and binding to bring the grain back into the barns.

Then, after the harvest was taken in, the men withdrew, leaving the women and children to glean.[290]

Work drew women together: Craig Muldrew's careful research into the ubiquitous practice of spinning has demonstrated its importance as a key source of household earning.[291] Likewise, albeit for a later date, Peter King has shown the critical role in the maintenance of the economy of the rural proletariat played by gleaning, a task that was largely carried out by

---

[288] L. Thatcher Ulrich, '"A Friendly Neighbor": Social Dimensions of Daily Work in Northern Colonial New England', *Feminist Studies*, 6, 2 (1980), 392, 393–4, 395. Miranda Chaytor also argues for a strong model of the sexual division of labour; see M. Chaytor, 'Household and Kinship: Ryton in the Late Sixteenth and Early Seventeenth Centuries', *History Workshop Journal*, 10, 1 (1980), 25–60.

[289] A. J. Flather, 'Space, Place and Gender: The Sexual and Spatial Division of Labor in the Early Modern Household', *History and Theory*, 52 (2013), 348, 349, 353.

[290] Ibid., 351.

[291] C. Muldrew, 'An Early Industrial Workforce: Spinning in the Countryside, c.1500–50', in R. Jones and C. Dyer (eds.), *Farmers, Consumers, Innovators: The World of Joan Thirsk* (Hatfield, 2016), 79–88.

women, organized under the figure of the Gleaners' Queen.[292] And Nicola Whyte has made a forceful case for women's role in asserting other key customary rights, such as collecting fuel in the woodland, pasturing animals on the commons and collecting nuts, herbs and berries. These represented important contributions to the household economy, providing milk, cheese, butter, fuel, protein and – for a diet that was often bland – some flavour in the form of herbs. Fattening pigs in the autumn woodland – a customary right called pannage – allowed the animals to eat acorns, giving the pork and bacon they provided a richer taste. Despite the fact that the large bulk of the depositions presented in customary disputes was given by men (typically around 90 per cent), Whyte shows convincingly that women's assertion of these rights was a source both of significant earnings for the household economy and of a sometimes pugnacious sense of independence amongst women.[293] Here, then, were some of the ways in which women's labour fed into a shared sense of neighbourhood and collectivity.

Working together provided important opportunities for women's sense of neighbourhood. Flather provides the example of a group of Jacobean women who were to be found on the village common doing their knitting together.[294] Women's occupations – commoning and pasturing; midwifery; collecting fuel, nuts, berries and herbs; milk, cheese and butter production; brewing; tending to vegetable gardens; harvest work – all of this alongside the labour involved in the reproduction of the household in the form of childcare may often have created a sense of shared identity amongst women, perhaps generating a sense of collective, gendered neighbourhood. In some places, that sense may have been consciously handed down the generations, part of a social patterning of labour that defined women's work. In a mid-seventeenth-century account, an old woman comes to work in butter production. Asserting her greater wisdom and experience over a young woman, she 'told the maid what was wont to be done when she was a maid, and also in her mother's young time, that if it happened then butter would not come readily, they used a charm to be said over it':

> Come, butter, come,
> Come, butter, come,
> Peter stands at the gate

[292] P. King, 'Customary Rights and Women's Earnings: The Importance of Gleaning to the Rural Laboring Poor', *Economic History Review*, 2nd ser., 44, 3 (1991), 461–76. For more on gleaning, see Wood, *The Memory of the People*, 1–8.

[293] N. M. Whyte, 'Custodians of Memory: Women and Custom in Rural England', *Cultural and Social History*, 8, 2 (2011), 153–73.

[294] A. J. Flather, *Gender and Space in Early Modern England* (Woodbridge, 2007), 84.

> Waiting for a butter'd cake;
> Come, butter, come

This, said the old woman, 'being said three times, will make your butter come, for it was taught my mother by a learned churchman in Queen Marie's days, when as churchmen had more cunning and could teach the people a trick that our ministers now a days know not'.[295] We are dealing here with the long-term transmission of women's skills and memories; the same tradition was noted by a folklorist in 1900. Work, then, could be about much more than the labour process. In this case, it was also about skill, long-term collective memory and habit, all of them informing a shared, localized sense of women's knowledge. This was one way in which neighbourhood could be constantly refashioned. It was, therefore, maddening when butter failed to churn. Shakespeare's Puck ('Call'd Robin Goodfellow') was held responsible by Warwickshire milkmaids for sending milk sour or for setting a spell over butter churning or cheese production:

> Either I mistake your shape and making quite,
> Or else you are that shrewd and knavish sprite: are not you he
> That frights the maidens of the villagery;
> Skim milk, and sometimes labour in the quern
> And bootless make the breathless housewife churn.[296]

Then, there was dirt: what Mary Douglas called 'matter out of place'.[297] As Garthine Walker has shown, women's honour was tied to much more than their sexual identity alone – it attached also to their capacity to maintain a clean home and a functioning household economy.[298] All of these were ways in which women's sense of neighbourhood might be both asserted and argued over. Just like Puck's baleful influence over dairying, fairies could also inflict themselves on women's attempts to maintain a clean home. Written sometime after 1630, Robert Herrick's poem *The Fairies* records folk-belief in the fairy Mab, who watched over women's domestic work. Herrick warned that

> If ye will with Mab find grace
> Set each platter in his place
> Rake the fire up, and get
> Water in, ere sun be set.

---

[295] C. Burne, *A Handbook of Folklore* (London, 1914), 67–8.
[296] *A Midsummer Night's Dream*, act II, scene 1, lines 19–24.
[297] M. Douglas, *Purity and Danger: An Analysis of the Concept of Pollution and Taboo* (London, 1966).
[298] G. Walker, 'Expanding the Boundaries of Female Honour in Early Modern England', *TRHS*, 6th ser., 6 (1996), 235–46.

> Wash your pails and cleanse your dairies
> Sluts are loathesome to the fairies
> Sweep your house, who doth not so
> Mab will pinch her by the toe.[299]

Women's honour, readily attested to in the neighbourhood, was attached to this separation of cleanliness from dirt, part of an elemental structuring of their separation from the outside, from nature and from what might at least in some ways be conceived of as foul. Maintaining an internal, clean, industrious, homely home – one distinct from an outside dirty world – was one way in which female honour was made materially real – and, as Garthine Walker shows, failure to do so could render a woman's identity fragile within her neighbourhood.

Susan Harding argued long ago that women's gossip makes social worlds: in the 1970s, as the women of Oreol sat talking, they sewed together: 'They were mending their memories of village families with the thread of their talk, much as they were sewing up hems and cuffs and collars with the thread of their needles.'[300] It is easy – and all too clumsy – to slip into the notion that male worlds in the period were those of the literate, while women's (due to their lower levels of literacy) were fundamentally oral. The evidence of ballads suggests that there was a market for women's perspectives; and, in any case, women's literacy levels were rising. Moreover, as Adam Fox has made clear, divisions between orality and literacy were always very fuzzy.[301] Yet, there were ways in which women's communal engagement was built on a special engagement with oral culture: mostly, this lies beyond the written record. But sometimes, it becomes clear to us. Twelfth Day (7 January) structured women's worlds – it was the date on which, following Christmas celebrations, women were supposed to return to the lucrative trade of spinning wool. It was therefore known as Saint Distaff's Day. Women seem to have spun together – out in the street, in the open light – making a community that was their own. In *Twelfth Night*, reference is made to how

> The spinsters and the knitters in the sun
> And the free maids that weave their thread with bones
> Do use to chant it
> It is silly sooth,
> And dallies with the innocence of love,
> Like the old age.[302]

[299] A. Pollard (ed.), *Works of Robert Herrick*, 2 vols. (London, 1891), I, 252.
[300] Harding, 'Women and Words', 283.
[301] A. Fox, *Oral and Literate Cultures in England, 1500–1700* (Oxford, 2000).
[302] W. Shakespeare, *Twelfth Night*, act II, scene 4, lines 42–8.

In this respect, the women – singing together, while working in the open air – formed a 'singing community'.[303]

We are, then, a long way from the clumsy assumption that '[w]omen's position in late medieval and early modern English society was on the whole a subordinate one'.[304] Rather, women's experience of neighbourhood was rich, vital and potentially fulfilling. Outside observers noted the ways in which women's experience of mutual bonds defined their local interactions. In 1599, for example, Emmanuel van Materen observed that Englishwomen spent much of their time in 'visiting their friends and keeping company, conversing with their equals (whom they term gossips) and their neighbours, and making merry with them at child-births, christenings, churchings and funerals; and all this with the permission and knowledge of their husbands, as such is the custom'.[305] Women's social experiences were not the same as men's, and that fact helped to define their experience of neighbourhood. Perhaps the clearest statement of women's sense of local solidarity was to be found in the birthing chamber. Here, female friends and kin – 'gossips' – were to be found overseeing, hour after hour, that powerful process in which human life was renewed. Critically, the birthing chamber was a key site from which men were excluded, and within which the skill of the midwife ruled supreme. It was a place in which new friendships could be forged. It is therefore important that early modern women might have spent some one-third of their adult lives pregnant.[306] In his *Pleasant History of Thomas of Reading* (1623), Thomas Deloney provides a vivid picture of women's sociability in the birthing chamber:

Suttons wife of Salisbury which had lately bin delivered of a sonne, against her going to Church, prepared great cheare: at what time Simons wife of South-hampton came thither, and so did divers others of the Clothiers wives, onely to make merry at this Churching feast . . . and as the old Proverbe speaketh, Many women many words, so it fell out at that time: for there was such prattling that it passed: some talkt of their husbands frowardnes, some shewed their Maids sluttishnes, othersome deciphered the costlines of their garments, some told many tales of their neighbours: and to be briefe, there was none of them but would have talke for a whole day.[307]

[303] For the idea of a 'singing community', see C. Heppa, 'Harry Cox and His Friends: Song Transmission in an East Norfolk Singing Community, c. 1896–1960', *Folk Music Journal*, 8, 5 (2005), 569–93. See also G. Porter, '"Work the Old Lady out of the Ditch": Singing at Work by English Lacemakers', *Journal of Folklore Research*, 31 (1994), 35–55.

[304] R. A. Houlbrooke, 'Women's Social Life and Common Action in England from the Fifteenth Century to the Eve of the Civil War', *Continuity and Change*, 1, 2 (1986), 171.

[305] W. B. Rye (ed.), *England as Seen by Foreigners in the Days of Elizabeth I and James I* (London, 1865), 72.

[306] A. Shepard, 'Gender, the Body and Sexuality', in K. E. Wrightson (ed.), *A Social History of England, 1500–1750* (Cambridge, 2017), 339.

[307] Mann (ed.), *The Works of Thomas Deloney*, 260. See also Cressy, *Birth, Marriage and Death*, 84–7.

Pregnancy, birth, christening and churching were all social processes that were highly ritualized, and within which old friendships were renewed and new friendships forged. Bernard Capp cites an example from 1594 in which a London woman mentions how she and a woman who had helped at her child's christening two years earlier had since 'been of familiar acquaintance'.[308] All of this helped to construct a sense of neighbourhood that was distinctly gendered: men were no part of any of these networks; and they were powerful networks indeed. This was as true of the deathbed as it was of the birthing chamber. One early seventeenth-century ballad ran as follows:

> Draw near, kind friends and neighbours all
> Which now are come to see
> And bear witness of my death
> Give ear a while to me.[309]

Worries about the welfare of children might have led one woman to find fault with the apparently malicious intentions of another. Witchcraft accusations periodically emerged from worries for the welfare of a baby or small child. In June 1632, for example, Anna Kippax of Bolton (Yorkshire), the servant of the local gentleman Francis Malham, told the diocesan court that, 'betwixte hay time and harvest' in 1631, Mistress Atkinson, the family wet-nurse, came to the Malham household

and comeing into the chamber where this ex[aminan]te and her m[ist]ris ... were seemed to be desirous to speake some what to this ex[aminan]ts said m[istr]is w[hi]ch this ex[aminan]te p[er]ceivinge went her way forth of the Chamber and saith that upon this ex[aminan]ts comeing againe to her said m[istr]is her m[istr]ris told her that the childe w[hi]ch she had at Nurseing w[i]th the said Atkinsons wife was not well, and that ... the said Marie Atkinson had told her that ... Margaret Awcocke was the cause of it, and that she was a witch and had an evill ey[e], And saith that shortly after that the said Marie Atkinson comeing againe to the house of this ex[aminan]ts master in Elslacke art[iculat]e she this ex[aminan]te asked her the child did & howe her said m[ist]ris masters childe did wch she then had at nurseing, calling it by the name of mr Richard, to w[hi]ch she answered, that it was not well, but that she hoped that it mended, whereupon this ex[aminan]te asked what she thought might be the cause of its not being well, to w[hi]ch the said Marie Atkinson answered, that Awcocks wife, meaning the ar[ticula]te Margaret Awcocke was the cause thereof, saying further that she the said Magragett Awcocke was a naughty bad woman and had an [ev]ill ey[e].[310]

Here, then, we have that dangerous falling-out of women neighbours over accusations of witchcraft that blended questions concerning maternity, childcare and the bounds of the household. The great danger for

---

[308] Capp, *When Gossips Meet*, 51.    [309] Hallam, 'Turning the Hourglass', 68.
[310] BIA, CP.H.1734.

Margaret Awcocke was the possibility of a criminal case concerning witchcraft being brought against her, were the child not to prosper; she therefore sued before the church courts in order to regain her reputation.

Just as troubling was the vexed question of illegitimacy. The early modern period saw the hardening of attitudes towards unmarried mothers, as Janett Spence discovered in Hurworth (County Durham) in 1575. She had, as the widow Margaret Myddleton explained, been a servant in the house of Robert Warde, a respected member of the community. Yet, despite his status in the village, Warde had got the girl pregnant. Myddleton reported the matter thus:

> Janett Spenc[e] dwelt with the said Robert Warde this last yere, and was begotten and to all the neighbours ther[e], byfore she came frome the said Robert service[e]; and that the childe that she, the said Janett, was then with, was the said Robert Ward's, and never named any man or childe to be father of hir said childe but the said Robert Warde.

Warde put the girl out of his service and she was reduced, in her vulnerability, to sleeping in doorways and begging in the streets. As Myddleton continued the story,

> she, being a poor wench, sought hir relief emongst neighbours; and then she departyd frome the said Hurworth unto the tyme of the birth of her childe drew near, and then came again to Hurworth, and contynewed about the said Robert house and doors, and would not depart from thenc[e], still affirming the said Robert Ward to be father of hir childe.

When Janett Spence was about to give birth, 'like to be lost for women's help [as she] was then, at the mocion of the . . . parson and other good neighbours, [she was] taken into one Agnes Parker's house, a poor woman ther[e], and this examinat[e] was sent for by Margaret Clarke, a poore wench, to come to the said Janett and the good wyfes that were with hyr'. As the presiding midwife, Widow Myddleton told young Janett that she would have no help in her birth until she named the father of her child; yet again, Janett insisted that the father was her master. But some of the men of the village backed up Robert Warde. Christopher Stokton said that he '[h]aith well known the said Robert Warde this 20 yere, and the said Janet onlye this last yere – he shuld love the said Robert better, bycause he is commed of honest folks; and of a good fren[d]ship, yf his demeanour were accordingly'. Robert, it seemed from other witnesses, had offered the girl twelve pence to depart his threshold where she lay, weeping, in the closing stages of her pregnancy. In the end, Robert's wife intervened and assembled the older women of the neighbourhood to take control of the situation.[311] Robert Warde, as an insider,

---

[311] Raine (ed.), *Depositions . . . from the Courts of Durham*, 302–4.

retained the respect of men like Christopher Stokton. In contrast, Janett Spence now faced a life on the road. Neighbourliness had its hard edge: Warde had his place in the village, while young Janett had no such networks on which she could draw: for sure, under the aegis of Mistresses Warde and Myddleton, a birthing chamber was arranged in the end, but the older women still stood over the girl, demanding of her the name of the child's father while she was wracked in her labour pains.

The evidence concerning women's solidarities is complicated, contradictory and multi-faceted. But it would be wrong to assume from this that the search for women's solidarities lacks any historical basis.[312] For the women of Christchurch (Hampshire) in 1604, their loyalty to a deceased female neighbour was more important to them than her religion. It was recorded in the parish register that 'Christian Steevens, the wife of Thomas Steevens, died in childbirth and was buried by women, for she was a papishe'.[313] Note, then, the language of one resentfully misogynistic ballad that depicts a violent, abusive wife mistreating her mild husband. The husband complains:

> Then she goes foorthe a Gossiping
> Amongst her owne Comrades.
> And then she falls a bowsing
> With her merry blades.[314]

Who were this woman's 'comrades'? Perhaps one Kentish woman might have provided an answer when, in 1612, faced with another vicious beating from her husband, three of her female neighbours confronted her abuser.[315]

Early modern women were quite capable of standing up for one another. One ballad published around 1635 was clearly intended for a female readership, depicting a group of women in an alehouse, singing about the relative merits and failings of their husbands. It began:

> Of late within an evening tide,
> It was my chance to be
> Close placed beside a good fireside
> With a merry company
> Of kind good women, whose intent
> Was for to doe no wrong,
> But onely for to drink their drinke,

---

[312] For a useful survey of the women's solidarities and mutual support, see Capp, *When Gossips Meet*, 284–7.

[313] W. E. Tate, *The Parish Chest: A Study of the Records of Parochial Administration in England* (Cambridge, 1946), 65.

[314] Anon., *The Cruell Shrow* (1640?).

[315] A. Wall, *Power and Protest in England, 1525–1640* (London, 2000), 93.

And this was all their song:
This ale goes merrily downe, downe
This ale goes merrily downe
Since here we be good company
Let each wife drinke her round.[316]

In a culture in which memory enjoyed a special power, it was worth noting that some women recollected mothers who had refused to give way to the patriarchal norm. Hence, in 1579, in a dispute concerning the tithing customs of Upper Clatford (Hampshire), Emma Ashridge explained that

[s]he dwelt & was brought up in the p[ar]ish of upclatford . . . about xvi yeres & she dep[ar]ted w[i]th her husband owt of that p[ar]ish about xxvi yeres past. And all those yeres whilest this depo[nen]t was in that p[ar]ish one m[ar]garet Williams this depo[nen]ts mother was farm[er] of the p[ar]sonage there[.] And in those yeres one hopkyns & one Guy being farm[e]rs of the farme . . . called normans courte farme did subtract fro[m] her certayne tyth whete & barly growin in the common felds belonging to that farme by the space of two yeres. Whereupon[n] this depo[nen]ts said mother sewed the[m] in the law for the said tyth & recovered it against the[m.] And after that recoverye whilest this depon[en]t dwelt in that p[ar]ishe the said farmers & there successors in that farme did quietly & justly pay ther tythe of all ther corne growen in the common felds belonging to that farme.[317]

The evidence suggests, then, that some women might hang on to memories of powerful older women in their lives, women like Margaret Williams who, in asserting themselves, had won out. Something similar may have been the case for religiously conservative (or even recusant) women in Protestant England. In 1589, for example, the gentleman James Ryther wrote of the women of York that many were recusants, sometimes in defiance of their husbands, adding that 'the whole Countrie is muche adycted [to Catholicism], the Citty more, the women moste'. The women of York sought, as they saw it, 'to save their husbands sowles, som[e] of thes[e] by a secret consent, som[e] by a settled constraint, som[e] against their husbands wills'.[318] Likewise, an Elizabethan discussion of the religious loyalties of the populations of Berwick-on-Tweed and Northumberland noted that 'the women . . . have like conversing and meetings at gentlewomens labours childrens christenings and by such other means', and that these female verbal networks helped them, as a body, to hold to their conservative faith.[319]

It is important, then, that women had many public roles in the life of their communities. When the parish clerk of Attleborough (Norfolk) noted the 1625 burial of Mary Greene, the hostess of an alehouse called

---

[316] Anon., *The Gossips Feast: or A Merry Meeting of Women* (London, c.1635–6).
[317] HALS, 21M65/C3/8, p. 95.    [318] BL, Lansdowne Ms 119, fol. 112r (No. 8).
[319] HEHL, HAM67(10).

The Cock, he observed of her that she 'knew how to gain more by her trade than any other, and a woman free and kind for any in sickness, or woman in her travail or childbed, and for answering for anyone's child, and ready to give to anyone's marriage'.[320] Wealthier women were expected to have a particular role in the comings and goings of their neighbourhood. As Amanda Flather observes: 'The oft-repeated obligation of "good neighbourhood" ... meant many things but amongst them was the expectation that women be hospitable to neighbours and strangers who came to the house and that they should "visit such as stand in need" outside it, complicating constructions of the virtuous wife as solitary and enclosed.'[321] Introverted, quiet women found it hard to maintain social networks. In Elizabeth's reign, for example, Launcelot Robinson of Stanhope (County Durham) presented an ambivalent assessment of the local gentlewoman Isabell Bele's place. She was, he told the Durham consistory court,

a simple quiet woman and had a stamminge in her speech & used to speake seldome to any unlesse they demaunded question of [her.] And this ex[aminan]t did take her to be a woman of small discretion the rather for that she did not apply her selfe to such woorkes as other gentlewomen of the said p[ar]ish did but did use her selfe more privately seldom accompanyinge with any and sometimes used to com alone & not with the reste of the householde to church wherein she did shue a variable mynde in her selfe.

Margaret Key confirmed this assessment: she said that Isabell Bele 'was reputed to be of small estimacion by reason she estranged herselfe from company of other gentlewomen and never applied herselfe to any exercises or workes'.[322]

An acid test of women's place within their communities was the matter of male violence. Disputes between husband and wife were genuinely disturbing for their neighbours. Importantly, there was no sense that familial relations were private. It was necessary, where household values were threatened by internal discord, to put the matter right in public. Thus, in 1579, following gossip that she was involved in an adulterous relationship with a neighbour, the Essex woman Alice Kynge was ordered 'on Sunday [to] come sennight in the church to openly submit herself to her husband and to ask his forgiveness and to promise amendment'.[323] Households where a wife was felt to exercise undue power over her husband might be subject to a skimmington, in which both marital parties were led backwards through the streets of their community. Often, such occasions turned nasty, with the woman being beaten and dragged

---

[320] Thistleton-Dyer, *Old English Social Life*, 75.   [321] Flather, *Gender and Space*, 31.
[322] DUL, DDR/EJ/CCD/1/7, fol. 54, 57r.   [323] Emmison (ed.), *Elizabethan Life*, 67.

through the dirt.[324] Such skimmingtons were highly ritualized, partici-
pants presenting a collective statement of an upside-down world where
gender hierarchies had been inverted.[325] Thus, in Hadleigh (Essex), it
was reported in 1587 that there had been an 'outrage' following 'a mans
wieff beating her husband: there was hereupon a man in womans attire
and a woman in mans' who were 'caried on a cowle staff w[i]th a drumme
and Calyver and morise pikes on mens sh[o]ulders'.[326] Where it was
believed that a man and a woman were living together outside the
bonds of marriage, something similar might occur. In the deprived,
turbulent Norwich suburb of Pocklington, for example, a skimmington
took place in 1616 that involved drums, flags and a cuckold's horns, all of
it allegedly sanctioned by the local gentry.[327]

The public character of communal relationships meant that the apparently private authority of the patriarch to impose violent discipline upon
his household could be held up for effective criticism. Thus, in 1588, the
minister of Wenham (Suffolk) asked of his godly colleagues of the
Dedham Classis the sharp question of 'what shuld be done w[i]th a
wicked man that did beate his wieff and [tha]t was commonly knowen,
whether he shuld be received to the Communion w[i]thout publike confession'. He received no advice; rather the matter was 'deferred for this
tyme'.[328] In some circumstances, the common report of the neighbourhood might be mobilized against men who overstepped the perceived
mark of household discipline.[329] Unlike the Dedham Classis, ordinary
neighbours felt no embarrassment in intervening in household conflicts:
after the Londoner Ralf Pollard repeatedly beat his wife, he was 'divers
tymes' criticized by 'ye neighbours'.[330] Laura Gowing provides another
example from the London church court: in 1629, Margery Alyver and her
neighbours went to see Margaret Framer, who was sick in bed after
receiving a beating from her husband. As Alyver explained the matter,
'this deponent and the reste did plainly perceive that her sicknes came
only through her husbands cruell and harde delinge with her in beating
and brusing of her bodye ...[A]ll the neighbours there and abouts hath
made great complaint and spoke against Farmer for his ... ill dealing with
his wife.'[331]

---

[324] The best-known example of which is that at Calne (Wiltshire) in 1618, for which see
Howard Cunnington (ed.), *Records of the County of Wiltshire*, 64–6.

[325] S. D. Amussen and D. E. Underdown, *Gender, Culture and Politics in England, 1560–
1640: Turning the World Upside Down* (London, 2017).

[326] Usher (ed.), *The Presbyterian Movement in the Reign of Queen Elizabeth*, 63.

[327] NRO, NCR MS 453, T133A (folder 60).

[328] Usher (ed.), *The Presbyterian Movement in the Reign of Queen Elizabeth*, 71–2.

[329] Amussen, 'Being Stirred to Much Unquietnesss', 70–89.

[330] Archer, *The Pursuit of Stability*, 77.     [331] Gowing, *Domestic Dangers*, 216.

Communal values often overtook those based upon patriarchal authority. In 1611, one Norfolk man was taken before the Quarter Sessions because 'he beat his wife in sutch sort as if the constable had not beene he would have spoyled her'.[332] The magistracy heard in the same year from the neighbours of William Wright, who not only was constantly drunk and at war with those about him but (as they explained) 'he hath lyved very disquietly w[i]t[h] his wyffe & very many tymes in most rigourus manner beaten her And hath put her out of dores & kepte her out all the night'.[333] Violent husbands could also found themselves presented before the diocesan authorities. In 1575, the churchwardens of Ely presented William White for living 'evilly and disquietly'; his wife was in terror of him because, they explained, 'he is of that opinion that it is as lawful to kill a woman with child as a bullock or other beast, and standeth so stiffly in that opinion that he cannot be reformed'.[334]

And it was not only in their role as husbands that men would bring violence into the household. Fathers could show violence against their children as well, perhaps especially over matrimonial matters. In February 1571, twenty-year-old Janet Barras told the Durham church court that

a weik after mydsom[e]r wch was a twelvemonth viz in the yere off or lorde god 1569 . . . th[a]t Anth[ony] Barras hir father had put hir out of his house . . . bycause she wold not be content to tak[e] w[i]l[lia]m waldo als waldhome to hir husband betting hir and thretting hir, and also p[er]suadinge hir . . . to have and take the said w[i]l[lia]m to hir husband so th[a]t at the tyme aforesaid beinge the Monday next aft[e]r the said mydsom[e]rto hir remembrance she was handfast w[i][th the said w[i]l[lia]m waldhome in the presence of hir father aforesaid Th[omas] Johnson [Christophe]r walhome Edward waldoo w[i]l[lia]m andover Robert andro hir uncles Johis dalton [chritsophe]r stubbs & others w[hi]ch contract was maid one quarter of ayer & more aft[e]r th[a]t she . . . was contract wth Richard harrison for she . . . was contract wth the said Rich[ard] the week next after candlemas next byfore in his fathers house in the presence of john hedworth bailiff Rich[ard] harrison of whickh[a]m John Chrishep Janet walhouse.[335]

Despite being presented by an intimidatingly large body of adult men from her village, young Janet stood up to them, refusing to be bound by any marriage contract to William Waldo and preferring to be bound to Richard Harrison.

Violent male householders – for all their apparent patriarchal authority – could thereby be seen as problematic members of the neighbourhood. This was true of their violence not just towards their wives and children

[332] NRO, NQS/C/S3/17/1, articles against Everid.
[333] NRO, NQS/C/S3/17/2, articles against William Wright.
[334] Capp, *When Gossips Meet*, 108.      [335] DUL, DDR/EJ/CCD/1/2, fol. 212v.

but also towards servants and apprentices. On 5 March 1620, the Norfolk bench heard from William Woodward. He told them that his son had been bound apprentice to Richard Blanch, but that Blanch 'hath att sev[er]all tymes beaten the said John Woodward in an unreasonable manner and th[a]t he beate him att one tyme w[i]th a whipp of Five cords'. On another occasion, Blanch beat the boy so violently 'as that his eyes were so swollen as that he could not see'.[336] In a small community, these things would be noticed. The young lad's swollen eyes were a testimony to the excessive violence of his vicious master. All of this will have weighed heavily on Richard Blanch's reputation amongst his neighbours: far from being a Christian man, the neighbours had come to see him as violent and cruel. And it was not only men who were accused: on 21 June 1614, the Norfolk bench learnt that Agnes Mynnes of Methwold had beaten her servant Margaret Hodge so repeatedly that Margaret had ended up severely disabled.[337]

The evidence points to violent men worrying that their wives might receive succour and aid from their female friends. Here, perhaps, there was something akin to what we might want to call women's solidarity, along with the willingness of women to intervene in local disputes. In 1586, Thomas Browne of Wawne (Yorkshire) began to beat his pregnant wife, Anne. Threatened by the support she received from some of her female neighbours, he kept her from her clothes so as to detain her indoors and (in his own words) 'did forbid two or three women from keeping company w[i]th his wyffe in this R[esp]ondents howse for that this R[esp]ondent did suspect them to geve evell counsel to his wyffe'.[338] Faced by recurrent violence from her husband, in 1629, Anne Bytson of Narborough (Norfolk) brought the matter before the magistrates. She explained that her husband had attacked her while she was rocking her child in its cradle, breaking two of her ribs; on another occasion, the man had struck Anne with the tongs from the fireside. Importantly, Anne Bytson was supported by the women of her locality, who provided evidence of her husband's violence. The widow Margaret Mowlster, for example, told the bench that 'when she kept Anne Bytson the wife of Henrie Bytson in Child bed, her husband would allowe her noe victuals but a barl[e]y cake'; he had mocked her, 'sa[y]ing she was a whore; and common whore; and bid her bring up her bastard and carie it to Swaffham Market and sell it'.[339]

---

[336] NRO, NQS/C/S3/22, information of William Woodward. Things could cut both ways. For a vivid account of a fist-fight between a master and a servant, see NRO, NQS/C/S3/22, examination of Dorothy Hall.

[337] NRO, NQS/C/S3/18, certificate of inhabitants of Methwold.    [338] BIA, CP.G.2235.

[339] NRO, NQS/C/S3/27, information of Anne Bytson.

Where a woman had links within her neighbourhood, though, if faced by a violent husband, she might be able to draw upon female friends as Anne Bytson did with Margaret Mowlster. Similarly, if she lived in a community where she had close kin, she might fall back on them for support. Thus, early in Elizabeth's reign, Isabell Forlocke told the Durham church court that her daughter's husband

hath not used hir as an honest ma[n] ought to use his wyff. For she had no lib[er]tie of meat nor drink and this ex[aminant] beinge her mother ca[me] often tymes to hir the said agnes at w[hi]ch tymes she p[er]ceyved that yt was so ... and she saith further th[a]t hir daughter hath told hir that when he the said tho[mas] hir husband had company w[i]th hir he would gyve hir iiii.d w[hi]ch he said was the [payment] ... of a hoore ...[. S]he saith th[a]t she hath sein hir said daughters boddy blake and bloo w[i]th strooks.[340]

Early modern men worried over the possibility that women might stand together. Women's solidarity formed the basis of a ballad in 1633: another 'joke' that illuminated a wider anxiety. It begins with Nell hurrying through the village to attend to the birthing-chamber of a neighbour when she is stopped by Sisse, who asks:

> Whither away good neighbour
> What makes you to trudge so fast?
> Im going to Margeryes Labour,
> Im sent for in very great hast:
> Yet for all this your speed,
> I pray you goe softly a while,
> For I have a thing in my head
> That will hold us talking a mile:
> Heard you not lately of Hugh,
> How soundly his wife he bangd
> He beat her black and blew,
> O such a Rogue would be hanged

Nell and Sisse then discuss other cases of domestic violence, which appears to have been widespread in their village. In each instance, they condemn the brutality of husbands. Kett the Baker is cited as one example:

> Hee threatens his wife to forsake her
> ... Why what is his reason for that?
> In troth neighbour I doe not know,
> But when hees as drunke as a Rat,
> Then sheel act the part of a shrow
> Tush, that's such a catching disease
> Few women their silence can keepe,

[340] DUL, DDR/EJ/CCD/1/2, fol.83r.

> Let every one say what they please
> But a shrews better than a sheepe[.]

Women's assertiveness in the face of a drunken and unfaithful husband is held up in the ballad as praiseworthy. From this, the women draw the following conclusion:

> O fye on these dastardly Knaves,
> For those that will beate their wives
> They dare not with swords or staves
> Meet men in the field for their lives:
> But if my husband should
> Not use mee so well as he ought;
> My hands I should hardly hold
> For ide give him as good as he brought.[341]

Who sang this song? Most likely it was not the men of the Tudor and early Stuart village, but more likely their womenfolk, in their cups, as a collectivity, together.

Neighbours' negative reactions to domestic violence were noted in the ballad *A Hee-Divell*, which discusses the controlling cruelties of a husband who 'with his girdle' beat his wife 'though all the neighbours blame him'. Significantly, this husband is depicted as attempting to sever his wife from support from her female neighbours:

> If any neighbour me invite,
> To gossiping, or feasting,
> I dare not goe (is not this a spight)
> For feare of his molesting
> I forth to supper went one night,
> But that may be my warning,
> Heele not indure me out on's sight,
> He is so afraid of horning.[342]

'He is so afraid of horning': that is, of being cuckolded, that perennial male anxiety. Yet, some men found domestic violence amusing. In 1614, Richard Hutchins climbed into the minister's place in his parish church of All Cannings (Wiltshire) and announced that 'the one and twentieth chapter of Maud Butcher and the seventh verse: man, love thy wife and thy wife will love thee; and if she will not do as thou wilt, have her take a staff and break her arms and her legs and she will forgive thee'.[343]

---

[341] Anon., *Well Met Neighbour: or, A Dainty Discourse betwixt Nell and Sisse* (London, c.1633).

[342] Anon., *A Hee-divell* (London, 1630).

[343] M. Ingram, 'Ridings, Rough Music and Mocking Rhymes in Early Modern England', in B. Reay (ed.), *Popular Culture in Seventeenth-Century England* (London, 1985), 166.

But, in many cases, it was not only women who were appalled by male violence. Let us return to the ugly story of Thomas Browne of Wawne and his systematic cruelty to his wife, Anne. Thomas Browne's neighbour, the husbandman George Martyn, presented detailed testimony concerning Thomas's treatment of Anne. Martyn explained that for the past six months, 'Anne not daring to dwell w[i]th hir said husband did dep[ar]te frome him'. Martyn added that Browne's violence was common knowledge in Wawne. As Martyn put it, he 'hath hard it comonlie reported that the said Thom[a]s w[i]thin one quarter of a yere or thereabouts aft[e]r his mariag[e] to the said Anne did begin to use crueltie towards his said wife, & co[n]tinued the same till she dep[ar]tid from him'. Martyn explained that, some twelve months ago, he had been in the churchyard at Wawne with his neighbours when he heard Anne Browne, 'being in hir owne house sate nere to the said churchyard, cry most pitifullye, hir said husband being then beating of hir, as he & the rest of the hearers did verily believe, for they co[u]ld not see into the house, but might well here it to be so'. Later on, he saw Browne

beating his wife Anne Browne ... the said Anne lying upo[n] the ground & he standing ov[er] hir beating his wife w[i]th his fists & after this ex[aminan]t had so espied them & seeing that the said Thom[a]s did not cease to beat hir he went to them, & asked him what he meant so to deale w[i]th hir, who answered, I care not if I kill hir, & when this ex[aminan]te exhorted him to quietnes, saying that she was great w[i]th child as she was in deed answerid that he carid not if he killed hir & that in hir bellie[.]

Following Thomas's assault, Anne tried to drown herself in the village pond, but she was dragged out by George Martyn and his neighbor, Richard Watson. Martyn went on to tell his terrible story:

being so gotte[n] furth the said Thom[a]s Browne begonne to use evill speches against hir saying get th[e]e into the house thow art a whore & when she was in the house, he threatened hir most cruelie not anyway pittying hir being great w[i]th child & half dead, & then comandid this ex[aminan]te & the said Richard Watso[n] of[f] of his ground, saying what have yow to do betwixt me & my wife.

Significantly, when the matter came to the church court, Anne represented her husband's actions as a breach of Christian social values, saying that he behaved 'more lyke a Turke than a [Christ]ian', exercising 'extreme cruelty and tyranny' against her and on one occasion stuffing her mouth with his glove so that she could not be heard as he beat her. Thomas Browne was unembarrassed by his violence, discussing his cruelty in terms of what he saw as his legitimate right as the patriarchal head of the household to discipline its subordinate members. He told the church court 'that he this R[es]pondent hathe divers tyme corrected her

the sayd Anne, and upon juste cause hath beaten her w[i]th a Rodd
sometimes w[i]th his fiste, especially for that she the sayd Anne Browne
did confesse her selfe to be of unhonest behaviour and that she had
abused her bodye in fornicacion or adulterye'. Infuriated by this stain
on his masculine honour, Browne stated that he 'did chastise the sayd
Anne, and moderately beat her w[i]thowt any hurte to her bodye' and that
he 'did beate the sayd Anne, but not unreasonablye'. In this way, he
hoped to restore his patriarchal authority, telling the court that 'he ...
for the causes aforesaid did beate and chastise her the sayd Anne to th[e]
end to make her a duetifull wyfe', for she was 'a woman voyde of the feare
of god' who 'could not abyde any due correction'.[344] Thomas Browne
was not the only frustrated would-be patriarch who turned to his perceived legitimate right to beat his wife in order to reassert his failing
authority.

In some cases, though, patriarchy was trumped by neighbourhood:
persistently violent men could be frozen out of local communities. In
1599, the consistory court of Lichfield and Coventry heard of the yeoman
George Wilson's violence towards his wife, Mary. This was well known
'in the comon speache of the Cuntrye' around the Wilsons' home village
of Crich (Derbyshire). Knowledge of Wilson's ill-treatment of Mary came
initially from the gossip of his servants, who passed on word of the matter
to the women of the village, who in turn spoke to their menfolk. In
response, seeing him as a disruptive presence, Wilson's 'frendes' advised
him to stop beating Mary. When he failed to do so, he was bound over by a
magistrate; but still the violence continued. Finally, the matter appeared
before the church court. Notably, almost all of those who gave evidence
against Wilson came from Crich; in contrast, those who deposed on his
behalf came from further afield. The village had turned against him.[345]

[344] BIA, CP.G.2235.
[345] Lichfield Joint Record Office, B/C/5/1599: matrimony, Crich.

# 4     The Tongues of Men and Angels:
## Inclusion and Exclusion

### Newfangled Precisians: Neighbourhood and Religious Division

In his 1549 dialogue on the commonwealth, Sir Thomas Smith set the following words into the mouth of the Capper, angered by the pious reformist speech of the Doctor of Divinity:

I would set youe to the plowghe and cart, for the devell a whit the good doe ye with youre studies, but set men together by the eares. Some with this opinion and some with that, some holding this waye and some that waye, and some an other, and that so stifly as thoughe the truthe must be as they saye that have the upper hand in contention. And this contention is not the least cause of theise uprors of the people; some holdinge of the one learninge and some holdinge of the other. In my mynde it made no matter yf theare weare no lerned men at all ... for of diversitie thereof, comes divers opinions.[1]

Not for the only time, the words of Smith's imaginary disputants reflected real concerns. We will see in this section the ways in which radical Protestantism was contested by ordinary people, and how in the end they managed to defeat the Puritan project of radically reforming their culture.

There was an important achievement here, one that has a significance beyond the social history of England alone. In a powerful monograph, Philip Gorski has connected the organic, bottom-up process of state formation in the Dutch United Provinces to the emergent domination of Calvinism.[2] Gorski observes: 'The Calvinists ... aimed at nothing less than the establishment of an all-encompassing regime of moral and social discipline – a disciplinary revolution.' Inevitably citing Michel Foucault, he goes on to argue for a vision of state formation 'as a bottom-up process in which the capillaries and synapses of power within the social body are

---

[1] E. Lamond (ed.), *A Discourse on the Commonweal of this realm of England* (Cambridge, 1893), 21–22.
[2] Something similar, although less overt, underlies the argument in Steve Hindle's highly influential work: S. Hindle, *The State and Social Change in England, 1550–1640* (Basingstoke, 2000).

gradually plugged into and connected with the central circulatory and nervous systems of the state'. The difference between England and the United Provinces is that Calvinism was hegemonic in the Dutch Republic. In England, Puritan domination was never more than regional (for instance, in Essex, in parts of the West Country and in the West Riding) and sometimes narrowly parochial, or focused on a particular urban centre such as Colchester, Norwich or Dorchester. Deprived of national political influence, the English godly settled for the creation of local Puritan regimes. Drawing upon Max Weber, Gorski suggests that Calvinism 'tended to promote poor-law reform, political revolution, bureaucratization and social order more generally'. To any social historian of early modern England, this is all very familiar; he notes: 'The provincial diets could and did issue mandates regarding marriage, sexuality, criminality, vagabondage, poverty, unemployment, education, and other such matters.' But their enforcement was very much in the hands of local officials, who had interests and agendas of their own. It was they who registered the marriages, punished the criminals, dispensed poor-relief, built the schools and so on. The critical point is that subaltern groups in parishes dominated by the godly *permanently contested* the local hegemony of the godly – sometimes overtly, sometimes covertly and sometimes just by *being* – by holding on to some autonomy and dignity in the face of a Calvinist agenda that was informed by the idea of the 'disciplinary revolution'.[3]

What we see in Tudor and early Stuart England is the everyday contestation of this disciplinary revolution by poorer people, sometimes allied to religiously conservative elites. In the course of this struggle, concepts of neighbourhood became a terrain of conflict. That process of contestation developed prior to the emergence of Puritanism in the early Elizabethan period. In 1537, for example, a faction amongst the parishioners of Langham (Essex) wrote to the Council to denounce the questman John Vigorouse for his evangelical views. They said that although they sought only to 'lyve in peace and quyetnes', Vigorouse was a 'troublesome and disquyet neyboure'. The roots of division, the Langham petitioners felt, had been correctly identified by their priest, Master Warde. In a sermon, he had said of the new learning that 'there was in it newfanglenes, whereof he exhorted men shulde beware'. The arrival of the new learning in Langham had divided the young people of the village: 'One of vigorous servants at a tyme w[i]t[h]in this yeare didde quarelle & brawle w[i]t[h] other children many [of] whome he called heretykes and as children[n] be

[3] P. S. Gorski, *The Disciplinary Revolution: Calvinism and the Rise of the State in Early Modern Europe* (Chicago, IL, 2003), 22, 23–4, 28, 45–8.

lyte & wanton they called the sayde s[er]vante agayne pharyz[i]e.'[4] In these ways, communities split apart; many ordinary people disliked witnessing this, and blamed radical Protestants for the state of affairs.

In early sixteenth-century Sussex, parishioners sued their minister after he called one of their number a heretic; in the 1530s, people were reluctant to identify others as religious dissidents 'for fear of being "regarded in the sight of all as guilty of treachery against their neighbours"'.[5] Things were just as bad in some Kentish villages. In 1537, in one parish, the beadmen were held responsible for the introduction of divisive evangelical opinions into the village. The parishioners had agreed 'to stycke together like men and bete down [the] ... beidmen'. One man said that 'it wold never be well till they had killed iiii or v of us your beidman'. There were violent assaults and in the church it was declared that villagers would 'dryve thise heretike knaves out of the p[ar]ishe'. The result was that the beadmen dared not come out of their houses, for their neighbours paraded about with arms in their hands. There was opposition to the religious division of the parish. Thomas Sharp said 'that he was wery of all togethers for we cannot agree w[i]t[h]in our selfs[. W]ell[,] said Edward battarst[,] I pray god that all may be well that we may be lovers and freends[N]ay[,] said Thomas Sharpe[,] that will never be till v or vi be kylled of thise newe fellowes in our p[ar]ishe.'[6]

Elsewhere within Kent, there were still darker forces at work. When John Bland, minister of Adisham and later a Marian martyr, criticized the mass in a sermon, he was attacked by the churchwarden and his son-in-law, who

violently came upon me, and toke my booke from me, and pulled me down, & thrust me into the chauncell, with an exceding rore and crye: some cryed, thou heretycke: some, thou traitour: some, thou Rebel: & when every man had said his pleasure, & the rage was something past: be quiet good neighbours said I, and let me speake to you quietly.[7]

But of quietness there was little in many Kentish parishes in the Reformation period. Richard Baker, for example, asked his neighbour Thomasine Ashton, who sat in her pew while the rest of the parish of Westgate, Canterbury, went on a procession, 'Why follow ye not the cross?', adding, 'Ye be a heretic, will ye never leave your heresy?'.[8]

[4] TNA, E36/120, fols. 59r-64r.
[5] A. Walsham, *Charitable Hatred: Tolerance and Intolerance in England, 1500–1700* (Manchester, 2006), 273.
[6] TNA, E36/120, fol. 10r-v.
[7] J. Foxe, *Actes and Monuments* (London, 1563), V, 1288.
[8] Collinson, *The Birthpangs of Protestant England*, 51.

Perhaps especially within cities, the Reformation opened all sorts of fissures. On 1 July 1549, Robert Kyrke of the Norwich parish of St Mary Coslany said 'that the rich men had of the churche goodes & the pore men non[e]'. Geoffery Mitchell observed one parishioner denounce and attack another: he 'called the Rich men of the p[ar]isshe churles' and refused to pay the parish rates. The dispute ended with punches being thrown.[9]

The Reformation was connected to larger shifts in material relations. One constant theme pursued by the Commonwealth writers of the mid-sixteenth century was that the dissolution of the monastic houses had been a missed opportunity. The Dissolution, they felt, had been largely negative, removing from the poor the benefits of institutional charity and from tenants the easy lordship of the monasteries. Thomas Becon observed in 1553 that those who had bought monastic lands 'abhor the names of monks, friars, canons, nuns ... but their goods they greedily gripe. And yet, where the cloisters kept hospitality, let out their farms at a reasonable price, nourished schools, brought up youth in good letters', the new owners do 'none of all these things'.[10] The effects of these transformations endured. Writing in 1591, Michael Sherbrooke observed that, as a consequence of the Dissolution,

now there be so many sorts of inferior Persons made Gentlemen, by reason of the Fall of the Monasteries, Colleges and such like, that the said Gentlemen to maintain their Estate and Calling; and not being contented to live according to the rate of their Revenues, as other antient gentlemen in times past did, are compelled to raise their Rent so high that an acre of Ground, that might have been letten to farm before King Henry 8 times iiii.d. will now not be let for iii.s. And if there be any Peice of wast Ground, wherein their Tenants and others have used to have Common for their Cattle; all is taken in, and so enclosed from all others, that the poor Cottagers, that always before might have kept a Cow for sustaining of himself, his wife and Children and or xx.ty sheep towards their Cloathing, now is not able to keep so much as a Goose or a Hen.[11]

The confessional policies of the state – changing with each short alteration of regime in the mid-sixteenth century – were highly divisive. Amongst the 'enormities' in the realm that were listed in October 1550, it was observed:

The forme of religion is not used alike in all places but one useth on[e] fac[ti]on an other useth an other fac[ti]on diverselye as divers mens fantazies thinketh best ... The people give them selves more to seek mat[t]er in scriptures to maintain false disputac[i]ons and to condempn their neighboures liefs and conversac[i]on then

---

[9] NRO, NCR16A/4, fol. 65r.    [10] Ayre (ed.), *The Catechism of Thomas Becon*, 435.
[11] A. G. Dickens (ed.), *Tudor Treatises*, YASRS, 75 (Wakefield, 1959), 128–9.

thereby to knowe the benefites of Christe to them or to lerne their duetye to hym and theire neighboures or to travaille by their dedes to shew the same.[12]

Yet neighbourliness could be a barrier to the imposition of state policies that were deemed to be divisive or cruel. Whatever people made of evangelical reformers, there were many who saw the Marian persecutions as extreme and who disliked seeing neighbours betray one another. This offence against communal values was remembered in some places with considerable negativity. A century later, local tradition in Coddenham (Suffolk) had it that providence had struck down those who had betrayed their neighbours in the Marian persecutions, one of them losing his lands and dying 'full of lice'; another, though 'a great man in Estate[,] decayed little by little and left a small pittance to his children'.[13] Had the Marian regime lasted longer, pursuing religious policies that led to denunciations and executions, it may have become still more unpopular than the godly who, returning from exile in Calvinist cities on the Continent, brought with them new policies for social control and a second reformation.

If the Reformation seemed to many ordinary people to threaten the ideals of parochial unity with which they had been raised, the later emergence of Puritanism seemed like an existential threat to the values of good neighbourhood. Puritanism was inherently divisive. Pursuing their disciplinary revolution, many radical Protestants were unembarrassed by the challenge that their ideology represented to the neighbourly values that were embodied in traditional religion. There was much for common people to dislike in godly doctrine. By definition, the godly were thought to be the enemies of the values of neighbourhood. In 1629, one alehousekeeper admitted to voicing the opinion that 'he is a puritan that ... inventeth how to do his neighbour an ill turn'.[14] Puritans saw the alcoholic culture of good fellowship as a fundamental challenge to their disciplinary revolution. Richard Byfield stated categorically in 1630: 'Thou maiest not call him to the Alehouse or Taverne, to bibbe and drinke, or play the glutton, thou must not put thy bottle to him, and make him drunke. Woe to thee if thou doe it; this is cursed fellowship, which thou callest good fellowship.'[15] Likewise, in answer to the proposition that drinking together 'is said to be neighbourhood and good fellowshippe', William Perkins wrote: 'It is drunken fellowship. The right fellowship is in the doctrine of the

---

[12] BL, Egerton MS 2623, fol. 9r-v.     [13] BL, Add MS 15520, fols. 22v-3r.
[14] C. Haigh, 'The Character of an Anti Puritan', *Sixteenth Century Journal*, 35, 3 (2004), 683.
[15] R. Byfield, *The Light of Faith* (London, 1630), 419.

Apostles, praier, Sacraments, and the workes of mercie.'[16] In a later pamphlet, Perkins went on to condemn the widespread view that 'drunkennes' be 'counted good fellowship, & kinde neighbourhood'.[17] Yet other godly writers saw in neighbourhood a body of social norms that linked everyday practices and relationships with Christian social ideals. Richard Byfield observed in 1630 that 'it is an imputation cast upon religion and preaching, that it spoiles all good neighbourhood: yet in very deed it shall appeare, that this onely formes us hereunto, and destroyes nothing, but that bad·good-fellowship of rude, unmortified men, which is impious, uncivill, and pernicious'.[18]

All of this represented a wider attack on plebeian culture, something that the godly saw as entirely unproblematic. In Arthur Dent's 1601 text *The Plaine Man's Path-Way to Heaven*, one of his disputants, Antilegon ('a caviller'), observes: 'If neighbours meete together now and then at the Alehouse, and plaie a game or two at maw, for a pot of Ale, meaning no hurt: I take it to be good fellowship, and a good meanes to increase love amongst neighbours.' In response, Theologus ('a Divine') thunders: 'All drunkards are notorious reprobates and hell-hounds, branded of Sathan, and devoted to perpetuall destruction and damnation', adding that the consequence of poor men drinking all day was that their wives and children starved.[19]

And so, not without reason, the godly were seen by many ordinary people as the enemies of neighbourhood. Some of the godly recognized this: the Bermondsey minister Edward Elton noted in 1618 that

wee heare men say, There was never good world, since there was so much preaching and so much professing: Here is a vile place indeed, here is so much preaching and so much professing in it, as that men cannot now be merry in this place, and they cannot use that good neighbourhood in it as they were wont.[20]

Returning to that godly minister of Maldon (Essex) George Gifford, he put the following words into the mouth of a character who personified his conservative parishioners:

[G]odlinesse cannot bee suffered to come neere, for [the puritan] is a breake peace and a very unpleasant felow, hee is over rough and precise, and over captious, there was good neighbourhood and friendshippe before he came, they could be merie together, and bee in unitie, without anye jarre: had it not bene better to use

[16] W. Perkins, *A Commentarie or Exposition, upon the Five First Chapters of the Epistle to the Galatians* (London, 1604), 440–1.
[17] W. Perkins, *A Treatise of Mans Imaginations* (London, 1607), 136.
[18] Byfield, *The Light of Faith*, 416.
[19] A. Dent, *The Plaine Man's Path-Way to Heaven* (London, 1601), 186–7.
[20] E. Elton, *The Complaint of a Sanctified Sinner Answered* (London, 1618), 275.

gentlenesse and patience, then to have this broyle? for there is nothing better then love, and where that is not, there is nothing good.[21]

It was the opinion of his conservative parishioners, Gifford maintained, that Puritans disrupted the social order in manifold ways, coming into conflict with elementary social norms. He set the following words in a parishioner's mouth:

> There bee a number goe so farre they cannot tell what they may doe: they will not doe as their honest neighbours doe, they wilbe wiser then their betters: what shoulde they meddle with Gods woorde, it maketh them busie in checking every man. It was never merry since men unlearned have medled with the scriptures.[22]

In a similarly dialogic text written by the Lincolnshire vicar Thomas Granger, a plebeian critic of his Puritan minister says the following:

> But heere is the mischiefe, hee is too bold, and too indiscreet in his Catechizings and Sermons, he ... is alwaies roaving into Townes matters, and mens manners, that he hath nought to doe with: We are not so ignorant (as it pleases him to terme us sometimes) but we can see when he leaves his teske. What is it for him to stand telling us of such things as are not in the Scripture? We have some in our towne that can read indifferently well marry, and are good sensible men, that can finde no such matter in the Bible: Wherefore we thinke that hee is too precise and curious. It comes surely of pride, that hee would have all men ruled by him (and that our townes men know well enough) and that both his apparell and medling in high matters doth testifie; or it comes of malice, for hee hath no good neighbour-hood in him: or of envy, even as other poore men grudge at, and envy rich men.[23]

The consequence of the Puritan disciplinary revolution was to contest key aspects of the values of neighbourhood. In another dialogic text, the views of many parishioners of Puritan vicars were summarized as follows:

> [H]ee preacheth of malice, because he hath no good neighbourhood in him, because hee goes not to the Ale-house with you, and your hang-byes, haile-fellowes well met, to drinke and to game, and to preach over the pot (you would then heare him, with great devotion, and not say he preached prittle-prattle) therefore he hath no good neighbourhood in him. If you knew what good neigh-bourhood were, you should see none in any of you, so much as in him.

The conservative parishioner then demands of his godly neighbor, '[W]hat call you good neighbourhood[?]', to which the godly man answers as follows:

> If your fellowship and friendship be knit in God, it is good fellowship: If your feasting and meetings be as they were in the Primitive Church among Christians, using your selves as in the presence of God, there is good fellowship and

[21] Gifford, *Foure Sermons*, sig. D2r.

[22] Gifford, *A Briefe Discourse of Certaine Pointsbriefe discourse*, fol. 17v.

[23] T. Granger, *Pauls Crowne of Re[j]oycing* (London, 1616), 29.

neighbourhood. If you be affectioned to love one another with brotherly love, and in giving honour one going before another, that is good neighbourhood ... If your rich men prey not on the poore, by rent-racking, by small measures and great prizes, but releeve them before they fall, and helpe them up when they are fallen, then are you good neighbours. But if your good neighbour-hood be acted no where but at the Ale-house, in drinking and drunkennesse, ribaldry and swearing, in foolish [j]angling, rotten and unsavory speeches. In dissembling, lying, cousonage in bargayning, insnarings (called ale-house bargaines) wasting your good, then is it such like as S[aint] Peter speakes of ... It's like the meeting of swine at their trough.[24]

The most extreme Calvinist ideologues were clear that the concept of neighbourliness was itself inherently ungodly. John Dod, for example, had a dark reading of neighbourhood: 'Neighbours and kin are not to be depended upon; those who will help the godly in any Time of crisis are their co-religionists ... [. The godly should] associate our selves with godly men, for they will prove our surest friends. Vicinity and neighborhood will faile, and alliance and kindred will faile, but grace and religion will never faile.'[25] As Ronald Hutton has shown, the godly regarded the plebeian celebration of the ritual year as close to paganism. The frustrations of one godly minister might stand for thousands of his sort. In 1570, William Kethe presented a sermon at Blandform Forum (Dorset) in which he spoke of the sins of the 'multitude'. Not only did they ignore Protestant ministers' sermons, and not only did they hide in secret places the old Catholic rood screens, altars and statutes, but their year was structured around feasts that were at best popish and at worst pagan. For many, Kethe argued,

Shrost Tewsday was a day of great glottonie, surffeting & dronkennes, but by the Ashe Wensday at night, they thought God to be in their debt. On Goodfriday, they offered unto Christe egges, and bacon to be in hys favour till Easter day was past. The sinnes committed between Easter, and Whytsontyde they were fullye discharged by the pleasant walkes, and processions in the rogyng, I should say, Rogation Weeke. What offences soever happened from that tyme to Midsommer, the sumes of the friers dedicated to John, Peter and Thomas Becket the traytor, consumed them. And as for all disorders from that tyme to the begynnyng of Christmasse agayne, they were in this country all roonge away, upon all Hallowday and all Soules day at night last past.[26]

Puritanism therefore entailed an attack on ritual, festivity, good cheer – all of them neighbourly values that many celebrated.

Godly ministers may well have conferred amongst themselves on subjects such as 'peace and charity', but there remained a saying in early Jacobean England that 'a puritan is such a one as loves God with all his

---

[24] Ibid., 41–2.    [25] Dod, *A Plaine and Familiar Exposition*, 118.
[26] W. Kethe, *A Sermon Made at Blanford Foru[m]* (London, 1571), 19.

soul, but hates his neighbour with all his heart'.[27] The historian Diane Willen identifies Puritans as 'a self-fashioned community based on a strong degree of reciprocity, a patriarchal community which nevertheless blurred traditional lines of gender and, occasionally, of class'.[28] Critically, Puritanism was built into social structures: the godly perceived of themselves as distinct from those they called 'ignorant people', 'the common people', 'the common, ignorant sort of people', 'the multitude' and 'the ignorant multitude'.[29] Just as the godly criticized plebeian understandings of neighbourhood, so they thought of themselves as forming a neighbourhood of their own: one English translator of Calvin wrote of how the godly ought to comprise a 'mutual kindred or neighbourhood'.[30] Many ordinary people despised the godly for their seeming piety and for the division they brought to their villages. Some called them 'Scripture men' and 'precise fools'; others called them 'busie controllers'.[31] In a 1588 dialogue, an innkeeper complained of a godly preacher who 'setteth men by the ears, the town was never at quiet since he came, he teacheth such doctrine as some do like and some not, so they fall to variance'.[32] Thomas Tusser wrote against the godly, whom he saw as bearers of 'fantasticall scruplnenes'. He said of them:

> At this time and that time some make a great matter
> Som help not but hinder the poore with their clatter
> Take custome from feasting, what commeth then last,
> Where one hath a dinner, a hundred shall fast.[33]

Puritanism was widely seen as a driver of negative social change. Donald Lupton blamed the decline of gentry hospitality on 'pride, puritans, coaches and covetousness'.[34] In the 1630s, one Essex vicar told his congregation: 'It was never a merry world since there was so much preaching . . . for now all hospitality and good fellowship was laid abed.'[35]

---

[27] J. Ley, *Defensive Doubts, Hopes and Reasons for Refusal of the Oath Imposed by the Late Synod* (London, 1641), epistle dedicatory; P. Collinson, 'A Comment Concerning the Name Puritan', *Journal of Ecclesiastical History*, 31 (1980), 487.

[28] D. Willen, '"Communion of the Saints": Spiritual Reciprocity and the Godly Community in Early Modern England', *Albion*, 27 (1995), 20.

[29] Haigh, 'The Character of an Anti Puritan', 671. Haigh is quoting William Perkins.

[30] R. V., *A Commentarie of M. Iohn Calvine, upon the Epistle to the Colossians* (London, 1581), 80.

[31] C. Haigh, 'The Church of England, the Catholics and the People', in C. Haigh (ed.), *The Reign of Elizabeth I* (Basingstoke, 1984), 215; E. Duffy, 'The Godly and the Multitude in Stuart England', *The Seventeenth Century*, 1, 1 (1986), 37; Gifford, *A Briefe Discourse of Certaine Points*, epistle dedicatory, fol. 2v.

[32] Haigh, 'The Church of England, the Catholics and the People', 214.

[33] Tusser, *Five Hundred Points of Good Husbandry*, 64.

[34] Lupton, *London and the Country Carbonadoed*, 102–3.

[35] T. W. Davids (ed.), *Annals of Evangelical Nonconformity in the County of Essex* (London, 1853), 240, 439.

This connected to a wider sense that the teaching and preaching ministry represented an attack on neighbourhood. George Gifford recorded the common opinion of Puritans in Elizabethan Essex as follows: 'There be a number goe so farre they cannot tell what they may do: they wil not doe as their honest neighbours doe, they wilbe wiser then their betters: what should they meddle with Gods woorde, it maketh them busie in checking every man. It was never merry since men unlearned have medled with the scriptures.'[36] Importantly for later developments in the 1640s, during the reigns of James I and Charles I, the discourse of anti-Puritanism laid the basis for a sort of proto-royalism. This connected traditional gentry values of paternalism, good lordship and respect for the social hierarchy with a plebeian emphasis upon neighbourhood, beery fellowship and hostility to division. Thomas Randolph's comments on Puritans in his discussion of the Cotswold Games in 1636 are revealing:

> These teach that Dauncing is a [J]ezabell;
> And Barley-break, the ready way to Hell.
> The Morrice Idols, Whitsun-ales can be
> But prophane Reliques of a [J]ubilee!
> These in a Zeal, t'expresse how much they doe
> The Organs hate, have silenc'd Bag-pipes too;
> And harmlesse May-poles, all are rail'd upon
> As if they were the towers of Babilon.[37]

In many people's eyes, Puritans' failure to conform to communal religious norms made them unneighbourly. In particular, the tendency for the godly to bring division to communities made them appear deeply unattractive. In 1598, for example, after their new Puritan minister refused to wear the surplice or go on the Rogationtide perambulation, the churchwardens of Mapperton (Dorset) complained that, whereas before his arrival 'we lyved quietly in love and in charitie on[e] w[i]th an other', now there was only strife.[38] Twenty-six years later, the Wiltshire woman Susan Kent of Wylye observed of her parish that

we had a good parson here before but now we have a puritan ... a plague or a pox in him that ever he did come hither, and I would we had kept our old parson for he did never dislike with [games and dances] ... these proud puritans are up at the top nowe but I hope they will have a time to come as fast down as ever they came up.[39]

---

[36] Gifford, *A Briefe Discourse of Certaine Points*, epistle dedicatory, fol. 17v.

[37] T. Randolph, *Poems with the Muses Looking-Glasse and Amyntas* (Oxford, 1638).

[38] J. Hitchcock, 'Religious Conflict at Mapperton, 1597–99', *Proceedings of the Dorset Natural History and Archaeological Society*, 89 (1968), 230.

[39] Ingram, *Church Courts, Sex and Marriage*, 121.

The godly were unembarrassed by the divisions they brought. The wheat needed to be sifted from the chaff, they argued, and the elect set apart from the damned. Writing in 1612, Robert Wolcome said that there were two sorts of Christians, 'the one appearing and seeming, the other right and true ...[T]he visible and outward church in this world hath good and bad, worthy and unworthy, hath elect and reprobate.' Puritans differed over the proportion of the population that were to be saved; some thought one in twenty; others one in a thousand; the widely read writer Arthur Dent thought that if the godly were to be separated from the ungodly, 'I suppose we should not need the art of Arithmetic to number them'. In a sermon at St Paul's Cross, William Crashawe stated firmly: 'Wee must separate our selves from the wicked mans companie and societie as far as lawfully and conveniently we may, after we see him obstinate and incurable: this is Gods commandment.'[40] The godly were, as one Calvinist writer put it in the 1630s, to be distinguished by their 'reverent love and insatiable longing after the word preached and read, prayer, singing of psalms, meditation, conferences, vows, days of humiliation, use of good books, godly company, all God's ordinances and good means appointed and sanctified for our spiritual good'.[41] In particular, the godly were hostile to elemental aspects of neighbourhood and found fundamental aspects of popular religion wholly unacceptable. Puritans tended to dislike the clear, direct assumptions made by many people concerning the link between Christian belief and communal relations. In particular, they disliked religious opinions that drew upon practical common-sense notions of how the world worked or ideas that had been inherited from the past. William Perkins, for example, included amongst the 'great ignorance' of 'poore people' the following propositions:

1. That faith is a mans good meaning & his good serving of God
2. That God is served by the rehearsing of the ten Commandements, the Lords praier, and the Creede
3. That yee have believed in Christ ever since you could remember ...
11. That it is an easier thing to please God, than to please our neighbour ...
13. That it is the safest, to doo in Religion as most doo ...
18. That ye knowe al the Preacher can tell you: For he can say nothing, but that every man is a sinner, that we must love our neighbours as

---

[40] Collinson, 'The Cohabitation of the Faithful with the Unfaithful', 52–3, 61–2.
[41] P. Lake, '"A Charitable Christian Hatred": The Godly and Their Enemies in the 1630s', in C. Durston and J. Eales (eds.), *The Culture of English Puritanism, 1500–1700* (Basingstoke, 1996), 154.

our selves, that everie man must bee saved by Christ: and all this ye can tell aswell as he.

19. That it was a good world when the old Religion was, because all things were cheape.

20. That drinking and bezeling in the alehouse or tavern is good fellowship, & shews a good kind nature . . .

27. That if a man be no adulterer, no theefe, nor murderer, and doo no man harme, he is a right honest man.

28. That a man need not have any knowledg[e] of religio[n], because he is not book learn[e]d.[42]

Perkins therefore set himself against a plebeian community that was semiliterate, informed by a desire to get along together, rooted in local memories and hostile to division. Within this model of neighbourhood, that which was thought commonsensical was preferred to that which seemed to Perkins to be complex questions of theological principle. In particular, the notions that community and collective opinion was to be preferred over abstraction and division and that memory was the basis for community – 'That yee have believed in Christ ever since you could remember'; 'That it was a good world when the old Religion was, because all things were cheap' – all of these operating assumptions, the godly insisted, were in some way wrong.

For many people, the reality of Puritanism was that it brought with it division. George Sharp, vicar of Brigstock (Northamptonshire), wrote to the earl of Salisbury in 1610:

I find all the chief of the parish, with many of the inferior sort on both sides depending, to consist of puritans. I hope something conformable, and of papists, I fear refractory and obstinate. Between both there is outwardly scar[c]e a show of humanity, but inwardly mortal and unchristian malice of the rest, many rebukeable for their dissolute courses, others to be pitied for their very beggarly estates. I am grieved that where there is no agreement with contrarities, nor any communion with different religions, he whose part is to reconcile shall find his labours uneffectual or intolerable.[43]

The great historian of Puritanism Patrick Collinson was always aware that, in many communities, godliness was experienced as a divisive presence.[44] Collinson argued that 'in their more realistic moments,

---

[42] W. Perkins, *The Foundation of Christian Religion* (London, 1590), sigs. A2r-3r.

[43] HMC, Salisbury MSS, XVII, 67–8.

[44] Insufficient has been written about anti-Puritanism, and what has been produced mostly depends on contemporary printed material and has little to say about plebeian anti-Puritanism. See P. Lake, 'Anti-Puritanism: The Structure of a Prejudice', in K. Fincham and P. Lake (eds.), *Religious Politics in Post-Reformation England: Essays in Honour of Nicholas Tyacke* (Woodbridge, 2006), 80–97; P. Collinson, 'Antipuritanism', in J.

protestants and puritans knew that "the multitude", "the great unjust rude rabble", was not of their side'. He quoted the godly writer John Darrell in 1617, who believed that only one in twenty of the English people were 'christian indeed ... the greatest part being the worst'.[45] That the godly set themselves apart was apparent in the naming of their children. The curate of Warbleton (Sussex) christened his offspring with names such as Much-Mercy, Increased, Sin-deny, Fear-not and Constance. Nicholas Tyacke's work on the parish registers for that village show that between 1586 and 1596, while some 124 children were given non-Puritan names, 93 children received names that might be associated with godliness. Judged on the emotive subject of naming, this was a divided village.[46] Puritan naming practices were controversial elsewhere. A dispute over the naming of a child of a godly couple was important enough to write itself into local memory: it was noted by the town chronicler of Barnstaple in 1599 that 'John Symons[,] a petie Skolemaster of this Town[,] not very hardly witted, but one of the Anabaptistical & Precise Brethren[,] had a Child brought to the Church to be christend & calld it Doe well, the Vicar disliking it calld it John, which caused a great murmuring among the Brethren who said it came from the Hebrew word Abdeel'.[47] In many places, anxieties that Puritanism entailed division were far from baseless. In East Hanningfield (Essex) in the 1580s, the minister refused communion to half the parish on the grounds that they were unfit to receive it, while he met to read the Bible with the other half, whom the allegedly unregenerate called 'saints and scripture men'.[48]

One way in which the apparently 'ungodly' might articulate their opinions of Puritans, who were often in positions of local authority, was through the anonymous libel, pinned to the market cross or sung aloud in alehouses. The godly were presented in one such libel as a hypocritical 'holie Brotherhood' and as the self-appointed 'purer sort'.[49] Adam Fox has made a special study of the practice of libelling. He cites a dispute in Jacobean Nottingham that set Puritan members of the corporation

Coffey and P. C. H. Lim (eds.), *The Cambridge Companion to Puritanism* (Cambridge, 2008), 19–33. For some attention to plebeian anti-Puritanism, see C. Haigh, 'The Character of an Anti Puritan', *Sixteenth Century Journal*, 35, 3 (2004), especially 678–84.
[45] P. Collinson, *The Religion of Protestants: The Church in English Society, 1559–1625* (Oxford, 1982), 49–50.
[46] N. Tyacke, *Aspects of English Protestantism, c.1530–1700* (Manchester, 2001), 96. On naming and Protestantism, see S. Wilson, *The Means of Naming: A Social and Cultural History of Personal Naming in Western Europe* (London, 1998), 194–5.
[47] T. Gray (ed.), *The Lost Chronicle of Barnstaple, 1586–1611* (Exeter, 1998), 83.
[48] Collinson, *The Birthpangs of Protestant England*, 149.
[49] S. R. Gardiner (ed.), *Reports of Cases in the Courts of Star Chamber and High Commission*, Camden Society, 2nd ser., 39 (London, 1886), 149, 150.

against their conservative rivals. The godly clique was alleged to have maintained a secret conventicle in which its members catechized and prayed together 'after their own fashion'. In 1614, forty copies of the libel were spread about the streets, calling for the expulsion of the leading Puritan clergyman, Michael Purfrey: 'And then shall this towne be att peaceable rest / For being shut of such a member yt wilbe happie and blest.' Over the following years, three more libels were circulated, one of which focused specifically upon the divisive conventicling of the godly. It began:

> My muse arise and truth then tell,
> Of a Pure sect that sprang from hell,
> Who are so vaine soe false and fickle,
> They leave the Church to Conventicle.[50]

Libels often focused upon the divisiveness of the godly religion. One such document, circulated in Stratford-on-Avon (Warwickshire) in 1619 and entitled 'A Satyre to the Cheife Rulers in the Synagogue of Stratford', went on:

> Stratford is a Towne that doth prake a great shewe
> but yet it is governed but by a fewe.
> O Jesus Christe of heaven, I thinke they are but Seaven
> Puritans without doubt, for if ye knowe them they are soe stout
> their neighbours honeste to take
> In words, but within they are full of dissencion and discords.[51]

In early Stuart Dorchester, another town dominated by a self-appointed clique of Puritans, the merchant and public notary Robert Adyn told the Star Chamber that he had heard that

Mr White the precher of Dorchester had then lately preached that Christ was not the Savyre of the whole wolde but of his elected and chosen people onely And that alsoe that Christe dyed not for the synnes of the whole worlde but only for his sayd elected and chosen peple approving the same by this famylyar example that as everye sheapheard hath care and regard of his owne flocke and not more.

Angered by this exclusiveness, Adyn felt that he needed to defend 'the merytoryous passyon of Christ' and so, 'takinge penne in hand', he wrote a scurrilous libel against the godly of the town:

[50] A. Fox, 'Religious Satire in English Towns, 1570–1640', in P. Collinson and J. Craig (eds.), *The Reformation in English Towns, 1500–1640* (Basingstoke, 1998), 233–4. For more on this case, see High Court of Chivalry Database, case 199, *Eyre* v. *Keresforth*. For more on libeling, see A. Fox, 'Ballads, Libels and Popular Ridicule in Jacobean England', *P&P*, 145 (1994), 47–83.
[51] TNA, STAC8/26/10.

Thye mynd is high thie purse is small god knowes it to be trew
For were it not for other mens goodes thy state were of bad hue
Yow Puritans count yourselves the greatest men of all
But I trust in god ere longe to see all of yow to fall
... Is this the Puritans life that all of yow doe professe
The all your pure lyves are nothing but dissemblinge as I gesse
That shuld make shew of godlines but deny the lord Chr[i]ste
For your face and Countenance doth shew your dissemblers ar
... Yow Puritans all wheresoever yow dwell
Ymitateinge your master the dyvell of hell
leave of your devises the world to delude
last god from his blisse your soules doe exclude.[52]

Dorchester was only one place where the piety of the godly was held up for
public scorn. In Weymouth (Dorset) in September 1616, Richard
Chrismas

tooke up a cat in Sydlig street & set it on a post & said he would make the cat
preache & namd a Chap[ter] to the Co[r]inth[ians] for his text And then pincht it
by the eares & when the cat cryed he said it was as good a sermon As ext. but
named no body, and that if 500 people were in a church together 490 of them were
knaves or whores.

The following year, another Dorset man offered the opinion that 'all that
went to sermons were Bawdye knaves drunken knaves lecherous knaves
and thievish knaves, and did carry their strumpets and baggages to commit filthines by the way & under color of goeing to sermons did performe
their knavery'.[53] The truth was that the godly, with their exclusiveness,
piety and disciplinarianism, offered themselves up for accusations of
hypocrisy, authoritarianism, corruption and lechery. The libels that Fox
has studied were just one manifestation of a larger popular contempt for
the 'precisians' who seemed to many people to be a divisive force in their
communities. One Jacobean pamphleteer penned a vivid picture of the
typical puritan:

The false-hearted Puritan that (under the vaile of devotion) will commit all
villainy, take the forfeit of a poore mans bond, and dare affirme, that God sent it
to him: you shall know him by the ensuing liverie:

They run from church to church, through all the town
They weare a thin small ruffe, or bare blacke gowne
... They make long prayers, and goggle up their eyes
As if their zeale would teare God from the skies
They chide at every thing, we say, is good
(Excepting God) as Prince, as almes, as food:

[52] TNA, STAC8/94/17.    [53] BL, Harl 6715, fols. 19r, 22r.

> ... They speake to none that walketh in the street,
> Or with these words, God speed you, any greet.
> Not to looke up, but fixe on earth the eye
> Apparent signes are of hypocrisie.[54]

The hypocritical, unfriendly, unneighbourly Puritan who oppressed the poor and was mean with charity: this was a stereotype that, for many people, seemed to speak to their own experiences.

The divisions brought by the godly struck against some elementary social values. One of these was a respect for traditional forms of church worship. It hurt to hear the parson of Scoulton (Norfolk) preach in 1628, for example, that 'them that kneeled at the lords prayer at the Sacrament of Baptisme' were 'ridicul[o]us'. The minister refused to read Latin, reproved women who wore a veil when they came to the church, '& he saith it is a relick of the pope' and had taken away the ropes to the saints bell, 'wch was used to be runge when the Minister went to prayers to give the people knowledge that service was begun & saith it is poperie'.[55] All of this seemed to the parishioners of Scoulton to be an attack on the practices and traditions with which they had been raised. What is striking is that, in a culture that prized connections to the past, the godly were so often willing to sever links with local history. The preacher Anthony Lapthorne of Ebchester (County Durham), for example, while denouncing non-preaching ministers, asked of his flock, 'How many of your elders, thinke yow, are gone to hell through ignorance and for want of the word preached?'.[56] Sometimes, it was the very *novelty* of what the godly preached that offended local inhabitants: the prominent villager Jeremy Gleadall was reported by the churchwardens of Sutton (Cambridgeshire) for being 'vehemently suspected' to be 'of the heresye & scisme of the Novalistes and Puritanes, & sow the seedes of sedition in the hartes of the kings majesties subjects'.[57]

Given the centrality of the Scriptures to early modern conceptions of community, the question of exactly *which* Bible should be read could be contentious: in 1623, the churchwardens of Yapton (Sussex) presented John Waters for 'saying ... that a company of Puritans had lately translated the Bible and got the king to put his hand to it', adding that 'our ministers preach not the word of God, but other men's words, and their own phantasies. And further he hath given it forth that the people need not to bee so strict and carefull in keeping the Sabbath day, for it is

---

[54] Anon., *Muldsacke*, sig. B3r. See also sig. Dr.
[55] NRO, NQS/C/S3/26, statement of John Woodcock.
[56] Longstaffe (ed.), *The Acts of the High Commission within the Diocese of Durham*, 190.
[57] C. Marsh, 'Order and Place in England, 1580–1640: The View from the Pew', *JBS*, 44 (2005), 12.

abolished, and that every day in the weeke is a Christian's Sabbath.'[58]Perhaps most fundamentally, Puritans seemed, to many, to be hostile to basic neighbourly values. In 1614, John Parker, the constable of the Hundred of Thornbury, interrupted a revel in the village of Rangeworthy (Glocestershire), a popular festivity that he described to the court of the Star Chamber as a great riot involving hundreds of people. In reply, his opponents described Parker as 'a precision' who took upon himself 'a singularytie of sanctitie and Religion'. He was, the court was told, a constant, litigious irritant: Parker failed to follow established ecclesiastical practices, dragged villagers before the law courts and created 'great distraccon in religion' from which 'sc[h]isms have ensued, and great & manie suites and troubles have be[e]n stirred thereby in the hundred of Thornburie . . . between Neighbor & freindes'. In contrast to Parker's factious divisiveness, his opponents represented their traditional revel as an expression of neighbourly community. They told the Star Chamber:

By all the time whereof the memorie of man is not the contrarie there hath be[e]n a use and custome in Rangworthye . . . that a general feast or meetinge of Friends called a Revell hath be[e]n used and accustomed to be held & kept in Rangworthy . . . upon the Sondaie next after whitsondaie & upon the Mondaie then following which revel or feast hath be[e]n used . . . aswell for the refreshinge of the mindes & spiritts of the countrye people being enured and tyred w[i]th husbandrye and continuall labour as alsoe for the invitacon and entertainment of one friend & kinsman w[i]th another for preservacon of mutuall amytie acquaintance and love and deciding and allaying of strifes, discords and debates between neighbour and neighbour.[59]

Parker the 'precisian', the people of Rangeworthy believed, was the enemy of the values that were celebrated in their revel. Then there was the matter of the disruption of a parish feast by some of the godly of Goodrich (Herefordshire) in 1610. Again, the Star Chamber listened to testimony that presented Puritans as opponents of commensality and neighbourliness. The feast in question brought together one hundred people, after dinner, in the churchyard, 'who did meete then and there to be merrye in most neighbourly and friendly sorte accordinge to the antient custome of the said towne and Countrey those holy daies tyme out of mynde used with mirth musique and dancing without entent of hurt to anye person but to make peace and love betweene all neighbours if any debate were'.[60]In Goodrich, just like in Rangeworthy, it seemed as though the godly were determined to set themselves against local culture.

---

[58] Johnstone (ed.), *Churchwardens' Presentments*, 66.      [59] TNA, STAC8/239/3.
[60] TNA, STAC8/234/10.

Yet, for all that Puritans fell easily into distinctions between the godly and the vulgar, some amongst their ranks knew the damage that such easy divisions did to their cause. The minister of Elizabethan Dedham (Essex), Edmund Chapman, for example, was critical of 'the inordinate zeale of some, who thinke yt a greate peece of religion to [j]udge and exclude others whom they love not', suggesting instead that the godly should 'growe to a more general conference for unity both in affection and [j]udgment if yt may be, that we may see and feele more comforte in ourselves and in our brethren'.[61] But Chapman was in the minority amongst his co-religionists.

In contrast to the division that most of the godly brought to their parishes, Catholic households seem often to have been tolerated by their neighbours. Alexandra Walsham has detected a '"tolerance of practical rationality" at the grass roots' of English society, arguing that 'there is much to suggest that historians have underestimated both the extent and the capacity of an instinct for concord, harmony and peace to shape social relations'.[62] This everyday tolerance of religious difference – so long as it remained understated and didn't confront communal norms – militated against the emphasis in the post-Reformation polity upon religious uniformity. But many common people seem not to have cared. A lot of the time, the popish Antichrist seemed at a certain remove from the lives of ordinary people. Many late Elizabethan and early Stuart villages included one or two recusant households. But there is little evidence of their harassment or worries about how they fitted into the village community, other, perhaps, than periodic, magisterially driven offences against recusancy at the Quarter Sessions.[63] Catholics certainly did fall out with their Protestant neighbours, and at such moments their doctrinal identities were invoked; but this seems to have been surprisingly rare. In Pontop (County Durham) in 1635, the spinster Catherine Meaborne 'abused the children of Tho[mas] Hopper ... and called them "heretickes and hell-ratchettes", they all being good Protestants'.[64] Recusancy could, in some circumstances, be a cause of division. On 7 May 1587, Isabell Raffells of Beverley (Yorkshire) told the York consistory court that her neighbour Agnes Brand 'had one or two children in fornication before she was married and hath shewed her selfe a liker and favorer of popish ceremonies and will nowe and then speake words as if she scould tell howe longe children should live and what forme they should have'. This combination

---

[61] Usher (ed.), *The Presbyterian Movement in the Reign of Queen Elizabeth*, 96.
[62] Walsham, *Charitable Hatred*, 231.
[63] For an exception, see Longstaffe (ed.), *The Acts of the High Commission within the Diocese of Durham*, 52–3.
[64] Ibid., 119.

of popery with magic was dangerous enough. But, in 1586, Brand upped the stakes, circulating amongst her neighbours 'two p[i]eces of partchment th[e] one having a Jesus and the other some other popish device written or painted upon them w[i]th blood wch she said came from Rome and were popes p[ar]dons and th[a]t she had them sent from a Sister and cosin of hers wch were in prison in york castle for religion'. In reply, Raffells 'said they were wichcraftes and papistrye'. Yet other neighbours were willing to stand up for Brand. The bricklayer Richard Williamote, for example, said that she 'is an honest woman of good lyfe and conversation and so accompted of emongest her neighbours and so fare as this ex[aminan]te haith hard she was never detected of any notorious crime'.[65] In this case, Williamote implied, it was Raffles' accusations of witchcraft and recusancy that had disrupted the quietude of the community.[66] Yet other Catholics went out of their way to demonstrate their contempt for the established religion. In a visceral rejection of Protestantism in 1578, Elizabeth Milner 'did put the sacramental bread forth from her mouth and spewed forth the wine'.[67] But such individuals seem to have been the exception. What is remarkable, given the intensity with which the wars of religion were being waged on the Continent, was the uncontroversial acceptance of recusants and religious conservatives within many post-Reformation English villages.

Indeed, Catholics emphasized the ways in which they felt that Protestantism had undermined communal values. The recusant gentleman Thomas Hale of Walthamstow (Essex) was accused in 1594 of writing the following 'wrytten ballad or ryme':

Weepe, weepe, and still I weepe, for who can chuse but weepe to thinke howe England styll in synne and heresy dothe sleepe, The Christian faythe and Catholick is everye where detested, the holye servyce and suche like of all degrees neglected, The sacraments are taken awaye and holy orders all Religious men do begg a straye, to ground their howses fall. . . . Nowe favour hyndreth equytie, and ryches rule the roste, In vayne the poore crye Charytie, god healpe you saye the moste.[68]

Charity, then, in Protestant England, had been driven to the margins of civil society: a world in which the 'poore crye Charytie', their pleas unheard by 'the moste'. One recusant ballad played upon the sense that Protestant ministers failed in their duty to the poor. It ran:

[65] BIA, CP.G.2456.
[66] In Puritan Dorchester, it was those who accused their neighbours, not the accused witch, who fell foul of the town authorities for disrupting neighbourly values. See D. Underdown, *Fire from Heaven: Life in an English Town in the Seventeenth Century* (London, 1992), 78–9.
[67] P. J. Winstone, 'A History of the Church in Clapham', *Journal: North Yorkshire Country Record Office Publications*, 29 (1982), 36.
[68] Cockburn (ed.), *Calendar of Assize Records: Essex Indictments*, no. 2576.

> The tyme hath beene the prelate's dore
> Was seldome shott against the pore,
> The time is now, so wives so fine
> They take not thought the beggar kyne.[69]

Another ballad, this time transcribed by the Yorkshire recusant gentleman Richard Shanne, extolled the link between the old faith and social
unity. It spoke of how, since the Reformation, gentry hospitality had
grown cold, and that where

> Houses where musicke was wonted to ringe,
> Nothinge but Batts, and Ouls now do singe
> ... Christmas bread and beefe is turned into stons, into stons, into
>    stons,
> Into stones and silken ragges.
> ... Places where Christmas revells did keep
> Are now become habitations for sheep.
> ... tilliges doth decay, doth decay, doth decay,
> doth decay in everie towne
> Landlordes their rentes so highly Inhance
> That peares the plowman, barefoote doth daunce.
> ... Farmers that Christmas woulde Intertaine,
> hath scarselie withall them selves to mantaine,
> ... Go to the protestant, hele protest, hele protest, hele protest,
> he will protest and bouldlie boaste,
> And to the Puritine, he is so hote, he is so hote, he is so hote,
> He is so hote he will burne the Roast,
> The Catholike good deedes will not scorne,
> nor will not soe pore Christmas fore lorne.
> ... Since Holines no good deedes will do,
> Protestantes had best turn Papistes too.[70]

Anti-Puritanism made some aspects of early Stuart religious policies
popular amongst ordinary people. David Underdown has argued that the
civil war was in some respects a cultural war, a struggle that pitted
different visions of England against one another.[71] A pastoral proto-
royalism presented merry England as the site of good cheer, neighbourliness and social hierarchy, all of which were threatened by an individualistic Puritanism. Thus, Ben Jonson wrote of the Cotswold Games, with
their celebration of bucolic rusticity:

---

[69] T. E. Gibson (ed.), *Crosby Records: A Chapter of Lancashire Recusancy*, Chetham Society,
    2nd ser., 12 (Manchester, 1887), 29.
[70] BL, Add MS 38599, fols. 142r-143r.
[71] D. Underdown, *Revel, Riot and Rebellion: Popular Politics and Culture in England, 1603–
    1660* (Oxford, 1985).

How they advance true love and neighbourhood
And doe both Church and Common-wealth the Good,
In spite of Hipocrites, who are the worst
Of subjects. Let such envie till they burst![72]

In an early statement of what was to become the Laudian case, the Lincolnshire minister Thomas Grander wrote in 1621:

As for a feast, that is made for laughter, for a recreation of the minde and body at certaine convenient times, and to preserve common societie and neighbourhood, or rather to testifie friendship and love one towards another, though particular businesses and necessities have distracted them, and drawne euery man ... to care for his owne things· of the use whereof feasting and common meetings testifie a certaine communitie, such as in this disordered world, and miserable condition of man can be had.[73]

In discussions of cultural policy that strongly support Underdown's theory, one of the things that the Laudians wanted to reinstate was a sense of a connection between the Church and the festive culture of the common people. Thus, Bishop Piers of Bath and Wells wrote to Archbishop Laud, on 5 November 1633, concerning Puritan-inspired attempts to abolish parish feasts. Piers argued that parochial commensality strengthened vertical social bonds. As he put it,

it is fit and convenient there feast dayes should be continued, for a memoriall of the dedications of their severall churches, for the civilizinge of people, for their lawfull recreations, for the composing of differences by occasion of the meetinge of friends, for the increase of love and amity, as beinge Feasts of charity, for the releife of the poore, the richer sort keeping then in a manner open house[.]

Piers believed that in defending parish feasts, he had the common people on his side, explaining that

the people generally would by noe meanes have these feasts taken away for when the constables of some parishes ... told their Neighboures that the Judges would put downe these feasts, they answered that it was very hard if they could not entertayne their kindred and friends once in a yeere, to prayse God for his Blessings, and to pray for the Kings Ma[jes]tie under whose happy Governement they injoyed peace and quietnesse ... many suites in law have bin taken up at these feasts by mediation of friends, wch could not have bene soe soone ended in Westminster Hall.

In Piers' analysis, it was only the 'p[re]ciser sort' – that is, Puritans – who opposed the village feasts. The consequence of abolishing

[72] C. Whitfield, *Robert Dover and the Cotswold Games: A New Edition of the Annalia Dubrensia* (London, 1962), 134.
[73] T. Granger, *A Familiar Exposition or Commentarie on Ecclesiastes* (London, 1621), 274–5.

feasting, he argued, would be criticism of state affairs or perhaps the growth of religious divisions. He warned Laud that 'if the people should not have their honest and lawfull recreations upon sundayes after evening prayer, they would goe either into tipling houses, and there upon their ale-benc[h]es talke of matters of the church or state; or els[e] into conventicles'.[74]

Here, there was a vision of pastoral England that was directly at odds with the godly's disciplinary revolution. Feasts, festivities and rituals were not merely isolated events; rather, they comprised what Bob Bushaway has called a 'holistic' set of folk beliefs.[75] The Laudian achievement in the 1630s was to link this local, plebeian sense of good neighbourhood with a larger vision of social hierarchy. Here were established some of the deeper roots of civil war allegiance.

### Community Turned Inside Out: Witches, Gossips and Informers

There were many ways in which communal values could be transgressed, and the court records are full of examples of disputes in which both sides claim to be standing for neighbourly values. The vexed question of whether neighbours should inform on one another's doings was a special source of tension in many communities. The literature on state formation has emphasized the ways in which loyalty to the Crown and engagement with the law courts fostered a popular engagement with the state. Yet there were times when loyalties to one's neighbours came into conflict with loyalty to the Crown.[76] One example of this was the practice of tale-bearing: carrying malicious gossip about one's fellow inhabitants. Notably, without the willingness of ordinary people to tell tales on one another, the legislation around seditious and treasonable speech would have been unworkable.[77]

Accusations of seditious speech put ordinary people in a difficult position: in 1538, for example, one critic of Henry VIII's policies was warned by those around him that, if questioned by magistrates, he should take

---

[74] TNA, SP16/250/56. For more on this, see T. G. Barnes, 'County Politics and a Puritan Cause Celebre: Somerset Churchales, 1633', *TRHS*, 5th ser., 9 (1959), 103–22.

[75] B. Bushaway, *By Rite: Custom, Ceremony and Community in England, 1700–1800* (London, 1982).

[76] For constables' dilemmas in this regard, see K. E. Wrightson, 'Two Concepts of Order: Justices, Constables and Jurymen in Seventeenth-Century England', in J. Brewer and J. Styles (eds.), *An Ungovernable People: The English and Their Law in the Seventeenth and Eighteenth Centuries* (London, 1980), 21–46.

[77] For a fuller discussion, see A. Wood, '"A Lyttull Worde Ys Tresson": Loyalty, Denunciation and Popular Politics in Tudor England', *JBS*, 48, 4 (2009), 837–47.

more care over his opinions, '[f]or and yf thow confesse them or any of them Thow wylt be hanged onleste thy neghbors be good to the[e]'.[78] The same was true of economic regulation. Offences such as usury could be prosecuted because of the willingness of common people to bear tales about their neighbours. The records of the Palatinate of Durham in the bleak years of the 1590s attest to this. George Baxter of Wolsingham informed 'as well for the quean as for him selfe' that a number of his neighbours were practising usury. John Spayn of Gateshead informed against a long list of people who he said had offended against market regulations for offences such as 'by[i]ng of corn before it cam[e]to the market' and maintaining illegal alehouses. Other County Durham informers presented their neighbours for buying sheep that they resold at a substantial profit or for selling underweight loaves of bread.[79] These were all ways in which economic regulation was tied into social morality.

In many contexts, the state assumed that ordinary people would not hesitate to inform on their neighbours when necessary. In 1557, the Privy Council wrote to the magistrates to instruct them to appoint overseers in every parish, who would come together with 'one or two honest neighbours' and visit 'every house that they shall think meet within their charge nightly, or at the least once or twice in the week, and that as secretly as they may ... there peruse and view the people of the house'. If anyone of the household was missing, they were to be brought before the magistracy to explain their absence.[80] In his 1596 charge to the Maidstone Quarter Sessions, William Lambarde warned:

[C]onsidering that in these days of ours hardly any man is found that will inform against offenders, either for the love of virtue or for the good of others but only for the relief of himself and to be revenged upon some adversary, so much the more ought your ears to be open to all as such do complain.[81]

The author of a 1549 tract likewise asked, '[W]hat quiet person will take upon hime the slanderous name of a promouter, or what honeste man will in that cause procure the utter undoing of his neighbor[?]'.[82] The expectation that neighbours might betray one another's words and deeds to the authorities, while current in governmental circles, was more contested in terms of everyday life.

There was a lot of watchfulness within early modern communities. In 1623, for example, the Archbishop of York's visitation learnt that a

[78] TNA, SP1/128, fol.110r–v.
[79] TNA, DURH17/1, pt. 1, 1599 roll, piece 4; TNA, DURH17/1, pt. 1, 1599 roll, unnumbered, rolls 6 and 11.
[80] HMC, Various Collections, II, 90.
[81] Read (ed.), *William Lambarde and Local Government*, 126.     [82] *TED*, III, 332.

question hung over Henry and Elizabeth Bilcliffe 'for liveinge together as man and wife it being not knowne whether they be married or no'.[83] Tudor and Stuart villages could be anxious places, where everyone watched their backs. This was partly a result of the material environment within which early modern people lived their lives, cheek-by-jowl, their houses abutting onto one another, with compartments that could easily be breached by some officious neighbour. In 1562, for example, the aged man John Fowler of Kirby Overblow (Yorkshire) was called to testify as to a neighbourly dispute. In his deposition, he emphasized the close proximity of the parties and how this intense situation had generated the conflict: in Fowler's account, the plaintiff and the defendant were described as 'p[ar]chioners and dwell of the p[ar]yshe ... p[ar]te of their dwelling howses is under one Rofe and the Reaste standeth joined unto the same and thus have they continued theis two yeares'.[84]

The anthropologist Karen Brison has noted the importance of such 'tale-bearing': she observes that 'gossip and rumour seem to be particularly feared in small isolated communities where people have relatively few ties with the outside world and so are dependent on their neighbours for many things'.[85] Thus, in 1595, the Staffordshire tailor Thomas Wooddall was deemed to be a bad neighbour because he 'hathe many tymes apon verie malice practised to sett discord and discention ... betwixt loving neighbours and betwixt husband and wyffe'.[86] In Leominster (Herefordshire) in 1578, the borough jurors presented Philipp Bennett as 'an Eavesdropper and doth harbour under the wall and windows of his neighbours'.[87] Thirty-four years later, the jurors of Holt Hundred (Norfolk) presented Elizabeth Newton because she 'did listen under the window and eves of the house of Allic[e] Lampkins of Langham the iii day of July at night and did publish abro[a]d the speeches which she hard'.[88] And, in 1623, the inhabitants of Newton (Norfolk) presented one of their neighbours because he was 'a common tale be[a]rer betwixt the lord and tenants and also betwixt the minister and the p[ar]ishioners wherof commeth much strife and controv[er]sie'. If anyone in the town was quarrelling or involved in a legal case, he was 'a common tale caryer and meddler betwene them intending thereby to continewe and add striffe upon striffe and offereth him selffe to be a

---

[83] BIA, V.1623, fol. 102.    [84] BIA, CP.G. 1066.
[85] K. J. Brison, *Just Talk: Gossip, Meetings and Power in a Papua New Guinea Village* (Berkeley, CA, 1992), 1.
[86] Burne (ed.), *The Staffordshire Quarter Sessions Rolls, III: 1594–97*, 101–3.
[87] G. Fyler Townsend, *The Town and Borough of Leominster* (Leominster, n.d.), 312.
[88] NRO, NQS/C/S3/18, presentment of the Holt Hundred.

wytnes For eyther p[ar]ti[e]s or For one of them'.[89] When, in 1553, the Norwich labourer William Warlowe told the city authorities that Elizabeth Newman had said to Mistress Gallow on their way to St Giles' Church, 'God that dyed at Styrbrydge Fayer and spred his armes upon a chese I pray god save you Jenny Bareleggs you maynteyne hores and theves', and that, at the funeral of Mr Cokks' daughter, Elizabeth called another mourner a 'pocke marked chorle', did he maintain proper moral values any more than he offended against communal norms of charity towards neighbours? In such ways, neighbourliness was constantly contested.[90]

Women and men who denounced their neighbours could, in some circumstances, be seen as upholding the proper standards of the authorities. Yet, in other contexts, they could be seen as troublesome barrators and gossips, disrupting the easy-flowing life of the ideal community, and so be subject to neighbourly sanctions or even – ironically – to being themselves presented to the authorities. Hence, the churchwardens of Great Sampford in Elizabethan Essex presented a villager who 'used railing speeches against some of his honest neighbours, calling them dogs, sly whelps, and they might have barked before they bit'.[91] Likewise, in 1621, the churchwardens of West Itchenor (Sussex) presented 'Thomas Styant to be a malicious, contentious, and uncharitable person, one that seekes the unjust vexacion of his neighbours, a common swearer and such a one as is not fitt to be harboured in any parishe'.[92] Four years earlier, the Norfolk man John King had found himself in trouble at the Quarter Sessions because he made trouble between neighbours

especially betweene many men and theire wyves Rayling of them calling the men cookhol[d]s and their wyves [w]hores ...[H]e hath often when he hath wanted monys gone to dyvers men to borrowe as of some xii.d of some les[s] And if they would not Lend him, he would threaten eyther to put them into the Exchequer, Hundred Corte or the Commissary Corte as he have done to Warnes, Fell, Brettingh[a]m & Tudd[e]nam.

King had given 'fryvol[o]us Informacons' against them and thereby made them spend money in their defence.[93] Back in 1604, the Chichester Archdeacon's court was told that Thomas Northe was 'a sower of discord and debate between neighbours and friends by carrying of lies and tales from one to another; neither is a man of any credit amongst his neighbours; neither doth any man of honest conversation almost make any account of his saying'. Thomas Northe and John Northe were, it was said,

[89] NRO, NQS/C/S3/24 (Box 1), complaint of the inhabitants of Newton.
[90] NRO, NCR16A/6, p. 285.      [91] Emmison, *Elizabethan Life*, 49.
[92] Johnstone (ed.), *Churchwardens' Presentments*, 18.
[93] NRO, NQS/C/S3/21, articles against John King.

'not men that are in charity with their neighbours'; they were 'men of small credit'.[94]

In 1619, the inhabitants of Hockwold and Wilton (Norfolk) combined to complain about the speech of the labourer William Taylor. They told the bench that he was a 'barrator, that he picked quarrels and was a common Rayler and ... [was] verye foule mouthed'. In particular, one incident stood out: on 12 March 1619, when the inhabitants of both parishes had returned from their Rogationtide perambulations 'and in friendlie and neighbourlike sorte mette together', William Taylor, 'intrudinge himself into our companye', started to shout about the casting out of a woman who had rented a room with him. He accused the minister of Hockwold of fathering a bastard child upon her, saying:

It is one of your bastards and I will keepe none of your bastards and also It is one of your calves but I will keepe non[e] of your calves, and againe a lit[t]le while after, It is one of your tythe lambs, but I will keepe non[e] of your tithe lambs ...[. A]fter all this he rayled upon the whole company sayeing th[a]t they all hated him but he cared for none of them, noe, for never a name of them all with manye other foule words the most and best of the inhabitants of both the p[ar]ishes being then and there present.[95]

Men's tongues, then, could be 'busy', leading to accusations of barratory.[96] In 1612, for example, Richard Collier of Topcliffe (Yorkshire) told his neighbour Edmund Stephenson that he was a 'hollow harted man, monesworne man, monesworne fellow and foresworne knave, a lyer, a lying fellow and naught'. Invoking the sense that Stephenson was a bad neighbour, Collier went on, adding that Stephenson 'was a damn[e]d fellow, and damn[e]d villaine. And such a naughty and vildebad fellow, as was not worthy to dwel in a towne Raw or to be amongst any good and honest Company'.[97] But women's words could be seen as a source of neighbourly strife. Early modern people felt there was a special power to women's speech. F. G. Emmison noted the regularity with which women appeared in the church courts of Elizabethan Essex for their dangerous words: it was noted of one woman that 'she causeth strife' between married couples, that another woman was 'a breeder of strife' or 'a setter of discord through her evil

---

[94] Wilkinson (ed.), *Chichester Archdeaconry Depositions*, 25, 27.

[95] NRO, NQS/C/S3/21, Complaint of the inhabitants of Hockwold and Wilton.

[96] While female defamation has received some attention, accusations of male barratory remain less well understood. It would be possible to write a history of plebeian speech that linked barratory, scolding and neighbourly disputes to the record of seditious speech concerning religion, the state and the social order. Such a project would necessitate linking of church court material with that of the criminal courts, plus borough records and state papers. It would be difficult, but very revealing.

[97] BIA, CP.H.888.

tongue' or 'a troublesome person amongst her neighbours by her unquiet-
ness of tongue' or 'abused her tongue' or 'a malicious, contentious and
uncharitable woman', 'a sower of discord between her neighbours and a
carrier of tales between party and party', 'a notorious common scold and
makebate between her neighbours', 'uncharitable scolding with her
neighbours and a blasphemer of the Word of God' or 'suspected to live
incontinently and to be busy with her tongue and unquiet'. Then there
was Barbara Driver of Stock (Essex), who, in 1583, was presented to the
visitation, '[s]uspected of living incontinently by common report with
divers persons . . . [. I]t is noised that she hath had a bastard and was never
punished for it; also[that she was] a maker of debate between neighbour
and neighbour and a common scold and brawler.'[98] Women's speech was
partly, then, about the contestation of neighbourhood; but it was also
about agency.[99] In a patriarchal society, in which women were meant to
be silent, to speak was to become an agent.

The expectation that women should be silent in the face of male power
was always unrealistic. But men persisted in presenting women's conversation as a threat to neighbourly norms. So, in 1619, George Webbe argued:
'It is the tongue which breaketh the peace betweene neighbours, giveth
shrewd wives sharpe weapons to fight against their husbands, breedes
quarrels among servants, and setteth men together by the eares.'[100] In his
discussion of women's conversations, Thomas Deloney noted 'the old
Proverbe . . . Many women many words.'[101] Shakespeare's patrician anti-
hero Coriolanus refers to his wife as his 'gracious silence'.[102] It seemed to
Thomas Wilson self-evident that women's words threatened the proper
order of things. He demanded of his readers a set of rhetorical questions:
'What becometh a woman best, and first of al? Silence. What seconde?
Silence. What third? Silence. What fourth? Silence. Yea if a man should
aske me til dowmes day, I would still crie silence, silence.'[103]

Such prescriptive norms did more than merely float in the ideological
ether of patriarchy and its unlikely ideals. They informed the ways in
which women's words were understood in everyday life. As Jane

---

[98] Emmison, *Elizabethan Life*, 24, 65.

[99] There is an important parallel here with Susan Harding's research on the Aragonese
village of Oroel in the 1970s. She comments: 'In a legally and ideologically subordinate
position and without recourse to effective institutions of their own that they can manip-
ulate, women must defend and advance themselves with whatever everyday verbal skills,
such as squabbling, finesse, and gossip, they may develop.' See Harding, 'Women and
Words', 284.

[100] Webbe, *Arraignment of an Unruly Tongue*, 28.

[101] T. Deloney, *Thomas of Reading* (London, 1612), sig. H3r-v.

[102] *Coriolanus*, act II, scene 1, lines 184–7.

[103] T. Wilson, *The Art of Rhetoricke for the Use of All Such as Are Studious of Eloquence*
(London, 1553), 400–1.

Kamensky has suggested with reference to early New England, early modern people were preoccupied with speech. For them, speech was 'part of the dynamics of face-to-face communities in which the small scale of daily life makes words loom large'. Kamensky argues: 'The white inhabitants of Massachusetts imbued the act of speaking with dramatic and fearful power: power to symbolize and to shape the relationships that made up their daily lives.'[104] As Laura Gowing has shown, this was also true of the world that New England folk had left behind.[105] In 1611, Catherine Parson of Sheringham (Norfolk) was said by the men of the village to 'dayely stur up sedic[i]on and stryfe betwixt man and wife & betwixt neighbour and neighbour, so that the neighbors cannot live peaceably by her'.[106] Some women became notorious for their disruption of communal relations. In July 1608, the York consistory court heard from Jane Simpson that 'she thinketh that ther is little or no scolding in Tarhen town but diane fording & Betha[ny] Burley are either beginners of it'.[107] In 1617, the widow Joane Makam was felt to be making trouble between neighbours, telling Winifred Williams that 'she would be sworne' that Winifred's husband and Goodwife Tawney were having sex and that Mr Williams had got Thomas Tawney's wife pregnant, 'then let Thomas Tawney goe get his wife w[i]th child & then they may goe horne in horne'.[108] Whether accurate or not, these stories of male cuckoldry cut into the core of patriarchal values. Women's words were seen by some men as inherently dangerous, and their tongues needed to be controlled if, on both the everyday and the ideological level, patriarchal ideals were to remain dominant. And so, it mattered that some women could be defended from the accusation of scolding. In July 1621, the male inhabitants of Swaffham (Norfolk) wrote to the Quarter Sessions to inform them that they had known Anne Isacke, a widow, for thirty years and in all that time 'she hath lived very orderly and honestly amongst us w[i]thout controv[er]sie or brablinge w[i]th any others'.[109]

Like all social norms, neighbourliness excluded some and included others. Women who bore bastard children were one easy group upon whom richer people turned. In January 1614, the overseers of Wedmore (Somerset) told the Quarter Sessions that Isabel Day had borne five illegitimate children 'and doth live very idly, and is very troublesome to her neighbours on any small occasion'. They had decided that Day was to be sent to the Bridewell. People like this could easily find themselves

---

[104] Kamensky, *Governing the Tongue*, 5, 12.    [105] Gowing, *Domestic Dangers*.
[106] NRO, NQS/C/S3/17/1, articles against Catherine Parson of Sheringham.
[107] BIA, CP. H. 5024.    [108] NRO, NQS/C/S3/21, articles against Joane Makam widow.
[109] NRO, NQS/C/S3/23, certificate of the inhabitants of Swaffham.

driven out of the community.[110] Elsewhere, those that crossed the bounds of neighbourly conduct could – if they were sufficiently marginal – simply be driven away. In 1521, Beatrice Atwode of Norwich spread gossip that 'Richard Clerk and Jone his wife were of such evill disposicion that thei were driven out of Saint Stevyn parisshe'. In the same year, rumour reached Walsingham (Norfolk) that Robert Gottes had been 'dryven out of Norwich with bonys and stones and boys'.[111] Even those with roots in a community could find themselves frozen out. In 1575, Robert Aire of Whitbarn (County Durham) was accused of having sex with his sister-in-law, Margaret Nicolson. He found it hard to get any local supporters: Robert Wright observed that 'the matter was so manifest and known to neighbours that the said Robert c[o]ulde not cleir hym self ther[e]of, nor any of his neighbours wold goo with hym to take ooth in that matter'.[112] A year later, Thomas Colson of Stranton (County Durham) told the consistory court that he knew, 'as all his neighbours doe', that Edward Johnson had sex with Jennet Slaiter 'and that he haithe kept hir, and doethe kepe hir still, as his leman'. Colson had warned Johnson 'that the neighbours wold put hir out of the parishe and Johnson aunswered that he wold place hir. And she, beinge so put out of the parishe, was placed by him in his owne house.' Despite the opprobrium against him and Jennet, Johnson would not give her up. His love for the woman overcame any sense of neighbourly duty to the village order. To the shame of others, Johnson said openly that he regularly committed 'whoredom' with Jennet and 'that if there were a hundrethe harnessed men set betwixt him and hir, with drawen swerds in the[i]r hands, that he wold run through them all to hir; and that, if ther[e] were a hundrethe devels of hell betwit him and hir, with fleshe croks in the[i]r hands, that he wold run through them all to hir'. Upon the parish minister reproving him, 'Johnson aunswered that he hoped that he was an evill man wold never amend'.[113]

Edward Johnson and Jennet Slaiter stuck together. But there were other ways in which emotional ties could be fractured. In 1630, Matthew Mearne's neighbours of Avington (Somerset) petitioned the county bench to explain that

he having a Daughter which went from him without his consent about three yeares since unto one Joane Kidgell … [she] beinge an invective enemy of … Matthew Mearne and a molestor of the most part of her neighbours in suits of law being

[110] Bates (ed.), *Quarter Sessions Records for … Somerset: Vol. I, James I, 1607–1625*, 110.
[111] Stone and Cozens-Hardy (eds.), *Norwich Consistory Court Depositions*, nos. 238, 267.
[112] Raine (ed.), *Depositions … from the Courts of Durham*, 308–9.
[113] Raine (ed.), *Depositions … from the Courts of Durham*, 312–13.

presented any the wardens of the said parish for suspicion of incontinency, the said Mathew Mearne beinge then one of the wardens that presented her, And that the said Joane Kidgell insinuats with his said Daughter in siche sorte that she will not acknowledge him to be hir father nor speake unto him.[114]

All of this was upsetting to Matthew Mearne: no father would want to be cut dead by his daughter. But in the public world of the neighbourhood, for a father to be brushed aside was disruptive to the order of the whole village, undermining age and gender hierarchies.

Cases like this, in which Matthew Mearne's 'invective enemy' had stolen away his daughter's love, perhaps confirm Lawrence Stone's view that Tudor and Stuart communities were 'filled with malice and hatred'.[115] On the other hand, they also confirm the enduring value of affective, neighbourly and social bonds. Matthew Mearne's neighbours seem to have been genuinely shocked that his daughter had shunned him. Certainly, they explained this in terms of local enmities within their small world. But underlying this was a larger sense of how the world *should* be – that children – even if grown – owed an enduring debt to their parents, that village societies were held together by social bonds that were underwritten by family, household and neighbourhood. Once again, it is in the breach of social values that we see them most clearly articulated.

Some people were so antisocial in their dealings with their neighbours that they seemed to represent the reverse of neighbourhood values. In October 1640, a group of Cheshire villagers came together to complain against Elizabeth Tushingham. They told the county bench that she

hath been a wandering idle person over the country for the space of these twenty years and more, being a woman of very light and incontinent life and a stirrer up of many suits in diverse courts for these fourteen years last past against her father, brother and brother's son without any just cause ... and hath threatened to burn [her nephew's] house and to kill and destroy the cattle ...[s]he being a vile and willful obstinate woman, the neighbours have often entreated her to live in peaceable sort and honest fashion but could not prevail ...[s]he is also a woman that hath not the fear of God before her eyes [for] she has not come to her parish church this ten or twelve years ... [nor] stands upon any religion, but a very atheist.[116]

Tushingham seemed to be the antithesis of everything that village society stood for, representing the personification of the anti-neighbour. She was mobile, wandering about and difficult to track down. She was 'idle', 'light', 'incontinent'. She stirred up trouble within the village. She even

---

[114] Bates (ed.), *Quarter Sessions Records for ... Somerset: Vol. II, Charles I, 1625–1639*, 110.
[115] L. Stone, *The Family, Sex and Marriage in England, 1500–1800* (London, 1977), 95, 98.
[116] T. C. Curtis, 'Quarter Sessions Appearances and Their Background: A Seventeenth-Century Regional Study', in J. S. Cockburn (ed.), *Crime in England, 1550–1800* (Princeton, NJ, 1977),139.

took male members of her family to court, offending against patriarchal authority. Terrifyingly, she threatened the village with fire. And she seemed not to have any religion but to be an atheist, that disturbing category of folk who placed themselves outside of God's mercy.

Irreligion was, for many ordinary people, quite shocking.[117] Episodically, the records of the church courts and the criminal jurisdictions yield cases of the rejection of the Protestant religion. There was the butcher Walter Dennys from Bromsgrove (Worcestershire) who, in 1623, appeared before the Quarter Sessions because he had 'depraved and abused the ... most blessed sacrament by reverently holding in his right hand a crooked pin and ... malicioulsy and wickedly spoke these words "Take thee this" (the aforesaid pin) "in remembrance that Parkins of Wedgebury died for thee and be thankfull"'.[118] Excommunication – the separation of an individual from godly communion with her or his neighbours – might be the result of such behaviour. In 1628, the Archdeacon of Taunton wrote to the minister of Luccombe (Somerset) ordering:

Whereas Walter Pugslie, Moses Pugslie, and John Anton ... have been longe time justlie excommunicated and for excommunicate persons openly denounced in the face of the Church at the time of divine service in which dangerous estate without feare of God or shame of [th]e world they still remain in contempt of lawe and lawful magistrates. We therefore will and require yow that the next Sabbath day or holiday ensuing the Receipt hereof in your said Parish Church at the time of divine service before the whole congregation assembled yow shall publiquely denounce those Walter Pugslie Moses Pugslie and John Anton for aggravated persons and also then and there yow shall admomish all Christian people by virtue hereof that they and any of them henceforth eschewe and avoide the society, fellowship and company of the said persons and neither eate, nor drink, buy, sell or otherwise by any other manner of Means communicate with them, being members cut off from all Christian Society under the payne of excommunication by lawe in this behalf provided until they shall submit themselves to be reconciled.[119]

But if the informers, gossips, barrators and the irreligious seemed like a threat to the collectivity of the parish, the greatest anti-neighbour, epitomizing the reverse of all the social values with which early modern people had been raised, was the witch. As Malcolm Gaskill has suggested, witches were understood to represent the inversion of ideas of good neighbourhood.[120] The evidence strongly supports his view. In Warnham (Sussex), a woman

---

[117] The subject requires fuller study, especially from the bottom up. This would require extensive work in church court records and ecclesiastical records, along with criminal courts and state papers.

[118] Bund (ed.), *Calendar ...*, *Vol. I: 1591–1643*, 360.     [119] Tate, *The Parish Chest*, 148.

[120] M. Gaskill, 'Witchcraft and Neighbourliness in Early Modern England', in S. Hindle, A. Shepard and J. Walter (eds.), *Remaking English Society: Social Relations and Social Change in Early Modern England* (Woodbridge, 2013), 211–32.

threw dirt on her neighbours from her gate, reviled them and prepared a 'posnett of scalding water' to pour on them. The culmination of her anti-neighbourliness was her prosecution for witchcraft.[121] In 1617, Thomas Cooper suggested that householders should distance themselves from alleged witches, advising his reader 'to bee straight-handed towards them, not to entertaine them in our houses, not to relieve them with our morsels'. The line of community was thereby drawn, with the witch on the other side of the line from her or his neighbours.[122] Following Stuart Clark's proposition that early modern people understood the world in terms of polarities – God and the Devil, light and darkness, Catholic and Protestant – the witch was thereby constituted as a kind of anti-neighbour, full of malice towards those around them. Thus, it was said of a Northamptonshire witch in 1612, who was born to poor parents, that she was 'ever noted to be of an ill nature and a wicked disposition, spiteful and malicious, and many years before, she died both hated, and feared among her neighbours'.[123]

Gaskill quotes the minister George Gifford, who explained how, in Elizabethan Essex, rumours of witchcraft might easily spread amongst neighbours:

Wel, mother W doth begin to bee very odious & terrible unto many [of] her neighbours, [who] dare say nothing but yet in their heartes they wish shee were hanged. Shortly after an other falleth sicke and doth pine, hee can have no stomacke unto his meate, nor hee can not sleepe. The neighbours come to visit him. Well neighbour, sayeth one, do ye not suspect some naughty dealing: did yee never anger mother W? truly neighbour (sayeth he) I have not liked the woman a long tyme.[124]

Witchcraft accusations, then, drew upon a wider sense that the witch was an enemy of the neighbourhood and that his or her activities formed the antithesis of Christian, communal living.[125] In 1583, Richard Baker and his wife managed to combine a series of unchristian stereotypes. They were condemned by their neighbours of Romford (Essex) for 'using of

---

[121] A. Fletcher, *A County Community in Peace and War: Sussex, 1603–1660* (London, 1975), 163.

[122] T. Cooper, *The Mystery of Witchcraft* (London, 1617), 288.

[123] C. L'Estrange Ewen, *Witchcraft and Demonianism* (London, 1933), 206.

[124] Ibid., 220–1.

[125] For the traumatic local effects of witchcraft prosecutions, see DeWindt, 'Witchcraft and Conflicting Visions of the Ideal Village Community', 427–63; Gregory, 'Witchcraft, Politics and "Good Neighbourhood"', 31–66. For a brilliant micro-history of one witchcraft case, see M. Gaskill, 'Witchcraft and Power in Early Modern England: The Case of Margaret Moore', in J. Kermode and G. Walker (eds.), *Women, Crime and the Courts in Early Modern England* (London, 1994), 125–45.

their talk something savouring of false doctrine; and she something of witchery'. Baker was alleged to have remarked that 'he never read the Scriptures, and Christ's Godhead was given him of the Father; only that Christ said "My Father is greater than my father"; and being demanded whether a Jew or a Christian is best, he answered that it made no matter whether he were a Jew or a Christian, seeing that he do well'.[126]

Cursing – one of the weapons of the poor – could slide easily into accusations regarding the deployment of the black arts. In 1633, for instance, Isabel Oxley was accused of cursing her neighbour George Fenwick, crying out, 'Godes curse, Godes plague, light of the[e] and all thine.' Ralph Fenwick of Heddon On The Wall (Northumberland) told the High Commission: 'About August or September last Isabell, in the townegaite of Heddon and neere unto the doore of Reede, did revile, and curse, and said unto him Godes plague and Godes curse light of the[e] and thine beates, and God let never they nor anie thing thou hast prosper nor doe well.' Mabell Carrock had also been cursed by Oxley, who said to her: 'The Devill goe with thie father and my grandmother.' Neighbours confirmed that Isabel Oxley's tongue was a weapon: Margaret Hall said that 'Oxley is accompted for a lewd woemann of her tonge'; another witness added that 'einge neighbour unto Isabell, [he] hath verie often hea[r]d and observed her cursinges'. Since no ill effects had followed Oxley's curses, the dispute remained a matter of church law. In what might be seen as a means of ritually binding the communal wounds opened by Oxley's words, the High Commission ordered that 'in penetentiall manner, in the church of Heddon', she should 'confesse her irreligious course of life in cursinge and swearinge'.[127]

In contrast, the gossip amongst the women of Thwing (Yorkshire) spoke powerfully of the vitality of cursing amongst their number. On 17 June 1608, the thirty-year-old Dinah Fording told the York consistory court that, at Easter that year, she had been present in the birthing chamber of one of her neighbours when Susan Bossall 'began to talke of ... Robert Constable and said he had brought all the Towne to trouble'. These comments spurred a dramatic response in Margaret Parrett, who

did curse and banne the said Robert Constable and his children, and wished that if he the said Robert Constable were than a sleepe he shoulde nev[er] wake and that he should nev[er] wake and that he should nev[er] come to Thweng againe. And said furder that the devil had beene long in fetching of him, but now she hooped he would not be long in fetching of him, and wished that nether he nor his should come to a good end or prosp[er], and the aforesaid Susan Bossall said Amen. And

[126] Emmison (ed.), *Elizabethan Life*, 110.
[127] Longstaffe (ed.), *The Acts of the High Commission within the Diocese of Durham*, 72–4.

then . . . Susan Bossall did also curse . . . Robert Constable and wished that the plague might light upon him, and that if he were then a slepe he should nev[er] awake, and that he should nev[er] come to Thweng againe, and said furder that the devell had beene long in fetching of him, but now she hoped he would but be long in fetching of him, and she wished that his necke might breake.[128]

These were dangerous words, spoken publicly amongst the other women of the village, as one of their number was caught up in childbirth. Neighbours were appalled by cursing, seeing in it as powerful an attack on communal norms as could be imagined, apart from witchcraft. Hence, the Yorkshire currier William Daniell of Wetherby (Yorkshire) recalled how, on Saint Bartholemew's Eve in 1611, he and John Wood had been sitting before the door of Wood's house when Hellen Hiley 'kneeled her downe upon her knees and said a vengeance of god light upon the[e] wood (meaning the art[iculat]e John Wood) and all thy children, and I shall trule pray this praier for the[e] so long as I live'.[129]

Cursing – calling dark forces into a neighbourhood – might work the other way, forming an instrument against a witch. Jane Spark, for example, told the York consistory court that her neighbour 'Susan Powell, did in cursing mann[er], saie unto the saide Jane Sparke, woe worthe the[e], woe worthe the[e], for thou haist hart eaten me and my ba[i]rnes for we never thrive[d] since thou came hither to dwell And saith moreov[er] yf I shuld speake what I thinke, thou art a witche'.[130] The boot was now on Jane Spark's foot: should she let the matter lie, leaving it to fester, and perhaps years later result in an accusation of witchcraft at the criminal courts? Or should she see it as a matter of slander and haul Susan Powell before the church court? She chose the latter option.

Witchcraft accusations could become powerful social dramas and those making such accusations had to be warned as to the gravity of their words. In July 1590, for example, the butcher Walter Barwick recalled how he had been at work in his father's shop when he heard the widow Fraunces Browne arguing with some other neighbours. William Plumber told her to

hold yor peace Dame Browne you have said ynough And she . . . then asked him what have I said, And will[i]am Plumber said you have called Mergery Thomlinson . . . wytche and you must prove it And Frauncis Browne . . . aunswered and said, I have called her witch, I will call her witch, . . . And I will stand to it, Then and there being p[rese]nt with the ex[aminan]t in the said shop Agnes Barwick this ex[aminan]ts wife Tho[mas] Mornhouse Willi[i]am Plumber and Robert Ellison and div[er]se others w[i]thin and w[i]thout the said shop to the number of halfe a dozen whose he now remembreth not . . . this ex[aminan]t saith that of his knowledge the said m[ar]gery Thomlinson is worse thought of by

[128] BIA, CP. H. 5024.    [129] BIA, CP. H. 758.    [130] BIA, CP. H. 841.

meanes of the words af[oresai]d For he hath h[e]ard diverse children it said that since the speaking of the words af[oresai]d diverse children of the towne of hard-wood af[oresai]d have called hir witch.[131]

This was, then, a public event in the life of the village, and it would have been hard for Frances Browne to back down from her words. Were she able to prove her case before a criminal court, the consequences would have been serious. But here, before the church court, this remained a matter of slander, and one where Margery Tomlinson had the opportunity to reject the accusation.

Those who had a reputation for what contemporaries called 'witchery' worried their neighbours. In October 1621, the Yorkshireman Thomas Steare explained to the church court his worries about Grace Darvell. As he put it, 'having understood by himself, and some of his Neighbours, that ... Grace Darvell had used charming of horses, and Cattell, of other mens, and undertaken to mend them', he was disturbed to encounter her 'while driving his draught in a Laine'. Darvell crossed in front of his cattle; Steare,

doubting & suspecting some harde measure about his Cattell to be used by the said Grace, said unto her, arrant thou Charmer, dost thou thinke to weaken my Cattell, and thereupon the said Grace, p[er]ceiving shee could do them noe harme, att that instant, dep[ar]ted from them For wch said Offence and some others, she hath beene compleyned upon u[n]to a Justice of Peace within the Eastridding of the county of yorke, and ther being exa[min]ed hath confessed that people did resorte unto her for cattell, to do them good, and that shee used certeine prayers to that purpose.[132]

Grace Darvell, then, saw herself as a white witch: she believed herself to possess magical powers, but only to 'do ... good'. Thomas Steare, in contrast, saw her as a disturbing figure, who in threatening his cattle threatened also his material prosperity.

Reputation was critically important in witchcraft trials. Where a person was unable to mobilize local support, where they were marginal to the community or where, contrarily, he or she was well-known – but as a witch – then this weighed against them. Consider the case of the Lancashire woman Anne Spencer, whose neighbours informed the magistracy, in 1638, that she was 'as all the neighbours conceave ... a knowen wich'.[133] A general reputation as a bad neighbour could provide the basis from which accusations of witchcraft might gradually emerge. A sense that someone failed to live up to their neighbourly duties, was known for cursing, uttered blasphemous speech – these were all things that shocked neighbours,

---

[131] BIA, CP. G. 2564.      [132] BIA, CP.H.1475.      [133] HMC Kenyon, 55.

creating a feeling that the individual in question was excluding themselves from the moral community of the neighbourhood. In 1628, for example, John Personn and his wife Ann were presented to the Worcestershire Quarter Sessions for a variety of sins. The Personns were, their neighbours explained, disordered, lewd and of evil fame amongst the people of Stourbridge. While John Personn was said to be 'a common drunkard sorcerer slanderer quarreler and one that taketh upon him to tell fortunes and destinies', Ann Personn was 'a common slaunderer or curser'. The Worcestershire magistracy learnt not only that she had tried to cut the nose off Thomas Jeffries wife but also that she 'hath of late affirmed that she can and will make some of her honest neighbours to scrape and creep and those whom she hath curses have not prospered and that those whom she shall curse will never prosper'.[134] Ann Personn ended up before the Quarter Sessions; but, from her cursing, she had gained remarkable power over her neighbours, for whom witchcraft represented an existential threat, and whom she had said she would destroy.

Accusations of witchcraft could spring up in the course of everyday conflicts, imploding within a community's life. The twenty-three-year-old weaver William Skailes of the York parish of St John's Micklegate explained how one such local quarrel spiralled suddenly into talk of witchcraft. In 1586, he explained to the consistory court

that upon the munday nexte before the feaste of pentecoste laste paste and aboute thre[e] or foure a clocke in the after noone the same day this ex[aminan]te beinge sittinge at his masters doore in north streete wyndinge yarne neere unto William gambles doore before wch doore . . . the said Elizabeth gamble and Jane Fawcett were chidinge together aboute weeds wch the servaunts of the said Elizabeth gambles husbands broughte home to the said gambles house and as thay were chydinge together he saith he h[e]ard the said Elizabeth gamble call the said Jane Fawcett Black witche saying further thow blacke witche I thinke thow haiste bewitched our horse and oure kow for thay did never thryve since thay eate those weeds.[135]

A dispute over fodder for a woman's horse and cow had suddenly turned into something much more serious. Were Elizabeth Gamble able to show evidence that Jane Fawcett had indeed bewitched her animals – calling, amongst other things, on Fawcett's reputation in that intense world of the urban parish – Fawcett might find herself before the criminal courts.

A case that appeared before the Norfolk Quarter Sessions in 1614 provides a case-study of how everyday struggles between villagers might turn into accusations of witchcraft, in which the alleged witch came to stand for the reverse of neighbourly values. On 28 May 1614, Anthony

[134] Bund (ed.), *Calendar . . ., Vol. I: 1591–1643*, 459.    [135] BIA, CP.G.3129.

Leland of Saxlingham told Sir Nathaniel Bacon that William Cheeseman and his wife were both suspected of witchcraft. On a number of occasions, Anthony Leland felt that Mistress Cheeseman had bewitched her neighbours' cattle and pigs, adding 'that thes[e] losses in his cattell have fallen out by the undue practise & witching of Chesemans wife as he is p[er]suaded in his conscience. He saith that he hath dwelt in Saxlingham between 4 & 5 yeares And at his first coming he heard amongst his neighbours that shee was taken for a witch.' John Robinson of Saxlingham added: 'He saith that he is in feare of Cheseman and his wife for witchery. For he hath divers times had his cattell often die upon falling out w[i]th them and upon threates . . . [. H]e hath lived nere 5 yeres at Saxlingh[a]m now laste, And before that have also, And they have been suspected for witches thes[e] 20 yeares.'[136] John Robinson's fear, combined with the steady accumulation of a negative reputation on the part of the Cheesemans, had brought the matter as far as the Quarter Sessions.

A reputation for witchcraft could build up over the years on the basis of ill fortune, village enmities, the fear of men like John Robinson and subtle, nagging innuendo. In March 1620, for instance, the mayor of Castle Rising (Norfolk), in an almost thoughtless manner, threw out the comment that the wife of William Barker, 'a poore silly man', was not just 'reputed to be a woman of light behav[i]or' but was also 'suspected to be a wi[t]ch'.[137] Witchcraft accusations were sometimes rolled up into a general indictment of a person for violence, drunkenness, obscenity, disrespect and cursing. Margaret Wood of Barton Bendish, for instance, was presented to the Norfolk magistracy in 1628 as 'a great curser & banner & A very evill tonged woman, wch causeth her neighbors to have a very hard opinion of her'; her local opponent said that she 'prayed god the devile might fetch hir awaye'.[138] In the same year, the Norfolk magistracy also learnt of the manifold sins of Matthew Loose of Dalling. First, they were told that Loose was a disruptive presence: 'he is a common Raylor upon his Neybors as well in publick as in private assemblies and a breeder of much disquiet amongst them'. More seriously, just like the accusations against Margaret Wood, 'he useth frequently and most forcefully to sweare, bann, and curse his neybors and is disobedient to all authorytie and hath vowed w[i]th many dylvlyshe imputac[i]ons and wyshes uppon himself to be the death of the constable or any other that shall serve any warrant on him'. Loose had threatened to burn the

[136] NRO, NQS/C/S3/19, examinations of Anthony Leland and John Robinson.
[137] NRO, NQS/C/S3/22, information of John Hawkeswell, Mayor of Castle Rising, 19 March 1620.
[138] NRO, NQS/C/S3/17/1, articles against Margaret Woode.

village, was constantly drunk and beat his wife.[139] In all these respects – and with the implication that he was receiving diabolic inspiration in his antisocial actions – Loose represented the inverse of a Christian neighbour.

Witches brought fear into communities. In May 1617, the neighbours of the Winter family of Grimston (Norfolk) complained to the Quarter Sessions. They said that Annea Winter and her two daughters, Edina and Margaret, were all witches. The women had cursed their neighbours, following which misfortune had befallen them. Amongst other things, the village constable, Thomas Watters, had fallen sick after Edina Winter cursed him as he took her to the House of Correction. The Winter family had become a source of communal anxiety: Henry Clemente told the magistrates 'that his wife & children are affrayd to goe in the streetes, for that ... Annea winter & her daughters have threatened them'.[140] If the Winter women were feared by their neighbours, Elizabeth Busher of Henton (Somerset) was identified as someone who actually *hated* the social values prized by Christian people. The Somerset Quarter Sessions learnt that not only was she of 'lewde life and conversac[i]on ... the mother of divers basse children, the suspected maintainer of incontinencie in her owne house, the continuall Disturber of her neighbors quietness and threatening of mischieffe against them' but she was also 'both reputed and feared to be a dangerous witch thorow the untimely Death of men, woemen and children wch she hath hated, threat[e]ned and handled ... And so doth live about woods and obscure places w[i]thout obedience to the lawes of god and this land, And to the terror of her neighbors.'[141] Running throughout the complaint against Elizabeth Busher is the sense that she represented the antithesis of the values of neighbourliness, charity and common interest that many Tudor and Stuart people saw as the basis for the endurance of a Christian commonwealth – be that commonwealth the small world of the village or the larger world of the country and the realm. Busher, it seemed to the men who drew up the complaint against her, opposed all of those values that they held dear. She had borne illegitimate children, maintained a disorderly household, lived on the margins of the village and, through her dark powers, brought death to those whom she 'hated'.

So, then, witchcraft can also be thought of as the antithesis of all the things that Tudor and Stuart people held dear: the values that they instilled in their children and that they rehearsed in catechisms and church services. Witchcraft prosecutions bring us close to the dark fantasies and terrors of ordinary English people – fears that the drunk and the dissolute might grow

---

[139] NRO, NQS/C/S3/26, articles against Matthew Loose.
[140] NRO, NQS/C/S/3/26, articles against Annea Winter.
[141] Bates (ed.), *Quarter Sessions Records for ... Somerset: Vol. I, James I, 1607–1625*, 96–7.

into individuals such as Elizabeth Busher, a woman who, overcome with hatred for her neighbours, had apparently sealed a diabolic covenant that granted her the powers to destroy her enemies in the little commonwealth of the village.

As we have seen, much church court litigation was about closing wounds in local communities. Merely by testifying to a consistory court, many people would feel that they had had their say and would pursue the matter no further. But with a crime such as witchcraft, where the potential outcome could be a noose, there could be no easy solution to neighbourly conflicts. The case of the Norfolk man William Colles provides a stark example of how the execution of a witch could deepen, rather than heal, divisions within the locality. Around 1620, the magistracy learnt that Colles had abused his neighbours, sometimes in the church and some-times in the churchyard, and had denounced the minister, Thomas Howes, saying 'that hee hathe noe honesty, conscience, nor goodness', charging him to be forsworne. The matter was that of the condemnation of his wife for witchcraft. As the neighbours complained to the bench:

The said Colls hathe vowed and p[ro]tested upon his salvacion that yf his weiffe weare a wytch: that hee is a wizard and had found about him a charme beinge a blasphemous one ...[.] Colls hathe impudentlie and slanderouslye abused the lorde Cheife Justice, the Jurye, and all the witnesses, that were sworne againste his weiffe saying, that hee will avouch itt befor[e] the Cheife Justice of England that his weiffe was most unjustly condemned.[142]

Although witchcraft accusations can be seen as an indicator of social conflict within local communities, they also generated evidence that reveals the ways in which neighbourliness was understood. When the minister of Pulham (Norfolk) and six of his neighbours wrote to the magistrate Robert Buxton in 1590 concerning the allegations of witch-craft that had been levelled against Margaret Grame, their petition spoke to the values she embodied – her 'good life and conversation' – and her embeddedness within village life. Critically for Margaret, she was cer-tainly not a marginal figure in village life and was able to call on a social network that could sustain her against accusations of witchcraft. The minister wrote to Buxton:

Truth it is ... that I have had conference with three women with whom she have been very well known for the space of 26 years, and right sisters to the wife of ... Richard Cole, who is this complainant, and they do affirm in all their knowledge she have never been named or suspected for such a one, neither any ways guilty of such a horrible crime.

[142] NRO, NQS/C/S3/22, articles against William Colles.

At the bottom of the petition, Buxton scribbled a note that, following receipt of the document, he had discussed the case with John Prenice, 'one of the chief of the parish', adding that Prenice was also prepared to testify on behalf of Margaret Grame.[143] Witchcraft accusations often succeeded or failed on the basis of the alleged witch's reputation and the depth of their connections within the neighbourhood. Although we do not know the outcome of the trial of Margaret Grame (assuming the matter ever reached court), her capacity to draw on her deep social networks – the minister, the chief men and three women whom she had known for twenty-six years – would have significantly strengthened her defence.

There are similar examples to be found elsewhere of people standing up for neighbours who had been labelled as witches, invoking communal norms in support of the accused. In 1618, for instance, the eighteen-year-old Dorothie Hudspeck of North Dalton (Yorkshire) told the church court that Isabell Morris for these

seven yeares last and more hath lived and yet doth live in the same towne where this ex[aminan]te for all that time hath dwelt dureinge all wch said time she saith That she the said Isabell hath bene and is comonlie accompted for an honest woman of good life and con[vers]acion w[i]thin the towne and p[ar]ishe of North Dalton . . . and other places thereabouts of this ex[aminan]tes certin hearing being her neighbor as aforesaid, and saith she never knew or h[e]ard the con[trar]y.[144]

The patriarchs of Padstow (Cornwall) were mustered in 1581 to defend Anne Piers against the allegation of witchcraft; they explained that they never knew Piers to 'practize witchcrafte or had the name to be a witche'. The petition originated from amongst 'some of the better sorte & of most credite' who listed their names, along with their ages – most were in their sixties and seventies. The petition was further signed by the minister and three local gentlemen.[145] The order of the town – founded on class, age and gender – was therefore invoked in order to defend a neighbour against that most harmful of accusations.

In the same way, powerful social norms – charity, godliness and conscience – were invoked in 1627 by the neighbours of the Lancashire woman Elizabeth Londesdale in their defence of her against charges of witchcraft. They told the Assize Judges:

[W]ee her neighbours (or not farr remote) having knowne and crediblie heard of her Life and con[ve]rsa[i]con past by the space of twentie yeres or above doe hold orselves bound in conscience and charitie to certifie the truth unto yor Lo[rdshi]ps The said Elizabeth dureinge the tyme afor[e]said hath Lived orderly and

[143] HMC, Various Collections, II, 244.    [144] BIA, CP.H.1327.
[145] TNA, SP12/150/96.

Religeously amongst her neighbours Duelie repareinge to the church and hearing
divine service and sermons & receaving the blessed Sacrament of or Lords supper
and till this accusac[i]on ... w[i]thout touch or impeachm[en]t of her credit or
reputac[i]on. And wee are perswaded in or conscience[e]s that shee is no witche
Sorceresse or user of Charmes ... but a good honest & orderly neighbour All wch
in neighbourly compassion and confidence of her innocencie wee have presumed
to certifie unto yor Lo[rdshi]ps.[146]

It is difficult to find a stronger statement of the values of neighbourhood
than this, founded as it was on reputation, name, conscience, religious
duty and charity.

Those who made accusations of witchcraft that fell flat could find
themselves prosecuted before the church courts for slander or being
presented by officers as a disquieter of the neighbourhood. In 1601,
David Tarver of Great Oakley (Essex) appeared before the visitation for
'being a most troublesome, disquiet and slanderous fellow among his
honest neighbours, for calling the wife of James Bean witch'.[147]
Witchcraft allegations set neighbour against neighbour, sometimes indi-
vidually and sometimes across the parish as a whole. In 1606, in
Pulborough (Sussex), Elizabeth Hitchcocke said that Thomas Herold
'was a witch and did bewitch her, her husband's cattle and her children
that nothing they had could prosper with them'. As a result, Thomas
Herold initiated a slander action at the church court. As the case
unfolded, it revealed a deeply divided village: William Hitchcocke, for
example, said: 'That['s] true it is that Edward Talmye, Simon Talmye,
Alice Talmye and Margery Fivian are capital enemies to Elizabeth
Hitchcocke ... and are the especial good friends and favorites of
Thomas Herold and have not deposed a truth, but lies, falsehood and
things to truth altogether contrary.'[148] This was not how early modern
people wanted to live their lives; in communities riven by conflict and
enmities.

One way of overcoming an allegation of witchcraft – and so settling the
matter – was litigation. This was especially true of defamation cases
involving witchcraft allegations heard by church courts. In the 1560s,
some of the women of Southampton were discussing how moths had
eaten one of their garments when Mistress Singleton, standing at her
door, entered the conversation. Mistress Dingly then said to Mistress
Singleton, '[A]rt thow come hither to scould[G]et the[e] hence thow
witche and clere thy selfe thou knowest what it is well inoughe for I will

---

[146] Lancashire Record Office, DDKE/HMC/82.
[147] Emmison (ed.), *Elizabethan Life*, 66. For another example, see Major, 'The Lincoln
Diocesan Records', 59.
[148] Wilkinson (ed.), *Chichester Archdeaconry Depositions*, 230–2.

never take the[e] for other then a witche till thow hast cleerd thy
selfe.'[149] Should Mistress Singleton 'clear' herself through the process
of litigation, Mistress Dingly's implication was that she would cease to
chide her with accusations of witchcraft. Another means by which the
lacerations inflicted by witchcraft could be bound was through the
public confession of the alleged witch. He or she was lucky to avoid
execution. See, for instance, the case of the yeoman Ralph Milner of
Rashe (Yorkshire) who, in 1606, 'being accused of sorcerie, witchcraft,
inchantment, and telling of fortunes', was required to 'make his submission at Mewkarr Church upon Sonday next, in the tyme of Divine
Service and confesse that he hath heighlie offended God and deluded
men, and is heartily sorie, and will offend no more'.[150] In this way,
through litigation, social ties could be reasserted and neighbourliness
re-established.

Magic could be useful, and many villages had a cunning man or a
white witch to whom neighbours could turn in times of trouble. Some
people acquired reputations for warding off evil spirits. Janet Pereson
of Elizabethan Washington (County Durham), for example, was
known amongst her neighbours for employing 'wytchcraft in measur-
inge of belts to p[re]serve folks frome the Fayries'. Pereson acquired a
reputation for exorcism: it was common knowledge in Washington that
when Thomasine Blackberd's child fell ill, she had turned to Janet
Pereson, who had cast out the 'farye' that had possessed her little
one.[151] Having a woman like Pereson in the neighbourhood could,
then, be very useful. But elsewhere the practice of having recourse to
cunning men and white witches was something that wealthier people
were starting to see as contemptible. When the church goods of
Henrician Holbeach (Lincolnshire) were stolen, John Patriche sought
the aid of the local cunning men 'occupying the craft of inchantement
and wichecraft' to track them down. This impaired his credit amongst
his neighbours. Patriche found that although he held land worth forty
marks per year, 'convenient to his degre[e] and more that many other
ther have', and although he had always been taken of 'good nature
fame honeste credens and estimacion', his association with the local
magicians had 'browght [him] to infamy slander and owte of
credens'.[152]

---

[149] HALS, 21M65/C3/5, pp. 214–15.
[150] E. Cooper, *Muker: The Story of a Yorkshire Parish* (Clapham, 1948), 35–6.
[151] DUL, DDR/EJ/CCD/1/2, fols. 36v–8r.    [152] TNA, STAC2/17/64.

## The Plight of Thomas Barebones: Settlement, Place and Neighbourhood

The detailed register kept in the early seventeenth century for the parish of Hamwell (Hertfordshire) allows some insight into the ways in which community was understood. Central to belonging was having a sense of place, defined by Christian morality, long residence, common association, credit, trustworthiness and communal entitlement. The register chronicles the baptisms, marriages and burials within the parish, marking the passing away of well-known people. Reputation continued to matter after death. Mary Kyngsland, 'a woeman too well deserving, too dearly beloved to bee soone forgotten', was buried on 19 August 1613 in the chancel, 'awaitinge the resurrection of the just'. Edmund Hales, 'an antiant man and of good worth and estimation amongst us', was interred on 6 April 1615. William Westwood, 'an antiant man of honest report', was buried on 11 February 1616. Marke Hopkins of Amwell Streete, 'an honest poore labouring man and a good churchman', was buried on 8 August 1630. In contrast to Hopkins, Philip Winchley of Ware, 'an owld notorious bedlam roge', took his negative reputation to the grave on 12 October 1615. Another bad neighbour, William Robinson, 'a miserable poore man', commonly called 'Wicked Will', was buried on 7 November 1628. Some poor folk had a notable place within the community. The eighty-year-old John Allen, 'a laboringe man and of good and honest reputation ... living allwayes poorelye but never miserable, died and was buried' on 1 December 1634. He was 'a pentioner to the Newe River to clense and keepe the head, and old servant to the church to guarde the chappell doore, to controle unrulye boyes and correct intruding doggs'. Six months later, Edward Shadbolt was buried, 'a labouring man of above threescore and ten yeares of age, allwayes a good laborer, no spender, without children, selldome eate good meate or drinke or wore good cloathes, yet lived and dyed very poore and miserable'. Life may have been hard for Edward Shadbolt, but he had his name and his place.[153]

This sense of place was embedded in the material culture of the village: in its houses, streets, fields, commons, woodland, moors, manorial and parochial boundaries, and in its parish church.[154] Critically, this was a landscape that was imbued with spiritual meaning: the church, the parish bounds, the tithes paid on particular holdings, all linked the economics of village life to its spiritual identity. There was no distinction here between the sacred and the profane: rather, Christian morality informed everyday

---

[153] Doree (ed.), *The Parish Register*, 94, 95, 96, 116, 118, 125, 126.
[154] For local memory in Amwell, see Wood, *The Memory of the People*, 131, 226.

social practices, and its authority was written into the spatial arrangements of the parish. Indeed, the burial register of Hamwell points to the
ways in which the physicality of the church was central to the material
commemoration of those who had passed away: rich folk buried in the
chancel, poorer folk buried in the churchyard; both interred in a material
environment that was simultaneously sacred and everyday. Some people
had their place within the village, but not one fixed in any particular
house: in 1600, George Soveraigne, 'an owld man a bagpipe player of
no certayne dwellinge', was laid into the ground. Interment within the
churchyard meant that parishioners retained that place long after their
death. And a sense of the place of the deceased within the local hierarchy
was also retained for the more prominent members of the community.
Nicholas Thurrood was 'a man of the age of threescore yeares and uppe-
ward' who had drowned after falling into a ditch; he was buried in
September 1601 'in Amwell church ... betwixt the great stone and
chaunccell doore in the chaunccell'. In death as in life, the parish church
was a theatre for the symbolic structuring of the social order, written into
sacred space. Mr John Goodman, for example, 'a cownseller and a justice
of the peace', was buried on 8 August; mourning continued for the next
seven days, and it was noted that 'Hee lyeth in the chaunccell under the
communion table next to the grave of owld Hale's wife new covered with
paving tiles'.[155]

And then there were those who had no place: those migrant poor who
seemed faceless to the folk of Hamwell. The clerk registered children born
to travelling people as the offspring of a 'pore travailinge woeman', of 'a
traveller', as the 'sonne of a strange poore woman', '[a] poore woeman's
child'.[156] Some distinct tragedies experienced by the tramping poor
found their way into the record: on 27 March 1631, it was recorded:

One Anthonye Barnes of Sedgebrooke alias Seabrooke in Lincolnshire, travelling
towards London with Amye his wife great with childe, shee fell in travel at
Amweall Hill and at the howse of Richard Davis was delivered of a manchild
the first daye of Aprill, which child beinge in great danger of death (beinge it seems
borne before the tyme) was at theire instance baptized the same daye and named
Robert, and dyed shortlye after.[157]

---

[155] Doree (ed.), *The Parish Register*, 77, 78, 82, 84, 85, 86–7, 88, 93.
[156] Ibid., 4, 9, 12, 15. For another parish register that speaks powerfully of the placelessness
and anonymity of the wandering poor, see D. M. Palliser, 'Dearth and Disease in
Staffordshire, 1540–1670', in C. W. Chalklin and M. A. Havinden (eds.), *Rural
Change and Economic Growth, 1500–1800* (London, 1974), 64.
[157] Doree (ed.), *The Parish Register*, 41.

Hamwell seems to have been a community in which most people knew their place, yet through which others – anonymous, marginal, hungry people – moved.

The parish registers of the coal-mining parish of St Oswald's, located at the edge of the city of Durham, suggest a more complicated picture, one in which established neighbours went to their grave with respect, in which the anonymous poor featured in some numbers, but also where despite the fact that the local poor were known, they were sometimes left to die in the street. Such evidence represents a powerful challenge to the values of neighbourhood as they have been described in this book and needs to be considered in its own terms.

Early in the summer of 1614, the parish buried some of its most valued inhabitants. On 20 May, Jennett Hopper, 'beinge a woman of a very great aige', was interred. In September, George Man, 'a verie honest nighbore', went to his grave. Then there was 'John Richardson, public notary, a verie honest nighbore and a good willer both for the good of this Churche and for the good of this parish, whose soule the lord Jesus receive in to his Kingdome, Amen'. He went to his grave on 8 November 1614. Two days before Christmas, it was the turn of Mistress Graie, 'a verie honest nighbore and about the aige of one hundredth yeares of their aboure'. The following year, 'Anne Mann, wife of George Man, a verie honest nighbore', was buried. We might go on: over successive years, men and women were interred whose neighbourliness and charity were widely recognized. They included people identified in the following terms: 'a verie honest nighbore'; 'a man godlie, good to the mentenance of the poore and especial a verie honest man amonge his nighbours'; 'a verie honest man amongst his nighbors'; 'a verie honest nighbore'; 'a most wordy houskeper both for riche and poore'; 'a verie honest nighbore and good to the powre'; 'a verie old woman who levede verie honestly just and godly'; 'verie bountefull for house kepinge both for rich and power'; 'a verie zelous godly gentlewoman'; 'a verie honest nighbore, verie bountefull and good to the power. God send hime a joyfull resurrection'; 'a verie honest and religious gen[tleman], good to the power'; 'a verie good nighbore, and good and bountefull to the power and nedy'; 'a verie religious gentleman, bountefull to the poore and nedy'.[158]

In contrast to such local worthies' interments, burials were also recorded of the anonymous, rootless poor, desperate folk on the road who died while in search of food and shelter, or perhaps in search of work in the burgeoning coal industry. St Oswald's parish stretched into the

---

[158] A. W. Headlam (ed.), *The Parish Registers of St Oswald's, Durham* (Durham, 1891), 53, 54, 55, 57, 59, 60, 61, 62, 63, 69, 77, 89, 93.

Great North Road and its clerk noted a considerable number of such burials. On 19 May 1577, '[a] power man, spendyd by water', was buried. On 20 July 1584, the parishioners interred '[a] poore man a stranger'. The coal-mining village of Shincliffe, located within the larger parish, featured regularly as the domicile of the poor. Again, many seemed to be unknown to the parish clerk. On 30 April 1586, '[a] poor child from Shynkeleye' was buried. On 27 June 1587, an entry read: 'A poore woman buryde from Shyknklye bakhowse.' On 9 October 1599, there was '[a] childe fownd dede at Shinklife'. On 5 March 1608, 'Umfrey, a poore child borne in Shinckclif backhouse', was buried. On 5 August 1612, the clerk noted that '[a] poor woman dyed at Shinckcliffe, hir name was I know not, a stranger'. Twelve years later, there was the case of '[a] power traveller, a younge man, dyed in John Engglebie barne in Shinckcliffe'. Migrants from Sunderland were also noted. On 24 June 1584, '[a] collyers chylde from Sunderlande' found his or her way to the grave. On 28 July 1587, '[a] poor chylde from Synderlande' was buried. Nine days later, another 'poore chylde from Synderland' was interred. On 11 August 1587, there was buried '[a]nother poore woman from Sunderland [tha]t dyed in the streete'. On 18 November 1587, '[a] poore man from Synderland' was buried. It seems 1587 was a busy year for the gravediggers of St Oswald's. That same year, on 13 August, '[a] poore woman died in Ratten Row'. On 9 October 1587, '[a] poore man dyed upon [Elvet] brydge'.

The cause of these deaths was not merely high food prices: in truth, rather than being about food scarcity, it was about the way in which scant resources were socially distributed. The rich did not die from starvation; their lives were not blighted and shortened by chronic malnutrition; their children lived beyond babyhood in greater numbers. Instead, choices about resource distribution were made by richer folk that left their poorer neighbours dying in large numbers. The parish clerk recorded in the marriage register:

Thys yeare a[nn]o 1587 the pryce of corne was as folowyth, and the gretest parte of last yeare before goinge, so th[a]t many poore people were supposed to dye for lacke of bredde, notw[i]t[h]standing greate store in the handes of the hard harted carles, th[a]t styll raysed the pr[i]ce untyll harvest at the wyche tyme the pr[i]ce of corne beganne to fall. The p[ri]ce of Rye xiii.s. iiii.d. the busshell: wheat at xvi.s. iiii.d. the busshell: haver at v.s ix.d. the busshell; byg at vi.s. the busshell; pease at xii.s the busshell; halffe malt at v.s vi.d the busshell; but the next Somer wheate was at iiiis. 4d. the busshell & ikewyse rye, & payse at iiii.s. the busshell, otes ii.s the busshell, byg at 3s.4d the bussehell.'

The anonymous poor continued to find their way into the parish register into the following year. On 20 January 1588, '[a] poore man from the brome' died 'in M[istre]ss Stevensons house'. Two weeks later, there the 'poore man buryed th[a]t dyed on the bridge end'. Plague hit the parish in the following year, resulting in twenty-four burials. Things seemed to settle down in the early 1590s; but in 1598, the community was devastated by the return of the plague. The deaths were so numerous that the parish clerk made no effort at individual registration, noting only: 'The number of them that died within Elvitt streates – 344.'

The record of the parish register speaks powerfully to the placelessness of many of the poor. On 2 April 1600, '[a] pore Boye, beinge a stranger to the parishe' was buried. Three years later, '[a] poor man [was] fownde spent at Botterbe'. In 1611, '[a] poor woman ... dyed in the almes house'. In 1622, a 'power woman that dyed in the backhowse att Aldernedge' went to her grave. In the following year, there was the case of the 'power man that dyed in the almosse house, his name not knowne'. On 13 April 1623, 'a power man who dyed in Baxter wood his name not knowne' was buried; likewise, four months later, there was '[a] power man who dyed in Alton field, his name not knowne'. The wandering poor also imposed themselves on the baptismal record of St Oswald's. On 14 February 1615, the christening was noted of 'William White, so[n] of Robert White, dwelling in Penrathe in Cumberland a tynckker by his traide. Godfather William Dawson of Elvitt potter'. The following year, the christening of 'Anthony Gibson, s[on] of Edmunde Gibson, a poore man goinge abrod for his almosse' was recorded.[159]

Yet it is highly significant for our understanding of neighbourhood that the starved poor were not always rootless and anonymous. When, in 1622, a 'poore man' was recorded as found dead 'in the field neare Brome', it was known that he had been 'borne in Branton in Gilsland'. And amongst the wandering poor, some were known to the parish: Roger Makecrown was known to be of Sunderland when he was buried on 25 February 1600; so too, a day following, was Gerrard Lydle known to be from the township of Toddy in the parish of Brancepeth. Elisabeth Woodend and Margaret Winter were both buried on 29 March 1603. Although they were recorded as being 'both strangers to the parishe', yet they were known to the clerk. On 24 March 1622, the burial was recorded of 'Barbary Felton, wife of Thomas Felton, power people sekinge releiffe. She the saide Barbary Felton dyed at Butterbye.' Then there was Roger Trolopp, who was buried in 1628 'beinge a childe who dyed in this streete of Elvit destituted of frindes'. The following year, the burial of 'Grace Hallman of Norton, spinster' was recorded, 'dying in this streete'. The implication in both cases is that they were known to the parish, yet had been left to die in the open streets. Then there was Jayne Mugge,

[159] Ibid., 23, 28, 30, 31, 32, 37, 38, 39, 41, 51, 54, 56, 66, 67, 68, 69.

described as merely 'a poore wench' when she was buried on 21 July 1634. What are we to make of this entry? Did she have a place in the parish? People knew her name; but she was clearly a young woman – and poverty stricken at that.[160] The poor, then, were not always nameless. Their names and faces were known to those who allowed them to die in the streets, fields and parish porches of their communities. This was a known social reality: writing in 1631, Henry Peacham observed that 'the poore of parishes are faine to bee relieved by the Farmer, the Husbandman and the middle rank, or else they must starve, as many upon my own knowledge did this last Snowie-winter'.[161]

Every community has its own history, its own stories of feuds, trials, labour, love, children, customs, beliefs, allegiances, friendships and betrayal. But there are certain typicalities to the early modern community that command our attention. The poor who moved, anonymous and desperate, through Amwell and St Oswald's, their presence only very occasionally inscribing itself into the parish register, were one particular issue with which all early modern communities had to deal. In London, the issue was especially pressing. A. L. Beier comments that 'London's burial records abound with references to vagrants dyng in the streets and near-by fields'. He provides some examples from St Botolph's without Aldgate from the 1590s: 'Edward Ellis, a vagrant who died in the street. A young man not known who died in a hay-loft. A cripple that died in the street before John Awstren's door.'[162] In outlying London parishes, the poor were dying in the fields: the clerk of Elizabethan St Dunstans-in-the-West noted, in February 1586, 'a maide buried out of the field'. Three years later, there was 'a poore maide that died in the fielde'. Then, in 1593, there was 'a childe that died in the fielde'. Rural parish registers speak similarly of poor men and women dying on the road, in streets, in fields and on commons, and on moorland in the winter snow. It may have been a relatively unsurprising sight for a farmer to walk his cattle onto the common and there find the body of some poor traveller. And the evidence of socially specific famine is also to be found in parish registers, including in some of the richest parishes in the realm, such as St Margaret's, Westminster. Here, in 1557, the parish clerk recorded people who 'died of very poverty' or of 'very famine'.[163]

As we have seen in Hamwell and St Oswald's, Durham, many of the poor seemed like faceless, anonymous wanderers through a world in

[160] Ibid., 38, 42, 66–7, 76, 78.
[161] C. Bridenbaugh, *Vexed and Troubled Englishmen, 1590–1642* (Oxford, 1968), 377.
[162] A. L. Beier, *Masterless Men: The Vagrancy Problem in England, 1560–1640* (London, 1985), 46.
[163] Thistleton-Dyer, *Old English Social Life*, 184.

which they had no friends, no neighbours or kindred, no *place*. Parish registers across the realm speak to this sense of placelessness, of social anomie and near-collapse during crisis times. In 1580, the clerk of Orpington (Kent) recorded the burial of '[a] Poor Childe wiche died in an oxe stall at my Lady Hart's house'. Then there was an entry in the parish register for Poyning (Sussex) for 1 April 1608. On that day 'was buried John Skerry a poore man that died in the place stable, and being brought half naked with is face bare, the parson would not burye him soe, but first he gave a sheete and caused him to be sacked therein, and they buried him more Christian like, being much grieved to see him brought soe unto the grave'. And there were those children who were on the run from the institutions that had been placed in authority over them. In October 1589, there was the burial in Mitcham (Surrey) of 'William a little boy in a blew jerkine and a blew paier of gaskins, being the livery of Bridewell, buried out of William Swillinghurst his barne, he was supposed to be a Cheshire boy as he reported'. Some wandering children crawled into communal ovens and brick kilns in order to stay warm. In Thorington (Suffolk) in 1591, there was the sad matter of 'one Derrowe a ladde of the age of viii.th yeares whoe as he saide came from Bunggaye and was there borne, he dyed at our bricke kell and was buried the viii.th of December'.[164] In plague years, the deaths of the anonymous poor overwhelmed parish clerks who were meant to record names and places in the burial process. During the Newcastle plague of 1636, some fifty-six of those buried in the poor parish of St Andrews had no name, recorded only as 'a power one', 'a powre child' or '2 powre ones'.[165]

In Kendal (Westmorland) during the 1596–7 dearth, some were indeed anonymous. The parish clerk recorded the interment of '[a] poor cripple whose name none of Hutton could tell' and '[a] poore child which dyed upon the Kirkland, which came out of Lancashire'.[166] At the same time, in Holme Cultram (Cumberland), the parish clerk noted the following burial: 'A daughter of Tho. Burghe she dyed in the Church porche.'[167] Poor folk, devoid of any other shelter, often took refuge in the porches of parish churches. Some were wanderers; some had roots in the village, yet were left shivering in the parish porch.[168] Some were ejected by the parish

[164] J. C. Cox (ed.), *The Parish Registers of England* (London, 1910), 98, 120.

[165] Wrightson, *Ralph Tailor's Summer*, 108.

[166] G. E. Moser, 'Kendal Parish Church Registers', *TC&WA&AS*, 1st ser., 3 (1878), 54.

[167] W. F. Gilbanks, 'The Oldest Register Book of the Parish of Holm Cultram, Cumberland', *TC&WA&AS*, 1st ser., 10 (1889), 185.

[168] For a fuller study, see S. Hindle, 'Destitution, Liminality and Belonging: The Church Porch and the Politics of Settlement in English Rural Communities, c.1590–1660', in C. Dyer (ed.), *The Self-Contained Village? The Social History of English Rural Communities, 1250–1900* (Hertford, 2006), 46–71.

authorities; others froze and died.[169] But – again – they were not all unknown. In Holm Cultram, the burial register noted 'one man child brought up in the town which no man could show ought him buried'. So the boy was part of the village, yet had no known name. Many others were not anonymous: the burial register noted the interment of '[a] poor woman called Black Meg, of the highgate ... Michael Robby, a poore vagrant stranger ... Richard Peill, a poor child, a vagabond person ... William, which God sent us, a poore ladd who dyed at Jefferey Crosbies, Highgate'.

So, this presents the historian of neighbourhood with a dilemma: for all that parish authorities ran a relatively effective system of poor relief, there were always a few folk – established in the village – who lived such marginal lives that they might end up shivering in the parish porch or bedded down in a farmer's barn or seeking warmth in the bakehouse. These people were known to their neighbours – there was Black Meg and the 'poore lads' William and Richard Peill – but they were so marginal that they were just left to die. Communities are about exclusion as well as inclusion; neighbourhood extended only so far and was constructed within sometimes coldly brutal social structures. Class always matters.

The frequently stated doctrinal notion that all Christians were neighbours placed many propertied parishioners in a difficult position, for the increasingly harsh logic of welfare provision distinguished between the resident and the mobile poor: parish governors were expected by magistrates to care for those poor who were 'neare dwellers' but were meant to be harsh to those whom they found on the road.[170] Yet, despite this, many people provided care to the indigent poor. In his study of Warwickshire vagrants, A. L. Beier found some 100 cases where travellers lodged with friends, kin, alehousekeepers and gentlemen.[171] Ilana Krausman Ben-Amos cites examples of travellers being offered help during fast-days, harvest, sheep-shearing, revels, Christmas and other holidays, churching and funerals. She notes householders who gave hospitality to the poor in their barns, sometimes for weeks or months, and numbering over twenty.[172] Understanding that a warm lodging might mean the difference between life and death during a cold northern winter, in 1572, the manor court of Dilston (Northumberland) ordered that the common bakehouse was to be 'kept onelie for lodgeing a power bodie

---

[169] For examples, see J. Bruce, 'Extracts from the Accounts of the Churchwardens of Minchinhampton in the County of Gloucester', *Archaeologia*, 35, 2 (1854), 436, 437.

[170] Hindle, *On the Parish?*, 70.

[171] A. L. Beier, 'Vagrants and the Social Order in Elizabethan England', *P&P*, 64 (1974), 16–17.

[172] Krausman Ben-Amos, '"Good Works" and Social Ties', 129.

travellinge'.[173] In some places, pitying the poor, locals took them into their community. In 1610, the villagers of Warbleton (Sussex) informed the magistracy that a poor family were currently living in a barn, explaining: 'The case of the poore man & his wife & his iiii children doth pyttie us all for they have lyen in an ende of a barne this last month.'[174]

Yet the generous folk of Jacobean Warbleton and Elizabethan Dilston seem to have been in the minority. Building upon a series of carefully contextualized local studies, Steve Hindle has shown that attitudes amongst the propertied towards the mobile poor hardened in the face of an increase in the numbers of people on the road and a magisterial and governmental drive that criminalized poor migrants as vagrants.[175] In particular, Hindle's study of parish affairs in Layston (Hertfordshire) points to the ways in which the governors of communities made sure that poor travellers faced closed doors. The objective in this village was to control in-migration by preventing tenants from erecting cottages for the poor, who might become sub-lessees, pay rent to the tenant and thereby establish themselves within the village. When Alexander Strange, the minister of Layston, addressed his neighbours, he spoke of the poor householder as a figure called 'Thomas Barebones' who was a burden on the parish. In particular, Strange was anxious to 'keepe out rude & disordered poor which may here after be a Charge to our parish'.[176] Deploying such commanding evidence, Hindle has argued that 'however conciliatory the poor law may have been within the community of the parish, chief inhabitants were necessarily coercive to those poor strangers who stood at its margins. "Community" implied "exclusion".'[177]

Something similar was going on in cities. Jeremy Boulton observes: 'The poorer sort [of London] were vulnerable to parochial harassment'; they had few links within social networks upon which they could draw to protect themselves. Boulton cites the report of the Southwark searcher for inmates who explains that of 'William Milwood his wife and 2 children being come to dwell in Horsehead Alley I made it known to the churchwardens, and afterwards warned them to put in sureties, and being notable for fear of further troubles they left this parish, and went to dwell in St George's parish, and so we were rid of them'.[178] There was little neighbourhood here.

[173] Healey, 'The Northern Manor', 233.     [174] BL, Add MS 33058, fol. 54r.
[175] For the heavy investment of ratepayers in the poor rate, see S. Hindle, 'Power, Poor Relief and Social Relations in Holland Fen, c.1600–1800', Historical Journal, 41, 1 (1998), 67–96.
[176] Falvey and Hindle (eds.), 'This Little Commonwealth', 68, 71.
[177] Hindle, 'Exclusion Crises', 126.     [178] Boulton, Neighbourhood and Society, 221.

One consequence of this institutional drive – intimately related to early modern processes of state formation – was to *test* ideas about community. The people of Tudor and early Stuart England were well aware of these forces, not least because they were active agents within them – whether opposing socially restricted visions of community, supporting such ideas or exploiting them for their own purposes. Consequently, the language of neighbourliness became a *battleground* between opposing individuals, groups and interests. Notions of insider and outsider were constructed around social ideals concerning belonging, place, neighbourhood and social morality. These contested notions suggest that community was an *idea*: it formed part of a discourse about mutuality and social identification that people built up in words and actions, sometimes against one another.

Neighbourliness might seem like the softest of social concepts, drawing people together into some rose-tinted picture of shared norms and values and supportive social systems. But there were always those who were excluded from this supporting umbrella, and they were not always the indigent poor. Just as they were about movement, questions of insider and outsider were always about class, gender and power. Steven Evered of Metton (Norfolk) petitioned the Jacobean bench, offering a tale that spoke to some of the ways in which the poor might be excluded from local belonging. Evered told the magistrates that he had been born 'lame' and yet had always done 'his uttermost inde[a]vor by his labor to get his lyvinge'. Nonetheless, given his disability, he had been unable to earn sufficient to support his family and had fallen back on the parish for relief, 'wch some of the Inh[ab]itants and the overseers of the poore of ... metton p[er]ceyvinge and supposing that they might be charged w[i]th yor said supplicant yf he should there remayne' had expelled him from the village. Now, he and his family were 'compelled to lodge in dykes and carthowses where they are in great danger this winter season to starve and perishe'.[179] Truly, charity had grown cold in this Norfolk village.

Where people like Steven Evered failed to gain succour from their richer neighbours, they might petition the county magistrates. Sometimes this worked; sometimes it didn't. No outcome is recorded for the petition of the 'poor labourer' James Hurde who wrote to the Somerset bench in 1612 to complain about his treatment by the governors of his home village of West Cranmore. He explained that, for two years, he and his family had lived in a rented house in the village, noting that he had never become chargeable to the parish. Then Hurde cut to the rub: despite his place, 'yet the parishioners and churchwardens there, Do

[179] NRO, NRO, NQS/C/S3/20, petition of Steven Evered.

indeavor and threaten' to evict him and his family unless he gave sufficient sureties never to become chargeable upon them, 'which he canot by reason he is but a poor Labourer'. Hurde therefore requested that the magistrates allow his family to live in the parish for so long as they were not chargeable to the parish, 'otherwise he and his family are like to perish'.[180] Then there was the practice of banning pauper marriage, according to which richer villagers would ensure that their poor rates stayed low by preventing poorer folk from marrying and so raising children who would become beholden to the parish.[181]

Neighbourliness – despite its apparently warm hues – was no more straightforward than any other social norm. Rather, it was constantly struggled over, guaranteeing as it did access to place, agency, safety and access to resources. It should, then, be no surprise to find that those deemed to be 'neighbours' might exclude many others from the term, or that this ran down class lines. In Wolverhampton (Staffordshire) in 1597, for example, a crowd of 200 'very lewd & dissolute p[er]sones, Naylors, & smithes, of very base trades & Condicions' sought to impose an affordable price on the food in the town's market; they were opposed in this by the constable, 'accompanied by the best sorte of his honest neighbors'.[182] Who stood for community here? Likewise, in the London parish of St Martin Ludgate, the parish paid for a feast on the anniversaries of Elizabeth's accession, the defeat of the Armada and the failure of the Gunpowder Plot. Those who were to sit at the table as the feast was conducted included the preacher, the churchwardens, the two chief constables and two of the 'auncientist' of the parish, 'as well for the continuence of brotherly love and kind neighbourhood amongst them'.[183]

Social networks – and the definition of neighbourhood itself – in such instances became socially restricted. Neighbourliness could provide a way of squeezing out the poor and needy. And yet, in some places, birth and propinquity ensured support for the poor amongst villagers. This was evident in those cases where parishioners petitioned magistrates and lords to secure accommodation for poor members of the community who sought to construct cottages on the commons.[184] In 1615, the Somerset

---

[180] Bates (ed.), *Quarter Sessions Records for ... Somerset: Vol. I, James I, 1607–1625*, 94.
[181] S. Hindle, 'The Problem of Pauper Marriage in Seventeenth-Century England', *TRHS*, 6th ser., 8 (1998), 71–89.
[182] TNA, STAC5/C41/16.
[183] M. Berlin, 'Reordering Rituals: Ceremony and the Parish, 1520–1640', in P. Griffiths and M. S. R. Jenner (eds.), *Londinopolis: Essays in the Cultural and Social History of Early Modern London* (Manchester, 2000), 57, 59.
[184] Under an Act of 1589, paupers were allowed to petition the Quarter Sessions for permission to build cottages on commons so long as the lord of the manor consented. For a local study of the construction of pauper cottages on common land, see D. H.

bench heard from Thomas Orchard of Widcombe, where he had lived for twenty years, 'being a very poor man without a house to receive and succor himself his wife and children, yet hath the consent and goodwill of the inhabitants'. He was allowed to build a cottage on the common. A year earlier, Thomas Macye of Winsham (Somerset) presented a petition to the magistracy subscribed by the most part of the parishioners showing that he, his wife and children were all born there, 'and ever behaved themselves very well, and by hard labour maintained themselves', but he had become lame and so he asked permission to build a cottage on the waste.[185]

The need of such families was great, and parishioners were often willing to open their hearts to long-established poor folk. Hence, the inhabitants of Mountfield (Sussex) petitioned their lord Pelham to allow a poor old man to build a cottage on the common. They explained: 'The man is ould & his worke near done, he hath lived honestly amonge us a longe time . . .[. U]nlesse youre favoure bee shewed unto hime, he shall hardly keape his kynes, wch are his cheefest healpe unto his living.'[186] Only a truly hard-hearted lord, the petitioners implied, could turn down such a request.

## The Better Sort and the Domination of Parish Politics

So, who ruled early modern England? Looked at from the top, the answer seemed obvious: the monarch and her or his privy council, and around them a tight circle of nobility, higher clergy and upper gentry. But, in reality, little could be achieved without the active participation, on the level of small communities, of the 'better sort of people' who dominated parish politics. Fundamentally, what this represented was the *localization* of administrative affairs and of social relations. Writing in 1588, John Case felt that although 'bakers, tavern-keepers, cobblers and other man of the basest sort' might hold village office, 'such men dispute better about ale-cups than laws, more fitly about Aesop's fables than the tables and statutes of the commonwealth'.[187] Office, Case suggested, lay below politics. Many early modern office-holders would have disagreed: routinely, they had to enforce the monarch's laws, and from this they gained a sense of agency that was underwritten by a practical sense of governance, of the nature of authority – and so, also, of politics.[188]

Tankard, 'The Regulation of Cottage-Building in Seventeenth-Century Sussex', *Agricultural History Review*, 59, 1 (2011), 18–35.
[185] Bates (ed.), *Quarter Sessions Records for . . . Somerset: Vol. I, James I, 1607–1625*, 145, 185.
[186] BL, Add MS 33058, fol. 2r.
[187] N. Dauber, *State and Commonwealth: The Theory of the State in Early Modern England, 1549–1640* (Princeton, NJ, 2016), 141.
[188] For middling sort claims to embody civic virtues of rationality and order, see E. H. Shagan, *The Rule of Moderation: Violence, Religion and the Politics of Restraint in Early Modern England* (Cambridge, 2011), 220–53; E. H. Shagan, 'The Two Republics:

The gentry could not be expected to govern England alone: they represented only a tiny fraction of the population. A survey of Huntingdonshire in 1613 suggested that less than half of its parishes had any resident gentry.[189] In the populous county of Kent, on the eve of the civil war, the gentry – including lesser or 'village' gentry alongside the 40 or so men who held the Commission of the Peace – came to only around 800 households. In Leicestershire, a county about half the size of Kent, that figure stood at around 350.[190] The number of magistrates rose during Elizabeth's reign; A. G. R. Smith suggests that 'at the beginning of the Tudor period there were, on average, less than ten [Justices of the Peace] ... per shire, but by the middle of Elizabeth's reign the average was perhaps forty or fifty'. In 1580, there were 1,738 Justices of the Peace across England as a whole.[191] But even given this expansion, the magistracy remained a very small body of men. In total, those holding the Commission of the Peace were estimated in 1587 as numbering around 1,500. Eight years earlier, Burghley had counted no more than 100 men amongst 'the inner core of county notables, peers and gentlemen'.[192] Moreover, whereas the greater gentry tended to encounter the poor – or even their tenants – on calculated occasions of stage-managed social performance such as Christmas feasts, it was really the 'better sort' of inhabitants who managed everyday social interactions with those at the bottom of the social hierarchy. They did so as patrons, benefactors, employers and – critically – as village officers.

Recent studies of English state formation have emphasized the active participation of wealthier social fractions in a 'bottom-up' process that combined the institutional, social and economic power of the better sort in local communities. This is very close to what Gorki argued for the role of middling groups in the disciplinary revolution whose course he has charted in the United Provinces. If the state expanded in its powers, those powers were made *real* – manifest in everyday social relations – on the level of the locality. One of the outstanding characteristics of both state formation and social relations in early modern England was, therefore, their embeddedness in the *local*. Day-to-day patterns of interaction amongst richer, middling and poorer people occurred in face-to-face

Conflicting Views of Participatory Local Government in Early Tudor England', in J. F. McDiarmid (ed.), *The Monarchical Republic of Early Modern England: Essays in Response to Patrick Collinson* (Aldershot, 2007), 19–36.

[189] J. Bedells, 'The Gentry of Huntingdonshire', *Local Population Studies*, 44 (1990), 35.

[190] A. Everitt, *The Community of Kent and the Great Rebellion, 1640–60* (Leicester, 1966), 33–4.

[191] A. G. R. Smith, *The Government of Elizabethan England* (London, 1967), 90.

[192] W. T. MacCaffrey, 'Place and Patronage in Elizabethan Politics', in S. T. Bindoff, J. Hurstfield and C. H. Williams (eds.), *Elizabethan Government and Society* (London, 1961), 99.

situations in which the rich typically held greater agency. Drawing middling social groups into the process of governance had the great advantage
of combining their formal authority as office-holders with their less formal
status as employers and patrons. One translator of the eminently pragmatic Jean Bodin observed in 1606:

> Whereas a great Commonweale is much more hardly divided; for that betwixt the
> great Lords and the meanest subiects, betwixt the rich and the poore, betwixt the
> good and the bad, there are a great number of the middle sort which bind the one
> with the other, by meanes that they participate both with the one and the other, as
> having some accord and agreement with both the extreames.[193]

It was a habitual response on the part of magistrates and rulers, when
faced with a difficulty, to turn to the local 'middle sort'. When the
magistracy of the West Country needed to look into local supplies of
food, for example, it was to 'the most honest and substantial inhabitants'
of each parish that they turned.[194] Similarly, in 1597, it was the churchwardens 'and other discreete men of the parish' upon whom the bishops
depended to monitor their clergy's contribution to the poor relief.[195]
Likewise, lords found it easier to negotiate the terms of common rights,
emparkment, enclosure and tenure with the wealthier yeomanry
than they might with the village poor. The yeomanry, then, were drawn
into the ongoing conversation between lord and tenant; the poor were
meant to watch, and stand silent.[196] When the lord of Cottenham
(Cambridgeshire) arrived at a settlement concerning the common rights
in the village in 1580, he did so with the 'greatest number of welthiest and
substancyialist inhabitants and tenants of Cottenham in the behalf of
themselves and of all the rest of the inhabitants of the said town'.[197]

The process by which institutional arrangements for the government of
localities emerged is, in many cases, lost to historical scrutiny. In some
places, as Brodie Waddell has recently demonstrated, manor courts
remained a vital force for the assertion of the authority of landed villagers.[198]

[193] J. Bodin, *The Six Bookes of a Common-Weale* (London, 1606), 432.
[194] T. Gray (ed.), *Harvest Failure in Cornwall and Devon: The Books of Orders and the Corn
Surveys of 1623 and 1630–1*, Sources of Cornish History, 1 (Plymouth, 1992), xiv.
[195] S. Hindle, 'Dearth, Fasting and Alms: The Campaign for General Hospitality in Late
Elizabethan England', *P&P*, 172 (2001), 50.
[196] For a village dispute where the lord signically ignores the local poor, speaking only to the
wealthier villagers, see Wood, 'Some Banglyng about the Customes'. For a brilliant
discussion of speech, silence and social relations, see H. Taylor, '"Branded on the
Tongue": Rethinking Plebeian Inarticulacy in Early Modern England', *Radical History
Review*, 121 (2015), 91–105.
[197] W. Cunningham (ed.), 'Common Rights at Cottenham and Stretham in
Cambridgeshire', *Camden Miscellany*, 2nd ser. 12 (1910),193.
[198] Waddell, 'Governing England through the Manor Courts'.

Elsewhere, semi-formal authority passed to parish vestries or to ad hoc committees of wealthier folk who, over the years, developed customary arguments in favour of such arrangements. The earliest select vestry would appear to be that which governed Great St Mary in Cambridge, and whose activities can be dated from 1504.[199] Thereafter, at first in urban communities, such institutional arrangements became increasingly common. Local authorities took upon themselves, as it suited them, to rewrite the customary arrangements by which their village was governed. Vestry regulations were periodically drafted and redrafted in Layston (Hertfordshire) 'with the consent of the best sort of the inhabitants of Layston'.[200]

The social identity of those who held authority in the parish was sometimes as vague as the powers they claimed. In some places, decision-making may have been defined more by a sense of community than by social place: a difficult case concerning an illegitimate child was handled by 'the neighbours' of Checkley (Staffordshire).[201] The Devon village of Dean Prior was governed in the late sixteenth century by a very small council called the Four Men.[202] In Stoneleigh (Warwickshire) in 1580, the village seemed to have been relatively inclusive in that it was run by 'viij persones, were of iiij to be tenantes and the other iiij Cotyger'.[203] Yet elsewhere, there was a clearer correspondence between social and institutional authority; engagement in the running of a community was one way in which the aspirant middle sort might assert their authority. In Jacobean Braintree (Essex) the 'Company of the 24tie and the Vestry' were selected from amongst 'the cheife of the towne in generall'.[204] In Chiddingly (Sussex), authority was held in 1595 by 'the chiefe of the p[ar]ishe'.[205] In Tavistock (Devon) in 1519, power lay with the churchwardens and the 'most substancyall men'.[206] In Henrician Holbeach (Lincolnshire), the 'churchewardens and other the most honest and substanciall persones' ran affairs.[207] Glastonbury was regulated by 'the men of best qualetie there.'[208]

The middle sort sometimes complained about the responsibilities that the state had laid upon them: in 1601, one sympathetic assessment of the significance of parish office-holding observed plaintively: 'It is a common oversight in this age, that in most cases of impositions, taxations, &c. the square of equalitie is dissolved, and men are charged as the dice chance . . .

---

[199] S. Webb and B. Webb, *The Parish and the County* (London, 1906), 174.
[200] Hindle, 'Exclusion Crises', 136.     [201] FSL, L.a. 969.
[202] Travers (ed.), *Robert Furse*, 78.
[203] Shakespeare Centre Library and Archive DR18/17/24/7.
[204] Emmison, *Early Essex Town Meetings*, 1.     [205] BL, Add 33058, fol. 42r.
[206] Duffy, *The Voices of Morebath*, 22.     [207] TNA, STAC2/17/64.
[208] Bates (ed.), *Quarter Sessions Records for . . . Somerset: Vol. II, Charles I, 1625–1639*, 148.

that is to say, the pore cannot, the rich will not, but the middle sort must pay all.'[209] But there was a nervousness about middle-sort authority that, in some places, drove the establishment of parochial vestries: in 1603, it was agreed by the governors of St Magnus (London) that henceforth 'for avoiding of tumult and future strife', parish affairs would be run by a Select Vestry of thirty-two men. Around the same time, the Select Vestry of St Saviour's (Southwark) observed that their authority did not arise from the 'consent of the parishioners' but rather from the ecclesiastical authorities, and that 'there would be great confusion if the whole parish should be electors' as this would 'incite the ruder sort to extreme liberty'.[210]

Within towns, formal authority was often more clearly oligarchic than in rural communities. Elizabethan Lewes (Sussex) was governed by the Twelve, drawn from 'the wealthier & discreeter sorte of the Townesmen'.[211] The 1549 founding ordinances for the government of the borough of Saffron Walden (Essex) stipulated that the governing council of the Twenty-Four was to be selected from amongst the 'most honest sober Auncyent & dyscreate men' who were to be 'an ensample of quyettnes & obedyens to their inferiourz'.[212] Lincoln's governors presented themselves in 1610 as 'menn of good abilitie and of the best reputac[i]on'.[213] The corporation of Kendal may have been a little more open in its governmental arrangements. Here, under its 1575 charter, the alderman (equivalent to a bailiff) was elected by 'all the inhabitants of the Burgh ... or greater part of them assembled' from two names submitted by the capital burgesses. Just to nail things down a little harder, a by-law added to the provision that there should be a council of twenty-four people 'or moo or Fewer off the moost honeste discrete sober wise and substanciall ... Inhabitants'. These arrangements were tidied up in a charter granted to the town in 1637, in which the alderman became the mayor, the capital burgesses became alderman and the council of Twenty-Four became capital burgesses.[214]

Tudor Worcester was governed by a council of twenty-four citizens, selected from a wider body of forty-eight men who comprised the 'most sad and sufficient' of the inhabitants. There were six wards in the city, each watched over by two constables who, excluding those 'of simple

---

[209] Anon., *An Ease for Overseers of the Poore* (London, 1601), 15.
[210] Webb and Webb, *The Parish and the County*, 191.
[211] W. H. Godfrey (ed.), *The Book of John Rowe, Steward of the Manors of Lord Bergavenny, 1597–1622*, Sussex Records Society, 34 (Cambridge, 1928), 120; BL, Add MS 5705, fol. 110r. For the context, see J. Goring, 'The Fellowship of the Twelve in Elizabethan Lewes', *Sussex Archaeological Collections*, 119 (1981), 157–72.
[212] Essex Record Office, T/A104/1.    [213] TNA, STAC 8/121/12.
[214] Ferguson, *A Boke off Recorde*, 274.

condition', were selected from amongst the 'good, honest, sad and discreet' citizens.[215] Worcester was not the only city in which honesty,
sadness and discretion were preferred over simplicity. In 1537, the
mayor, jurors and seventy-five of 'the most substantiall commons' of
Rye (Sussex) wrote to the Council in support of their minister whose
critics they described as of 'very simple and small substance rude both in
theyr communication and behavior not only agenst him but also agenst
the estate of the seyd towne'.[216] In 1505, the Star Chamber heard anxious
testimony from the 'xij men' of Stratford-on-Avon (Warwickshire). They
were used to being treated with deference: 'owt of tyme of mynd', the
Twelve Men had been selected from amongst the 'most substanciall and
honest persones of the same town to thentent that they shuld chose
substanciall men and men of honest co[nver]sacon to be constables and
Baylyffes'. But, as they complained to the Star Chamber, the deputy
steward, seeking his own gain, had chosen the borough jurors from
amongst 'the most senglest and symplest persones . . .[. S]ome of them
wer but younge servauntes and left the substanciall men owt of the same
Jury.'[217]

In 1573, the governing elite of Bridgnorth (Shropshire) – comprising
the 'xxiiii' men – laid down a set of ordinances, rules and customs for the
government of their town, around which their authority was set in stone.
This was legitimated by reference to a documentary sense of the history of
governance in the town, written up in 'ordre' established 'in the booke
called the Grene booke'. Above and beyond the 'xxiiii', there was a higher
council of the 'xii', comprising the 'moste Auncyent Burgesses'. The
governors of the town didn't like their proceedings to be known, ordering
that their discussions were to remain secret. The town governors were
equally sharp in their treatment of verbal dissent: anyone who did
'mysuse' or 'revyle' any of the bailiffs or the 'xxiiii' was to be gaoled for
a week and then to make submission before the 'xxiiii'.[218]

The elitism of urban government was axiomatic. In Thomas Deloney's
fictionalized treatment of the life of Jack of Newbury, it was only once his
'good government and discretion [was] noted of the best and substantial-
est men of the Town' that Jack rose within its institutional hierarchy.[219]
Proper governance could only flow from having the right people in position: when in 1616 the town authorities of Hallamshire decided to conduct a survey of its population, they turned naturally to 'twenty-four of
the most sufficient inhabitants'.[220] The establishment of select vestries in

[215] Dyer, *Worcester*, 196, 202.    [216] TNA, SP1/113/106–9; TNA, SP1/124/21.
[217] TNA, STAC1/2/66.    [218] Shropshire Archives, BB/C/4/1/1.
[219] Mann (ed.), *The Works of Thomas Deloney*, 3–4.    [220] Hunter, *Hallamshire*, 148.

London was closely related to processes of social polarization. In 1600, 'the worshipful and discrete' of St Dunstan's sought to limit membership of the vestry, excluding the 'meaner sort of the multitude' on the basis of their 'disquietness and hindrance'. Likewise, the governors of St Benet's Paul's Wharf complained of the 'confusion and disorderly carriage' that was brought to parish affairs by the 'poorer and weaker sort' who were liable to be swayed by 'the men of the better understanding'. And so, parish government passed to the 'more worshipful and discrete', those who were 'creditable men and of the best householders'.[221]

With power came expectations: in 1632, the Quarter Sessions learnt that the 'good and able men' of Totteridge (Hertfordshire), 'some of them of great rank and quality and very rich', were failing in their duties to provide for the growing numbers of poor.[222] No less than in the royal court, power corrupted. In early Tudor East Dereham (Norfolk), some of the inhabitants – calling themselves 'the most parte of the Substanciall p[er]sons' of the town – laid charges of corruption against the Steward, Thomas Mowtyng. They said that he had used great 'extorcon and brybory to the grete hurte and charges of the comons within the seyd towne'. Mowtyng's critics laid claim to local memory: traditionally, they told the Star Chamber, the steward was 'an honest man of good name' and, by 'old ant[iq]uitie', the local offices were held by different people; but to the harm of 'the comon well of this pore town and hundredth', Mowtyng had taken into his hands the offices of steward, bailiff, reeve, heyward and gaoler and had imposed an 'Ignorant p[er]son w[i]t[h]out any Lernyng' as under-bailiff.[223] The power that men like Mowtyng might wield within their local community provided the tawdry basis for one of the proverbs recorded by John Smyth in 1639:

Be-gis, be-gis, it's but a mans fancy—A frequent speach which thus arose: William Bower of Hurst Farme, had each second yeare one or more of his maidservants with childe, whom, with such portions as bee bestowed vpon them, hee maryed either to his menservants, (perhaps also sharers with him,) or to his neighbors sonnes of meaner ranke: Some yeares past, it was demaunded of A: Cl: why hee beinge of an estate in wealth well able to live, would marry one of Bowers double whores, (for by her hee had had two bastards,) whereto A. Cl: soberly replyed, Begys, Begys, its but a mans fancy, Its but a mans fancy: meaninge, &c. take which of the constructions you please; In both senses it's comon with vs hundreders.[224]

Some communities, perhaps especially those with a broad distribution of wealth, were relatively inclusive in their governmental arrangements.

[221] Berlin, 'Reordering Rituals', 52–53.
[222] Le Hardy (ed.), *Calendar to the Sessions Books ... of Hertford, Vol. V: 1619–1657*, 154.
[223] TNA, STAC2/14/1.
[224] J. Maclean (ed.), *The Berkeley Manuscripts*, 3 vols. (Gloucester, 1885), III, 28.

Wigston Magna (Leicestershire), with its solid copyholders, was one such. In 1602, the village was governed according to 'an ancient custom and order' by which the greater part of the inhabitants had an annual meeting at which they would 'agree upon divers and sundry orders and bylaws for the good ordering and preservacions of the profits of their lands and commons within the Fields of Wigston'.[225] Everyday arrangements for the use of the meadows appear to have been a source of consensus, drawing villagers into a knot. In a lawsuit of 1574 over tithes before the consistory court, Walter Pawley of Wigston Magna deposed 'that in somer when the [inhabitants] use to mowe there grasse the parisheners beinge togeather doe amongste thym selves agree and saye let us begin and mowe longe medowe suche a day and soe that day they doe mowe longe medowe and [the meadow called] halters slade togeather as one meadowe'. The landholding villagers were not to be crossed: in a twenty-year dispute beginning in 1586 in one of Wigston Magna's manors, the tenants combined in defeating a lord who was trying to undermine their customs. After they prevailed, the lord sold the manor to the tenants.[226] Jacobean Wigston Magna had emerged as a sort of copyholder republic. It was not unique in such relations.[227]

Everyday languages of social discrimination perhaps most often reveal themselves where contemporaries discussed the institutional arrangements for the government of their communities. Sometimes, these could be rather vague. Elizabethan Condover (Shropshire) seems to have been governed by a small oligarchy known as 'the viii men'. That group had responsibility for selecting the minister of the parish.[228] In Jacobean Ombersley (Worcestershire), decisions were made by 'the most and chefest of the said p[ar]ishe'.[229] The 1604 arrangements for the government of the Liberty of Romney Marsh (Kent) rested on gender, status and office-holding. Power lay with the twenty-four 'freemen' of the marsh villages who were to be selected from the 'chiefest, substantialist, most sufficient, discreetest and richest inhabitants of the commonalty'.[230] It was of such men and women that one of the proverbs recorded by John

---

[225] W. G. Hoskins, *The Midland Peasant: The Economic and Social History of a Leicestershire Village* (London, 1957), 97. For examples of copyholders acquiring manors, see Wood, *The Politics of Social Conflict*, 130; Lindley, *Fenland Riots*, 10; R. B. Manning, *Village Revolts: Social Protest and Popular Disturbances in England 1509–1640* (Oxford, 1988), 95–6.

[226] Hoskins, *The Midland Peasant*, 104–14.

[227] For a similar example, see BL, Harl Ms 98, fols. 124r-127r.

[228] Shropshire Archives, 6001/377.         [229] TNA, E134/17ChasI/Mich30.

[230] S. Hipkin, 'The Worlds of Daniel Langdon: Public Office and Private Enterprise in the Romney Marsh Region in the Early Eighteenth Century', in A. Long, S. Hipkin and H. Clarke (eds.), *Romney Marsh: Coastal and Landscape Change through the Ages* (Oxford, 2002), 183.

Smyth of Nibley spoke: 'Hee's like the master Bee that leades forth the swarme – alludinge to the prime man of a parish, to whose will all the rest agree.'[231]

Much of the authority that followed from being regarded as an 'honest', 'sad', 'substantial', 'auncient' or 'sufficient' person was informal and went unrecorded. Every so often, though, the mediating role of the middling people of early modern England becomes apparent. When rumours concerning the misconduct of the curate of Old Buckenham (Norfolk) reached the ears of the Bishop of Norwich in 1555, his immediate response was to consult the office-holders and 'the moost substancyall men of the parryshe'.[232] Later in our period, on matters concerning the government of the parish, the godly looked instinctively not just to the minister but to 'the chief of the parish'. Thus, when one member of the Dedham Classis wondered what was to be done about those parishioners who failed to come to Communion, '[i]t was answered that the auncientes in the towne shuld deale w[i]th them and professe an earnest dislike of their course'.[233] The consolidated authority of local elites did not, then, precede Puritanism – rather, in counties like Essex, the godly took local systems of class-based administration and adapted them to their specific purposes. The rules for the government of Elizabethan Dedham (Essex), as agreed between the town's godly minister and the 'Auncients of the Congregation', stated that the minister 'and the auncients of the towne' should 'conferre of matters concerning the good government of the towne'. These 'auncient' and 'chief' inhabitants were distinguished from the 'common ignorant people'. Puritan householders were to assist the minister in checking on the poor: it was ordained 'that every quarter' the ministers 'w[i]th two or three of the auncients of the towne, always accompanied w[i]th one of the Constables, do visit the poore and chiefly the suspected places, that understanding the miserable estate of those [tha]t wante and the naughtie disposition of disordered persons, they may provide for them accordinglie'.[234]

The power held by wealthier people over local affairs was often at best semi-formal, embedded in loose customary arrangements rather than given any specific codification; perhaps it suited them best that it was so. But all over England, rulers made the common assumption that governance depended, on the local level (which was, after all, where it really mattered), upon the participation of the 'better sort'. Thus, a set of orders agreed by the Elizabethan Norfolk bench specified that at Acle, the

---

[231] Maclean (ed.), *The Berkeley Manuscripts*, III, 28.
[232] BL, Cotton MSS, Titus, BII, fol. 142r.
[233] Usher (ed.), *The Presbyterian Movement in the Reign of Queen Elizabeth*, 41, 47, 61–2, 68.
[234] Ibid., 83, 99, 100.

Bishop of Norwich should meet at least every month 'with certan gentlemen and chief yomen ... and spend one howre in prayer and preachinge, the chief effect wherof is to perswade love, obedience, amitie, concorde, etc'.[235] The relationship between the lord and the village poor might be negotiated by the substantial inhabitants. This was the case in Haddenham (Buckinghamshire) in 1558. Every year, 'by the consent and discretion' of four men 'counted the moste discreetest and most substanciall men in the p[ar]ishe', the poor received a dole of wheat, barley and pease from the lord.[236] In this way, seigneurial patronage fed the poor while at the same time sustaining the authority of the wealthier villagers.

Magistrates also relied on the informal cooperation of the wealthier people. In 1631, after receiving news of a 'stirringe up of the poore about Uppingham to A mutinye and Insurreccon', the county bench of Rutland saw to it that unemployed paupers were 'set to Labour w[i]th those of the richer sort'.[237] When, in 1527, the Duke of Norfolk was asked by Cardinal Wolsey to look into the attitudes of the 'light people' of Lavenham (Suffolk), Norfolk turned to the 'most substaunciall men' for an answer. They explained that since they had expelled from the town John Porter, who had been a leader of the 1525 events, there had been no trouble. Just to be certain, Norfolk assured Wolsey that 'I dyd enqure off them yff there wer[e] any In that towne or In any other towne nere unto them that used secretly or openly Any sedicious words ... assembl[i]es murmures or any disobeysaunt maner In worde countenaunce or dede', but that other than John Porter the town was in good government and in particular that the young people were obedient.[238] In March 1528, three years after the Lavenham rebellion of 1525, renewed social tensions developed as a result of a new depression in East Anglia's textile regions. In response, the Duke of Norfolk summoned forty of the most substantial clothiers of the area around Stoke-by-Nayland (Suffolk) and 'with the best wordes I could use perswaded them to conynew the settyng of their workfolkes on werk'.[239] Even for a great man such as the Duke, it was hard to get the business of government done without the assistance of the 'substantial men'. The bottom-up process of state formation depended upon communication up and down the social scale. Thus, in 1530, the high price of food brought 'many bre[w]ers [as well] as merchauntes, clothmakers and handy craft men' to complain to the Ipswich

[235] Smith, 'Justices at Work in Elizabethan Norfolk', 104.     [236] TNA, REQ2/129/45.
[237] TNA, SP16/185/55.     [238] TNA, SP1/45, fol. 266r.
[239] G. W. Bernard, *War, Taxation and Rebellion in Early Tudor England: Henry VIII, Thomas Wolsey and the Amicable Grant of 1525* (Hassocks, 1986), 143.

bailiffs.[240] The expectation was that their complaints would be listened to and, if necessary, passed further up the hierarchy.

As Steve Hindle and Mike Braddick have shown in a pair of powerfully argued monographs, early modern government rested upon the participation of village elites.[241] When they really considered the organic nature of the polity, early modern commentators recognized this as well.[242] The Tudor and early Stuart state depended upon the institutional and informal participation of the middling sort – but, emphatically, not of the poor. In his charge to the grand jurors at the Maidstone sessions in 1599, William Lambarde wished 'th[a]t none be suffered to occupy the place of constable over an hundred but such only as can both write and read and is withal assessed to the subsidy at 6 or 8 li. lands, or at the double thereof in goods at the least'. Five years earlier, speaking again to the grand jury, Lambarde assumed that he was addressing men 'that be of the middle sort'.[243] Orders such as that from the magistracy of Essex in 1598 that the Overseers of the Poor were to be selected from amongst 'the most discreet and principal persons' litter the files generated by the administration of the common law.[244]

Being an office-holder gave many people an added sense of their standing. The husbandman William Beake observed of John Northe of Houghton (Sussex) in 1605 that he 'hath been chosen churchwarden of Houghton three or four times and is now high constable of the hundred of Bury; and hath and doth well sufficiently and honestly discharge his office therein and doth as good credit and fashion as other men do'.[245] In most early modern villages and towns, there were a wide range of offices to be filled each year – headborough, aleconner, bailiff, vestryman, churchwarden, overseer of the poor, constable, parish clerk, jurors on the courts leet and baron – such that historians of office-holding can be deceived into seeing the distribution of institutional power as more diffuse than it actually was.[246] Eamon Duffy has found that, of the fifty-five

---

[240] J. Webb, *Great Tooley of Ipswich: Portrait of an Early Tudor Merchant* (Ipswich, 1962), 128.

[241] M. J. Braddick, *State Formation in Early Modern England, c.1550–1700* (Cambridge, 2000); Hindle, *The State and Social Change*.

[242] See the tongue-tied and contradictory discussion of the polity provided by T. Smith, *De Republica Anglorum* (London, 1583). Smith was no fool and so his lack of clarity in discussing the structure of the Elizabethan state speaks volumes.

[243] Read (ed.), *William Lambarde and Local Government*, 138, 167.

[244] Hunt, *The Puritan Moment*, 66.

[245] Wilkinson (ed.), *Chichester Archdeaconry Depositions*, 42.

[246] Jan Pitman's finely graded study of a group of Norfolk communities brings out the diffuse nature of officeholding very well. See J. Pitman, 'Tradition and Exclusion: Parochial Office-Holding in Early Modern England, a Case Study from North Norfolk, 1580–1640', *Rural History*, 15 (2004), 27–45.

taxpayers named in the 1524 lay subsidy for the village of Morebath (Devon), some thirty-five held office during their lifetime. But, significantly, he also found that the village was dominated by what he calls a 'parish plutocracy' known as the 'Four Men' or 'Five Men'. It was amongst this informal grouping that the big decisions were made. Moreover, in the latter half of the sixteenth century, office-holding narrowed in Morebath.[247]

If this was true of relatively communal Morebath, it was all the more true of socially polarized villages such as Terling (Essex) for which Keith Wrightson and David Levine have pointed to the emergence of an oligarchy of literate officeholders drawn from amongst the Puritan, landholding elite.[248] A similar pattern has been found for other Essex villages.[249] This middle rank had sufficient clout within their communities to enforce deference from the poor; but they did not always win the respect of those above them in the social hierarchy. Hindle notes that in Essex in 1616, '[a]lthough those who became the "great governors" of rural parishes were "rich and sufficient men" ... their lack of gentility meant that "all others do not respect them accordingly"'.[250] In Terling, as in many Essex communities, the social authority of the 'better sort' of inhabitants was bolstered by their godliness, and a powerful alliance might emerge between Calvinist ministers and the 'chief inhabitants'. But not everywhere. In at least one Essex village, the minister found cause to find fault with the greed of the rich: in 1613, the minister of Great Totham (Essex) was alleged to have compared the 'cheifest parishioners' to the sinners of Sodom and Gomorrah. He singled them out for their 'pride fullnes of bread idlenes not strengtheninge the hand of the needye And they thinke to rule the minister and the whole parishe'.[251]

Essex represented an extreme case of a more general phenomenon. In many parishes across England, if oligarchy was not already embedded within local power relations, the sixteenth century saw a drift towards it. Typically, the poor were excluded from holding office: this basic assumption was rendered by one witness to the Chichester church court who, in 1604, observed '[t]hat all the parishioners of

---

[247] Duffy, *The Voices of Morebath*, 30, 31.
[248] K. Wrightson and D. Levine, *Poverty and Piety in an English Village: Terling, 1525–1700* (New York, 1979), chapter 5.
[249] Hunt, *The Puritan Moment*, 24–85.
[250] S. Hindle, 'Exhortation and Entitlement: Negotiating Inequality in English Rural Communities, 1550–1650', in Braddick and Walter (eds.), *Negotiating Power in Early Modern Society*, 120. There was something distinct about Essex, where parochial elites seem to have been defined by a profound solidarity. For stark examples, see Hunt, *The Puritan Moment*, 143.
[251] Gowing, *Domestic Dangers*, 55.

Madehurst are not all chosen in their courses to be churchwardens, sidesmen, or constables, for they omit the poorer sort'.[252] Mike Braddick makes a similar point: 'Office not only reflected social status but also confirmed it and this was a motive, sometimes perhaps the chief one, for seeking office.'[253] Agency and office-holding went together: Discussing the management of the town of Wakefield (Yorkshire) in 1597, Henry Arthington explained that it lay in the hands of 'the most able forwarde men of that Towne'. In that hungry year, they had established a general assessment of the wealth of 'everie able householder', on the basis of which they paid into a parochial poor rate and supported a regular 'supper' for the poor.[254]

It was common in County Durham, Northumberland, Cumberland, Westmorland and parts of Lancashire and Yorkshire for parishes to be governed by village councils known (variously) as 'The Twelve', 'The Sixteen', 'The Twenty-Four' or 'The Thirty Men'.[255] The first reference to the 'XVI Men' who governed Holm Cultram (Cumberland) is to be found in 1553. In 1640, the deponent John Chamber explained that 'the XVI men are chosen of the best and ablest men of understanding and of qualities, fower in every Q[uarte[r]'.[256] In Pittington (County Durham), the parish was governed by a council of twelve villagers, assisted by the local gentry.[257] Such bodies were responsible for a wide variety of matters. In Eppledon (County Durham), for example, the churchwardens reported to the Twenty-Four, who also had responsibility for regulating the seating plan in the parish church. Their authority, in the words of one Elizabethan witness, depended upon the 'report in th[o]s[e] his fathers daies' upon which 'ancient custom' depended, 'and this is & haith been the comon voice & report wthin the said p[ar]ish tyme out of any ma[n]s remembruance'.[258]

There was a council of 'Thirty Men' in Kirkham (Lancashire) who oversaw the fifteen townships that comprised their very large parish. It is explained by Kirkham's local historian that '[t]he oath which they took was administered by the civil and not the ecclesiastical authority, and

[252] Wilkinson (ed.), *Chichester Archdeaconry Depositions*, 60.

[253] Braddick, *State Formation in Early Modern England*, 77.

[254] Arthurton, *Provision for the Poore*, sig. Cr.

[255] For the government of northern parishes by groups of men called the 'Four and Twenty', or sometimes 'The Twelve', see Webb and Webb, *The Parish and the County*, 175, 179; B. L. Thompson, 'The Windermere "Four and Twenty"', *TC&WA&AS*, 2nd ser., 54 (1954), 151–64. For examples of councils of Twenty-Four at work in County Durham, see DUL, DDR/EJ/CCD/1/2, fols. 95r, 135r.

[256] Grainger and Collingwood (eds.), *The Register and Records of Holm Cultram*, 223.

[257] Barmby (ed.), *Churchwardens' Accounts*, 69.

[258] DUL, DDR/EJ/CCD/1/2, fols. 86v-90r; see also fols. 96v-97r.

once elected, they held office for life or until they desired to resign. Upon a vacancy occurring, the remainder selected the new member; they were above the churchwardens, whom they appointed, and acted as guardians of the parish property.'[259] In Elizabethan Mitford (Northumberland), a body called 'the 12' chose the Churchwardens and 'the 24' were in charge of the allocation of seats in the church.[260] It was the same in West Rainton where by 'auncient custome ... no parishioner in that parish can build any stall in the church of Houghton, or take any away, with[out] the licenc[e] and consent of the 24 and the churchwardens'.[261] In Darlington around the same time, the sixty-seven-year old chandler Marmaduke Fairbairn explained that for all his remembrance '& before by the report of ancient men', the churchwardens were chosen by the Twenty-Four of the town. The Twenty-Four received yearly accounts from the churchwarden and also oversaw the administration of the grammar school.[262]

The institutional arrangements described were above all *class* arrangements. Parish authority was built upon the social power wielded by the wealthier social fractions of the neighbourhood. Such arrangements consolidated the otherwise fuzzy and informal powers wielded by middling people over their poorer neighbours. If a poor person demanded excessive wages in harvest time, or stood up for themselves in defence of rights to fuel or pasture, she or he might be denied parish relief in the winter, when employment was scare and the times hard. In this way, middling-sort participation in state structures rendered concrete their social authority as masters, employers and patrons. Again, we return to the *localization* of social relations. In Essex, in particular, there was a wide overlap between institutional arrangements and the material interests of the middle sort of people. The employment of the poor was one particular point of concern. The policies followed by the parish vestry and officers of Braintree (Essex) represent a case in point. In September 1625, they announced that 'there shalbe a meeting of all the cheife inhabitants of the towne in the church to confer of some course to be taken to set the poore on worke this hard time, & notice shalbe given in the church the Saboth before where & when they shall meet'.[263]

Just as it was in the interests of wealthier people as ratepayers to find employment for the poor, so it was in their interests as employers that the poor be subject to more effective labour discipline and to lower costs. An

---

[259] See R. Cunliffe Shaw, *History of Kirkham in Amounderness* (Preston, 1949), 138. Their activities are documented in R. Cunliffe Shaw (ed.), *Records of the Thirty Men of the Parish of Kirkham* (Kendal, 1930).
[260] Raine (ed.), *Depositions ... from the Courts of Durham*, 93.    [261] Ibid., 106.
[262] DUL, DDR/EJ/CCD/1/2, fol. 101v.
[263] Emmison, *Early Essex Town Meetings*, 32–3.

important element in this programme of economic, social and moral reform lay in the monitoring of the lives, attitudes, speech and behaviour of the poor. This entailed an increasing urge towards surveillance. The Braintree governors, who had allotted to each of their number a particular part of the village for his special attention, ordered: 'Every one in the Companye shall walke his particular circuit and collect the gratuityes of the towne, & withal take notice of the pore, & take their names.' In February 1622, they agreed that 'the towne shalbe surveyed by the towns-men to the Company, according to the devision agreed upon & bring in account what disordered persons are crept into the parish & what inmates are either intertained already or coming in'. In 1633, they decided: 'Every man in his severall walke shall doe his best indeavour to fynde out such persons as absent them selves from churche, and to take a course to force them to come and that the porer sorte that take collection shalbe abated in their collection until such tyme as they shalbe reformed in it.' Such policies had real consequences for the poor. In 1620, the town governors observed: 'Browne being growne very filthy and troublesome shall have his collection denied him until he reforme himselfe.' Likewise, it was arranged that 'Widdow Ingrams boy that should be taken from her and put into the hospital, and shee being incorrigible in her idle and vicious course shee shalbe sent to the house of correction'. In February 1623, at a time of high food prices, a beadle was appointed 'to gather up about diner & supper time all that beg at mens doores both of our towne & other townes, except such as the overseers thinke fit to permit'.[264] In these ways, the interests of the wealthy folk of Braintree in creating a cheap, flexible, dependable, diligent, disciplined and quiescent workforce, and in keeping poor rates low, connected directly with their role in state formation.

For all that parish vestries were sometimes dominated by the godly, they shared the episcopacy's hostility to the rule of the poor. Thus, a group of vestrymen petitioned against the 'great confusion' that might develop 'if the whole parish should be electors'; an electorate made up of '£3 subsidy-men' would be 'popular, and excite the ruder sort to extreme liberty'. The consequence could only be that '[t]he inferior and meaner sort of the multitude of the inhabitants, being in greater number [would] . . . cross the good proceedings of the church and parish'.[265] Given the power of wealthier folk in the administration of local affairs, it was unwise for poorer people to stand up against them. In 1601, for example, there was a bequest of money 'to keepe the poore people of Amesbury

---

[264] Ibid., 4–5, 12–13, 14, 19, 68, 86, 96, 86, 107.
[265] Webb and Webb, *The Parish and the County*, 184–97.

[Wiltshire] in woorke, the stocke for ever to remain the gaines the poores; to be disposed by the masters of the Towne or fit men of the parishe'.[266] If any poor man or woman wished to secure help from this fund, they had to be careful not to cross the 'masters' and 'fit men'. There were all sorts of contexts in which the poor might receive some small handout from parish officers, contexts in which, if they had offended their betters, they might be denied help.[267] Likewise, in Cawston (Norfolk) in the hungry year of 1596, access to stocks of food for the 'poorer sort' were handled by the village governors.[268] A necessary harshness was expected of village officers in matters such as the passage of poor people through the town, or the lodging of vagrants. In 1622, the grand jury for the Hundred of Launditch found that the constable of Langham 'doo fro[m] time to time lodge wand[e]ring and vagra[n]t people and suffer them to dep[ar]t unpunished'.[269] This was not to be accepted: the indigent poor were to be whipped and moved on.

From the second half of the sixteenth century, it seems not to have been lords who developed the most antagonistic attitudes to the rural poor, but middling people. This seems to have been an earlier phenomenon in towns and cities. These were the people who – even if they remained unwedded to Calvinism – were driving the 'disciplinary revolution' in later sixteenth- and early seventeenth-century England. The greater gentry – the men who made up the county commission – may well have felt secure in their distance from the world of the village and inclined to grant lordly patronage to requests from the poor for housing, food, land or fuel. The richer neighbours of poor folk often felt very differently, and it is within these micro-political local encounters between the desperately poor and their moderately better-off neighbours that we find everyday social conflicts frequently manifest. The local poor were often in a state of dependence upon their better-off neighbours, needing help in the form of cash handouts or gifts of fuel or food: such poor folk needed what they called 'the charity of good neighbours', depended upon 'their neighbours pity' and on 'local charity' or on what 'well dispos'd Christians' might give them.[270] Moreover, it was the richer villagers who controlled the purse-strings of the parish, in the form of either endowed charities or institutional poor relief. Finally, yeomen farmers, wealthier artisans, lesser gentry and minor merchants – the 'middle sort' – were also in control of

---

[266] S. Hobbs (ed.), *Gleanings from Wiltshire Parish Registers*, Wiltshire Record Society, 63 (Chippenham, 2010), 8.
[267] For examples, see W. B. Rix, *Swaffham: Bygone Gleanings and Present* (Norwich, 1931), 49; BL, Add MS 33058, fol. 18r.
[268] NRO, MC 254/2/1.    [269] NRO, NQS/C/S3/23a, verdict for Launditch.
[270] Hindle, *On the Parish?*, 61.

local labour markets, deciding on who might get work and who might not. It was hard, then, for the village poor to stand up to their wealthier neighbours. Nonetheless, some tried.

One poor man stood up for himself in 1631. In that year, Lyonell Wills petitioned the Somerset bench, explaining that he had lived in Tintenhull for five years, 'three years whereof he served as a laboring servant, and the two last yeares as a married man, although not with the consent of some of the p[ar]ishe'. Wills was here raising the painful question of pauper marriage: some of the richer members of the community, he indicated, had opposed his marriage, presumably feeling that any household he headed would become dependent upon the poor rate and so a charge upon themselves. Were such opposition to be officially voiced, it would be in the parish church, at the reading of the banns.[271] Christian notions of belonging and neighbourhood might never have been more contested at such moments. Wills went on, explaining that once he was married, he tried to find a house, yet without seeking any financial support from the parish. But now, 'some of the p[ar]ishe hath forbidden him to remayne there any longer, and thret[e]neth him and those that would sett or let him any house whereby he is inforced to travel from place to place with his wife and children, and thereby doubteth [i.e., fears] that he shall in th[e] end bee taken as a vagrant'.[272]

A similarly outraged sense of entitlement underwrote the appeal that John and Alice Dampier of Kingsdon submitted to the Somerset Quarter Sessions in 1628. They complained that John had lived in the parish for four years and that Alice was born there and that they 'liveth by their labour without any charge or trouble to any ... no way misbeheavinge themselves but living orderly and mainteyninge themselves and their family by their carefull industry and labour'. John and Alice made a powerful claim to be part of the village community: Alice had been born there, they lived without any charge on the parish and they contributed to the local labour force. And yet, John and Alice explained, many other parishioners, 'combyninge themselves together[,] doe deny them any place of aboade within their said parish for their money threatening to expulse and drive them out of their said p[ar]ish and to shifte for a dwelling in other places they desiring nothinge of them but for their ready money'. The bench, guided by the institutionalized paternalism of the early modern state, called the Overseers of the Poor before them to explain.[273] And for a moment, we hear the voices of the labouring poor,

---

[271] Hindle, 'The Problem of Pauper Marriage', 71–89.
[272] Bates (ed.), *Quarter Sessions Records for . . . Somerset: Vol. II, Charles I, 1625–1639*, 139.
[273] Ibid., 80.

contesting their exclusion from the community of the village despite their honesty, hard labour and propinquity.

The mobile poor were monitored and their settlement prevented. The erection of cottages upon common land by the poor could be an especially sharp source of anger amongst landed inhabitants. In 1615, some of the inhabitants of Midsummer Norton (Somerset) complained that too many cottages had been built there 'and many tenants and under-tenants [are] people very poore and of lewd disposition which do offend and annoy the inhabitants'.[274] Perhaps those treated with the greatest harshness were wandering pregnant women, especially those close to birth. In communities in which birth was otherwise represented in Church as a sort of elemental miracle, village officers found no trouble in sending 'Big women' onto the road. At Rishton (Lancashire), for example, there was an order that any pregnant single woman be expelled from the village; anyone housing such a woman was to forfeit twenty shillings.[275] Parish authorities repeatedly drove poor pregnant women away, fearing that any child born in their parish would become dependent upon them. In Pattingham (Staffordshire), for example, the constable recorded that he had conveyed a woman to the next parish who was 'soe greete with child that I was feereful shee would have cryed out before I should have bee[n] shut of hir'. Other Pattington constables led pregnant women to neighbouring villagers, the women 'being readie to crie out' or even already in labour.[276] Similarly, in 1608, the constable of Wimeswold paid tuppence 'to a Bygg belly woman to goe forth of the towne'.[277] In the parish of All Hallows Barking (Essex) in 1628, there was 'paid two poor women for carrying a big bellied woman out of the parish, 1s.; paid to the women herself, 6d'.[278] Then there was the stark example of Katheryne Fullwood: she was driven from the community into which she had been born. The village officers, it seems,

[d]id violentlye take one, Katheryne Fullwood, borne in Ightham aforesaid and did carrye her into a bye lande not farre from the beacon in the said parishe and she being verye great with child and havynge not passinge a fortnight to reccon or thereabouts of the tyme of her deliverye, did verye cruellye and unjustly against lawe, nature and humanitye, whipe and beate the said Kateryne.[279]

[274] Bates (ed.), *Quarter Sessions Records for . . . Somerset: Vol. I, James I, 1607–1625*, 125.
[275] C. Watson, '"To Beare the Towne Harmless": Manorial Regulation of Mobility and Settlement in Early Modern Lancashire', *Rural History*, 28, 2 (2017), 127.
[276] J. R. Kent, 'Population Mobility and Alms: Poor Migrants in the Midlands during the Early Seventeenth Century', *Local Population Studies*, 27 (1981), 37.
[277] J. C. Cox (ed.), *Churchwardens' Accounts from the Fourteenth Century to the Close of the Seventeenth Century* (London, 1913), 341.
[278] C. Pendrill, *Old Parish Life in London* (Oxford, 1937), 190.
[279] E. Melling (ed.), *Kentish Sources: IV: The Poor* (Maidstone, 1964), 35.

There remains in the archival record a palpable sense of anger at attempts by local authorities to drive poor folk onto the road. In December 1610, the Norfolk man Nicholas Arnold kicked back at those who would deprive him of a home in the Marshland village of Terrington. As the magistracy learnt from the village governors, Arnold 'hathe lyved owte of servis at his pleasure very suspiciously ever since easter last'. The constable had already told Arnold 'to departe his house and lyve some other wher[e]', but he refused to do so. Finally, '[t]he said Arnold being Asked by Francis Chevelly what he did in terrington sayed what had he to do w[i]t[h] it sa[y]ing further he wold lyve ther in despite of them that sayd nay whatsoever'.[280]

All early modern communities had to deal with the problem of the migratory poor, those whom contemporaries called 'baggage people' or 'the poor walking people'.[281] The 'baggage people' represented a conceptual as well as a material challenge. Powerful elements of early modern concepts of neighbourhood were long residence and propinquity. When a poor family passed through their village, notions of neighbourhood were challenged, for these people had no place, nowhere within a social structure within which they could find home. The churchwardens of Felpham (Sussex) articulated this sense in 1621 when they presented Thomas Nicholson for giving shelter to 'one Joane Capelen, as shee calleth her self, who being with childe is thereof lately delivered; wee know not whence shee came nor what she is, but she saith she is married and comes from Burleigh near Rochester in Kent'.[282] The exigencies of a developing market economy, with its basic demands for a mobile labour force, not for the first time represented a powerful challenge to everyday senses of neighbourhood, generating a sense that the community was threatened by the social disintegration represented by the mobile poor.

In some parishes, the wandering poor were met not with a whip or the stocks but with small cash payments from the village officers in return for a promise to move on. In May 1630, for example, a total of one shilling and three pence was disbursed by the constable of Stathern (Leicestershire), upon twenty-four wanderers, some of them comprising whole families, others isolated 'poore men'. Some parishes combined coercion with charity, flogging the mobile poor at the pillory and then passing them a couple of pence as an incentive to move on.[283] In late Elizabethan St Mary Woolnorth (London), for example, the parish officers paid for migrants to be whipped and then placed small cash sums in

---

[280] NRO, NQS/C/S3/17/1, articles against Nicholas Arnold.
[281] Hardy (ed.), *Hertford County Records*, 35; Cressy, *Birth, Marriage and Death*, 443.
[282] Johnstone (ed.), *Churchwardens' Presentments*, 4.
[283] For examples, see Cox (ed.), *Churchwardens' Accounts*, 338.

their hand as an incentive to be on their way.[284] In Hexham (Northumberland), poor travellers were allowed to stay for one night in the almshouse but 'no longer unless it be the extremity of weather'.[285] Travellers deemed to be legitimately upon the road procured certificates or testimonials from local worthies or parish authorities.[286] In 1585, the churchwardens of Ecclesfield (Yorkshire) paid four pence to a poor man who passed through with a testimonial from Lord Darcy and a further twelve pence to another pauper who held a similar note from the earl of Derby.[287] This allowed them to seek the goodwill of those parishes through which they passed. Thus, in 1607, the Pittington (County Durham) churchwardens gave twelve pence 'to a poore man with a testimonial, a Scottish man that was robbed'. In 1612, they gave twenty pence '[t]o a poure widow of Barwicke that had her house burned with fier'. In 1618, they gave twelve pence 'to a poore woman whose husband was taken by the Turkes'.[288]

Unsurprisingly, the poor were unhappy about being cast onto the road: here, too, there was a sort of agency. On 19 May 1615, Margaret Halesworth wrote to the Norfolk magistracy to complain about her imminent ejection from the village of Weasenham. What she had to say spoke to the importance of women's networks, in this case the sense of an obligation that a mother-in-law might owe to the widow of a deceased son. Margaret explained that she, her husband and their two small children had moved to Weasenham to live with his parents. Her husband had subsequently died, 'after which death ... her mother in lawe, hired a house of a butcher in weasenh[a]m for the rent of three shillings she thinketh; and in the said house did place the said margarett & her two children w[i]th such implements of household stuffe as she had'. So set up, perhaps Margaret Halesworth felt herself safe. But her troubles multiplied: within ten days, the landed inhabitants of Weasenham had procured a warrant to send her back to Blickling, the place of her birth.[289] Margaret Halesworth probably feared ending up on the road, denied a place in either village. She realized that she would be without any friends or kin to support her and her little ones. In October 1618, another Norfolk woman, Mistress Dickerson, faced such a prospect. She and

[284] Pendrill, *Old Parish Life in London*, 202.

[285] A. Rossiter, *Hexham in the Seventeenth Century: Economy, Society and Government in a Northern Market Town* (Hexham, 2010), 192.

[286] For examples, see B. Clarke, 'Norfolk License to Beg: An Unpublished Collection', *Norfolk Archaeology*, 35 (1970–3), 327–34.

[287] J. Eastwood, *History of the Parish of Ecclesfield* (London, 1862), 219.

[288] Barmby (ed.), *Churchwardens' Accounts*, 74. For similar payments, see ibid., 57, 64, 76, 77, 291, 303.

[289] NRO, NQS/C/S3/20, examination of Margaret Halesworth.

her husband Nicholas Dickerson had lived in Wigenhall St Mary for a while, where some six years earlier she had given birth to a daughter. Drawn perhaps by the promise of employment or maybe the support of kin, in 1614 the family had moved to Wiggenhall St Germans. Here, her husband, 'waxing poore', had deserted the family for a life on the road, and no one knew of his fate. Worse followed for Mistress Dickerson, for, as she explained it,

> thereupon the people of Germans, did send [her] to her Frendes, being borne att West Acre & sithence wch tyme she hath wandred aboute the Countrie and now being come againe to Wiggenhall St Germans they threttened to whipp her and to send her awaie againe and have sent the child to Wigenhall St Maryes and [Mistress Dickerson] to Westacre.[290]

So, one poor family broke apart.

Steve Hindle's richly detailed study of poor relief focuses on what he calls 'the known neighbourhood poor', whom he distinguishes from the wandering, transient poor.[291] Hindle shows that the 'known neighbourhood poor' made claims to a set of material resources that were central to their capacity to sustain their households. These included not just formal doles from the parish poor box but also a wide array of other resources that were administered by the parish, including housing, parochial charity, loans and milk from the parish cows. On top of such provisions – which parish governors saw as in their gift, but which some of the poor sometimes perceived of as entitlements or even rights – there were also customary claims that the poor made to common rights (nutting, pannage, turbary, housebote, pasture, gathering herbs and fruit, gleaning for shards of corn after the harvest) over which the poor sometimes came into conflict amongst one another or sometimes with their betters. Then there were informal handouts from established villagers or the gentry – gifts of food, drink, clothing, low-interest loans. Perhaps most importantly, there was employment, in an economy where the agrarian proletariat was becoming increasingly numerous: in the harvest season, the demand for labour was overwhelming and farmers found themselves forced to bargain with harvest workers over payments and perquisites. But in the winter months – what contemporaries called the 'dead time of the year' – employment was scarce, and having a good reputation might allow a member of the village-poor access to paid work that could keep their family off the poor rate.[292]

---

[290] NRO, NQS/C/S3/21, information of William Westbrooke of Wiggenhall St Mary.
[291] Hindle, *On the Parish?*, 14.
[292] For the 'dead time of the year', see *Calendar of Patent Rolls, Elizabeth I, 1568–72*, no. 1818.

All of this – formal and informal relief, employment, housing, common rights – might depend upon the poor showing proper deference to their local superiors. Moreover, it required the poor to have links within their community, connections on which they could draw with wealthier neighbours, employers and parish officers, built on propinquity, obligation and neighbourhood. These mutual interdependencies might be conceptualized in terms of clientage; certainly, they were about power relations. But they were also about a shared sense of neighbourhood, belonging and common interest. Most importantly, such clientage links required the poor to keep their place, not to be 'froward' or to demand excessive wages or to insist too forcibly upon their rights to common resources. Fundamentally, these mutually reinforcing local ties of deference, subordination, clientage and paternalism formed iron links that – on the micro-political level – bound English society together.

Being an insider didn't guarantee an easy life. But it may well have at least guaranteed shelter, even of the most minimal form. In his study of poor relief in Lancashire, Jonathan Healey provides the examples of Anne Wolfenden of Chadderton, who, in 1632, lived with her four children for a year in a barn, and of Agnes Denny of Halton, who, in the following year, was reported to the magistracy because, for six years, she 'hath dwelt in a little chamber in the end of a firehouse of Lawrence Huttons'.[293]

Kinship links really mattered.[294] For example, when Robert Smethurt's brothers were left orphaned in 1627, they were 'provided for in some smale sort by meanes of theyr mothers frendes & other well disposed neighbores'.[295] Having a place within a community meant that, in times of dearth, poor folk might be able to make claims on wealthier neighbours, securing cheap food while elsewhere there may have been famine: John Walter notes that those country labourers who had a place in their community could depend upon cheap prices from farmers selling grain from their doors. He quotes one source from Sussex in 1631: '[T]hose who have any corne to spare sell it better cheape at home to their poore neighbors then in the markets.'[296] A powerful set of reciprocities informed the everyday practice of social relations within the

---

[293] J. Healey, *The First Century of Welfare: Poverty and Poor Relief in Lancashire, 1620–1730* (Woodbridge, 2014), 155–6.

[294] D. Cressy, 'Kinship and Kin Interaction in Early Modern England', *P&P*, 113 (1986), 38–69.

[295] Healey, *The First Century of Welfare*, 153. Albeit for a later period, Steve King's work concerning Calverley (Yorkshire) shows that those without co-resident kin were more likely to need poor relief than those with kin in the township. See S. King, 'Reconstructing Lives: The Poor, the Poor Law and Welfare in Calverley, 1650–1820', *Social History*, 22 (1997), 331.

[296] Walter, 'The Social Economy of Dearth', 101.

local community, the site where need, obligation and authority collided. Such reciprocities entailed the rich extending (for example) credit, gifts, handouts or food sold at below the market price, and the poor returning this with deference. In this way, poor folk became entrapped within local webs of dependency and obligation.[297] To this effect, Walter quotes the words of the Cambridge corn merchant John Veppen, who, in 1597, explained to the Star Chamber that he sold barley to his poor neighbours at rates 'better Cheape then they could buye anye in the markett' and 'for relieffe of therire neecssitye did gyve Credit for the same'.[298]

Ironically, years of high food prices might create circumstances in some areas where social norms were *reasserted* rather than contested. John Walter observes that 'harvest failure must have played a vital role in underwriting the value of neighbourliness, one of whose most important springs was the need for mutual aid to combat the threat posed to all by an uncertain environment'.[299] In the dearth of 1596–7, for example, it was the 'able sort' who relieved the 'poorer sorte' of their communities, taking them into their houses and feeding them. These richer folk were said to have been 'very charitable herein', contributing in a manner that was 'plentiful', 'charitable' and 'sufficient'. In return, it was anticipated that the 'poorer sort' would not 'grudge against God nor envy at their rich neighbours'.[300]

Critically, social relations were conducted face to face. In 1631, the Privy Council received a missive from the Norfolk magistracy. Their letter argued against sending corn out of their county, noting that 'every town knows their own poor and their own wants'.[301] Values of neighbourhood and the obligations that such values required of richer folk were central to the negotiation of social relations. A Wiltshire constable observed in 1626 that when two poor women begged at his door, 'he punished [them] not, for that they were old and neighbours'. In Norfolk in 1631, it was observed that 'if any do beg, they are but near dwellers'.[302] But the dominant pattern of face-to-face relationships between richer neighbours and Hindle's 'known neighbourhood poor' cut both ways. The

---

[297] For the wider context, see this prescient essay: M. Fafchamps, 'Solidarity Networks in Preindustrial Societies: Rational Peasants with a Moral Economy', *Economic Development and Cultural Change*, 41, 1 (1992), 165–6.

[298] Walter, 'The Social Economy of Dearth', 104.

[299] J. Walter, 'Subsistence Strategies, Social Economy and the Politics of Subsistence in Early Modern England', in A. Häkkinen (ed.), *Just a Sack of Potatoes? Crisis Experiences in European Societies, Past and Present* (Helsinki, 1992), 69.

[300] Hindle, 'Dearth, Fasting and Alms', 65, 69, 71.

[301] J. Thirsk and J. P. Cooper (eds.), *Seventeenth-Century Economic Documents* (Oxford, 1972), 36, 343–7.

[302] Beier, *Masterless Men*, 71.

*localization* of charitable arrangements meant that it was possible for those administering such funds – generally the governing classes of a locality – to discern between those who were deserving and those undeserving of help. For example, recipients of help from one of Ipswich's leading charities were, in 1589, required to be 'inhabitauntes [of Ipswich] ... bi the space of xxx.ti yeres and more and of honest fame and reporte'. Having a supporter within the village or town government who could attest to a poor person's local standing could mean the difference between life and death. In 1589, Johane Lawrence, 'a poore olde woman [who] was borne yn this towne, being of honeste fame and reporte', and Robert Cawston, 'a poore, aged and lame man, beynge of honeste fame and reporte', were allowed doles from one of the charitable foundations administered by the Ipswich authorities.[303]

The village poor might be granted latitudes that were denied to the transitory poor. In Elizabethan Walden (Essex), for example, the prominent men of the village were required to select such poor people 'soche as for charit[i]e sake shalbe appointed' who would be allowed, in contravention of the normal regulations, to graze their cattle on the borders of lanes and streets.[304] This was a small mercy from the rich, but meaningful to the poor, providing their households with milk, cheese and butter; some of it to be consumed within the household; some to be sold to neighbours, generating a small but important pocket of cash. Irrelevant to the greater gentry and their superiors, these things mattered to the vulnerable households of the poor. They are owed our attention just as much as any great matter of state. For the dominant practice of face-to-face social relations – providing for those poor who fitted with the social order and were known to do as they were told – informed an important shift in the provision of formal charitable bequests, away from general provision and towards a more discriminatory system whereby those poor who were known to accept their place were allowed access to parish charities.[305] Ian Archer observes that in London,

testators did insist on increasing discrimination in the distribution of their relief. Relief should be confined to the 'godly religious poor', 'the honest godly poor', the 'godlie, aged, and well disposed', 'the godly poor of the church of god', the 'godliest poor', 'poor freemen of best report', 'such as have greate neede indeede and be of honest behavyour and good conversacion and no drunkarde nor swearer', 'labouring and industrious persons of honest life and conversation',

[303] Ibid., 26.

[304] K. C. Newton and M. K. McIntosh, 'Leet Jurisdiction in Essex Manor Courts during the Elizabethan Period', *Essex Archaeology and History*, 3rd ser., 13 (1981), 10.

[305] For a sustained discussion of discretionary charity, see Hindle, *On the Parish?*, 120–34. Hindle sees the 'last post of indiscriminate charity' as being sounded in 1655.

'old people of honest life such as have been willing to take pains for their living formerly'.[306]

Increasingly, charities required of the poor not just their deference and appropriate conduct but also, passed into the hands of village officers or richer villagers, the responsibility of disbursing charitable funds. One grant of cottages to the poor folk of a Sussex village in 1623 stated categorically that the fund was to be administered by three of the 'principall inhabitantes' and that if any tenant of the cottages 'shall usually and unlawfully take any other mens woodes underwoodes or hedges and become common hedge breakers or trespasse in woodes or shalbe otherwise notoriously wicked or scandalous in life or conversacon that then after reasonable admonition and warning given in his behalf (and noe sufficient reformaicon followeinge) [, it] shall be lawfull' then, in these circumstances, for those who had 'oversight of the aforesaid poore people' to expel them from their cottage.[307]

Over the course of the period between the accession of Henry VII and the calling of the Short Parliament, it became apparent in one community after another that access to parish or town resources ought to be regulated by the richer members of the place. Under the terms of the 1550 refoundation of the almshouses at Saffron Walden (Essex), it was specified that the houses were to be governed by a treasurer, a chamberlain and 'the xxiiii of the beste and moste descret', who were to appoint 'two of the honest men' of the town to be responsible for their day-to-day running.[308] So, also, the provision of hot meals to the local poor was conditional upon their displays of godliness: one of the orders decided upon by the 'Auncients' and the minister of Dedham (Essex) in 1587 was that 'so many as be of habilitie invite to their howses one couple of such of their poore neighbours as have submitted themselves to the good orders of the Churche, and walke Christianly and honestlie in their callings'.[309]

Likewise, when Robert Easton, a tanner from Oundle (Northamptonshire), a village dominated by its godly presence, made his will in 1585, he left forty shillings to 'the poor people of Oundle'. He thought of the local poor as part of his Christian neighbourhood, calling them 'the poor needy members of Christ'. But this was not a general charity: the purse-strings were controlled by the Puritan ministry and by Easton's Calvinist friends, whom he identified as 'the most godly and

---

[306] Archer, 'The Charity of Early Modern Londoners', 233.

[307] East Sussex Record Office, AMS5813/5.

[308] F. W. Steer, 'The Statutes of the Saffron Walden Almshouses', *Transactions of the Essex Archaeological Society*, 2nd ser., 25, 2 (1955–6), 208.

[309] Usher (ed.), *The Presbyterian Movement in the Reign of Queen Elizabeth*, 100.

approved Christians inhabiting the same town'.[310] In its own way, this emphasis upon the godliness of the poor gave them a discourse within which they could lay claim to charity. In 1618, one pauper appealed to Christ's suffering for humanity in justification of her appeal for charity: Margaret Biddle complained to the Worcestershire bench that the Overseers of the Poor of Droitwich had failed to pay her the eight pence weekly dole that they had been ordered to, asking for 'their pitiful consideration and the rather that the poor creature whom Christ Jesus has dearly bought should perish which otherwise she can by no means afford'.[311] Richer people often understood their duties as local officers or more prosperous neighbours according to 'the Lawe and equitie of conscience'.

Just like Margaret Biddle's reference to the manumission of Calvary, so 'Lawe', 'equitie' and 'conscience' might weigh heavily on the minds of parish officers when disbursing relief. These were important matters that entailed not just an investment in the social order but also the capacity to distinguish between deserving and undeserving – and that needed local knowledge.[312] But when officers such as John Waters of Terrington (Norfolk) failed to live up to his role as Overseer of the Poor, his neighbours complained against him: writing to the magistracy in 1631, they observed that he had denied pasture rights to Widow Daniell. She was, they explained, 'a poore woman' with four small grandchildren and had nothing to relieve her save two cows and a heifer; she had no winter feed to maintain them. 'It was gen[er]ally agreed amongst the cheifest of the Inhabitants' that Waters should pay forty shillings for the pasturing of the widow's cattle, but nothing had been done.[313] Again, there were a set of micro-political relationships at work here – a parish officer who was failing in his duties to the poor; a needy widow and her grandchildren; the obligations of the 'chiefest' of the village. Such infrapolitical swirls ended with the 'chiefest' asserting themselves, securing what they saw as justice for a poor widow and thereby winning her gratitude and deference.

In such ways, the fortunes of the poor came to depend upon the goodwill of their richer neighbours. One way in which this mattered was the willingness of richer folk to seek help from the wider authorities for the sustenance of the poor. The neighbours of David Osborne, 'a verie poor mann' of Sedgford (Norfolk), wrote on his behalf to the county bench. They explained that Osborne had 'a great charge of smale children and

---

[310] W. J. Sheils, *The Puritans in the Diocese of Peterborough, 1558–1610*, Northamptonshire Records Society, 30 (Northampton, 1979), 136, 142.
[311] Bund (ed.), *Calendar of the Quarter Sessions Papers, Vol. I: 1591–1643*, 266.
[312] NRO, NQS/C/S3/20, examination of Thomas Anderson.
[313] NRO, NQS/C/S3/28a, remonstrances against John Waters.

now[,] wanting an habitacon by reason whereof he is constrained to lie manie tymes in the streets', he had received 'the helpe and charity of good disposed people to erect and build him a smale cottage w[i]thin the same town of Sedg[e]ford', but that he could only do so with licence under the 1589 Act from the magistrates. Osborne's neighbours therefore 'beseech [ed] and humblie ... crave[d] yor worshippes favour to this pore mann'. Were the Justices to help Osborne, then they were assured that 'the pore man according to his bounden dutie shall daylie praie to Allmighty god for all yor worshippes he[a]lth w[i]th all happiness and increase of your worshippe'.[314] Within this negotiation, there was a triangular set of power relations at work: David Osborne and his family gained a house; his neighbours gained his gratitude and deference; the magistrates received the prayers of a poor man – a powerful thing in a Christian culture in which the prayers of the poor carried a real weight.

### Robin Starveling and the Destroying Angel: Famine, Disease and the Limits of Neighbourhood

William Shakespeare's *A Midsummer Night's Dream* is all too easily read as a bucolic frolic through the romantic imagination. Yet the world of the *Dream* is profoundly disturbed – kings and queens are at odds, men and women lose their bearings, human feelings lie at the mercy of magical beings. And hanging over all of this is the weather. Shakespeare wrote the play in the mid-1590s, at a time of soaring food prices and (for the poor) deteriorating living standards. Some of this had to do with the exploitative social system that was early capitalism; but much of it had also to do with the vagaries of the weather as a succession of wet summers led to crop failures and the spread of cattle disease.[315] The only consequence could be a steep rise in the price of food. In Shakespeare's play, Titania reflects on the disturbed nature of the weather, of the economy and of society:

> The ox hath therefore stretch'd his yoke in vain,
> The ploughman lost his sweat, and the green corn
> Hath rotted ere his youth attain'd a beard;
> The fold stands empty in the drowned field,
> And crows are fatted with the murrion flock;

[314] NRO, NQS/C/S3/17/2, the humble petition of the inhabitants of Sedgford; see also NRO, NQS/C/S3/28a, petition of Isabel Anderson; NRO, NQS/C/S3/31, petition on the behalf of William Lee.

[315] In 1596–8 it was not just the human population of England that was punished; murrain (cattle disease) also spread across the country in those years. See H. Barnes, 'Visitations of the Plague in Cumberland and Westmorland', *TC&WA&AS*, 1st ser., 11 (1889), 158–86.

> The nine men's morris is fill'd up with mud,
> And the quaint mazes in the wanton green
> For lack of tread are undistinguishable:
> The human mortals want their winter here[.]

Just as diseased cattle were tracked by carrion birds and as unripened wheat rotted in the fields, so neighbourhood – exemplified here in the form of the field game of Nine Men's Morris – perished. Titania's speech has received little critical attention.[316] Yet the interjection of a blunt statement about economic fragility into a play that is, at least on the surface, a pastoral comedy commands our attention. Not for the first time, Shakespeare emerges as a profound commentator on the material conditions of his day.[317]Early modern people – magistrates, aldermen, farmers, husbandmen, labourers and the poor – were painfully attuned to the price of food. On 11 April 1587, the chronicler of Barnstaple (Devon) observed: 'The dearthe of corne yet remains, wheate at viiix & yet this countrye is dailey charged with ammunition & harness, expecting & p[ro]viding for invasions and warrs which maketh the common sort [to] fall into poverty for want of trade, so that div[er]s fall to robbynge & stealing, the like hath never been seen.' This left the town authorities watching the weather with mounting anxiety. The clerk noted: 'About May. Little or no raine hath fallen for vi or viii weeks whereby more Dearthe and Scarcity is to be lookt for.'[318] The town, if not all of its population, escaped famine. Nine years later, food prices rose still further, leading the clerk to observe in August 1596: 'By reason of the continual rain there is great leare [i.e., shortage] of all sorts of corn, but little comes to market.' The next mention of food supply is terse and anxious: '[S]mall Quantitie of corn brought to market townsmen cannot have corn for money.'[319] Every summer provoked anxiety about food supply: were prices going to be low enough for the poor to afford? When the antiquarian Roger Dodsworth visited Royston parish church (Yorkshire) on 11 July 1621, he noted a stained-glass window that depicted '[a]n angell holding a plough drawne by 4 oxen and another angell driving. Above written: God speed plough And send us corne enough.'[320] The stained-glass imagery and text easily preceded the early modern period: but it spoke to Tudor and Stuart people, just as much as it did to their ancestors.

---

[316] For an exception, see S. Thomas, 'The Bad Weather in a Midsummer-Night's Dream', *Modern Language Notes*, 64, 5 (1949), 319–22.
[317] C. Fitter, *Radical Shakespeare: Politics and Stagecraft in the Early Career* (London, 2012); A. Patterson, *Shakespeare and the Popular Voice* (Oxford, 1989).
[318] Gray (ed.), *The Lost Chronicle of Barnstaple*, 63.    [319] Ibid., 77.
[320] J. W. Clay (ed.), *Yorkshire Church Notes, 1619–1631: by Roger Dodsworth*, YASRS, 34 (no place of publication, 1904), 132.

Everyone knew what would happen if God failed to 'send us corne enough': the fact that the issue found its way into medieval stained glass spoke of the persistent nature of the question; for the nutritional experiences of the 'poorer sort' were characterized by constant, endemic malnutrition, punctuated by potentially fatal periods in which food prices rose above their capacity to feed themselves. They did not need to be told by preachers that the author of the Book of Lamentations had foretold that '[t]hey that be slain with the sword are better than they that be slain with hunger: for these pine away, stricken through for want of the fruits of the field'.[321] The absence of the 'fruits of the field' in years such as 1596, when *A Midsummer Night's Dream* was probably written, told the poor that food prices might become unaffordable. Is it significant that one of the 'rude mechanicals' in Shakespeare's play is a character called Robin Starveling? Or that, at the end of another of Shakespeare's works of the mid-1590s, *Henry VI Part II*, the rebel leader Jack Cade says that it is not the gentleman Alexander Iden who has slain him but 'famine'?[322]

The household economies of the very poor were built on such shaky foundations that, even outside years of high food prices, some might just collapse under pressure. In 1613–14, years that was not marked by dearth conditions, there were tragic stories such as that of William Grewsold who buried a chrisom child on 25 November 1613, together with a little girl of seven months, and finally was himself interred on 25 June 1614. V. H. T. Skipp says of such folk that they 'have the look of people being pushed beyond the limits of subsistence'.[323] Then there were villages such as Brailes (Warwickshire) of which it was written by a local gentleman in 1599 that

> we have above thirtie poore people that did beg, or somebodie for them (they not beinge able) wch 30, not any of them, can get any parte of their lyvinge. Also wee have above three score & tenne of old people and children that are not able to get the one half of their lyvinge, yf they have worke fytt for them, wee have also fowrscore & tenne laborars, and the greater p[ar]te of them (for wante of worke) have bine compelled to begge, and yf they should not have good help now, they must steale or starve.[324]

Local governors paid close awareness to the variegation of poverty and the ways in which it plotted social structures. In 1616, a survey conducted in Sheffield concluded that the population numbered some 2,207 people. Of them, there were '725 which are not able to live without the charity of

---

[321] Lamentations, 4:9.    [322] Wood, 'Brave Minds and Hard Hands'.
[323] V. H. T. Skipp, *Crisis and Development: An Ecological History of the Forest of Arden, 1570–1674* (Cambridge, 1978), 33.
[324] HEHL, STT 110.

their neighbours. These are all begging poore.' Above this wholly destitute group, there were '160 householders, not able to relieve others.
These are such (though they beg not) as are not able to abide the storme
of one fortnight's sickness, but would be thereby driven to beggary.'
These people were vulnerable, hovering on the edge of ruin, but still
able in most years to keep things together. Then there were a mere '100
householders which relieve others. These (though the best sort) are but
poore artificers: among them there is not one which can keep a teame on
his own land, and not above ten who have grounds of their owne that will
keepe a cow.' Like all early modern communities, the place was overrun
by small children – yet their life courses too were marked in most cases by
poverty: the surveyors noted that there were '1222 children and servants
of the said householders: the greatest part of which are such as live of
small wages, and are constrained to worke sore, to provide them
necessaries'.[325]

Economic historians are agreed that the 1500–1640 period was a time
of deteriorating real wages for working people and their families. Stephen
Rappaport suggests that, over the sixteenth century, real wages for
London workers fell by 25 per cent. Still more starkly, Phelps Brown
and Hopkins' price index points to a 40 per cent deterioration.[326]
Between the early sixteenth and the mid-seventeenth centuries, the cost
of essential foodstuffs rose sevenfold. Yet wage rates increased only by a
factor of three.[327] In other words, even outside of years of high food
prices, there was a certain proportion of the population of any given
locality who, as one generation followed another, were subject to chronic,
inter-generational malnutrition. There is clear evidence for a linkage
between poverty and low fertility, which entailed a lower number of
conceptions than amongst richer folk, along with a higher proportion of
stillbirths and miscarriages. Finally, there was the likelihood that the
children of the poor were more prone to infant mortality.[328] In his
important study of the proto-industrial villages of the Forest of Arden,
V. H. T. Skipp showed that poor women gave birth to fewer children than
did their richer neighbours and that subsequent child mortality was
higher amongst the poor than the rich. It was not only miscarriages and
stillbirths that found their way into the record, the consequence of endemic poverty and malnutrition, but actually the collapse of fertility
amongst the poor. Skipp goes on:

[325] Hunter, *Hallamshire*, 148.      [326] Rappaport, *Worlds within Worlds*, 123–62.
[327] C. G. A. Clay, *Economic Expansion and Social Change: England, 1500–1700*, 2 vols.
(Cambridge, 1984), I, 41–2, 49, 217–18.
[328] S. Scott and C. J. Duncan, 'Marital Fertility at Penrith, 1557–1812: Evidence for a
Malnourished Community?', *TC&WA&AS*, 2nd ser., 96 (1996), 111.

[A]t the heart of the crisis (1615–17), the food-base becomes so inadequate that many of the poorer women are unable to conceive at all. Finally, with its gradual abatement, they again begin to do so; but now, such as is the backlog of malnutrition, as it were, that a significant proportion of them are unable to retain the foetus for a full term in the womb.[329]

Poverty, then and now, is a tragic predictor of child mortality. Clark and Hamilton observe: 'We find that wealth at death (as a proxy for income and material living conditions) was powerfully connected with reproductive success.'[330] This is evident from readership of parish registers: as poor women moved from malnutrition to near-starvation conditions, their fertility declined or ceased altogether.[331] In their work on the parish registers of Penrith, Scott and Duncan suggest that 'the possible deleterious effects of high wheat prices during pregnancy in 1622 ... may subsequently have caused severe infant mortality' in the following year. Moreover, that high level of infant mortality was combined with a disastrous collapse of fertility amongst the poor: they suggest that '[m]any of the fetuses of the poorer classes may have aborted pre-term because of poor nutrition and stress during pregnancy'.[332] Hunger and poverty were bodily, as well as social, experiences: women's menstrual cycles ceased; premature and stillborn births increased; in the end, the poor died from what contemporaries called 'the bloudie flux', a fatal form of diarrhoea in which, as starving people had thirty or forty bloody stools a day, the unoccupied intestinal tract became non-functional and their internal organs disintegrated.[333]

For some decades, early modern demographic, economic and social historians have asked the question (to use Peter Laslett's formulation) 'Did the peasants really starve?'. For all the undergraduate examination papers it has informed, Laslett's question is badly posed. For there were no 'peasants' in early modern England. Dearth, just like disease, was experienced in ways that were structured by class arrangements amongst the poorer and middling sort of people. The reactions of Laslett's 'peasants' to high food prices were determined by their radically different class positions. In times of dearth, richer farmers pulled in their horns, the more cynical amongst them holding corn back from the market in order to boost their income when they did sell. Some yeomen drew down their

---

[329] Skipp, *Crisis and Development*, 35.

[330] G. Clark and G. Hamilton, 'Survival of the Richest: The Malthusian Mechanism in Pre-industrial England', *Journal of Economic History*, 66, 3 (2006), 710, 730.

[331] A. B. Appleby, *Famine in Tudor and Stuart England* (Liverpool, 1978), 128–9.

[332] S. Scott and C. J. Duncan, 'The Mortality Crisis of 1623 in North-West England', *Local Population Studies*, 58 (1997), 18.

[333] Palliser, 'Dearth and Disease in Staffordshire', 54–75.

living-in workforces, so that service opportunities became scarcer in periods of dearth, as farmers worried over the number of mouths they had to feed.[334] Husbandmen and their families may well have been badly hit, losing their land as they became unable to pay the rents.[335] But, probably, they did not die from hunger; for if any did starve, it was the village poor, many of whom took to the roads for towns and cities where they might hope to be able to beg for their succour. Readership of the city accounts for Newcastle reveals the following entries:

Dec[ember] 1596, Paid for the charge of burying 7 poore folke which died in the streete, for winding them, grave making and carrying to the church ... Sept[ember] 1597. Paide for the charges of bur[y]inge 9 poore folks who died for wante in the streets ... Oct[ober] 1597 Paid for the charge of bur[y]inge 16 poore folks who died for wante in the streettes.[336]

These laconic entries hint at an unfolding horror. Their significance is confirmed by a correspondent to the Privy Council who wrote from Newcastle in 1597, mentioning 'sundry starving and dying in our streeets and in the fields for want of bread'.[337]

How, then, did the poor feed themselves and their families? In some places, driven by what Annabel Paterson has called 'the involuntary vegetarianism of the rural poor', labouring people ground acorns in order to make flour from which to bake bread.[338] In 1623, the Lincolnshire gentleman William Pelham wrote:

Our country was never in that want that now it is, and more of money than corn, for there are many thousands in these parts who have sold all they have even to their bedstraw and cannot get work to earn any money. Dog's flesh is a dainty dish and found upon search in many houses, also such horse flesh as hath lain long in a deke for hounds. And the other day one stole a sheep who for mere hunger tore a leg out, and did eat it raw. All that is most certain true and yet the great time of scarcity not yet come.[339]

[334] Robert Loder noted in 1614: 'I judge it good (in such dearth yeares) to keep as few servants as possible.' G. E. Fussell (ed.), *Robert Loder's Farm Accounts, 1610–1620*, Camden Society, 3rd ser., 53 (London, 1936), 90.

[335] Hindle, 'Exclusion Crises', 130; P. Edwards, 'The Decline of the Small Farmer: The Case of Rushock, Worcestershire', *Midland History*, 21 (1996), 73–100; M. Spufford, *Contrasting Communities: English Villagers in the Sixteenth and Seventeenth Centuries* (Cambridge, 1974), chapters 2–4, and 165–6.

[336] M. A. Richardson (ed.), *Reprints of Rare Tracts and Imprints of Antient Manuscripts &c., Chiefly Illustrative of the History of the Northern Counties*, 3 vols. (Newcastle, 1847–9), III, 44.

[337] HMC Salisbury, VII, 295–6.

[338] A. Patterson, *Reading Holinshed's Chronicles* (Chicago, 1994), 84; J. Schofield (ed.), *The Works of James Pilkington* (Cambridge, 1842), 611–12.

[339] Thirsk and Cooper (eds.), *Seventeenth-Century Economic Documents*, 24.

In Gloucestershire in April 1586, at Framilode, rioters had seized a load of malt, saying that they had to feed their children on cats, dogs and nettle roots.[340] The Essex minister William Harrison observed that, in normal times, 'poore neighbours in some shires are inforced to content themselves with rie or barleie, yea, and in time of dearth, maniewith bread made either of beans, peason, or otes, or of altogether and some acornes'.[341] The horrors of famine conditions even worked their way into the Cavalier poetry of Robert Herrick, who wrote of how, in times of dearth, the poor were expected

To taste boil'd nettles, colworts, beets and eat
These and sour herbs as dainty meat.[342]

Some deep, dark memories provoked the following warning from the Diggers of Warwickshire in 1607: '[I]f it should please God to withdrawe his blessing in not prospering the fruites of the Earth but one yeare (wch Godd forbidd) there would a worse, and more fearfull dearth happen then did in K. Ed, the seconds tyrne, when people were forced to eat Catts and doggs flesh, and women to eate theyr owne children.'[343]Richer folk, aware of 'the common proverbs: the belli[e] hath no eares; honger is sharper than thornes', may have stared into the hollow eyes of the poor and shivered.[344] Cannibalistic fantasies, some believed, hovered in the minds of the poor as they looked upon the fat bodies of their richer neighbours. In 1623, the poet John Taylor described Salisbury as 'so much overcharged with poore, as having in three Parishes neere 3,000 besides decayed men a great many . . . the poore being like Pharoah's lean Kine, even ready to eat up the fat ones'.[345]

In a seminal essay, John Walter established that in corn-producing areas, dearth was often ameliorated by the willingness of farmers and landlords to sell grain at low prices directly to the village poor or even to give away such food as was deemed necessary.[346] In this respect, Walter suggests, the established poor of agrarian England did not perish from lack of food. Yet one key text from 1631, a ventriloquism of the voice of the poor, complains:

---

[340] TNA, SP12/188/47.
[341] F. J. Furnivall (ed.), *Harrison's Description of England* (London, 1877), 153.
[342] Pollard (ed.), *Works of Robert Herrick*, I, 44.
[343] Halliwell (ed.), *The Marriage of Wit and Wisdom*, 140–1.
[344] T. Becon, *The Fortresse of the Faythfull* (London, 1550), sig. F.r.
[345] P. Slack, 'Poverty and Politics in Salisbury, 1597–1666', in Clark and Slack (eds.), *Crisis and Order in English Towns*, 171. For rumours of cannibalism amongst the 'poorer sort' of English colonists in Jamestown during the 'starving time' of 1609, see R. B. Herrmann, 'The "Tragicall Historie": Cannibalism and Abundance in Colonial Jamestown', *William and Mary Quarterly*, 68, 1 (2011), 47–74.
[346] Walter, 'The Social Economy of Dearth'.

Alas! What shall I doe? I have beene at goodman – such a one's house; from him I went to goodman – such a one . . . I have beene over the Parish, I have beene out of the Parish, with money in my hand, and cannot get a pecke of Barley: they have it, but they say they cannot spare it. O miserable condition! The poore man is put to a double labour; first, to get a little money for Corne, and then to get a little Corne for money, and this last is the hardest labour: he might have earned almost halfe a Bushell, while he runnes about begging to buye halfe a pecke.[347]

Sometimes, the sheer numbers of the starving poor seemed overwhelming. Despite the strenuous efforts of wealthier householders to provide for the poor in Buckinghamshire during the dearth of 1596–7, some felt that such relief failed to provide sufficient support owing to the 'extreme poverty and great multitude' of the poor.[348] Some richer folk responded to these crisis conditions with an increased willingness to prosecute thieves, vagrants and other transgressors of the social order.[349] Wherever meaningful runs of data are available to historians of crime, it seems that prosecutions for property crime roughly parallel the price of food: whether this was a result of 'real' crime, in which an actual increase of theft took place amongst the desperate poor, or it is reflective of a diminished willingness on the part of property-owners to tolerate such offences is hard to say. Agnes Slade of Melksham (Wiltshire), for example, was prosecuted during the dearth years of 1622–3 for stealing a sheep 'for want, and she had not food to relieve her and her child, being almost famished . . . for which offence she is sorry and desireth favour'. She was sentenced to be whipped.[350] Then there was Robert Whitehead of Terling (Essex) who explained to the bench in the winter of 1623 that he had stolen a sheep, 'beinge a very poore man and having a wiefe and seven smale children and being very hungery'.[351] Or there was William Cooper, who, 'beinge hungrie', took some bread, butter and cheese from an outhouse owned by William Smith of Ashill, husbandman.[352] Or, in 1601, there was Jane Meere, who picked the pocket of a man sleeping at a Kent alehouse, as she told the magistrates, because 'she had no shoes for her feet'.[353] Even in good years, the poor were sufficiently hungry to transgress an episodically brutal criminal code. The number of capital punishments handed out by the courts, as Jim Sharpe shows, increased

[347] Fitz-Geffrie, *The Curse of Corne-horders*, 36–7.
[348] Hindle, 'Dearth, Fasting and Alms', 71.
[349] P. G. Lawson, 'Property Crimes and Hard Times in England, 1559–1624', *Law and History Review*, 4 (1986), 95–127.
[350] Ingram, 'Communities and Courts',133.
[351] Thompson, *Mobility and Migration*, 21.
[352] NRO, NQS/C/S3/31, information of William Smyth. For a similar case, see NRO, NQS/C/S3/31, information of Christopher Graie.
[353] Clark, *The English Alehouse*, 146.

during years of food scarcity, pointing to not just a rise in real crime but also an increased willingness of (generally relatively wealthy) criminal court jurors to send their poorer neighbours to the gallows.[354]

That modern historians have judged that '[f]amine was above all a regional problem' does not relieve it of any of its terror.[355] In times of high food prices, it must have seemed to contemporaries as though their worlds were collapsing. This fear of social disintegration is powerfully apparent in the parish register of Kendal (Westmorland). In 1597, the clerk noted burial of 'a pore man died in the Underdarrowe his name not known'; '[a] poore child who dyed upon the Kirland who came out of Lankestere'; '[a] poore wife wch dyed at Staveley her name unknowne'; '[a] poore crippell whose name none of Hutton could tell and died there'; 'a poore child dyed in Stricklandgt'; '[a] poore woman died upon the Kyrkland her name not known'; '[a] poore cryple wch dyed in Almesse House'; '[a] poore woman of Heversham her name not knowne'; '[a] power woman died in Hutton'.[356] In 1623, another year of perilously high food prices, the anonymous poor returned to haunt the parish clerk as he scratched the following entries into the burial register: '[a] poore travailer'; '[a] young man unknowne'; '[a] poore child'; '[a] poore man'; '[a] woman being a poor traveller'; '[a] poore begger unknowne'; '[a] poore childe unknowne'; '[a] cripple a woman unknowne'; '[a] yonge woman unknowne'; '[a] child of a stranger of Natland'; '[a] d[aughter] unbap[tised] of an Irish travellor'; '[a] woeman begger from Natland unknowne'; '[a] travaileing man from Lamrigg'; '[a] poore woeman that dyed at Longsleddall'; '[a]nother poore woeman unknowne'; '[a] poore man unknowne'; '[a] woeman unknown of Stramongate'; '[a] woeman th[a]t dyed in Hiegate'; '[a] woeman unknown who dyed in Whinfell'; '[a] man begging unknowne'; 'Jennet unknowne'; '[a] poore wench called Alice'; '[a] poore cripple unknown a boy'.[357] Here, too, there was a story about neighbourhood: in this case, of neighbourhood refused.

In the years before the civil wars, the two great challenges to neighbourhood were famine and disease. Faced with either or both of these challenges, communities turned inwards, many protecting their own poor but rejecting those who were on the road. During the 1622–4 dearth that struck so hard in the North, the manor court of Lowick, near Ulverston (Lancashire), ordered that the millers should not allow 'anie person to linger in the said milnes' and that 'noe persons cominge to the said milnes

[354] J. A. Sharpe, *Crime in Early Modern England, 1550–1750* (Harlow, 1984), 58, 60–1, 64.
[355] Walter, 'The Social Economy of Dearth', 79.
[356] R. N. Birley (ed.), *The Registers of Kendal*, III–IV, Cumberland and Westmorland Parish Register Society, 36 (Penrith, 1952), 73–82.
[357] Ibid., 340–352.

to grynde theire corne as aforesaid shall give anie almes to anie poore folks to forfeite for it xii.d'. Likewise, the manor court of Rishton (Lancashire), near Blackburn, ordered, in October 1624, that 'yf any tenaunte within this mannor shall or doe hereafter gyve any almes to any beggars at the holte mylne that everie one so offending to forfett x.s.'.[358] Just like in earlier years of high food prices, concern over the settlement of poor inmates was most intense during the 1622–4 famine.[359]

The 1622–4 famine was felt most grievously in Cumberland, Westmorland, County Durham, Lancashire, north-east Cheshire and in the West Riding of Yorkshire, especially around Halifax.[360] What is noteworthy here is the clear correspondence between rural industry and mortality crisis. For industrial communities were especially vulnerable to harvest failure. In many cases, villages dominated by mining, textile production or small-wares manufacture were located either in areas of thin soil or in forest regions. In both cases, these were places that consumed grain produced beyond their regions.[361] The geography of food marketing around Warwick provides clear evidence of the dependence of pastoral-industrial regions upon food supplies from outside. Here, during the dearth of 1586–7, food supplies came from a rough circle around the town. But buyers in the Warwick market were very heavily concentrated in the industrial regions north of the town, especially in the Forest of Arden.[362] The poor of the Forest of Arden – a classic pastoral-industrial region dominated by small-handicraftsmen – were therefore especially sensitive to shifts in the price of food. A similar sensitivity can be found in other industrial communities. Of one coal-mining parish in County Durham, its historian observes:

Ryton was not a very prosperous parish; its relatively poor arable land and its wastes and commons, despoiled by pits and crossed by tracks, made it dependent on imported grain to feed its large non-food-producing population. During the four successive harvest failures of the late 1590s, exacerbated by cattle sickness

[358] A. J. L. Winchester, 'Response to the 1623 Famine in Two Lancashire Manors', *Local Population Studies*, 36 (1986), 47.

[359] Watson, 'To Beare the Towne Harmless', 124.

[360] M. Long and M. Pickles, 'An Enquiry into Mortality in Some Mid-Wharfedale Parishes in 1623', *Local Population Studies*, 37 (1986), 19–35; Scott and Duncan, 'The Mortality Crisis of 1623 in North-West England', 14–25; R. Hoyle, 'Famine as Agricultural Catastrophe: The Crisis of 1622–3 in East Lancashire', *EcHR*, 2nd ser., 63 (2010), 974–1002; P. Millward, 'The Demographic Crisis of 1623 in Stockport, Cheshire', *Historical Social Sciences Newsletter*, 1 (1983).

[361] The starting point for any discussion of rural industry remains J. Thirsk, 'Industries in the Countryside', in F. J. Fisher (ed.), *Essays in the Economic and Social History of Tudor and Stuart England* (Cambridge, 1961), 70–88.

[362] M. J. Kingman, 'Markets and Marketing in Tudor Warwickshire: The Evidence of John Fisher of Warwick and the Crisis of 1586–7', *Warwickshire History*, 4, 1 (1978), 21–4.

and an outbreak of plague in 1597, the price of grain rose by 83% and many starved to death.[363]

Faced with a bad harvest, farmers in corn-producing areas often sold within their region. This still further inflated grain prices in pastoral-industrial, grain-consuming regions. The result was not generalized hunger – gentry, clothiers, merchants and rich sheep farmers buckled their belts and survived – but rather *socially specific* famine amongst the numerous landless or near-landless poor.

Just like disease, famine drove many onto the road, while others shut their doors to this wandering population. The court leet at Shap (Westmorland) was only one place where the local elite were at pains to prevent the migratory poor from settling in their village. In 1622, at that time of famine in the North, they ordered that 'noe Tenn[an]t or any other person shall take or entertaine any Foreigners or poore people into the parish that have not formerly beene Inhabitants'.[364] The famine continued into 1623, and there would have been many people on the road.[365] In that year, the manor court of Dilston (Northumberland) appointed 'two sufficient persons weicklye to wache the streetes comynge to the town of Dilston all such traveling people & especiallie the poore except such as allowed to be relyved in this parishe'.[366]

When plague and famine struck together or the one followed the other, some communities were pushed to the brink of collapse. In large parts of the North, dearth and plague ripped local societies apart, forcing the poor onto the road in search of shelter and food. In January 1597, the Dean of Durham Cathedral noted that, as towns and cities in the North were filled with poor wanderers, with many migrants living under the same roof, so '[w]ant and waste have crept in Northumberland, Westmorland and Cumberland; many have come 60 miles from Carlisle to Durham to buy bread'.[367] Later that same year, Sir John Carey wrote to the Privy Council from Berwick. He explained:

So as this towen is shortely like to be in a pretty case, wiche is allredy belegared about with the plage in so extreme a maner, as that it is in all the towenes in the conterey rownd about, even to the verey gates of the town, so as we nether dare suffer aney of the conterey to come into us, nether dare we not kepe any market whereby to have aney susteynans out of the conterey. So as beseydes beinge besieged with the plage in such sort as we knowe not what towenes in the conterey is free, we ar like enofe to be well stored in the towen with famine, whereof all the conterey is allredy well furnished ... unlest ther be better regarde had for the

---

[363] Chaytor, 'Household and Kinship', 31.    [364] Whiteside, 'Paines Made at Shap', 154.
[365] Hoyle, 'Famine as Agricultural Catastrophe', 974–1002.
[366] Healey, 'The Northern Manor', 233.
[367] C. Creighton, *History of Epidemics in Britain*, 2 vols. (Cambridge, 1891–4), I, 358.

provision of the palles then I see yet aney likelyhud of ... Out of the conterey we are to loke for no relefe, wiche is, by the plague, the famine and the Scottes, almost layed waste allredey.[368]

Such a combination of famine and plague could devastate a community. In the last years of Elizabeth's reign, the northern border counties seem to have been especially cursed. During the outbreak of the plague between 1597 and 1598, the towns of Kendal (Westmorland) and Penrith (Cumberland) experienced something like a 50 per cent population loss. For Penrith, the arrival of the plague was but one disaster amongst many: in 1587, its population stood at about 1,700 in 1587, falling to 1,500 in 1596 (probably as a result of an outbreak of typhus) and then to 1,350 by 1597 as a consequence of famine then finally to around 858 in 1598, in the aftermath of the plague.[369] The plague was not just an assault upon communities; it was also an attack upon the durability of the household as the key building block of society. In Penrith, sixty-three households became extinct and seventy-nine were left with only one surviving parent. This was out of a total of 224 households. Infected households were boarded up, the residents left to die or sent to inhabit temporary shacks on moorland where they passed away in large numbers. Most of those who died in Penrith were buried in a common trench. Others were interred in the churchyard, some in the schoolhouse yard and some in their own gardens. This represented a further threat to communal values.

For early modern people, it mattered a lot that the dead were properly buried. Burials, as David Cressy has pointed out, were creative social moments, just like birth and marriage. The rite of burial was a way of dealing with the passing of a loved one or a neighbour, and the community was meant to come together to observe such events. Anthony Giddens provides an eloquent summary of Durkheim's view of the subject: 'mourning is a duty imposed by the group. The social function of mourning is to draw the group together when its solidarity is threatened by the loss of one of its members.'[370] Mass graves in un-consecrated land on marginal areas of the parish spoke of the collapse of neighbourhood. It is therefore significant that, when a community experienced the plague, burials were conducted at night.[371] Likewise, the miracle of birth seemed

---

[368] Tomlinson, *Life in Northumberland*, 43–4.

[369] C. B. Phillips, 'The Plague in Kendal in 1598: Some New Evidence', *TC&WA&AS*, 2nd ser., 94 (1994), 140; S. Scott, C. J. Duncan and S. R. Duncan, 'The Plague in Penrith, Cumbria, 1597/8: Its Causes, Biology and Consequences', *Annals of Human Biology*, 23, 1 (1996), 3, 15.

[370] A. Giddens, *Durkheim* (London, 1978), 96; E. Durkheim, *The Elementary Forms of Religious Life* ([1912 Eng. trans.] Oxford, 2001), 290–4.

[371] R. Sharpe France, 'A History of the Plague in Lancashire', *Transactions of the Historic Society of Lancashire and Cheshire*, 90 (1938), 32.

denied to those whose communities were suffering from a protracted plague outbreak. The parish clerk of Manchester, for example, recorded in August 1605 that for three months there had been 'no christenings by reason of the extremitye of the sicknes' raging in the town.[372]

There was a clear pattern of the spread of plague *within* households: as Scott, Duncan and Duncan note, 'if one member of a household died from the plague there was a very high probability that other members of the family would be rapidly infected'.[373] The experience was burnt into the mind of the parish clerk of Penrith, who recorded that there was '[a] sore plague in new castle, durrome & Dernton in the yere of our lord god 1597' followed by '[a] sore plague in Richmond Kendal Penreth Carliell Apulbie & ther places in Westmorland and Cumberland in the year of our lord god 1598'. The sense remains in the clerk's entry of an anxious watchfulness, as the plague moved westwards from Northumberland and County Durham.

One way in which contemporaries understood the arrival of the plague was as a judgment of God. On 22 September 1597, for example, the parish clerk of Penrith recorded: 'Here begonne the plage (God punismet) in Penrith.' The Council of the North offered no relief from this preoccupation with sin: on 30 November 1597, they wrote to 'our very loving Frends the Maior and Aldermen of the Cyttye of Carleslie' to explain their collective opinion that the plague 'proceed[ed] from the Lord's wrathe powred downe for sinne'.[374] So, also, in a sermon delivered in the aftermath of the Kendal plague, the town's godly minister Richard Leake blamed the infection upon 'the masse and multitude of our sins, in rebelling against the holie one of Israel, these (I say) have been the provokers of the Almightie, to make us drinke of the cup of afflictions, these have pulled upon us al these plagues, and brought upon us all these fearefull and afflicted times'. Leake saw dearth and plague as linked: both were rods wielded by an angry God. The minister reminded his parishioners that over the preceding decade 'the Lord hath beaten us blacke and pale, by his severe punishments of dearth and pestilence'. In Leake's analysis, God's anger had been stirred up by the people's continued attachment to the old religion, their drunkenness and whoreishness, and their attachment to magic and witchcraft.[375]

---

[372] T. S. Willan, 'Plague in Perspective: The Case of Manchester in 1605', *Transactions of the Historic Society of Lancashire and Cheshire*, 132 (1982), 29.

[373] Scott, Duncan and Duncan, 'The Plague in Penrith', 4, 10.

[374] J. Hughes, 'The Plague in Carlisle, 1597/8', *TC&WA&AS*, 2nd ser., 71 (1971), 55.

[375] E. M. Wilson, 'Richard Leake's Plague Sermons, 1599', *TC&WA&AS*, 2nd ser., 75 (1975), 155–6. At this time, Kendal was dominated by a clique of Puritans. See M. A. Clark, 'Kendal: The Protestant Exception', *TC&WA&AS*, 2nd ser., 95 (1996), 137–52.

Richard Leake was far from alone in seeing the arrival of infectious disease as a divine judgement. When the sweating sickness arrived in 1551, the Privy Council ordered bishops to set the people to prayer, 'to refrain their greedy appetites from that insatiable serpent of covetousness, where with most men are so infected, that it seemeth each one would devour another without charity or any godly respect to the poor, to their neighbours, or to the Commonwealth'.[376] This was a macro-explanation of infection, rooted in a reading of mid-Tudor social conflicts. For a micro-explanation of the arrival of disease, one that focused on the particular failings of an individual, we might turn to the words of the parish clerk of Cranbrook (Kent):

In this year following, 1597, began the great plague in Cranbrook, the which continued from April the y[ea]r af[oresai]d to July 13, 1598. 1st, it was observed that before this infection that God, about a year or two before, took away by death many honest and good men and women. 2. That the judgment of God for sin was much before threatened, especially for that vice of Drunkenness which abounded thar. 3. That this infection was in all quarters of the Parish except Hartly quarter. 4. That the same begun in the house of one Brightelling, out of which much thieving was committed, and that it ended in the House of one Henry Grynnock, who was a pott companion, and his wife much noted for incontinence, which both died excommunicated. 5. That this infection gott almost into all the Inns and Suckling Houses of the Town, places then of much misorder, so that God did seem to punish that himself which others did neglect and not regard. 6. Together with this infection there was a great dirth at the same time, which was cause also of much wailing and sorrow. 7. This was most grievous unto me of all, that this judgment of God did not draw people unto repentance the more, but many by it seemed the more hardened in their sin ... Now also this year others of the plague were buried near to their several dwellings, because they could get none to carry them into the Church, for it was the beginning of this infection, so that none would venture themselves. The certain day of their burials one could not learn.[377]

Thus, it was no mere formulary that led the clerk of the court leet of Manchester to write in October 1625:

The Jurye of this present Leete duelie considering the great perell of theis contagious tymes, and the fearefull miseries whereunto the poore inhabitants of this towne are like to be exposed if Almightie god do send the plague of pestilence amongst us, is earnestlie desireinge (if it bee gods will) to prevent the first, or to the latter, by good order, to give some ease (if god doe soe afflict us), have thought fit to nominate, and doe hereby order and appoint theis twelve persons whose names are hereunder written.[378]

[376] D. MacCulloch, *Tudor Church Militant: Edward VI and the Protestant Reformation* (London, 2001), 153.
[377] Thistleton-Dyer, *Old English Social Life*, 84–5.
[378] Sharpe France, 'A History of the Plague in Lancashire', 58.

One account of the arrival of the plague in Manchester in 1632 described how '[t]he Lord sent his destroying Angell' into the town.[379] Likewise, it seemed self-evident to a commentator on the London plague of 1636 that 'the destroying Angel hath unsheathed his sword and brandished it over us of this Citie, us of the whole Land ... Yea, the black Horse of the Pestilence with pale Death on his backe, hath beene and is, est-soones, prauncing and trampling in the streets of our Citie at midnight.'[380]

Those afflicted with the plague looked about themselves and asked why they had been so visited, what moral failings they had displayed that the Almighty chose to punish them. In September 1622, for example, the leading inhabitants of Harpley (Norfolk) petitioned the magistrates for an order suppressing all alehouses in their village, 'we finally being perswaded that the unthriftynesse prophanesse and unrulynesse of our towne hath come especially from owr Alehowses'.[381] A year earlier, some of the same men had asked the magistracy to suppress their alehouses,

> it being the observatio[n] of those which be ancyent amongst us that our towne was farr better to passe when it had noe such howses; whereas now, of (about) six and fiftye severall hows[e]houlders we have scarce any (two or three at the most) which use trading or occupacio[n]. Also the extraordinary mortalytye which lately by the providence of God befell us, we have cause to think was in great measure increased by alehowse drinkings the greater part of them which soe dyed being of the poorer sort and growen to that kind of riot ... Soe showld we hope to have our people more paynefull, thryvyng and fearing God then now they are or ever [a]re lyke to be, these howses continuing.[382]

God, then, had visited Harpley with the plague as punishment for their drunken ways. Moreover, critically, the alehouses of Harpley were seen as a problem in that they created alternative centres for sociability amongst the 'poorer sort'.

The Destroying Angel brought with it an existential threat to fundamental social values. Most of all, the plague was an attack upon the idea of neighbourhood. Looking back on the plague of 1636, the Newcastle minister Robert Jenison told his flock that the plague 'makes a man stranger to his own house, to his dearest friends; yea, as it were an enemie to them, and an instrument of death to wife, children, friends; and it deprives a man of comforters in his greatest agonie and need'.[383] Likewise, a Jacobean preacher felt that the plague 'was more destructive than discord or hunger', because 'comfort and company' were denied to

---

[379] Ibid., 76

[380] I. D., *Salomon's Pest-House, or Tower-Royall* (London, 1636), preface.

[381] NRO, NQS/C/S3/23a, letter of the inhabitants of Harpley.

[382] NRO, NQS/C/S3/23, petition of the town of Harpley.

[383] Wrightson, *Ralph Tailor's Summer*, 57.

the infected and 'the comfort of nature, the expectation of love among those that are left alive, is utterly dissolved'.[384]

For some folk, the consequence of the arrival of the plague was to break communities, disgorging poor people onto the roads. Thus, the Lancashire gentleman Alexander Rigby wrote during the 1631 epidemic that 'the sicknes in these partes increaseth much and disperseth ... so that the inhabitants ... leave their howses and seeke and resort to forrin places'.[385] For those who remained behind, the plague cut into the elementary values with which they had been raised. One of these concerned the decent treatment of the sick and the poor: Christian social values that in normal times might seem self-evident were, during periods of infection, broken down. In times of plague, Paul Slack notes: 'Above all, the sick themselves were shunned ... Corpses of travellers were refused burial in churchyards and interred in the road instead. In the country, some of those "suspected to die of the plague" were buried in their own gardens; there was no welcome for them anywhere else.'[386] Fears around the collapse of neighbourhood drew upon awareness that some plague-stricken communities could no longer sustain themselves – that they had, functionally, fallen apart. Hence, in 1631, the governors of Preston (Lancashire) explained that there were 887 people in their plague-stricken town, of whom some 756 were dependent upon a weekly dole, and that the few remaining independent folk could not survive the winter without help towards their fuel costs. The householders who had once contributed greatly to the town and county were now themselves poverty-stricken: 'What tax shalbee laide will fall as heavie on us as others; yet theire miseries are enough by the plague; yt were pittie famine should also destroy them. Soe wee heave them to Godes mercie.'[387] The plague orders followed by urban authorities from the later Elizabethan period onwards assumed that normal patterns of social interaction had, in the face of disease, broken down. Yet the enforcement of plague regulations – nailing up infected houses and forcing the poor to live in pesthouses on the outskirts of towns and cities – were deeply unpopular with the infected and perceived of as an arbitrary proceeding.[388]

---

[384] P. Slack, *The Impact of Plague in Tudor and Stuart England* (London, 1985), 20.
[385] Sharpe France, 'A History of the Plague in Lancashire', 12.
[386] Slack, *The Impact of Plague*, 19.
[387] Sharpe France, 'A History of the Plague in Lancashire', 7.
[388] K. L. S. Newman, 'Shutt Up: Bubonic Plague and Quarantine in Early Modern England', *Journal of Social History*, 45, 3 (2012), 809–34.

Looking back on his early days, William Lilly recalled how, during the London plague of 1625, '[p]eople [were] dying in the open Fields and in the open Streets'.[389] The clerks of plague-ridden London parishes noted the demise of '[a] poor body that died in Chancery Lane' and 'a poor woman that lay in the street all night'.[390] For those few who ventured into the street, their nostrils were assailed by the scent of burning pitch, believed to drive away infection, a harsh stench that was mitigated in some places by the use of frankincense and incense. Venturing into a parish church, here, too, the visitor might find a barrel of pitch burning.[391] A memoir of the London plague of 1625 described how

> When at high Noone one passing by, should meet
> A Mid-night Darke, and silence in the street;
> When in the ways well-pav[e]d and worne before
> By frequent steps of men, there now grew store
> Of uncouth Grasse; and Harvests now apace
> Grew where they once were sold i[n] th[e] Market-place:
> When as no Marryments, no Sports, no Playes
> Were knowne at all, and yet all Holy-dayes
> No Papers then over the doores were set,
> With *Chambers readie furnish'd to be let;*
> But a sad, *Lord have mercie upon us,* and
> A bloody Crosse, as fatall Markes did stand,
> Able to fright one from the Prayer. The time
> Then held it an inexpiable Crime,
> To visit a sicke friend; Strange Stoure, wherein
> Love was a fault and Charitie a sin
> When Bad did feare infection from the Good
> And men did hate their cruell Naighbour-hood.[392]

The materialities of urban street-life – so richly rewarding to everyday communal relations in normal circumstances – were extinguished by the plague. In 1610, for example, the Lincoln authorities noted that one consequence of a collective fear of the plague was that households had ceased to interact.[393] The Liverpool authorities ordered in 1540 that, following the outbreak of plague in the town, the inhabitants should 'kepe theym on the backsydes of theyr howsies, and keape theyr doores and wyndoys shutte on the streete syde . . . that no other person or persons be of famulie conversacion or dwell with theym upon payne of imprisonement, and to kepe [to] theyr owne howsies. And that they walke in noe

---

[389] W. Lilly, *Mr William Lilley's History of His Life and Times* (London, 1715), 18.
[390] Slack, *The Impact of Plague,* 17.
[391] Cox (ed.), *Churchwardens' Accounts,* 317, 318, 319.
[392] I. D., *Salomons Pest-House,* 61.    [393] HMC, 14th Report, VIII, Lincoln MSS, 84.

stretes excepte a reasonable cause.'[394] Such regulations represented the temporary death of the urban neighbourhood, with its swirl of life and intercourse and gossip – in the streets, at the threshold, at shopfronts. All of this ceased in towns that were experiencing disease. Industry was also badly affected by the arrival of the plague. In April 1617, the mayor and the vicar of Dudley (Worcestershire) wrote to the Quarter Sessions, noting that the plague had been present for nine months, such that 'our towne standing principally upon poore handicraft's men who are nigh impoverished and now themselves waite ayde who heretofore did contribute to the refuge of the poore sorte'. The people of Dudley awaited 'further impoverishment and imminent danger of famishment of many amongst us'.[395]

The fundamental bonds of local society were threatened by the arrival of disease. So, too, were economic and social interconnections between communities broken by infectious disease. The passage of what contemporaries called 'traffick' – the movement of people, goods, capital and ideas – died out as a result of the plague.[396] Critically, the plague followed road networks that linked the English economy and polity into an intricate web of trading patterns that, in particular, enmeshed small market towns with one another as the critical nodes of commerce and early capitalism.[397] The results were catastrophic not just for the economy of an urban centre but also for its 'country' thereabouts. In Liverpool in 1558, faced with the arrival of the plague from Manchester, St Martin's Fair was cancelled and for three months no market was held.[398] In 1517, it was reported from Chester that the consequence of the arrival of the sweating sickness had been to leave grass to grow 'a foot high at the Cross', this being the material and symbolic centre of the city, located at the crossroads of the old Roman streetscape.[399] The Newcastle man John Fenwick reminded his audience of how, in 1636, the plague had 'made thee almost desolate, thy streets grown greene with grasse, thy treasure wasted, they trading departed'.[400] As they learnt that plague was alive on the roads, communities shut down, 'traffick' dying in the face of

---

[394] Sharpe France, 'A History of the Plague in Lancashire', 30.
[395] Bund (ed.), *Calendar of the Quarter Sessions Papers, Vol. I: 1591–1643*, 229.
[396] For the concept of 'traffick', see D. Rollison, 'Discourse and Class Struggle: The Politics of Industry in Early Modern England', *Social History*, 26, 2 (2001), 166–89. On the importance of exchange in the development of human societies, see R. E. Blanton and L. F. Farger, *How Humans Cooperate: Confronting the Challenges of Collective Action* (Boulder, CO, 2016).
[397] For the geography of the spread of plague in the northern borders in 1597–8, see Scott, Duncan and Duncan, 'The Plague in Penrith', 12.
[398] Sharpe France, 'A History of the Plague in Lancashire', 31.     [399] Ibid., 16.
[400] Wrightson, *Ralph Tailor's Summer*, 44.

254    4   The Tongues of Men and Angels

the arrival of suspicious wandering strangers. In Manchester in June 1605, for example, those coming into the town had to certify that they were not diseased.[401] The Council of the North told the Carlisle authorities in November 1597 that they were worried about 'the more dispersed by the recourse of people from towns and places infected unto suche as are free from the same and also by carryeinge of goods from place to place, without obsevinge anye good order'.[402]

Certainly, the pale rider's scythe cut down the rich; but it was at its sharpest amongst the poor. Paul Slack's study of the relationship between poverty and epidemic disease in Norwich, just like that of Keith Wrightson in Newcastle, shows that it was in the poorest parts of those towns where mortality was highest.[403] Plague was, if not socially specific, then certainly related to poverty: the rich had homes outside afflicted urban centres to which they could flee and extensive social contacts on which they could draw. The poor inhabited cramped, claustrophobic tenements within which the plague spread all too easily. Poverty was recognized as related to disease; if neighbours were worried that the plague might arrive in their community, it was the poor they watched. Paul Slack provides the example of 'a poor man' called Dobson who, living on the edge of the parish of Westerham (Kent), took in a lodger who subsequently died of the plague. The lodger sold 'a coat ... not well aired or purified, unto one Wexe of Westerham, a poor man also, who by that coat was infected and died of the pestilence'.[404] The trade in second-hand clothes – one of the ways in which poor folk might engage in commerce, passing cash and garments to and fro – had become a fatal practice. With the construction by town and city authorities of temporary shacks on nearby wasteland or commons within which the infected poor could be left to die, the marginality of poverty became literal and self-evident. It was noted in Newcastle upon Tyne that during the plague of 1558–9, '[t]he sick poor were sent out of the town and encamped on the waste grounds'.[405] In Manchester in October 1605, the infected were left to die in cabins on Collyhurst Common.[406]

Contemporaries were well aware that it was in the poor suburbs and backstreets, where the urban poor congregated, that disease often struck first and with greatest ferocity. The impetus of disease was directed

---

[401] Willan, 'Plague in Perspective', 31.
[402] J. Hughes, 'The Plague in Carlisle, 1597/8', *TC&WA&AS*, 2nd ser., 71 (1971), 55.
[403] Wrightson, *Ralph Tailor's Summer*, 36.     [404] Slack, *The Impact of Plague*, 11.
[405] Barnes, 'Visitations of the Plague', 173 176.
[406] Willan, 'Plague in Perspective', 31. For a detailed discussion of the construction of cabins for the infected poor on the commons of Carlisle, see Hughes, J., 'The Plague in Carlisle', 60.

towards 'the rude multitude' and 'the ignorant sort'. This inspired pity in some and a cruel satisfaction in others: one commentator saw the plague as 'a broom in the hands of the Almighty with which he sweepeth the most nasty and uncomely corners of the universe'. William Gouge felt that the reason that God selected 'the poorer and meaner sort' as the prime victims of the plague was 'because they are not of such use' and so 'may better be spared'; another writer saw plague as a blessing in that its main victims were 'of the baser and poorer sort, such whose lives were burdensome, whose deaths are beneficial'. But why should the poor be so chosen? To some observers, the answer was obvious. Citizens of late Tudor Oxford and Chester felt that the spread of plague was due to 'the most lewd and dissolute behavior of some base and unruly inhabitants'. 'Divers nasty poor people' were thereby taken away by the plague.[407] As Paul Slack observes in his seminal study: 'By the beginning of the seventeenth century plague was recognized as one element in that generalized threat which the "rough poorer sort" presented to the respectable sections of English society ...[. I]t was precisely because the "base sort of people" were seen as carriers of contagion that they were so much feared in the sixteenth and seventeenth centuries.'[408]The plague threatened familial bonds. The assumption that brothers would aid one another was rendered problematic by the arrival of the plague in one Norfolk village in 1636. William Handy explained to the church court, after his brother Roger fell sick with the plague (of which he died), that

beinge intended to settle his estate and to p[ro]vide for his children ... Roger said that he would have him this respondent and ... Thomas [Handy] to take care of his children and to p[ro]vide for them and he desiered that they should take his goods and assist one another ther[e]in: And the same beinge made knowne to the wife of ... Thomas Handy she altogether disliked ther[e]of, & p[er]swaded her ... husband not to meddle eith[e]r w[i]th the children or goods of ... Roger for she said she was sicklye & the troble of lookeinge to & p[ro]videinge for the said children would light upon her And after wch the said Roger haveinge notice or knowledge of the unwillingnes[s] of his said sister in lawe, said I hope I shall finde other or better Fr[i]ends.[409]

Certainly, as he lay in his infected deathbed, Roger Handy was not out of place in expecting 'freindship' from his kin. For there were those who, in the face of the affliction of their villages and towns, still held to communal norms as the moral basis of their actions. One diseased Wiltshire man was better served than Roger Handy: in this case, his sister-in-law was called

[407] Slack, *The Impact of Plague*, 195, 232, 239–40, 305.   [408] Ibid., 307.
[409] NRO, DN/CON/15, part 3, 1636 depositions regarding the last testament of Roger Handy.

upon by her neighbours to remain 'no nearer to the house wherein he lay sick than about the distance of the breadth of an acre and a half', but she told them that she would go to him, 'live or die'. Paul Slack observes that 'the poor thought it a "matter of conscience" and a "Christian" duty to visit their neighbours when infected'.[410] Thus, in February 1593, the neighbours of Margaret Benton of Vernham Dean (Hampshire) appealed to her not to go and visit her plague-ridden sister and brother-in-law, 'but she answered she wold goe to the[m] live or dye'.[411]

For richer folk, their response to the arrival of the plague was sometimes to stay put and to fight it, standing alongside their poorer neighbours. Richer people in Carlisle in 1598, for example, stayed with their neighbours, raising over £209 for the relief of the diseased poor. Likewise, in Nottingham in 1591, leading townspeople gave substantial quantities of food and money 'for releyffe of the poore and disseisyd infected' of Nottingham.[412] Following the 1636 Newcastle plague, the minister Robert Jenison reminded his congregation that the infection

should much more have prevailed with multitudes of the poorer sort among us, were it not that by Gods blessing and the care of our Magistrates in disposing the revenues of our Chamber weekly, in great summes for their reliefe; as also by their and other Inhabitants free loanes, and some good help and assistance made freely by kind neighbours, they were competently provided for.[413]

One print commentator advised those amongst his readers who had fled an infected community: 'Omit no dutie of charitie and benefice: if thy person be removed, leave thy purse behind thee, & thy best help, as one that knowest thou art not loosed from the common law of neighbourhood.'[414] For many people, such neighbourhood values triumphed over the urge to escape or to leave the infected nailed up in their homes or left to die on the moorland.

Keith Wrightson's evocative discussion of the Newcastle plague of 1636 shows the ways in which a sense of community was sustained in the city in the face of the plague. Focusing upon testamentary practices and what these show about the endurance of neighbourhood, he provides examples such as John Wason, who heard the will of the infected Clement Curry, 'being [his] neighbor'; he had known Clement's family for twenty years. Likewise, Mary Finlay, 'neighbor to Mabel Walker att the time of her death' for nine years 'did voluntarily goe to the dore of [Mabel's]

[410] Slack, *The Impact of Plague*, 289, 301.    [411] HALS, 21M65/C3/10, p. 296.
[412] Hughes, J., 'The Plague in Carlisle', 54; Stevenson et al. (eds.), *Records of the Borough of Nottingham*, IV, 236–7.
[413] Wrightson, *Ralph Tailor's Summer*, 47.
[414] T. Taylor, *An Answer to that Question: How Farre It Is Lawfull to Flee in the Time of the Plague* (London, 1636).

house ... being a neighbour to heare her said will'. Likewise, three neighbours visited William Cooke and heard his will 'before the dore of his house'; they were all healthy and so 'durst not come to [him] after the writeing thereof'. Cooke 'desired them to goe to a neighbours house and there to drinke twoe or three pottes of beere' on his behalf.[415]

And after the plague? The sermons preached by Richard Leake in 1599 speak to the sense of relief – apparent in the restoration of neighbourhood – that came with the end of the plague. He noted 'that then might be heard amongst us, mirth in stead of mourning, songs in stead of doleful sighings; gladsome salutations in meetings, in stead of diligent shunning each of others presence, for feare of infection'.[416] Survivors gave thanks to their Lord, passing comment on the wickedness that had led to the visitation of the plague. The parish clerk of Nantwich (Cheshire) wrote in July 1604:

This yeare together with the former yeare and the year following this Realme of England was visited with a contagious plague generally: whereof many thousands in London, and other townes and Cities dyed of the same. The said plague begane in our Towne of Namptwich about the 24th June 1604, being brought out of Chester and here dispersed diversly, soe th[a]t presently our Market was spoyled, the town abandoned of all the wealthy inhabitants, who fled for refuge into divers places of the Country adjoyninge. But of those which remained at home ther Dyed from the 12th June till the 2nd March following about the number of 430 persons of all diseases. Now seeing God in mercy hath withdrawn his punishing hand, and hath quenched the spark of contagious infection among us, God graunt that we by Repentaunce may prevent further punishment & that the remembrance of this plague past may remain in our hearts for that purp[o]se for ever. Amen.[417]

Survivors remarried, sometimes a widower marrying a widow, blending into a new household those children, nephews, nieces, servants and apprentices that had survived the plague. Early modern households – seeming so fixed and patriarchal – in such times were perhaps at their most fluid. T. S. Willan notes that in many north-west communities, high mortality in one year was followed by high levels of marriage in that which followed.[418] Survivors married and they had babies: human life contin-ued. Andrew Appleby's work on Cumberland and Westmorland shows that, in the aftermath of mortality crises, levels of baptisms were unusually high.[419] And post-plague communities were refreshed by the arrival of immigrants. Penrith's population recovered in the early Jacobean period, as 65 new families moved into the town by 1610, boosting the town's

---

[415] Wrightson, *Ralph Tailor's Summer*, 98–100.
[416] Wilson, 'Richard Leake's Plague Sermons', 160.
[417] Thistleton-Dyer, *Old English Social Life*, 86.     [418] Willan, 'Plague in Perspective', 32.
[419] A. B. Appleby, 'Disease or Famine? Mortality in Cumberland and Westmorland, 1580–1640', *EcHR*, 2nd ser., 26, 3 (1973), 414.

population from its post-plague population of around 858 to 1,150. Severe famine followed again in 1623, but by 1642, the population had recovered to number 1,233.[420] Early modern people, like the communities they made, were resilient.

Yet, it was hard for people to forget. The signs of the Destroying Angel were, in the early days, apparent to all. There were the mass graves on the surrounding commons. The remains of the pesthouses alongside those graves. The burial-places of neighbours, interred in their own gardens. The burnt remains of houses and barns that had been torched in the hope of removing any lingering infection. The barrels of tar that had been burnt as a failing protection against the spread of the disease. The empty houses, their doors still daubed with the fatal words – Lord Protect Us From This Evil. Perhaps most of all, the mass graves. Memories of the passage of the plague were scorched into the official record: along with years of dearth and famine, one of the recurrent themes in urban chronicles is an attention to the outbreak of infectious disease.[421] Plague also endured in popular memory. In 1601, the eighty-year-old Northamptonshire tailor Nicholas Loasbie told the Exchequer Court that

he dothe remember ther was a great plague in Okelie ... fyftie viij yeares past or thereabouts at wch tyme there wer[e] divers of the Inhabitants of great okelie ... fledd into great Okelie woods and there dwelte and uppon a sondaie or hollidaie he well remembreth there wer[e] divers of the Inhabitants of Okelie ... wch hadd fledd into the woods came to the Church in Geddington ... to heare devine service whome the Inhabitants of Geddington by reason of the plague denyed and then the said Inhabitants of great Okelie chalenged themselves to be of the p[ar]ishe of Geddington whereuppon they were admitted to stand in the west end of the church to heare prayer and to see the elevation [of the host].[422]

I have suggested elsewhere that Loasbie's story represents a *usable* past: that is, his story communicates meaning, as well as historical information, one that, in this case, was important for the consolidation and retention of communal memory, telling a tale that was about survival.[423]

Elsewhere, there were strong memories of the passage of the plague, constructing memories that lasted for generations. In the course of a dispute between the parishes of St Margaret's and St Oswald's (Durham) in the 1570s, for example, aged witnesses spoke about the burial of the dead in 'the plage tyme, within this 40 years, when sick folks had lodges maid upon the more'. Another old man, who had dwelt in Elvet street beside St Oswald's parish church for at least forty years,

---

[420] Scott, Duncan and Duncan, 'The Plague in Penrith', 3.
[421] I hope to write more fully about urban chronicles and civic memory in the future.
[422] TNA, E134/43Eliz/Trin8.     [423] Wood, *The Memory of the People*, 278.

recalled 'the great dead tyme about 37 or 38 yeres ago' when too many people were buried in the churchyard of St Oswald's.[424] In the aftermath of the 1598 plague, a carved stone was erected by the people of Penrith in St Andrew's church. The earliest surviving account of the text on the stone comes from the antiquarian William Nicolson, who, in 1704, observed: 'On the outside of the North Wall of the Vestry, in a rude and slovenly Character: Petis fuit, A.o. 1598. Unde moriebantur apud Kendal, 2500. Richmond, 2200. Penrith, 2266. Karliol, 1196.'[425] Alongside the figures for the dead, Ezekiel 18:32 was also cited ('For I have no pleasure in the death of him that dieth, saith the Lord God: wherefore turn yourselves, and live ye').[426] So, remember, turn away and live on. Yet the memory of the plague was inscribed in the shared memory of the community. In 1599, a sequence of historical notes was scored into the parish register of Penrith, apparently copied from some earlier register. Events noted included the Battle of Flodden; the Pilgrimage of Grace; the arrival of the plague in Penrith and Kendal in 1554; the Northern Rising of 1569; plagues in London, Nottingham, Derby and Lincoln in 1593; plagues in Newcastle, Durham and Darlington in 1597; and the plague in Westmorland and Cumberland in 1598.[427]

Memories of the plague in Kendal and Penrith were textual, material and local all at once. Writing in 1832, Cornelius Nicholson observed the tradition that the site of a Roman fort called Coneybeds on Hay Fell above Kendal was the location of the continuation of traffick. Here, Nicholson wrote, '[i]n the time of the plague which desolated the kingdom in 1597–98, provisions were brought to this spot by the country people, and deposited for the inhabitants of Kendal, which was their only intercourse during that destructive period'.[428] Something similar was at work in local memories following the plague in Penrith. In that town, there still stands a large block called the plague stone, where food had been brought by rural people to be sold to the plague-infected town. The stone is twelve inches square and ten inches deep, intended to hold disinfecting liquid such as vinegar. It may be the reworked base of a pre-Reformation cross: no one knows. In this trough, the townspeople's money was laid and, after being cleansed, it would be taken by the country people. In Keswick, there was a

---

[424] Raine (ed.), *Depositions . . . from the Courts of Durham*, 278, 280–1.
[425] R. S. Ferguson (ed.), *Miscellany Accounts of the Diocese of Carlile* (London, 1877), 154. The church was rebuilt in the eighteenth century and the stone replaced with a brass plaque. The figures for the dead of Kendal, Penrith, Carlisle and Richmond probably refer to the rural deaneries as well as the towns themselves.
[426] Barnes, 'Visitations of the Plague', 172–3. See also Scott, Duncan and Duncan, 'The Plague in Penrith', 1–21.
[427] Barnes, 'Visitations of the Plague', 169–70.
[428] C. Nicholson, *The Annals of Kendal, with Biographical Sketches* (Kendal, 1832).

tradition noted in 1887 that during the plague, owing to the collapse of marketing as a result of the infection, rural folk brought the clothes they had made to a conspicuous stone on Armboth Fell. Here they traded their goods. The object still goes by the name of the Web Stone. Traffick continued, but at a distance. The local tradition observed in the Victorian period was that when the plague was in Keswick, the country people would come as far as Ciddy Beck but no further. Just like the story that Nicholas Loasbie told to the Court of Exchequer, these were *usable* memories: they told a story that was partly about God's wrath and his punishment of the Lakeland district but also about *survival*; the survival of traffick, of exchange and intercourse, of community and neighbourhood. This usable past told the people of Keswick, Penrith and Carlisle who they were – that they had stood *together* and *survived*.

Keswick, Penrith and Carlisle folk, then, resisted the swift scythe of the pale rider: terrible losses were sustained, but neighbourhoods retained intact. Yet, all the time, there were those who were excluded from the social equation that was neighbourhood. The great contradiction in the history of neighbourhood is that, while it remained so discursively dominant, it sat at a certain remove from the material realities of growing social polarization. Over the course of the period with which we have been engaged, poor folk were in many places crushed by the social structures that they inhabited. Their voices are notoriously difficult to access.

Maybe the best thing to do is to listen to the silences. One silence remains in the records of the magistracy of Jacobean Norfolk. It is an examination conducted on 24 April 1612 into Margerie Clove of Burnham Westgate. Mistress Clove tells us that

upon Saterdaye morning Last before sun rising she dep[ar]ted from her house w[i]th one dorithie Clove her daughter (the said dorithie carrying her base childe w[i]th her) by a back lane next the howse and at the end therof towards the Field, this ex[aminan]t gave the said dorithie her blessinge & soe Returned from her home to her owne house and what is become of the said dorithye and her child she knoweth not.[429]

The precise context is lost, but the implication is clear: in bearing her bastard child, Dorithie Clove had offended the moral norms of Burnham Westgate, and so her mother – out of shame or perhaps the worry of another mouth to feed – had set her girl upon the road. How much did a mother's blessing matter to Dorithie and her little baby? As she walked onto the 'back lane next the howse ... towards the Field', did Dorithie have cause to doubt the Christian community of her village or to wonder

[429] NRO, NQS/C/S3/18, examination of Margerie Clove.

how her mother's hearth had grown so cold? Perhaps she and her baby died on the road. Perhaps some bored parish clerk recorded Dorithie's burial as that of merely another nameless pauper, as he was now put to the irritating expense of finding a grave. Or perhaps Dorithie headed for some place where she had friends, somewhere that she might begin anew, to create a life of her own. Maybe she set out for one of the great cities of the realm – perhaps even as far as London. Can we ever know? For as Dorithie Clove began her journey, she left her neighbourhood behind. Faith passed away. Of hope, there seemed nothing left, other than that which she might will up within herself. Charity was frozen cold. As Dorithie passed onto the road bearing no more than her mother's blessing, she knew that, for her, neighbourhood was truly dead.

# Bibliography

## Contemporary Printed Works

Abbot, G., *An Exposition upon the Prophet Ionah* (Oxford, 1600).

Adams, T., *The Happines of the Church* (London, 1619).

Anon., *A Goodly Treatise of Faith, Hope and Charit[i]e* (Southwark, 1537).

*The Prayse and Commendacion of Suche as Sought Comenwelthes* (London, 1548?).

*A Balade Declaring How Neybourhed, Love and Trew Dealing Is Gone* (London, 1561).

*A New Yeres Gyft* (London, 1571).

*Cyvile and Uncyvile Life: A Discourse Very Profitable* (London, 1579).

*The Life and Death of Jack Straw* (London, 1594).

*A Knacke to Knowe a Knave* (London, 1594).

*The Crie of the Poore for the Death of the Right Honorable Earle of Huntington* (London, 1596).

*A Right Godly and Christian ABC, Shewing the Duty of Every Degree* (London, 1601?).

*The Cruell Shrow* (London, 1640?).

*An Ease for Overseers of the Poore* (London, 1601).

*A Newe Ballad, Composed in Commendation of the Societie, or Companie of the Porters* (London, 1605).

*A Health to All Good-Fellowes* (London, c.1615).

*Pasquils Palonidia* (London, 1619).

*Muldsacke, or the Apologie of Hic Mulier* (London, 1620).

*Newes Good and Newe* (London, c.1623).

*A Dialogue between Master Guesright and Poor Neighbour Needy* (London, c.1624).

*A Pleasant Countrey New Ditty* (London, 1625?).

*Pitties Lamentation for the Cruelty of this Age* (London, c.1625).

*A Merry New Ballad I Have Here to Shew* (London, c.1630).

*A Hee-Divell* (London, 1630).

*The Country Mens Chat* (London, c.1632).

*Mondayes Worke: or The Two Honest Neigbours Both Birds of a Feather* (London, 1632).

*Well Met Neighbour: or, A Dainty Discourse betwixt Nell and Sisse* (London, c.1633).

*The Gossips Feast: or A Merry Meeting of Women* (London, c.1635–6).

Arthurton, H., *Provision for the Poore* (London, 1597).

Bodin, J., *The Six Bookes of a Common-Weale* (London, 1606).

Bird, S., *Lectures* (London, 1598).

Braham, H., *The Institution of a Gentleman* (London, 1568).

Breton, N., *Olde Mad-cappes New Gally-mawsrey* (London, 1602).

*The Court and the Country* (London, 1618).

Burton, H., *Israels Fast* (London, 1628).

Byfield, R., *The Light of Faith* (London, 1630).

C. C., *A Commentary upon the Prophecie of Isaiah* (London, 1609).

Caesar, P., *A General Discourse against the Damnable Sect of Usurers Grounded uppon the Worde of God* (London, 1578).

Camden, W., *Britain, or A Chorographicall Description of the Most Flourishing Kingdomes, England, Scotland, and Ireland* (London, 1637).

Carew, T., 'A Caveat for Craftesmen and Clothiers', in T. Carew, *Certaine Godly and Necessary Sermons* (London, 1603).

Carey, W., *The Present State of England* (London, 1626).

Cartwright, T., *The Second Replie of Thomas Cartwright: Agaynst Maister Doctor Whitgiftes Second Answer, Touching the Churche Discipline* (London, 1575).

Chapman, G., *Al Fooles a Comedy* (London, 1605).

Chettle, H., *Piers Plainnes Seaven Yeres Prentiship* (London, 1595).

Cleaver, R., *A Briefe Explanation of the Whole Booke of the Proverbs of Salomon* (London, 1615).

Conway, W., *An Exhortacion to Charite* (London, 1550?).

Cooper, T., *The Mystery of Witchcraft* (London, 1617).

Cotta, J., *A Short Discoverie of the Unobserved Dangers of Severall Sorts of Ignorant and Unconsiderate Practisers of Physicke* (London, 1612).

Crooke, S., *The Guide unto True Blessednesse* (London, 1613).

Daneau, L., *True and Christian Friendshippe* (London, 1586).

Day, M., *Doomes-Day: or, A Treatise of the Resurrection of the Body* (London, 1636).

De La Perrière, G., *The Mirrour of Policie* (London, 1598).

de Mornay, P., *A Woorke Concerning the Trewnesse of the Christian Religion* (London, 1587).

de Serres, J., *A General Inventorie of the History of France* (London, 1607).

Dent, A., *The Plaine Man's Path-Way to Heaven* (London, 1601).

Dod, J., *The Bright Star which Leadeth Wise Men to Our Lord Jesus Christ* (London, 1603).

*A Plaine and Familiar Exposition of the Eleventh and Twelfth Chapters of the Proverbes of Salomon* (London, 1607).

Dod, J. and Cleaver, R., *A Treatise or Exposition upon the Ten Commandments* (London, 1603).

Downame, G., *The Christians Sanctuarie* (London, 1604).

Downame, J., *The Plea of the Poore* (London, 1616).

Dyke, J., *A Worthy Communicant* (London, 1636).

Elton, E., *An Exposition of the Epistle of St Paule to the Colossians Deliuered in Sundry Sermons* (London, 1615).

*The Complaint of a Sanctified Sinner Answered* (London, 1618).

E. P., *A Harmonie upon the Three Evangelists, Matthew, Mark and Luke* (London, 1584).

Ferne, J., *The Blazon of Gentrie* (London, 1586).

Fenton, R., *A Treatise of Usurie Divided into Three Books* (London, 1611).

Fitz-Geffrie, C., *The Curse of Corne-Horders* (London, 1631).

Foster, T., *The Scourge of Covetousnesse* (London, 1631).

Fuller, T., *The Holy and Profane States* (Cambridge, 1831).

Garey, S., *A Manuall for Magistrates: or A Lantern for Lawyers: A Sermon Preached before Judges and Justices at Norwich Assizes, 1619* (London, 1623).

Gascoinge, G., *A Hundredth Sundrie Flowres* (London, 1573).

Gifford, G., *A Briefe Discourse of Certaine Points* (London, 1582).
     *Foure Sermons upon the Seven Chiefe Vertues or Principall Effectes of Faith* (London, 1582).

Gomersall, R., *The Levites Revenge* (London, 1628).

Gore, J., *Certaine Sermons Preached upon Severall Occasions* (London, 1636).

Greene, R., *A Quip for an Upstart Courtier* (London, 1592).

Granger, T., *Pauls Crowne of Re[j]oycing* (London, 1616).
     *A Familiar Exposition or Commentarie on Ecclesiastes* (London, 1621).

Harris, R., *Abners Funerall, or a Sermon Preached at the Funerall of . . . Sir Thomas Lucie* (London, 1641).

Heylyn, P., *The History of the Sabbath in Two Bookes* (London, 1636).

Heywood, J., *An Hundred Epigrammes* (London, 1550).

Hooker, T., *Foure Learned and Godly Treatises* (London, 1638).

I. D., *Salomon's Pest-House, or Tower-Royall* (London, 1636).

Jorden, E., *A Briefe Discourse of a Disease Called the Suffocation of the Mother* (London, 1603).

Kethe, W., *A Sermon Made at Blanford Foru[m]* (London, 1571).

Lambard, W., *Eirenarcha: or Of the Office of the Justices of the Peace* (London, 1599).

Ley, J., *Defensive Doubts, Hopes and Reasons for Refusal of the Oath Imposed by the Late Synod* (London, 1641).

Lupset, T., *A Treatise of Charitie* (London, 1533).

Lupton, D., *London and the Country Carbonadoed and Quartred into Severall Characters* (London, 1632).

Lupton, T., *A Dreame of the Devil and Dives* (London, 1615).

M. S., *Greevous Grones for the Poore* (London, 1621).

Mulcaster, R., *Positions wherein Those Primitive Circumstances Be Examined, which Are Necessarie for the Training Up of Children* (London, 1581).

N. L., *Politeuphuia: Wits Common Wealth* (London, 1598).

Nelson, T., *A Memorable Epitaph . . . for the Death of Sir Francis Walsingham* (London, 1590).

Nowell, A., *A Catechism: or, First Instruction and Learning of a Christian Religion* (London, 1571).

Oldmayne, T., *Gods Rebuke in Taking from Us . . . Sir E[dward] Lewkenor* (London, 1619).

Palfreyman, T., *A Myrrour or Cleare Glasse* (London, 1560).

Palmer, T., *An Essay of the Meanes How to Make Our Travailes, into Forraine Countries, the More Profitable and Honourable* (London, 1606).

Patrizi, F., *A Moral Methode of Civile Policie* (London, 1576).

Peele, G., *The Old Wives' Tale* (London, 1595).

Perkins, W., *A Sermon Preached in the Cathedrall Church in Norwich* (London, 1590).

*The Foundation of Christian Religion* (London, 1590).

*A Commentarie or Exposition, upon the Five First Chapters of the Epistle to the Galatians* (London, 1604).

*A Treatise of Mans Imaginations* (London, 1607).

Pliny, *The Historie of the World* (London, 1634).

Plot, R., *The Natural History of Stafford-Shire* (Oxford, 1686).

Porter, H., *The Pleasant History of the Two Angry Women of Abington* (London, 1599).

R. C., *An Olde Thrift Newly Revived* (London, 1612).

R. V., *A Commentarie of M. Iohn Calvine, upon the Epistle to the Colossians* (London 1581).

Randolph, T., *Poems with the Muses Looking-Glasse and Amyntas* (Oxford, 1638).

Reeve, E., *The Communion Booke Catechisme Expounded* (London, 1635).

Rogers, F., *A Sermon of Love* (London, 1613).

*A Commentary upon the Whole Booke of Judges* (London, 1615).

Saltmarsh, J., *The Practice of Policie in a Christian Life* (London, 1639).

Sander, N., *A Briefe Treatise of Usurie* (London, 1568).

Sanderson, R., *Two Sermons Preached at Paules-Crosse* (London, 1628).

*XXXV Sermons*, 7th ed. (London, 1681).

Scoloker, A., *A Godly Dysputacion between a Christen Shoemaker and a Popysh Parson* (London, 1548).

Smith, T., *De Republica Anglorum: The Maner of Governement or Policie of the Realme of England* (London, 1583).

Stubbes, P., *Two Wunderfull and Rare Examples, of the Undeferred and Present Approaching Judgement of the Lord Our God* (London, 1581).

T. W., *A Short, yet Sound Commentarie; Written on that Woorthie Worke Called; the Proverbes of Salomon* (London, 1589).

Taverner, R., *Erasmus' Proverbes* (London, 1545).

Taylor, T., *Christ Revealed: or The Old Testament Explained: A Treatise of the Types and Shadowes of Our Saviour Contained throughout the Whole Scripture* (London, 1635).

*An Answer to that Question: How Farre It Is Lawfull to Flee in the Time of the Plague* (London, 1636).

Vaughan, W., *The Golden Grove* (London, 1608).

Vincent, P., *The Lamentations of Germany* (London, 1638).

Ward, R., *Theologicall Questions, Dogmaticall Observations, and Evangelicall Essays* (London, 1640).

Webbe, G., *Arraignment of an Unruly Tongue* (London, 1619).

Wilson, T., *The Art of Rhetoricke for the Use of All Such as Are Studious of Eloquence* (London, 1553).

Wither, G., *A Collection of Emblemes, Ancient and Moderne* (London, 1635).

## Editions of Manuscripts and Contemporary Printed Works and Calendars

Anon., *Practical Wisdom; or The Manual of Life* (London, 1824).

'A Description of Cleveland; in a Letter Addressed by H.R. to Sir Thomas Chaloner', *Topographer and Genealogist*, II (1853), 403–32.

Axton, R. (ed.), *Three Rastell Plays* (Woodbridge, 1979).

Ayre, J. (ed.), The Catechism of Thomas Becon . . . with Other Pieces Written by Him, Parker Society (Cambridge, 1844).

Bamford, F. (ed.), *A Royalist's Notebook: The Commonplace Book of Sir John Oglander Kt. of Nunwell* (London, 1936).

Barmby, J. (ed.), Churchwardens' Accounts of Pittington and Other Parishes in the Diocese of Durham from 1580 to 1700, Surtees Society, 84 (Durham, 1888).

Bates, E. H. (ed.), Quarter Sessions Records for the County of Somerset: Vol. I, James I, 1607–1625, Somerset Record Society, 23 (London, 1907).

Bates, E. H. (ed.), Quarter Sessions Records for the County of Somerset: Vol. II, Charles I, 1625–1639, Somerset Record Society, 24 (London, 1908).

Bateson, M. (ed.), *Records of the Borough of Leicester . . . 1509–1603* (Cambridge, 1905).

Bettey, J. (ed.), Wiltshire Farming in the Seventeenth Century, Wiltshire Records Society, 57 (Trowbridge, 2005).

Birley, R. N. (ed.), The Registers of Kendal, III–IV, Cumberland and Westmorland Parish Register Society, 36 (Penrith, 1952).

Brewer, J. S. et al. (eds.), *Letters and Papers, Foreign and Domestic, of Henry VIII*, 21 vols. (London, 1862–1910).

Brown, W. (ed.), Yorkshire Star Chamber Proceedings, III, YASRS, 51 (Leeds, 1914).

Brodie, D. M. (ed.), *The Tree of Commonwealth: A Treatise Written by Edmund Dudley* (Cambridge, 1948).

Bund, J. W. (ed.), Calendar of the Quarter Sessions Papers, Vol. I: 1591–1643, Worcestershire Historical Society, 22 (Worcester, 1900).

Burne, S. A. H. (ed.), *The Staffordshire Quarter Sessions Rolls, II: 1590–1593, Collections for a History of Staffordshire* (Kendal, 1932).

*Calendar of the Patent Rolls Preserved in the Public Record Office: Elizabeth I*, 9 vols. (London, 1939–86).

The Staffordshire Quarter Sessions Rolls, III: 1594–97, Collections for a History of Staffordshire (Kendal, 1933).

Carleton, G., 'Life of Bernard Gilpin', in C. Wordsworth (ed.), *Ecclesiastical Biography*, 6 vols. (London, 1818), IV, 158.

Clay, J. W. (ed.), Yorkshire Church Notes, 1619–1631: by Roger Dodsworth, YASRS, 34 (no place of publication, 1904).

Cockburn, J. S. (ed.), *Calendar of Assize Records: Essex Indictments, Elizabeth I* (London, 1978).

Cooper, J. P. (ed.), Wentworth Papers, 1597–1628, Camden Society, 4th ser., 12 (1973).

Cotton, W. (ed.), *An Elizabethan Guild of the City of Exeter* (Exeter, 1873).

Cowper, J. M. (ed.), Henry Brinklow's Complaint of Roderick Mors . . . and the Lamentacyon of a Christen against the Citye of London, EETS, 22 (London, 1874), 90.

(ed.), The Select Works of Robert Crowley, EETS, 15 (London, 1872).

Cox, J. C. (ed.), The Parish Registers of England (London, 1910).

Cox, J. C. and Markham, C. A. (eds.), The Records of the Borough of Northampton, 2 vols. (Northampton, 1898).

Cunningham, W. (ed.), 'Common Rights at Cottenham and Stretham in Cambridgeshire', Camden Miscellany, 2nd ser., 12 (1910), 173–289.

Cust, R. (ed.), The Papers of Sir Richard Grosvenor, 1st Baronet (1585–1645), Lancashire and Cheshire Record Society, 84 (1996).

Davids, T. W. (ed.), Annals of Evangelical Nonconformity in the County of Essex (London, 1853).

de Sola Pinto, V. and Rodway, A. E. (eds.), The Common Muse: Popular British Ballad Poetry from the 15th to the 20th Century (London, 1957).

Dennett, J. (ed.), Beverley Borough Records, 1575–1821, YASRS, 84 (Wakefield, 1933).

Dickens, A. G. (ed.), Tudor Treatises, YASRS, 75 (Wakefield, 1959).

Doree, S. G. (ed.), The Parish Register and Tithing Book of Thomas Hassall of Amwell, Hertfordshire Record Society, 5 (Cambridge, 1989).

Emmison, F. G., Early Essex Town Meetings (Chichester, 1970).

Falvey, H. and Hindle, S. (eds.), 'This Little Commonwealth': Layston Parish Memorandum Book, 1607–c.1650 and 1704–1747, Hertfordshire Record Society, 19 (Hertford, 2003).

Ferguson, R. S. (ed.), Miscellany Accounts of the Diocese of Carlile (London, 1877).

(ed.), A Boke Off Recorde or Register of the Burgh of Kirkby Kendal (Carlisle, 1892).

Ferguson, R. S. and Nanson, W. (eds.), Some Municipal Records of the City of Carlisle, TW&WA&AS, 4 (Carlisle, 1887).

Farington, S. M. (ed.), The Farington Papers, Chetham Society, 39 (Manchester, 1856).

Fletcher, W. G. D., 'Philip Kinder's Ms. "Historie of Darbyshire"', Reliquary, 23 (1882–3).

Forbes, A. P. (ed.), Winthrop Papers, 5 vols. (Boston, MA, 1929–47).

Furnivall, F. J. (ed.), Ballads from Manuscripts (London, 1868–72).

(ed.), Harrison's Description of England (London, 1877).

Fussell, G. E. (ed.), Robert Loder's Farm Accounts, 1610–1620, Camden Society, 3rd ser., 53 (London, 1936).

Gardiner, S. R. (ed.), Reports of Cases in the Courts of Star Chamber and High Commission, Camden Society, 2nd ser., 39 (London, 1886).

Gibson, T. E. (ed.), Crosby Records: A Chapter of Lancashire Recusancy, Chetham Society, 2nd ser., 12 (Manchester, 1887).

Godfrey, W. H. (ed.), The Book of John Rowe, Steward of the Manors of Lord Bergavenny, 1597–1622, Sussex Records Society, 34 (Cambridge, 1928).

Grainger, F. and Collingwood, W. G. (eds.), Register and Records of Holm Cultram (Kendal, 1929).

Gray, T. (ed.), The Lost Chronicle of Barnstaple, 1586–1611 (Exeter, 1998).

Harvest Failure in Cornwall and Devon: The Books of Orders and the Corn Surveys of 1623 and 1630–1, Sources of Cornish History, 1 (Plymouth, 1992).

Guilding, J. M. (ed.), *Reading Records*, 4 vols. (London, 1895).

Hall, E., *Hall's Chronicle: Containing the History of England during the Reign of Henry the Fourth and Succeeding Monarchs, to the End of the Reign of Henry the Eighth* (London, [1548]1809).

Halliwell, J. O. (ed.), *The Marriage of Wit and Wisdom, and Ancient Interlude, to which Are Added Illustrations of Shakespeare and the Early English Drama* (London, 1846).

Hamilton, G. H. (ed.), Books of Examinations and Depositions, 1570–1594, Southampton Record Society, 16 (Southampton, 1914).

Hardy, W. J. (ed.), *Hertford County Records: Sessions Rolls 1581 to 1698* (Hertford, 1905).

Harland, J. (ed.), Court Leet Records of the Manor of Manchester, A.D. 1586–1602, Chetham Society, 55 (Manchester, 1865).

*Three Lancashire Documents of the Fourteenth and Fifteenth Centuries*, Chetham Society, 74 (Manchester, 1868).

Hassall, W. O. (ed.), Wheatley Records, 956–1956, Oxfordshire Records Society, 37 (Banbury, 1956).

Headlam, A. W. (ed.), *The Parish Registers of St Oswald's, Durham* (Durham, 1891).

Historical Manuscripts Commission, 4th Report, X, Shrewsbury MSS.

Historical Manuscripts Commission, 14th Report, Appendix VIII, Lincoln MSS, Bury St Edmunds MSS.

Historical Manuscripts Commission, Montagu MSS.

Historical Manuscripts Commission, Salisbury MSS.

Historical Manuscripts Commission, Kenyon MSS.

Historical Manuscripts Commission, Various Collections.

Howard Cunnington, B. (ed.), *Records of the County of Wiltshire: Being Extracts from the Quarter Sessions Great Rolls from the Seventeenth Century* (Devizes, 1932).

Jarman, E. K. M. (ed.), Justice and Conciliation in a Tudor Church Court: Depositions from EDC 2/6, Deposition Book of the Consistory Court of Chester, September 1558–March 1559, Record Society of Lancashire and Cheshire, 146 (Bristol, 2012).

Johnstone, H. (ed.), Churchwardens' Presentments (17th Century): The Archdeaconry of Chichester, Sussex Record Society, 49 (Cambridge, 1947).

Kempe, A. J. (ed.), *The Loseley Manuscripts* (London, 1836).

Kingsford, C. L. (ed.), *A Survey of London by John Stow*, 2 vols. (Oxford, 1908).

Le Hardy, W. (ed.), *Calendar to the Sessions Books and Sessions Minute Books and Other Sessions Records of the County of Hertford, Vol. V: 1619–1657* (Hertford, 1928).

Lister, J. (ed.), West Riding Sessions Rolls, 1597/8–1602, YASRS, 3 (Worksop, 1888).

Longstaffe, W. H. D. (ed.), The Acts of the High Commission within the Diocese of Durham, Surtees Society, 34 (Durham, 1858).

Maclean, J. (ed.), *The Berkeley Manuscripts*, 3 vols. (Gloucester, 1885).

Mann, F. O. (ed.), *The Works of Thomas Deloney* (Oxford, 1912).

McKerrow, R. B. (ed.), *The Works of Thomas Nashe* (Oxford, 1966).

Melling, E. (ed.), *Kentish Sources: IV: The Poor* (Maidstone, 1964).

Minet, W., 'A Steward's Accounts at Hadham Hall, 1628–1629', Transactions of the Essex Archaeological Society, 15, 2 (1918), 138–48.

Palmer, C. J. (ed.), *The History of Great Yarmouth by Henry Manship Esq., Temp. Queen Elizabeth* (London, 1854).

Payne Collier, J. (ed.), *A Book of Roxburghe Ballads* (London, 1847).

Peyton, S. A. (ed.), The Churchwardens' Presentments in the Oxfordshire Peculiars of Dorchester, Thame and Banbury, Oxfordshire Record Society, 10 (Oxford 1928).

Pollard, A. (ed.), *Works of Robert Herrick*, 2 vols. (London, 1891).

Purvis, J. S. (ed.), Select XVI Century Causes in Tithe, YASRS, 64 (York, 1947). *Tudor Parish Documents of the Diocese of York* (Cambridge, 1948).

Raine, A. (ed.), York Civic Records, IV, YASRS, 98, 103, 106, 108, 110, 112, 115, 119 (York, 1939–53).

Raine, J. (ed.), The Injunctions and Other Ecclesiastical Proceedings of Richard Barnes, Bishop of Durham, from 1575 to 1587, Surtees Society, 21 (Durham, 1850).

Raines, F. R. (ed.), The Journal of Nicholas Assheton, Chetham Society, 14 (Manchester, 1848).

Richardson, M. A. (ed.), *Reprints of Rare Tracts and Imprints of Antient Manuscripts &c., Chiefly Illustrative of the History of the Northern Counties*, 3 vols. (Newcastle, 1847–9).

Rosetti, W. M. and Oswald, E. (eds.), Queene Elizabeth's Academy, EETS, 8 (London, 1869).

Rye, W. (ed.), *Depositions Taken before the Mayor and Aldermen of Norwich, 1549–1567; Extracts from the Court Books of the City of Norwich, 1666–1688* (Norwich, 1905).

Rye, W. B. (ed.), *England as Seen by Foreigners in the Days of Elizabeth I and James I* (London, 1865).

Sheils, W. J. (ed.), Archbishop Grindal's Visitation, 1575: Comperta at Detecta Book, Borthwick Texts and Calendars, 4 (York, 1977).

Simpson, E. M. and Potter, G. R. (eds.), *The Sermons of John Donne*, 10 vols. (Berkeley, CA, 1953).

Smith, J. E. (ed.), *A Catalogue of Westminster Records* (London, 1900).

Somerset, J. A. B., *Records of Early English Drama: Shropshire* (Toronto, 1994).

Stevenson, W. H. et al. (eds.), *Records of the Borough of Nottingham*, 7 vols. (London, 1885–1947).

Stone, E. D. and Cozens-Hardy, B. (eds.), Norwich Consistory Court Depositions, 1499–1512 and 1518–1530, Norfolk Record Society, 10 (Norwich, 1938).

Strype, J. (ed.), *The Life and Acts of Matthew Parker*, 3 vols. (Oxford, 1821).

Tawney, R. H. and Power, E. (eds.), *Tudor Economic Documents: Being Select Documents Illustrating the Economic and Social History of Tudor England* (London, 1924).

Thirsk, J. and Cooper, J. P. (eds.), *Seventeenth-Century Economic Documents* (Oxford, 1972).

Toulin Smith, L. (ed.), The Maire of Bristowe Is Calendar, Camden Society, 2nd ser., 5 (London, 1872).

Travers, A. (ed.), Robert Furse: A Devon Family Memoir of 1593, Devon and Cornwall Record Society, new ser., 53 (Exeter, 2012).

Tusser, T., *Five Hundred Points of Good Husbandry* (Oxford, 1984).

Twemlow, J. A. (ed.), *Liverpool Town Books*, 2 vols. (London, 1935).

Usher, R. G. (ed.), The Presbyterian Movement in the Reign of Queen Elizabeth, Camden Society, 3rd ser., 8 (London, 1905).

Webb, J. (ed.), Poor Relief in Elizabeth Ipswich, Suffolk Record Society, 9 (Ipswich, 1966).

Wheatley, H. B. (ed.), Merlin, or The Early History of King Arthur, EETS, 10, 21, 36, 112 (London, 1856–99).

Wilkinson, P. M. (ed.), Chichester Archdeaconry Depositions, 1603–1608, Sussex Record Society, 97 (Lewes, 2017), 206–8.

Williams, J. F. (ed.), Bishop Redman's Visitation, 1597, Norfolk Record Society, 18 (Norwich, 1946).

## Secondary Works

Amussen, S. D., *An Ordered Society: Gender and Class in Early Modern England* (London, 1988).

'"Being Stirred to Much Unquietnesss"': Violence and Domestic Violence in Early Modern England', *Journal of Women's History*, 6, 2 (1994), 70–89.

Amussen, S. D. and Underdown, D. E., *Gender, Culture and Politics in England, 1560–1640: Turning the World Upside Down* (London, 2017).

Appleby, A. B., 'Disease or Famine? Mortality in Cumberland and Westmorland, 1580–1640', Economic History Review, 2nd ser., 26, 3 (1973), 403–32.

*Famine in Tudor and Stuart England* (Liverpool, 1978).

Archer, I. W., *The Pursuit of Stability: Social Relations in Elizabethan London* (Cambridge, 1991).

'The Charity of Early Modern Londoners', TRHS, 6th ser., 12 (2002), 223–44.

Baker, P. and Merry, M., '"The Pore Lost and Good Frend and the Parish a Good Neighbour"': The Lives of the Poor and Their Supporters in London's Eastern Suburb, c. 1583–c.1679', in M. Davies and J. A. Galloway (eds.), *London and Beyond: Essays in Honour of Derek Keene* (London, 2012), 155–80.

Baldwin, E. M. S., 'Entertainments in East Cheshire before 1642', *Transactions of the Lancashire and Cheshire Antiquarian Society*, 89 (1993), 114–28.

Barnes, H., 'Visitations of the Plague in Cumberland and Westmorland', TC&WA&AS, 1st ser., 11 (1889), 158–86.

Barnes, T. G., 'County Politics and a Puritan Cause Celebre: Somerset Churchales, 1633', TRHS, 5th ser., 9 (1959), 103–22.

Barton, T., 'Notices of the Town and Parish of Watton', *Norfolk Archaeology*, 3 (1852), 394–414.

Battley, S. M., 'Elite and Community: The Mayors of Sixteenth-Century King's Lynn', PhD, State University of New York (1981).

Bedells, J., 'The Gentry of Huntingdonshire', *Local Population Studies*, 44 (1990), 30–40.

Beier, A. L., 'Vagrants and the Social Order in Elizabethan England', *P&P*, 64 (1974), 3–29.

*Masterless Men: The Vagrancy Problem in England, 1560–1640* (London, 1985).

Benbow, R. M., 'The Court of Aldermen and the Assizes: The Policy of Price Control in Elizabethan London', *Guildhall Studies in London History*, 4, 3 (1980), 93–118.

Berlin, M., 'Reordering Rituals: Ceremony and the Parish, 1520–1640', in P. Griffiths and M. S. R. Jenner (eds.), *Londinopolis: Essays in the Cultural and Social History of Early Modern London* (Manchester, 2000), 47–66.

Bernard, G. W., *War, Taxation and Rebellion in Early Tudor England: Henry VIII, Thomas Wolsey and the Amicable Grant of 1525* (Hassocks, 1986).

Bishop, J., 'Speech and Sociability: The Regulation of Language in the Livery Companies of Early Modern London', in J. Colson and A. van Steensel (eds.), *Cities and Solidarities: Urban Communities in Pre-modern Europe* (London, 2017), 208–24.

Blanton, R. E. and Farger, L. F., *How Humans Cooperate: Confronting the Challenges of Collective Action* (Boulder, CO, 2016).

Blomley, N., 'Making Private Property: Enclosure, Common Right and the Work of Hedges', *Rural History*, 18, 1 (2001), 1–21.

Bossy, J., 'Some Elementary Forms of Durkheim', *P&P*, 95, 1 (1982), 3–18.

*Christianity in the West, 1400–1700* (Oxford, 1985).

Boulton, J., *Neighbourhood and Society: A London Suburb in the Seventeenth Century* (Cambridge, 1987).

'Neighbourhood Migration in Early Modern London', in P. Clark and D. Souden (eds.), *Migration and Society in Early Modern England* (London, 1987), 107–49.

Bourdieu, P., *Outline of a Theory of Practice* (Cambridge, 1977).

Breen, T. H. and Foster, S., 'The Puritans' Greatest Achievement: A Study of Social Cohesion in Seventeenth-Century Massachusetts', *Journal of American History*, 60, 1 (1973), 5–22.

Braddick, M. J., *State Formation in Early Modern England, c.1550–1700* (Cambridge, 2000).

Bridenbaugh, C., *Vexed and Troubled Englishmen, 1590–1642* (Oxford, 1968).

Brigden, S., 'Religion and Social Obligation in Early Sixteenth Century London', *P&P*, 103 (1984), 67–112.

Brison, K. J., *Just Talk: Gossip, Meetings and Power in a Papua New Guinea Village* (Berkeley, CA, 1992).

Brodie, N. D., '"An Ancient Box": The Queen v. Robert Wortley and John Allen (1846); or, A History of the English Parochial Poor Box, c.1547', in A. M. Scott (ed.), *Experiences of Charity, 1250–1650* (Aldershot, 2015), 215–38.

Brooks, C., *Pettyfoggers and Vipers of the Commonwealth: The 'Lower Branch' of the Legal Profession in Early Modern England* (Cambridge, 1986).

Bruce, J., 'Extracts from the Accounts of the Churchwardens of Minchinhampton in the County of Gloucester', *Archaeologia*, 35, 2 (1854), 409–52.

Buckley, A., 'Neighbourliness: Myth and History', *Oral History*, 11, 1 (1983), 44–51.

Burne, C., *A Handbook of Folklore* (London, 1914).

Bushaway, B., *By Rite: Custom, Ceremony and Community in England, 1700–1800* (London, 1982).

Butterfield, R. P., *Monastery and Manor: The History of Crondall* (Farnham, 1948).

Campbell, M., *The English Yeoman under Elizabeth and the Early Stuarts* (New Haven, CT, 1942).

Capp, B., *When Gossips Meet: Women, Family and Neighbourhood in Early Modern England* (Oxford, 2003).

Chartres, J., 'The Marketing of Agricultural Produce, 1640–1750', in J. Chartres (ed.), *Agricultural Markets and Trade, 1500–1750* (Cambridge, 1990), 160–255.

Chaytor, M., 'Household and Kinship: Ryton in the Late Sixteenth and Early Seventeenth Centuries', *History Workshop Journal*, 10, 1 (1980), 25–60.

Clark, G. and Hamilton, G., 'Survival of the Richest: The Malthusian Mechanism in Pre-industrial England', *Journal of Economic History*, 66, 3 (2006), 707–36.

Clark, M. A., 'Kendal: The Protestant Exception', TC&WA&AS, 2nd ser., 95 (1996), 137–52.

Clark, P., *The English Alehouse: A Social History* (London, 1983).

'Migrants in the City: The Process of Social Adaptation in English Towns, 1500–1800', in P. Clark and D. Souden (eds.), *Migration and Society in Early Modern England* (London, 1987), 267–91.

Clarke, B., 'Norfolk License to Beg: An Unpublished Collection', *Norfolk Archaeology*, 35 (1970–3), 327–34.

Clay, C. G. A., *Economic Expansion and Social Change: England, 1500–1700*, 2 vols. (Cambridge, 1984).

Clutterbuck, F. H., 'State Papers Relating to the Cloth Trade, 1622', Transactions of the Bristol and Gloucestershire Archaeological Society, 5 (1880–1), 154–62.

Collinson, P., 'A Comment Concerning the Name Puritan', *Journal of Ecclesiastical History*, 31 (1980), 483–8.

*The Religion of Protestants: The Church in English Society, 1559–1625* (Oxford, 1982).

*The Birthpangs of Protestant England: Religious and Cultural Change in the Sixteenth and Seventeenth Centuries* (Basingstoke, 1988).

'The Cohabitation of the Faithful with the Unfaithful', in O. P. Grell, J. I. Israel and N. Tyacke (eds.), *From Persecution to Toleration* (Oxford, 1991), 51–76.

'Antipuritanism', in J. Coffey and P. C. H. Lim (eds.), *The Cambridge Companion to Puritanism* (Cambridge, 2008), 19–33.

Cooper, E., *Muker: The Story of a Yorkshire Parish* (Clapham, 1948).

Coster, W., 'A Microcosm of Community: Burial, Space and Society in Chester, 1598 to 1633', in W. Coster and A. Spicer (eds.), *Sacred Space in Early Modern Europe* (Cambridge, 2005), 124–43.

Creighton, C., *History of Epidemics in Britain*, 2 vols. (Cambridge, 1891–4).
Cressy, D., 'Occupations, Migration and Literacy in East London, 1580–1640', *Local Population Studies*, 5 (1970), 53–60.
    'Kinship and Kin Interaction in Early Modern England', *P&P*, 113 (1986), 38–69.
    *Birth, Marriage and Death: Ritual, Religion and the Life-Cycle in Tudor and Stuart England* (Oxford, 1997).
Cross, C., *The Puritan Earl: The Life of Henry Hastings, Third Earl of Huntington, 1536–1595* (London, 1966).
Cunliffe Shaw, R., *History of Kirkham in Amounderness* (Preston, 1949).
Curtis, T. C., 'Quarter Sessions Appearances and Their Background: A Seventeenth-Century Regional Study', in J. S. Cockburn (ed.), *Crime in England, 1550–1800* (Princeton, NJ, 1977), 135–54.
Darnton, R., *The Great Cat Massacre and Other Episodes in French Cultural History* (New York, 1984).
Dauber, N., *State and Commonwealth: The Theory of the State in Early Modern England, 1549–1640* (Princeton, NJ, 2016).
DeWindt, A. R., 'Witchcraft and Conflicting Visions of the Ideal Village Community', *JBS*, 34, 4 (1995), 31–66.
Dobson, R. B., *The Peasants' Revolt of 1381* (Basingstoke, 1970).
Douglas, M., *Purity and Danger: An Analysis of the Concept of Pollution and Taboo* (London, 1966).
Duffy, E., 'The Godly and the Multitude in Stuart England', *The Seventeenth Century*, 1, 1 (1986), 31–55.
    *The Voices of Morebath: Reformation and Rebellion in an English Village* (New Haven, CT, 2001).
Dumolyn, J., '"I Thought of It at Work, in Ostend": Urban Artisan Labour and Guild Ideology in the Later Medieval Low Countries', *International Review of Social History*, 62, 3 (2017), 389–419.
Durkheim, E., *The Elementary Forms of Religious Life* ([1912 Eng. trans.] Oxford, 2001).
Dyer, A. D., *The City of Worcester in the Sixteenth Century* (Leicester, 1973).
Dymond, D., 'A Lost Social Institution: The Camping Close', *Rural History*, 1 (1990), 165–91.
Earle, P., *The Making of the English Middle Class: Business, Society and Family Life in London, 1660–1730* (London, 1989).
Eastwood, J., *History of the Parish of Ecclesfield* (London, 1862).
Eckstein, N. A., *The District of the Green Dragon: Neighbourhood Life and Social Change in Renaissance Florence* (Florence, 1995).
Edwards, P., 'The Decline of the Small Farmer: The Case of Rushock, Worcestershire', *Midland History*, 21 (1996), 73–100.
Emmison, F. G., *Tudor Secretary: Sir William Petre at Court and Home* (London, 1961).
    *Elizabethan Life: Morals and the Church Courts* (Chelmsford, 1973).
Esser, R., 'They Obey All Magistrates and All Good Laws . . . and We Thinke Our Cittie Happie to Enjoye Them": Migrants and Urban Stability in Early Modern English Towns', *Urban History*, 34 (2007), 64–75.

Everitt, A., 'The Marketing of Agricultural Produce, 1500–1640', in J. Chartres (ed.), *Agricultural Markets and Trade, 1500–1750* (Cambridge, 1990).

Fafchamps, M., 'Solidarity Networks in Preindustrial Societies: Rational Peasants with a Moral Economy', *Economic Development and Cultural Change*, 41, 1 (1992), 147–74.

Farr, M. W., 'Midsummer Riding: A Seventeenth-Century Custom of the Millers of Warwick', *Warwickshire History*, 7, 3 (1988), 80–2.

Fenster, T. and Lord Smail, D. (eds.), *Fama: The Politics of Talk and Reputation in Medieval Europe* (Ithaca, NY, 2003).

Fitter, C., *Radical Shakespeare: Politics and Stagecraft in the Early Career* (London, 2012).

'"As Full of Grief as Age": Protesting against the Poor Law in *King Lear*', in C. Fitter (ed.), *Shakespeare and the Politics of Commoners: Digesting the New Social History* (Oxford, 2017), 217–35.

Flather, A. J., *Gender and Space in Early Modern England* (Woodbridge, 2007).

'Space, Place and Gender: The Sexual and Spatial Division of Labor in the Early Modern Household', *History and Theory*, 52 (2013), 344–60.

Fletcher, A., *A County Community in Peace and War: Sussex, 1603–1660* (London, 1975).

Fox, A., 'Ballads, Libels and Popular Ridicule in Jacobean England', *P&P*, 145 (1994), 47–83.

'Religious Satire in English Towns, 1570–1640', in P. Collinson and J. Craig (eds.), *The Reformation in English Towns, 1500–1640* (Basingstoke, 1998), 221–40.

*Oral and Literate Cultures in England, 1500–1700* (Oxford, 2000).

Fyler Townsend, G., *The Town and Borough of Leominster* (Leominster, n.d.).

Garrioch, D., *Neighbourhood and Community in Paris, 1740–1790* (Cambridge, 1986).

Garrioch, D. and Peel, M., 'The Social History of Urban Neighbourhoods', *Journal of Urban History*, 32, 5 (2006), 663–76.

Gaskill, M., 'Witchcraft and Power in Early Modern England: The Case of Margaret Moore', in J. Kermode and G. Walker (eds.), *Women, Crime and the Courts in Early Modern England* (London, 1994), 125–45.

'Witchcraft and Neighbourliness in Early Modern England', in S. Hindle, A. Shepard and J. Walter (eds.), *Remaking English Society: Social Relations and Social Change in Early Modern England* (Woodbridge, 2013), 211–32.

'Little Commonwealths II: Communities', in K. E. Wrightson (ed.), *A Social History of England, 1500–1750* (Cambridge, 2017), 84–104.

Giddens, A., *Durkheim* (London, 1978).

Gilbanks, W. F., 'The Oldest Register Book of the Parish of Holm Cultram, Cumberland', TC&WA&AS, 1st ser., 10 (1889), 176–85.

Goring, J., 'The Fellowship of the Twelve in Elizabethan Lewes', *Sussex Archaeological Collections*, 119 (1981), 157–72.

Gorski, P. S., *The Disciplinary Revolution: Calvinism and the Rise of the State in Early Modern Europe* (Chicago, IL, 2003).

Gowing, L., *Domestic Dangers: Women, Words and Sex in Early Modern London* (Oxford, 1996).

'"The Freedom of the Streets": Women and Social Space, 1560–1640', in P. Griffiths and M. S. R. Jenner (eds.), *Londinopolis: Essays in the Cultural and Social History of Early Modern London* (Manchester, 2000), 130–51.

Gregory, A., 'Witchcraft, Politics and "Good Neighbourhood" in Early Seventeenth-Century Rye', *P&P*, 133 (1991), 31–66.

Griffiths, P., Landers, J., Pelling, M. and Tyson, R., 'Population and Disease, Estrangement and Belonging, 1540–1700', in P. Clark (ed.), *The Cambridge Urban History of Britain: Vol. 2, 1540–1840* (Cambridge, 2000), 195–233.

Guest, J., *Historic Notices of Rotheram: Eccelesiastical, Collegiate and Civil* (Worksop, 1879).

Haigh, C., 'The Church of England, the Catholics and the People', in C. Haigh (ed.), *The Reign of Elizabeth I* (Basingstoke, 1984), 195–220.

'Communion and Community: Exclusion from Communion in Post-Reformation England', *Journal of Ecclesiastical History*, 51 (2000), 721–40.

'The Character of an Anti Puritan', *Sixteenth Century Journal*, 35, 3 (2004), 671–88.

Hailwood, M., 'Alehouses, Popular Politics and Plebeian Agency in Early Modern England', in F. Williamson (ed.), *Locating Agency: Space, Power and Popular Politics* (Newcastle, 2010), 51–76.

'Sociability, Work and Labouring Identity in Seventeenth-Century England', *Cultural and Social History*, 8, 1 (2011), 9–29.

'The Honest Tradesman's Honour: Occupational and Social Identity in Early Modern England', *TRHS*, 6th ser., 24 (2014), 79–103.

*Alehouses and Good Fellowship in Early Modern England* (Woodbridge, 2014).

Hallam, E. A., 'Turning the Hourglass: Gender Relations at the Deathbed in Early Modern Canterbury', *Mortality*, 1, 1 (1996), 61–82.

Harding, S., 'Women and Words in a Spanish Village', in R. R. Reiter (ed.), *Toward an Anthropology of Women* (New York, 1975), 283–308.

Hart, A. T., *The Man in the Pew, 1558–1640* (London, 1966).

Harrison, C., 'Manor Courts and the Governance of Tudor England', in C. W. Brooks and M. Lobban (eds.), *Communities and Courts in Britain, 1150–1900* (London, 1997), 43–60.

Heal, F., *Hospitality in Early Modern England* (Oxford, 1990).

Healey, J., 'The Northern Manor and the Politics of Neighbourhood: Dilston, Northumberland, 1558–1640', *Northern History*, 51, 2 (2014), 221–41.

*The First Century of Welfare: Poverty and Poor Relief in Lancashire, 1620–1730* (Woodbridge, 2014).

Heppa, C., 'Harry Cox and His Friends: Song Transmission in an East Norfolk Singing Community, c. 1896–1960', *Folk Music Journal*, 8, 5 (2005), 569–93.

Herrmann, R. B., 'The "Tragicall Historie": Cannibalism and Abundance in Colonial Jamestown', *William and Mary Quarterly*, 68, 1 (2011), 47–74.

Hindle, S., 'Exclusion Crises: Poverty, Migration and Parochial Responsibility in English Rural Communities, c.1560–1660', *Rural History*, 7, 2 (1996), 125–49.

'Power, Poor Relief and Social Relations in Holland Fen, c.1600–1800', *Historical Journal*, 41, 1 (1998), 67–96.

'The Problem of Pauper Marriage in Seventeenth-Century England', TRHS, 6th ser., 8 (1998), 71–89.

*The State and Social Change in England, 1550–1640* (Basingstoke, 2000).

'A Sense of Place? Becoming and Belonging in the Rural Parish, 1550–1650', in A. Shepard and P. Withington (eds.), *Communities in Early Modern England: Networks, Place, Rhetoric* (Manchester, 2000), 96–114.

'Exhortation and Entitlement: Negotiating Inequality in English Rural Communities, 1550–1650' in M. J. Braddick and J. Walter (eds.), *Negotiating Power in Early Modern Society: Order, Hierarchy and Subordination in Britain and Ireland* (Cambridge, 2001), 102–22.

'Dearth, Fasting and Alms: The Campaign for General Hospitality in Late Elizabethan England', *P&P*, 172 (2001), 44–86.

*On the Parish? The Micro-politics of Poor Relief in Rural England, c. 1550–1750* (Oxford, 2004).

'Destitution, Liminality and Belonging: The Church Porch and the Politics of Settlement in English Rural Communities, c.1590–1660', in C. Dyer (ed.), *The Self-Contained Village? The Social History of English Rural Communities, 1250–1900* (Hertford, 2006), 46–71.

'Beating the Bounds of the Parish: Order, Memory and Identity in the English Local Community, c.1500–1700', in M. Halvorson and K. Spierling (eds.), *Defining Community in Early Modern Europe* (Aldershot, 2008), 205–27.

'Self-Image and Public Image in the Career of a Jacobean Magistrate: Sir John Newdigate in the Court of Star Chamber', in M. J. Braddick and P. Withington (eds.), *Popular Culture and Political Agency in Early Modern England: Essays in Honour of John Walter* (Woodbridge, 2017), 123–44.

Hipkin, S., 'The Worlds of Daniel Langdon: Public Office and Private Enterprise in the Romney Marsh Region in the Early Eighteenth Century', in A. Long, S. Hipkin and H. Clarke (eds.), *Romney Marsh: Coastal and Landscape Change through the Ages* (Oxford, 2002).

'The Structure, Development, and Politics of the Kent Grain Trade, 1552–1647', *EcHR*, 2nd ser., 61 (2008), 106–19.

Hitchcock, J., 'Religious Conflict at Mapperton, 1597–99', *Proceedings of the Dorset Natural History and Archaeological Society*, 89 (1968), 227–30.

'A Decree of the High Commission, 1596', Transactions of the Bristol and Gloucestershire Archaeological Society, 88 (1969), 216–17.

Holford, M. L., '*Pro Patriotis*: "Country", "Countrymen" and Local Solidarities in Late Medieval England', *Parergon*, 23, 1 (2006) 47–70.

Holmes, C., 'The County Community in Stuart Historiography', *JBS*, 19, 2 (1980), 45–73.

Hoskins, W. G., *The Midland Peasant: The Economic and Social History of a Leicestershire Village* (London, 1957).

Houlbrooke, R. A., 'Women's Social Life and Common Action in England from the Fifteenth Century to the Eve of the Civil War', *Continuity and Change*, 1, 2 (1986), 171–89.

Hoyle, R., 'Famine as Agricultural Catastrophe: The Crisis of 1622–3 in East Lancashire', *Economic History Review*, 2nd ser., 63 (2010), 974–1002.

Hudleston, N. F., 'Elizabethan Paines Laid at Hutton John', *TC&WAAS*, 2nd ser., 69 (1969), 115–28.

Hudson, W., 'Assessment of the Hundred of Forehoe in 1621: A Sidelight on the Difficulties of National Taxation', *Norfolk Archaeology*, 21, 3 (1922), 285–309

Hughes, J., 'The Plague in Carlisle, 1597/8', TC&WA&AS, 2nd ser., 71 (1971), 52–63.

Hughes, D. O., 'Kinmen and Neighbours in Medieval Genoa', in H. A. Miskimin, D. Herlihy and A. L. Udovitch (eds.), *The Medieval City* (New Haven, CT, 1977), 95–111.

Hunt, A., 'The Lord's Supper in Early Modern England', *P&P*, 161 (1998), 39–83.

Hunt, W., *The Puritan Moment: The Coming of Revolution to an English County* (Cambridge, MA, 1983).

Hunter, J., *Hallamshire: The History and Topography of the Parish of Sheffield in the County of York* (1861).

Hutton, R., *The Rise and Fall of Merry England: The Ritual Year, 1400–1700* (Oxford, 1994).

*The Stations of the Sun: A History of the Ritual Year in Britain* (Oxford 1996).

Ingram, M. J., 'Communities and Courts: Law and Disorder in Seventeenth-Century Wiltshire', in J. S. Cockburn (ed.), *Crime in England, 1550–1800* (Princeton, NJ, 1977), 110–34.

[published as Ingram, M.] 'Ridings, Rough Music and Mocking Rhymes in Early Modern England', in B. Reay (ed.), *Popular Culture in Seventeenth-Century England* (London, 1985), 166–97.

*Church Courts, Sex and Marriage in England, 1570–1640* (Cambridge, 1987).

[published as Ingram, M.] 'Puritans and the Church Courts, 1560–1640', in C. Durston and J. Eales (eds.), *The Culture of English Puritanism, 1500–1700* (Basingstoke, 1996).

Jacob, W. M., '"In Love and Charity with Your Neighbours": Ecclesiastical Courts and Justices of the Peace in the Eighteenth Century', *Studies in Church History*, 40 (2004), 205–17.

James, M. E., *Family, Lineage and Civil Society: A Study of Society, Politics and Mentality in the Durham Region, 1500–1640* (Oxford, 1974).

Johnston, A. F., 'English Puritanism and Festive Culture', *Renaissance and Reformation*, 15, 4 (1991), 289.

Johnston, M., 'Doing Neighbourhood: Practising Neighbourliness in the Diocese of Durham, 1624–31', in B. Kane and S. Sandall (eds.), *The Experience of Neighbourhood in Late Medieval and Early Modern Europe* (London, forthcoming 2021).

Kamensky, J., *Governing the Tongue: The Politics of Speech in Early New England* (Oxford, 1997).

Karant-Nunn, S. C., 'The Women of the Saxon Silver Mines', in S. Marshall (ed.), *Women and Reformation in Counter-Reformation Europe* (Bloomington, IN, 1989), 29–46.

Kent, D.V. and Kent, F.W., *Neighbours and Neighbourhood in Renaissance Florence: The District of the Red Lion in the Fifteenth Century*, Villa I Tatti Series: 6 (Locust Valley, NY, 1982).

Kent, J. R., 'Population Mobility and Alms: Poor Migrants in the Midlands during the Early Seventeenth Century', *Local Population Studies*, 27 (1981), 35–51.

'"Folk Justice" and Royal Justice in Early Seventeenth-Century England: A "Charivari" in the Midlands', *Midland History*, 8, 1 (1983), 70–85.

King, P., 'Customary Rights and Women's Earnings: The Importance of Gleaning to the Rural Laboring Poor', *Economic History Review*, 2nd ser., 44, 3 (1991), 461–76.

King, S., 'Reconstructing Lives: The Poor, the Poor Law and Welfare in Calverley, 1650–1820', *Social History*, 22 (1997), 318–38.

King, W. J., 'Early Stuart Courts Leet: Still Needful and Useful', *Histoire Sociale/Social History*, 23, 46 (1990), 271–99.

Kingman, M. J., 'Markets and Marketing in Tudor Warwickshire: The Evidence of John Fisher of Warwick and the Crisis of 1586–7', *Warwickshire History*, 4, 1 (1978), 21–4.

Kishlansky, M. A., *Parliamentary Selection: Social and Political Choice in Early Modern England* (Cambridge, 1986).

Krausman Ben-Amos, I., '"Good Works" and Social Ties: Helping the Migrant Poor in Early Modern England', in M. C. McClendon, J. P. Ward and M. Macdonald (eds.), *Protestant Identities: Religion, Society and Self-Fashioning in Post-Reformation England* (Stanford, CA, 1999), 125–40.

Lake, P., '"A Charitable Christian Hatred": The Godly and Their Enemies in the 1630s', in C. Durston and J. Eales (eds.), *The Culture of English Puritanism, 1500–1700* (Basingstoke, 1996), 145–83.

'Anti-Puritanism: The Structure of a Prejudice', in K. Fincham and P. Lake (eds.), *Religious Politics in Post-Reformation England: Essays in Honour of Nicholas Tyacke* (Woodbridge, 2006), 80–97.

Lambert, J. M., *Two Thousand Years of Gild Life* (London, 1891).

Lawson, P. G., 'Property Crimes and Hard Times in England, 1559–1624', *Law and History Review*, 4 (1986), 95–127.

Layton, R., *Anthropology and History in Franche-Comté: A Critique of Social Theory* (Oxford, 2000).

Leader, R. E., *History of the Cutlers in Hallamshire, in the County of York*, 2 vols. (Sheffield, 1905).

Leonard, E. M., *The Early History of English Poor Relief* (Cambridge, 1900).

l'Estrange Ewen, C., *Witchcraft and Demonianism* (London, 1933).

Lindley, K., *Fenland Riots and the English Revolution* (London, 1982).

Loades, D. M., *Two Tudor Conspiracies* (Cambridge, 1965).

Long, M. and Pickles, M., 'An Enquiry into Mortality in Some Mid-Wharfedale Parishes in 1623', *Local Population Studies*, 37 (1986), 19–35.

MacCaffrey, W. T., 'Place and Patronage in Elizabethan Politics', in S. T. Bindoff, J. Hurstfield and C. H. Williams (eds.), *Elizabethan Government and Society* (London, 1961), 95–126.

MacCulloch, D., 'Kett's Rebellion in Context', *P&P*, 84 (1979), 36–59.

*Tudor Church Militant: Edward VI and the Protestant Reformation* (London, 2001).

Macfarlane, A., *The Family Life of Ralph Josselin: An Essay in Historical Anthropology* (Cambridge, 1970).

Manning, R. B., *Village Revolts: Social Protest and Popular Disturbances in England 1509–1640* (Oxford, 1988).

Major, K., 'The Lincoln Diocesan Records', TRHS, 4th ser., 22 (1940), 58–9.

Marsh, C., '"Common Prayer" in England, 1560–1640: The View from the Pew', *P&P*, 171 (2001), 66–94.

'Order and Place in England, 1580–1640: The View from the Pew', *JBS*, 44 (2005), 3–26.

MacMaster, N., 'The Battle for Mousehold Heath, 1857–1884: "Popular Politics" and the Victorian Public Park', *P&P*, 127 (1990), 117–54.

Meredith, R., 'The Eyres of Hassop, 1470–1640: I', *Derbyshire Archaeological Journal*, new ser., 84 (1964).

Mitson, A., 'The Significance of Kinship Networks in the Seventeenth Century: South-West Nottinghamshire', in C. Phythian-Adams (ed.), *Societies, Cultures and Kinship, 1580–1850: Cultural Provinces in English Local History* (Leicester, 1993), 24–76.

Morgan, V., 'The Cartographic Image of "The Country" in Early Modern England', TRHS, 5th ser., 29 (1979), 129–54.

Moser, G. E., 'Kendal Parish Church Registers', TC&WA&AS, 1st ser., 3 (1878), 49–63.

Muldrew, C., 'The Culture of Reconciliation: Community and the Settlement of Economic Disputes in Early Modern England', *Historical Journal*, 39, 4 (1996), 915–42.

*The Economy of Obligation: The Culture of Credit and Social Relations in Early Modern England* (Basingstoke, 1998).

'An Early Industrial Workforce: Spinning in the Countryside, c. 1500–50', in R. Jones and C. Dyer (eds.), *Farmers, Consumers, Innovators: The World of Joan Thirsk* (Hatfield, 2016), 79–88.

Nader, L. (ed.), *Law in Culture and Society* (Chicago, 1969).

*Harmony Ideology: Justice and Control in a Zaoptec Mountain Village* (Stanford, CA, 1990).

Newman, K. L. S., 'Shutt Up: Plague and Quarantine in Early Modern England', *Journal of Social History*, 45, 3 (2012), 809–34.

Newton, K. C. and McIntosh, M. K., 'Leet Jurisdiction in Essex Manor Courts during the Elizabethan Period', Essex Archaeology and History, 3rd ser., 13 (1981), 3–14.

Nicholson, C., *The Annals of Kendal, with Biographical Sketches* (Kendal, 1832).

Ogilvie, S., 'How Does Social Capital Affect Women? Guilds and Communities in Early Modern Germany', *American Historical Review*, 109, 2 (2004), 325–59.

Palliser, D. M., 'Dearth and Disease in Staffordshire, 1540–1670', in C. W. Chalklin and M. A. Havinden (eds.), *Rural Change and Economic Growth, 1500–1800* (London, 1974), 54–75.

*Tudor York* (Oxford, 1979).

'Civic Mentality and the Environment in Tudor York', *Northern History*, 18, 1 (1982), 107.

Patterson, A., *Shakespeare and the Popular Voice* (Oxford, 1989).

*Reading Holinshed's Chronicles* (Chicago, 1994).

Pendrill, C., *Old Parish Life in London* (Oxford, 1937).

Pennell, S., '"Pots and Pans History": The Material Culture of the Kitchen in Early Modern England', *Journal of Design History*, 11, 3 (1998), 201–16.

Phillips, C. B., 'The Plague in Kendal in 1598: Some New Evidence', TC&WA&AS, 2nd ser., 94 (1994), 135–42.

Phythian Adams, C., 'Ceremony and the Citizen: The Communal Year at Coventry, 1450–1750', in P. Clark and P. Slack (eds.), *Crisis and Order in English Towns, 1500–1700: Essays in Urban History* (London, 1972), 57–85.

*Re-thinking English Local History* (University of Leicester, Dept of English Local History, Occasional Papers, 4th ser., No. 1, 1987).

Pitman, J., 'Tradition and Exclusion: Parochial Office-Holding in Early Modern England, a Case Study from North Norfolk, 1580–1640', *Rural History*, 15 (2004), 27–45.

Pittman, S., 'The Social Structure and Parish Community of St Andrew's Church, Calstock, as Reconstituted from Its Seating Plan, c.1587/8', *Southern History*, 20 (1998), 44–67.

Porter, G., '"Work the Old Lady out of the Ditch": Singing at Work by English Lacemakers', *Journal of Folklore Research*, 31 (1994), 35–55.

Pounds, N. J. G., *The Culture of the English People: Iron Age to the Industrial Revolution* (Cambridge, 1994).

Read, C. (ed.), *William Lambarde and Local Government* (Ithaca, NY, 1962).

Richards, R., *The Manor of Gawsworth, Cheshire* (Congleton, 1957).

Riegelhaupt, J., 'Saloio Women: An Analysis of Informal and Formal Political and Economic Roles of Portuguese Peasant Women', *Anthropological Quarterly*, 40 (1967), 109–26.

Robb, H., 'Purses and the Charitable Gift', *Journal of Social History*, 49, 2 (2015), 387–405.

Robson, E., 'Improvement and Epistemologies of Landscape in Seventeenth-Century English Forest Enclosure', *Historical Journal*, 60, 3 (2017), 597–632.

Rollison, D., 'Discourse and Class Struggle: The Politics of Industry in Early Modern England', *Social History*, 26, 2 (2001), 166–89.

Rappaport, S., *Worlds within Worlds: Structures of Life in Sixteenth-Century London* (Cambridge, 1989).

Ross, J., 'The Noble Household as a Political Centre in the Early Tudor Period', Harlaxton Medieval Studies, 28 (Donington, 2018).

Rowse, A. L. and Henderson, M. I. (eds.), *Essays in Cornish History by Charles Henderson* (Truro, 1963).

Rix, W. B., *Swaffham: Bygone Gleanings and Present* (Norwich, 1931).

Rossiter, A., *Hexham in the Seventeenth Century: Economy, Society and Government in a Northern Market Town* (Hexham, 2010).

Scott, J. C., *The Moral Economy of the Peasant: Rebellion and Subsistence in Southeast Asia* (New Haven, CT, 1976).

Scott, S. and Duncan, C. J., 'Marital Fertility at Penrith, 1557–1812: Evidence for a Malnourished Community?', TC&WA&AS, 2nd ser., 96 (1996), 105–14.

'The Mortality Crisis of 1623 in North-West England', *Local Population Studies*, 58 (1997), 14–25.

Scott, S., Duncan, C. J. and Duncan, S. R., 'The Plague in Penrith, Cumbria, 1597/8: Its Causes, Biology and Consequences', *Annals of Human Biology*, 23, 1 (1996), 1–21.

Seaver, P. S., *Wallington's World: A Puritan Artisan in Seventeenth-Century London* (London, 1985).

Shagan, E. H., 'The Two Republics: Conflicting Views of Participatory Local Government in Early Tudor England', in J. F. McDiarmid (ed.), *The Monarchical Republic of Early Modern England: Essays in Response to Patrick Collinson* (Aldershot, 2007), 19–36.

*The Rule of Moderation: Violence, Religion and the Politics of Restraint in Early Modern England* (Cambridge, 2011).

Sharpe, J. A., '"Such Disagreement betwyx Neighbours": Litigation and Human Relations in Early Modern England', in J. Bossy (ed.), *Disputes and Settlements: Law and Human Relations in the West* (Cambridge, 1983), 167–87.

*Crime in Early Modern England, 1550–1750* (Harlow, 1984).

Sharpe France, R., 'A History of the Plague in Lancashire', Transactions of the Historic Society of Lancashire and Cheshire, 90 (1938), 1–175

Sheils, W. J., *The Puritans in the Diocese of Peterborough, 1558–1610*, Northamptonshire Records Society, 30 (Northampton, 1979).

Shepard, A., *Accounting for Oneself: Worth, Status and the Social Order in Early Modern England* (Oxford, 2015).

'Gender, the Body and Sexuality', in K. E. Wrightson (ed.), *A Social History of England, 1500–1750* (Cambridge, 2017), 330–51.

Siraut, M., 'Physical Mobility in Elizabethan Cambridge', *Local Population Studies*, 27 (1981), 65–70.

Skipp, V. H. T., *Crisis and Development: An Ecological History of the Forest of Arden, 1570–1674* (Cambridge, 1978).

Slack, P., 'Poverty and Politics in Salisbury, 1597–1666', in P. Clark and P. Slack (eds.), *Crisis and Order in English Towns, 1500–1700* (London, 1972).

*The Impact of Plague in Tudor and Stuart England* (London, 1985).

Smith, A. G. R., *The Government of Elizabethan England* (London, 1967).

Smith, A. H., 'Justices at Work in Elizabethan Norfolk', *Norfolk Archaeology*, 34, 2 (1967), 80–93.

'Puritanism and "Neighbourhood": A Case Study in Late 16th and Early 17th-Century Norfolk', in E. Royle (ed.), *Regional Studies in the History of Religion in Britain since the Later Middle Ages* (York, 1984), 93–110.

Snell, K. D. M., 'The Culture of Local Xenophobia', *Social History*, 28, 1 (2003), 1–30.

Spufford, M., *Contrasting Communities: English Villagers in the Sixteenth and Seventeenth Centuries* (Cambridge, 1974).

Steer, F. W., 'The Statutes of the Saffron Walden Almshouses', Transactions of the Essex Archaeological Society, 2nd ser., 25, 2 (1955–6), 161–221.

Stone, L., 'Social Mobility in England, 1500–1700', P&P, 33 (1964) 16–55.

The Family, Sex and Marriage in England, 1500–1800 (London, 1977).

Stoyle, M., West Britons: Cornish Identities and the Early Modern British State (Exeter, 2002).

Tadmor, N., The Social Universe of the English Bible: Scripture, Society and Culture in Early Modern England (Cambridge, 2010).

Tankard, D. H., 'The Regulation of Cottage-Building in Seventeenth-Century Sussex', Agricultural History Review, 59, 1 (2011), 18–35.

Tate, W. E., The Parish Chest: A Study of the Records of Parochial Administration in England (Cambridge, 1946).

Taylor, H., '"Branded on the Tongue": Rethinking Plebeian Inarticulacy in Early Modern England', Radical History Review, 121 (2015), 91–105.

Thatcher Ulrich, L., "A Friendly Neighbor": Social Dimensions of Daily Work in Northern Colonial New England', Feminist Studies, 6, 2 (1980), 392–405.

Thirsk, J., 'Industries in the Countryside', in F. J. Fisher (ed.), Essays in the Economic and Social History of Tudor and Stuart England (Cambridge, 1961), 70–88.

Thistleton-Dyer, T. F., Old English Social Life as Told by the Parish Registers (London, 1898).

Thomas, K., The Ends of Life: Roads to Fulfillment in Early Modern England (Oxford, 2009).

Thomas, S., 'The Bad Weather in a Midsummer-Night's Dream', Modern Language Notes, 64, 5 (1949), 319–22.

Thompson, B. L., 'The Windermere "Four and Twenty"', TC&WA&AS, 2nd ser., 54 (1954), 151–64.

Thompson, R., Mobility and Migration: East Anglian Founders of New England, 1629–1640 (Amherst, MA, 1994).

Tomlinson, W., Life in Northumberland during the Sixteenth Century (London, 1897).

Trotman, E. E., 'The Church Ale and the Robin Hood Legend', Somerset and Dorset Notes and Queries, 28 (1961–7), 37–8.

Turner, E., 'The Early History of Brighton, as Illustrated by the "Customs of the Ancient Fishermen of the Town"', Sussex Archaeological Collections, 2 (1849), 38–52.

Tyacke, N., Aspects of English Protestantism, c.1530–1700 (Manchester, 2001).

Tyler, P., 'The Church Courts at York and Witchcraft Prosecutions, 1567–1640', Northern History, 4, 1 (1969), 84–110.

Underdown, D., Revel, Riot and Rebellion: Popular Politics and Culture in England, 1603–1660 (Oxford, 1985).

Fire from Heaven: Life in an English Town in the Seventeenth Century (London, 1992).

Waddell, B., 'Governing England through the Manor Courts, c.1550–1850', Historical Journal, 55, 2 (2012), 279–31.

Walker, G., 'Expanding the Boundaries of Female Honour in Early Modern England', TRHS, 6th ser., 6 (1996), 235–46.

Wall, A., *Power and Protest in England, 1525–1640* (London, 2000).

Walsham, A., *Charitable Hatred: Tolerance and Intolerance in England, 1500–1700* (Manchester, 2006).

'Supping with Satan's Disciples: Spiritual and Secular Sociability in Post-Reformation England', in N. Lewycky and A. Morton (eds.), *Getting Along? Religious Identities and Confessional Relations in Early Modern England* (Aldershot, 2012), 29–56.

Walter, J., 'Grain Riots and Popular Attitudes to the Law: Maldon and the Crisis of 1629' in J. Brewer and J. Styles (eds.), *An Ungovernable People: The English and Their Law in the Seventeenth and Eighteenth Centuries* (London, 1980), 47–84.

'The Social Economy of Dearth in Early Modern England' in J. Walter and R. Schofield (eds.), *Famine, Disease and the Social Order in Early Modern Society* (Cambridge, 1989), 75–128.

'Subsistence Strategies, Social Economy and the Politics of Subsistence in Early Modern England', in A. Häkkinen (ed.), *Just a Sack of Potatoes? Crisis Experiences in European Societies, Past and Present* (Helsinki, 1992), 53–86.

'Public Transcripts, Popular Agency and the Politics of Subsistence in Early Modern England', in M. J. Braddick and J. Walter (eds.), *Negotiating Power in Early Modern Society: Order, Hierarchy and Subordination in Britain and Ireland* (Cambridge, 2001), 123–48.

Warnicke, R. M., *William Lambarde: English Antiquary, 1536–1601* (Chichester, 1973).

Watson, C., '"To Beare the Towne Harmless": Manorial Regulation of Mobility and Settlement in Early Modern Lancashire', *Rural History*, 28, 2 (2017), 119–35.

Webb, J., *Great Tooley of Ipswich: Portrait of an Early Tudor Merchant* (Ipswich, 1962).

Webb, S. and Webb, B., *The Parish and the County* (London, 1906).

Welford, R. (ed.), *History of Newcastle and Gateshead*, 3 vols. (London, 1884–7).

Whiteside, J., 'Paines Made at Shap', *TC&WAAS*, 2nd ser., 3 (1903), 150–62.

Whitfield, C., *Robert Dover and the Cotswold Games: A New Edition of the Annalia Dubrensia* (London, 1962).

Whyte, N. M., 'Custodians of Memory: Women and Custom in Rural England', *Cultural and Social History*, 8, 2 (2011), 153–73.

[published as Whyte, N.] 'Remembering Mousehold Heath', in C. J. Griffin and B. McDonagh (eds.), *Remembering Protest in Britain since 1500: Memory, Materiality and the Landscape* (Basingstoke, 2018), 25–52.

Wiesner, M. E., 'Guilds, Male Bonding and Women's Work in Early Modern Germany', *Gender and History*, 1, 2 (1989), 125–37.

Willan, T. S., 'Plague in Perspective: The Case of Manchester in 1605', *Transactions of the Historic Society of Lancashire and Cheshire*, 132 (1982), 29–40.

Willen, D., '"Communion of the Saints": Spiritual Reciprocity and the Godly Community in Early Modern England', *Albion*, 27 (1995), 20–41.

Williamson, F., *Social Relations and Urban Space: Norwich, 1600–1700* (Woodbridge, 2014).

Wilson, E. M., 'Richard Leake's Plague Sermons, 1599', TC&WA&AS, 2nd ser., 75 (1975), 150–73.

Wilson, S., *The Means of Naming: A Social and Cultural History of Personal Naming in Western Europe* (London, 1998).

Winchester, A. J. L., 'Response to the 1623 Famine in Two Lancashire Manors', *Local Population Studies*, 36 (1986), 47–8.

*The Harvest of the Hills: Rural Life in Northern England and the Scottish Borders, 1400–1700* (Edinburgh, 2000).

Winstone, P. J., 'A History of the Church in Clapham', *Journal: North Yorkshire Country Record Office Publications*, 29 (1982)

Wood, A., *The Politics of Social Conflict: The Peak Country, 1520–1770* (Cambridge, 1999).

'"A Lyttull Worde Ys Tresson": Loyalty, Denunciation and Popular Politics in Tudor England', *JBS*, 48, 4 (2009), 837–47.

*The Memory of the People: Custom and Popular Senses of the Past in Early Modern England* (Cambridge, 2013).

'"Some Banglyng about the Customes": Popular Memory and the Experience of Defeat in a Sussex Village, 1549–1640', *Rural History*, 25, 1 (2014), 1–14.

'Tales from the "Yarmouth Hutch": Civic Identities and Hidden Histories in an Urban Archive', in L. Corens, K. Peters and A. Walsham (eds.), The Social History of the Archive: Record Keeping in Early Modern Europe, *P&P*, 230, Supplement 11 (2016), 213–30.

'Brave Minds and Hard Hands: Work, Drama and Social Relations in the Hungry 1590s', in C. Fitter (ed.), *Shakespeare and the Politics of Commoners: Digesting the New Social History* (Oxford, 2017), 84–103.

Wrightson, K. E., 'Two Concepts of Order: Justices, Constables and Jurymen in Seventeenth-Century England', in J. Brewer and J. Styles (eds.), *An Ungovernable People: The English and Their Law in the Seventeenth and Eighteenth Centuries* (London, 1980), 21–46.

'The Politics of the Parish in Early Modern England', in P. Griffiths, A. Fox and S. Hindle (eds.), *The Experience of Authority in Early Modern England* (London, 1996), 10–46.

'The "Decline of Neighbourliness" Revisited', in N. L. Jones and D. Woolf (eds.), *Local Identities in Late Medieval and Early Modern England* (Basingstoke, 2007), 19–49.

*Ralph Tailor's Summer: A Scrivener, His City and the Plague* (New Haven, CT, 2011).

Wrightson, K. and Levine, D., *Poverty and Piety in an English Village: Terling, 1525–1700* (New York, 1979).

# Index